THE volumes of the Humanistic Series are published by authority of the Board of Regents of the University of Michigan. The contributors are chiefly, but not exclusively, members of the faculties or graduates of the University. The expense is borne in part by gifts, in part by appropriations of the Board of Regents. A list of the volumes thus far published or arranged is given at the end of this volume.

University of Michigan Studies

HUMANISTIC SERIES

VOLUME IX

THE NEW TESTAMENT MANUSCRIPTS IN THE FREER COLLECTION

THE MACMILLAN COMPANY
NEW YORK · BOSTON · CHICAGO
DALLAS · SAN FRANCISCO

MACMILLAN & CO., LIMITED
LONDON · BOMBAY · CALCUTTA
MELBOURNE

THE MACMILLAN CO. OF CANADA, LTD.
TORONTO

THE NEW TESTAMENT MANUSCRIPTS

IN THE FREER COLLECTION

PART I

THE WASHINGTON MANUSCRIPT
OF
THE FOUR GOSPELS

BY

HENRY A. SANDERS
UNIVERSITY OF MICHIGAN

New York
THE MACMILLAN COMPANY
1912

Norwood Press
J. S. Cushing Co. — Berwick & Smith Co.
Norwood, Mass., U.S.A.

Paperback ISBN: 978-0-472-75191-4

PREFACE

Over two years have elapsed since the publication of the first of the Biblical MSS in the Freer Collection, though it was then hoped that the remaining MSS would appear with less delay. My excuse is the great importance of the MS of the Gospels now published and the difficulty of gathering parallels to its remarkable readings so as to put a proper estimate and interpretation on the MS. Furthermore the great importance of the early Versions was soon discovered and necessitated a working knowledge of Syriac, Coptic, and Gothic. For Armenian and Ethiopic I have had to rely on secondary sources. It is hardly necessary to state that the admirable editions of the Old Syriac Gospels by Burkitt and of the Bohairic and Sahidic by Horner were of the utmost assistance.

In gathering the parallels to the special readings shown in the various lists the main object was to learn the degree of relationship to other MSS. Absolute completeness was therefore not necessary, nor was it attainable with the books accessible to me. In many cases reasons of space prevented printing all the parallels gathered; thus the conclusions are based on somewhat fuller material than is given the reader. On the other hand some parallels were inserted in proof, which had not been considered in the summaries.

I am under obligation to so many Biblical scholars that space will hardly permit the mention of all here; yet without belittling the assistance received from others, I wish to give special thanks to Professors Caspar René Gregory, Kirsopp Lake, and William H. Worrell, Dr. J. Rendel Harris, Sir Frederick Kenyon, and Mr. Herman C. Hoskier. To Mr. Hoskier I am also indebted for many suggestions and additions made in reading the proof, as well as for the loan of valuable books not elsewhere accessible to me. The libraries of Harvard University, Oberlin College, Hartford

Theological Seminary, and the Theological Department of the University of Chicago have been most kind in the loan of books and in granting special privileges for work. My most earnest thanks are likewise extended to Mr. Charles L. Freer for his interest in the work and his generous support of the publication.

HENRY A. SANDERS.

ANN ARBOR, MICHIGAN,
November 22, 1912.

CONTENTS

PLATE I

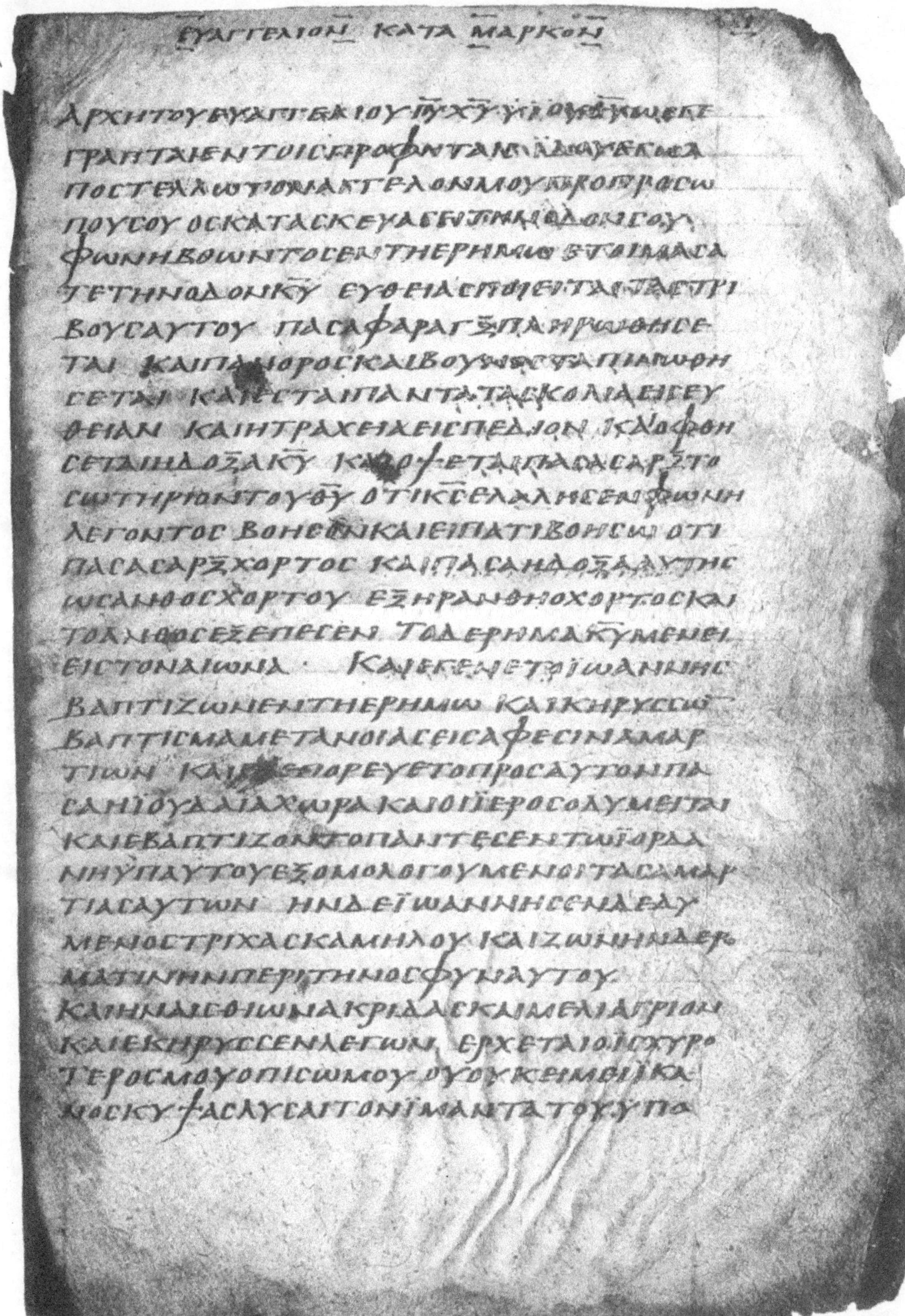

ΕΥΑΓΓΕΛΙΟΝ ΚΑΤΑ ΜΑΡΚΟΝ

ΑΡΧΗ ΤΟΥ ΕΥΑΓΓΕΛΙΟΥ ΙΥ ΧΥ ΥΙΟΥ ΘΥ ΚΑΘΩΣ ΓΕΓ
ΡΑΠΤΑΙ ΕΝ ΤΟΙΣ ΠΡΟΦΗΤΑΙΣ ΙΔΟΥ ΕΓΩ Α
ΠΟΣΤΕΛΛΩ ΤΟΝ ΑΓΓΕΛΟΝ ΜΟΥ ΠΡΟ ΠΡΟΣΩ
ΠΟΥ ΣΟΥ ΟΣ ΚΑΤΑΣΚΕΥΑΣΕΙ ΤΗΝ ΟΔΟΝ ΣΟΥ·
ΦΩΝΗ ΒΟΩΝΤΟΣ ΕΝ ΤΗ ΕΡΗΜΩ ΕΤΟΙΜΑΣΑ
ΤΕ ΤΗΝ ΟΔΟΝ ΚΥ ΕΥΘΕΙΑΣ ΠΟΙΕΙΤΑΙ ΤΑΣ ΤΡΙ
ΒΟΥΣ ΑΥΤΟΥ ΠΑΣΑ ΦΑΡΑΓΞ ΠΛΗΡΩΘΗΣΕ
ΤΑΙ ΚΑΙ ΠΑΝ ΟΡΟΣ ΚΑΙ ΒΟΥΝΟΣ ΤΑΠΙΝΩΘΗ
ΣΕΤΑΙ ΚΑΙ ΕΣΤΑΙ ΠΑΝΤΑ ΤΑ ΣΚΟΛΙΑ ΕΙΣ ΕΥ
ΘΕΙΑΝ ΚΑΙ Η ΤΡΑΧΕΙΑ ΕΙΣ ΠΕΔΙΟΝ ΚΑΙ ΟΦΘΗ
ΣΕΤΑΙ Η ΔΟΞΑ ΚΥ ΚΑΙ ΟΨΕΤΑΙ ΠΑΣΑ ΣΑΡΞ ΤΟ
ΣΩΤΗΡΙΟΝ ΤΟΥ ΘΥ ΟΤΙ ΚΣ ΕΛΑΛΗΣΕΝ ΦΩΝΗ
ΛΕΓΟΝΤΟΣ ΒΟΗΣΟΝ ΚΑΙ ΕΙΠΑ ΤΙ ΒΟΗΣΩ ΟΤΙ
ΠΑΣΑ ΣΑΡΞ ΧΟΡΤΟΣ ΚΑΙ ΠΑΣΑ Η ΔΟΞΑ ΑΥΤΗΣ
ΩΣ ΑΝΘΟΣ ΧΟΡΤΟΥ ΕΞΗΡΑΝΘΗ Ο ΧΟΡΤΟΣ ΚΑΙ
ΤΟ ΑΝΘΟΣ ΕΞΕΠΕΣΕΝ ΤΟ ΔΕ ΡΗΜΑ ΚΥ ΜΕΝΕΙ
ΕΙΣ ΤΟΝ ΑΙΩΝΑ· ΚΑΙ ΕΓΕΝΕΤΟ ΙΩΑΝΝΗΣ
ΒΑΠΤΙΖΩΝ ΕΝ ΤΗ ΕΡΗΜΩ ΚΑΙ ΚΗΡΥΣΣΩΝ
ΒΑΠΤΙΣΜΑ ΜΕΤΑΝΟΙΑΣ ΕΙΣ ΑΦΕΣΙΝ ΑΜΑΡ
ΤΙΩΝ ΚΑΙ ΕΞΕΠΟΡΕΥΕΤΟ ΠΡΟΣ ΑΥΤΟΝ ΠΑ
ΣΑ Η ΙΟΥΔΑΙΑ ΧΩΡΑ ΚΑΙ ΟΙ ΙΕΡΟΣΟΛΥΜΕΙΤΑΙ
ΚΑΙ ΕΒΑΠΤΙΖΟΝΤΟ ΠΑΝΤΕΣ ΕΝ ΤΩ ΙΟΡΔΑ
ΝΗ ΥΠ ΑΥΤΟΥ ΕΞΟΜΟΛΟΓΟΥΜΕΝΟΙ ΤΑΣ ΑΜΑΡ
ΤΙΑΣ ΑΥΤΩΝ ΗΝ ΔΕ ΙΩΑΝΝΗΣ ΕΝΔΕΔΥ
ΜΕΝΟΣ ΤΡΙΧΑΣ ΚΑΜΗΛΟΥ ΚΑΙ ΖΩΝΗΝ ΔΕΡ
ΜΑΤΙΝΗΝ ΠΕΡΙ ΤΗΝ ΟΣΦΥΝ ΑΥΤΟΥ·
ΚΑΙ ΗΝ ΑΙΣΘΙΩΝ ΑΚΡΙΔΑΣ ΚΑΙ ΜΕΛΙ ΑΓΡΙΟΝ
ΚΑΙ ΕΚΗΡΥΣΣΕΝ ΛΕΓΩΝ ΕΡΧΕΤΑΙ Ο ΙΣΧΥΡΟ
ΤΕΡΟΣ ΜΟΥ ΟΠΙΣΩ ΜΟΥ ΟΥ ΟΥΚ ΕΙΜΙ ΙΚΑ
ΝΟΣ ΚΥΨΑΣ ΛΥΣΑΙ ΤΟΝ ΙΜΑΝΤΑ ΤΟΥ ΥΠΟ

MARK i. 1-7.

I. HISTORY OF THE MANUSCRIPT

THE Washington MS of the Gospels (Greek MS III in the Freer collection, Detroit, Michigan) will eventually be transferred to the Smithsonian Institution in Washington, D. C., where it will be placed with the other collections in the gallery to be erected by Mr. Charles L. Freer. Gregory has named it W in his list (Die griechischen Handschriften des Neuen Testaments, Leipzig, 1908), and I shall use that designation for it in the following pages. It has the number ε 014 in von Soden's list. A complete facsimile edition of the MS is published simultaneously with this volume under the title: Facsimile of the Washington Manuscript of the Four Gospels in the Freer Collection, University of Michigan, 1912.[1]

The story of the purchase of these famous Biblical MSS has already been told[2] and I shall merely summarize it here. The four MSS[3] were bought by Mr. Freer of an Arab dealer named Ali in Gizeh, near Cairo, on December 19th, 1906. I saw them for the first time and recognized their value in October, 1907. It was at once determined not only to publish the MSS in full, but also to make a most diligent search for the missing portions and related finds, as well as for the original resting-place of the MSS.

The only hint as to origin or former owner found in the MSS themselves is the prayer for a certain Timothy in the subscription to Mark, p. 372 in the Facsimile.[4] I have already given my reasons[2] for connecting this with the Church of Timothy in the Monastery of the Vinedresser, which was located near the third pyramid (Abu Salih's Churches and Monasteries of Egypt, trans.

[1] Cited as Facsimile.

[2] Cf. University of Michigan Studies, Humanistic Series, vol. VIII, p. 1, where the earlier literature is also given.

[3] I, Deuteronomy and Joshua; II, Psalms; III, Gospels; IV, Fragments of the Epistles of Paul.

[4] Cf. Biblical World, vol. 31, no. 2, Fig. 1; Amer. Jour. Arch., vol. 13, pl. 3.

by Evetts and Butler, p. 190), but an outline of the previous argument with some additions may not be out of place here. The subscription in fifth-century semi-cursive hands reads:

> ⳩ χριστε αγιε συ μετα του δουλο(υ σου τιμοθεου ⳨)
> και παντων των αυτου ⳨

"Holy Christ, be thou with thy servant Timothy and all of his." With this as a whole we may compare the repeated notices by the scribe in MS ε 376 of von Soden (Gregory 579), of which the parallel portion is *την δουλην σου Ολυμπιαν . . . και παντος του λαου αυτης*. The reference is plainly to an abbess at whose order the MS was written, as von Soden, Schriften des N. T., vol. I, p. 179, notes. Therefore, if Timothy assumed the whole of our subscription when he inserted his name, it would seem that he was head of the monastery. A number of subscriptions, cited by von Soden in his list of MSS, show that it was common to indicate that MSS belonged to church officials, monasteries, or other owners; cf. MSS α 150, ε 178, ε 1036, ε 210, ε 2015, δ 304, δ 261, δ 411, δ 453, A 605. Also prayers for writer or owner appear, as ε 135 *κυριε βοηθει τω σω δουλω Γεωργιω πρεσβυτερω*; cf. also ε 1145, α 103, O 21. In our subscription the matter is made more complex by the changes and additions. The second line is by a different hand and in brown ink of a slightly lighter tinge than the first line, though that is lighter than any other writing in the MS. The words in parentheses are in jet black ink, like that used in the lectionary note on p. 35 of the Washington MS of Deuteronomy and Joshua, and they stand on an erasure; in fact a double erasure is plainly indicated for all the letters except *ου* of *σου*. It is clear that the second hand did not write *σου*, yet it was a word differing by the first letter only, so presumably *του*. The length of the erasure, reaching over the sign ⳨, shows that the second had a longer name or other words. There was room for at least fourteen letters in the place of the eleven of the third hand. We may compare the subscription in von Soden's ε 1222: *υπερ μνημης και αφεσεως των αμαρτιων του δουλου του θεου Ιωαννου μοναχου . . .* The reading *του θεου* for the second hand in our subscription is rendered a little more probable by the erasure of a long-tailed letter where the final *υ* would have stood. As the second line was added by this writer, it seems sure that he at least was the head of a monastery or some other church union. Of the first hand of the subscription we know still less. Manifestly neither του nor σου could have been original, as the ου, though belonging to both second and third hands, stands on an erasure. From the remnant χριστε αγιε συ μετα του δουλου . . . we cannot hope to establish much in regard to the earliest owner, who attached his name to the MS, though we may hazard the guess that the feminine article stood in the place of the later του and σου, and that the writer characterized himself as the servant of a monastery, or a church, or a female saint. The difference in writing shows that it was not the scribe of the MS who added the first subscription. Thus we have to do with owners of the MS, of whom the first two belonged to the fifth century and the third to the sixth, if we may judge from the similarity of ink noted above. The infrequency of notes in black ink in all four of the MSS indicates that the owners no longer used Greek readily.

We shall see later that the writing of our MS is rather closely related to the Enoch fragment found at Akhmîm in 1886, but that is the only evidence thus far found to support the first statement of the dealer, that the MSS came from Akhmîm. The text of W, to be sure, shows some affiliations with the Sahidic Version, but far more with the Old Latin and Syriac, while scribal errors point rather to Bohairic than to Sahidic influence. The dealer long since acknowledged that his statement about buying the MSS in Akhmîm was made merely to mislead. Through him Mr. Freer has been able to get in touch with the supposed finders, and various other purchases have been made of articles which are said to have come from the same ruined monastery, and which are entirely consistent with such an explanation. Of these I may mention a diminutive Coptic Psalter of the fifth or sixth century; a badly decayed cluster of parchment leaves with Coptic writing, out of which fragments of five or six different MSS, all diminutive, have been secured, notably a Psalter of the fourth (?) century; a single leaf of a Greek MS of an unknown church writer (Slavonic uncial of the eighth or ninth century); a small holder or seat having a curved top of wood inlaid with ivory, a fine piece of work, but badly decayed. The Copts were famous for their skill in ivory inlaying; compare the ivory inlaid book-chest of the White Monastery, mentioned by Abu Salih, op. cit., p. 239. While I am not as yet allowed to publish the exact spot where the MSS were found, the statements made by the finders fix it definitely and are consistent with the evidence gathered. The place would be a likely refuge for monks from the ruined Monastery of the Vinedresser, and diggers finding MSS there would naturally take them to Gizeh for sale.

II. PALAEOGRAPHY

1. Parchment, Quires, Ruling, and Writing

The ms is written on parchment of medium thickness and excellent quality, but it has suffered exceedingly from age, wear, and exposure. When first examined the leaves were very brittle, especially on the edges; this condition was doubtless due to their having been so dried and baked by sand and sun for many years. The ms has gained in strength and pliability since it has been kept in a place where changes in temperature and moisture are guarded against, and it can now be used without damage, if handled with care. The presence of thick board covers[1] prevented the decay from affecting anything except the edges of the leaves, so the text is everywhere legible.

The parchment is mostly sheepskin and has yellowed badly with age; yet in spite of this it is still rather transparent, so that the writing on the opposite side of the leaf is often visible. Some goatskin leaves occur, but they are usually hard to distinguish positively. In general it may be said that the flesh side of the goatskin leaves is whiter, and thus the difference in color between the two sides is greater. I have succeeded in seeing in a dozen or more leaves the branching veins characteristic of goatskin. Rough spots showing the hair roots sometimes occur, but only very rarely extend into the written portion of the page. The spots are smaller and nearer together in the goatskin leaves. A few weak spots and holes were mended by pasting on thin pieces of parchment; a good example may be seen on p. 337 of the Facsimile.

In the first quire[2] of John the parchment is all of sheepskin and seems to be of a somewhat different character. It is regularly a little thicker, but more worn and decayed. The flesh side of the parchment is as white as in the rest of the ms, but the skin side has yellowed more. In all of these respects, as well as in having

[1] For a description of the painted covers, see Professor Morey's section of the introduction to the Facsimile.

[2] This quire was written by a different scribe and at a different time, cf. pp. 8; 38; 135.

a slightly stronger odor, the parchment of this quire resembles that of the Greek Psalter in the Freer collection. A bit of wool, found between pp. 22 and 23, was probably a book mark.

The parchment varies in thickness from .05 to .20 mm., but the instances of extreme thickness or thinness are very rare. The general run of the leaves vary between .08 and .16 mm.; the average is .13 mm. The thinnest specimens seem to be goatskin. In the first quire of John the thickness varies from .13 to .20 mm.; the average is .16 mm. The largest leaves are eight and one-fourth inches in height by five and eleven-sixteenths inches in width (21 by 14.5 cm.), while the smallest measure eight by five and one-eighth inches (20.5 by 13 cm.); the common size is eight and three-sixteenths by five and five-eighths inches (20.8 by 14.3 cm.). The leaves of the first quire of John are all of the largest size, though the edges seem to show more loss by wear and decay.

There are at present 187 leaves or 374 pages, of which 372 are written. There are two blank pages at the end of John. The MS is divided into 26 quires, which had originally the quire numbers Α to ΚΓ placed on the upper right-hand corner of the first page of each quire. The numbers of the first seven quires have entirely disappeared through decay; of quire number Η there is a recognizable trace, and of the later quires the numbers can generally be read with certainty. Of quire ΙΓ the first two leaves are lost, but the opposite halves, forming the last two leaves of the quire, have been securely sewed in at some time when the MS had been taken apart, thus proving at least one rebinding. The missing leaves would have stood between pages 172 and 173 of the MS, as shown in the Facsimile. In quire ΚΓ the sixth leaf is missing (between pages 368 and 369) and the opposite half, the third leaf of the quire, has been carefully sewed in. The last leaf of quire Α was at one time torn out, but was repaired by pasting a fresh strip of parchment over the torn edges. Quires Α, Γ, ΙΒ, ΙΔ (end of John), and ΙΖ are of six leaves each. Quires Η (end of Matthew) and ΚΒ (end of Luke) have four leaves each. The remainder were all quires of eight leaves each, though two quires have lost leaves as above noted.

The leaves in the quires are so matched that flesh side of parchment is brought opposite to flesh side, and hair side opposite to hair side. I have noticed but one mistake in arrangement.

The middle double leaf of quire IZ is reversed. The resulting change in color between the pp. 230 and 231, and also 234 and 235, is not shown in the Facsimile, but the hair root marks distinguish the opposing sides. The leaves are so arranged in every quire that the flesh side of the parchment forms the outside of the quire. The ink is dark brown of approximately the shade shown in the plates; that used in the first quire of John is perceptibly darker, except where it has suffered from wear.

The writing is in one column of 30 lines to the page. In Matthew there are six instances where the scribe has written a single word or a part of a word on a 31st line. In three cases the extra word is placed at the beginning of the line and in three at the end. In Luke there are six similar cases of which four fall at the beginning of the line and two at the end. There are no cases in John or Mark. Pages 13, 14, and 15 of the first quire of John have 31 full lines each and show other signs of crowding.

Lines are ruled carefully and regularly 5.3 mm. apart. The ruling was done across the double pages before the quires were made up, and extends from the outer perpendicular of one page to the outer perpendicular of the other. The space between the writing and the binding edge of the MS is thus ruled, but the outer edge left unruled. Partial exceptions to the last statement occur once in Matthew and infrequently in the other gospels. In the first quire of John the horizontal rulings extend clear across the parchment. Perpendiculars are ruled to limit the ends of the lines of writing, and these extend regularly to the upper and lower edges of the parchment. Ruling was done on the light (flesh) side of the parchment, and rather lightly, as would be natural for thin parchment. Presumably the position of the lines was determined by compass points pricked in the parchment, but these are preserved only in the first quire of John, where they were placed quite a distance from the edge of the parchment.

The length of the written line as determined by the distance between the perpendiculars is three and seven-eighths inches (10 cm.). The writing sometimes extends slightly beyond the perpendicular. The number of letters in a full line varies between 27 and 30. The last quires of Luke run from 32 to 35 letters to the line. The letters are smaller, but the hand is the same. For some reason the scribe was crowding on these pages. Lines were not made longer for the sake of ending with a word or a phrase, yet the regular rules for syllable division at line ends are well preserved. Some irregularity is noted in regard to prepositions and prepositional compounds. Commonly we find *εκ|βαλλω*, *εισ|-ελθειν*, etc., but rarely *ε|ξελθειν* (Luke 14, 18) and even *ει|ς τον ουρανου* (Luke 15, 21); *ουκ* regularly attaches itself to the neighboring words; cf. *ου|κ ηδυναντο* Luke 8, 19 and often; even *αλ|λ' ουκ* John 3, 8. The writing is a graceful, sloping uncial of small size. It was evidently written with ease and rapidity. The ordinary letter is about 2.5 mm. in height, but *φ* and *ψ* are usually over 7 mm. and *ρ* and *υ* over 5 mm. in length.

The writer of the first quire of John was a less practised penman. The letters vary a little more in size and shape, and the line is followed less carefully. The average letter is about 3 mm. in height; *ρ*, *υ*, *ψ* are the same size as in the regular hand; *φ* is even larger, almost always touching or extending into the lines above and below. The various forms of the letters in the two hands are shown in the accompanying table; the more prevalent types have the first place. I have shown several types of each letter, even where the variations are slight, in order to better illustrate the general appearance. As might be expected in a hand written so rapidly, there are many slight variations, which I have not noted. The first column gives the regular hand of the MS, the second column, the first quire of John.

2. Abbreviations

The abbreviations used in Matthew are as follows: from *κυριος*, $\overline{\kappa\varsigma}$, $\overline{\kappa\upsilon}$, $\overline{\kappa\omega}$, $\overline{\kappa\nu}$, $\overline{\kappa\epsilon}$, always abbreviated when referring to God, otherwise not; cf. *κυριος* 10, 25; 18, 32; *κυριοις* 6, 24; from *θεος*, $\overline{\theta\varsigma}$, $\overline{\theta\upsilon}$, $\overline{\theta\omega}$, $\overline{\theta\nu}$; from *χριστος*, $\overline{\chi\varsigma}$, etc.; from *ιησους*, $\overline{\iota\varsigma}$, etc.; these three words are always abbreviated except as noted; from *πνευμα*, the forms $\overline{\pi\nu\alpha}$, $\overline{\pi\nu\varsigma}$, $\overline{\pi\nu\iota}$, $\overline{\pi\nu\tau\alpha}$ occur; I noted no cases of failure to abbreviate. In Matthew 8, 16 the scribe started to write *τα* $\overline{\pi\nu\alpha}$, but immediately corrected to *τα* $\overline{\pi\nu\tau\alpha}$; from *ανθρωπος*, $\overline{\alpha\nu o\varsigma}$, $\overline{\alpha\nu o\upsilon}$, $\overline{\alpha\nu\omega}$, $\overline{\alpha\nu o\nu}$, $\overline{\alpha\nu o\iota}$, $\overline{\alpha\nu\omega\nu}$, $\overline{\alpha\nu o\iota\varsigma}$, and $\overline{\alpha\nu o\upsilon\varsigma}$ all occur, yet there are a few instances of failure to abbreviate, in which all cases seem to be represented; from *πατηρ*, $\overline{\pi\eta\rho}$, $\overline{\pi\rho\varsigma}$, $\overline{\pi\rho\iota}$, $\overline{\pi\rho\alpha}$ are regular; $\overline{\pi\rho o\varsigma}$ occurs Matthew 10, 29, and *πατερ* is not abbreviated; cf. 6, 9; 11, 25; from *μητηρ*, $\overline{\mu\eta\rho}$, $\overline{\mu\rho\varsigma}$, $\overline{\mu\rho\alpha}$ occur, but *μητρος*, *μητρι*, and *μητερα* are also found; $\overline{\delta\alpha\delta}$ for *δαυειδ* occurs once at 12, 23 and *ισρλ* once at 27, 42; these words are elsewhere not

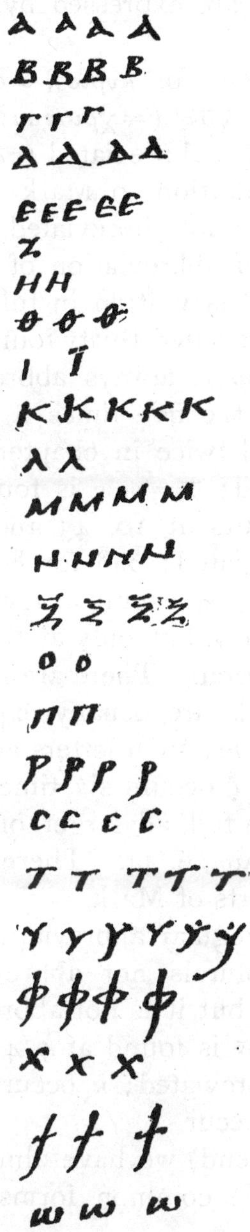

Forms of Letters in Major Portion of Manuscript

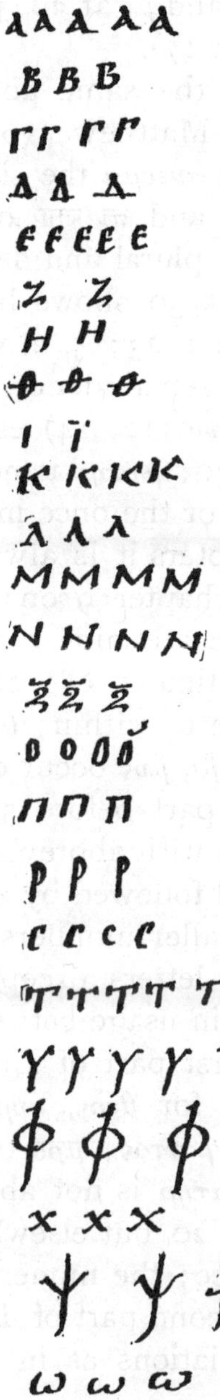

Forms of Letters in First Quire of John

abbreviated. κ_{3} for $\kappa\alpha\iota$, θ_{3} for $\theta\alpha\iota$, τ_{3} for $\tau\alpha\iota$ occur infrequently and generally only at ends of lines. NH̄ for $\nu\eta\nu$ is found at 27, 28, $\mathring{\mu}\upsilon$ at 20, 21, and $\mathring{\mu}\iota$ at 26, 53. Numerals are expressed by letters only twice (1, 17).

In Mark the same abbreviations occur for $\kappa\upsilon\rho\iota o\varsigma$, $\theta\epsilon o\varsigma$, and $\iota\eta\sigma o\upsilon\varsigma$ as in Matthew; $\chi\rho\iota\sigma\tau o\varsigma$ also has $\overline{\chi\rho\varsigma}$[1] (= $\chi\rho\iota\sigma\tau o\upsilon$?) once (9, 41); from $\pi\nu\epsilon\upsilon\mu\alpha$ the singular is always abbreviated ($\overline{\pi\nu\alpha}$, $\overline{\pi\nu\varsigma}$, $\overline{\pi\nu\iota}$); $\overline{\pi\nu\alpha\tau\omega\nu}$ and $\overline{\pi\nu\iota\kappa\eta\nu}$ occur in the addition to Mark 16, 14; otherwise the plural and derived forms are not abbreviated.

Mark 1 – 5, 30, shows but two cases of abbreviation of $\alpha\nu\theta\rho\omega$-$\pi o\varsigma$, viz., $\overline{\alpha\nu o\varsigma}$ 1, 23; 5, 2, while the word is written in full eight times; in the remainder of Mark it is abbreviated thirty-four times, only $\alpha\nu\theta\rho\omega\pi\omega\nu$ (12, 14) escaping. $\pi\alpha\tau\eta\rho$ is always abbreviated except at 1, 20; $\mu\eta\tau\eta\rho$ is not abbreviated the five times it occurs in chapter 3, or the once in chapter 5 and twice in chapter 6; in the later chapters it is always abbreviated; $\overline{\upsilon\varsigma}=\upsilon\iota o\varsigma$ is found six times from chapter 9 on; $\overline{\upsilon\iota\varsigma}=\upsilon\iota o\varsigma$ occurs at 10, 45 and $\overline{\upsilon\nu}$ at 14, 62; there are nine cases not abbreviated; $\overline{\delta\alpha\delta}$ for $\delta\alpha\upsilon\epsilon\iota\delta$ is found three times; $\overline{\overline{\delta\delta}}$[2] once, at 12, 35; κ_{3} occurs a few times at end of line or within; θ_{3}, τ_{3} occur rarely, but only at the ends of lines; $\mathring{\mu}\upsilon$, $\mathring{\mu}\iota$, $\mathring{\mu}\upsilon\varsigma$ occur once or twice each. There are no ligatures in the part before 5, 30. Numerals are usually expressed by the letters with abbreviation mark above; such letters are both preceded and followed by a slight space; $\bar{\zeta}$ occurs six times, $\epsilon\pi\tau\alpha$ twice; all smaller numbers are written in full, all larger ones are expressed by letters, except $\pi\epsilon\nu\tau\alpha\kappa\epsilon\iota\sigma\chi\epsilon\iota\lambda\iota o\iota$, 6, 44. There seems no variation in usage between the two parts of Mark.

In the first part of Luke (1 – 8, 12) regular abbreviations are always used for $\theta\epsilon o\varsigma$, $\kappa\upsilon\rho\iota o\varsigma$, $\pi\nu\epsilon\upsilon\mu\alpha$ (plurals not abbreviated), $\iota\eta\sigma o\upsilon\varsigma$, and $\chi\rho\iota\sigma\tau o\varsigma$; $\overline{\mu\rho\alpha}$ occurs at 2, 34, but it is not abbreviated six times; $\pi\alpha\tau\eta\rho$ is not abbreviated; $\overline{\alpha\nu o\varsigma}$ is found at 4, 4; $\overline{\alpha\nu o\upsilon\varsigma}$ 5, 10; $\overline{\alpha\nu\epsilon}$ 5, 20, but elsewhere is not abbreviated; κ_{3} occurs three times, θ_{3} twice; the numerals $\bar{\zeta}$, $\overline{\pi\delta}$, $\bar{\lambda}$, $\bar{\mu}$ occur.

In the second part of Luke (8, 13 to end) we have almost the same abbreviations as in Matthew. The common forms occur

[1] $\overline{\chi\rho\varsigma}$, $\overline{\chi\rho\upsilon}$, etc., occur in W (Luke 9, 20), in Oxy. Pap. vol. 2, no. 209; vol. 3, no. 402; they are regular in codex Bezae and the Old Latin MSS, and Horner's Coptic MSS show a few instances.

[2] This abbreviation is found in the Latin MSS dimma, mol, δ; it is noted by Traube, Nom. Sac., p. 105, as common in Latin MSS after the eighth century. A fourth century papyrus fragment of the Psalms at Leipzig also has it, as likewise Oxy. Pap. vol. 5, no. 840.

for *θεος*, *κυριος* (plural not abbreviated, also *κυριω* 14, 21), *ιησους*, *χριστος* ($\overline{\chi\rho\nu}$ occurs at 9, 20), *πνευμα* ($\overline{\pi\nu\alpha}$ = *πνευματα* at 10, 20, otherwise the plural is not abbreviated); *πατηρ* is abbreviated generally in the singular; $\overline{\pi\epsilon\rho}$ occurs seven times, unabbreviated four times; *πατρι* 9, 42, *πατερα* 9, 59, escaped abbreviation; *πατερες* 11, 47 and *πατερων* 11, 48 occur; *μητηρ* is not abbreviated (I noted nine instances); *ανθρωπος* is abbreviated in all cases and numbers, but unabbreviated forms occur almost as often (29 against 38 times); κ_3 occurs nine times, θ_3 twice, $\mathring{M}$ = *μου* four times, and τ_3, N_3, $\mathring{\mu}\iota$ once each; $\overline{\text{ϙ}\theta}$ (= 99) is found at 15, 4; 15, 7; otherwise numerals are written in full.

In John, excluding the first quire, we find the following abbreviations: $\overline{\theta\varsigma}$, $\overline{\kappa\varsigma}$, $\overline{\iota\varsigma}$, $\overline{\chi\varsigma}$, $\overline{\pi\nu\alpha}$, as also the oblique cases, are regular in the singular (*θεοι* 10, 34 *θεους* 10, 35 are the only plurals found); *πατηρ* is abbreviated regularly in the singular (yet *πατηρ* occurs once and *πατερ* five times); *μητηρ* does not occur often and is not abbreviated; *ανθρωπος* is regularly abbreviated in all cases and numbers; *ανθρωπον* is found three times; $\overline{\iota\eta\lambda}$ for *ισραηλ* is found once (12, 13); $\overline{\delta\alpha\delta}$ twice in 7, 42; $\overline{\upsilon\varsigma}$ once (20, 31); κ_3 and $\mathring{\mu}\upsilon\varsigma$ occur once each; $\overline{\kappa\epsilon}\,\eta\,\lambda$ of 6, 19 is the only numeral abbreviated.

In the first quire of John *θεος*, *κυριος*, *ιησους*, *χριστος*, *πνευμα*, *πατηρ*, *μητηρ*, *υιος*, and *ανθρωπος* have the regular abbreviations; $\overline{\iota\eta\lambda}$ occurs three times, $\overline{\text{ουρου}}$ four times, and $\overline{\text{ουρον}}$ twice; $\overline{\sigma\eta\rho}$ for *σωτηρ* is found at 4, 42, $\overline{\beta\lambda\epsilon\upsilon\varsigma}$ for *βασιλευς* at 1, 51, and $\overline{\beta\lambda\epsilon\iota\alpha\nu}$ for *βασιλειαν* at 3, 3; *βασιλιαν* is written in full at 3, 5; numerals are regularly represented by the letters, yet none of the ligatures occur except once, in the numeral $\overline{\mu}\,\kappa_3\,\overline{\eta}$. In 4, 25 for *χριστος* the scribe at first wrote χι, but immediately corrected to $\overline{\chi\varsigma}$; as *χριστος* is always abbreviated, it seems more probable that the scribe started to write $\overline{\chi\rho\varsigma}$, as at Luke 9, 20, Mark 9, 41.

These noteworthy variations in abbreviations cannot well be due to chance, especially as the changes coincide fairly well with the changes in text represented in the various parts of the MS. It seems clear that the scribe imitated the style of abbreviations of the parent MS, which, as we shall see later, was formed by joining parts of unrelated MSS. Judged on the basis of abbreviations alone, Matthew and the second part of Luke are the nearest related. The first part of Mark shows the fewest abbreviations, while Luke 1–8, 12, is not much inferior in this respect. The latter part of Mark shows similarity to John, having more abbreviations than the regular hand but less than the first quire. This foreign quire shows more abbreviations than any other part of the MS, but only four are peculiar to it. Of these $\overline{\sigma\eta\rho}$ is common and old in Biblical MSS; $\overline{\text{ουρου}}$, $\overline{\beta\lambda\epsilon\upsilon\varsigma}$, $\overline{\beta\lambda\epsilon\iota\alpha\nu}$ are not well known at any date, but the last two seem to point towards official documents in the early cursive, rather than to any literary hand; cf. $\overline{\beta\alpha}$ for *βασιλικω* in Oxy. Pap. vol. VII, no. 1028. The variation in the use of abbreviations for *πατηρ*, *μητηρ*, *υιος*, *ανθρωπος* in different parts of the same MS should warn us not to place too much reliance on the occurrence or non-occurrence of such abbreviations as criteria for dating.

The representation of *ν* at the end of a line by a stroke over the preceding vowel may be classed here with the abbreviations; it occurs with considerable frequency in all parts of the MS.

3. Punctuation

Punctuation is rather rare; a single dot in middle position is regularly used. In one or two instances the dot seems to approximate high position; cf. Matthew 24, 3 (Facsimile, p. 88, l. 30); Luke 2, 52 (Facsimile, p. 207, l. 1). The dot in lowest position (on the line) is not found. Hardly more than three or four punctuations occur on any one page, and the average is even less. They are most frequent in the first part of Luke, while Mark has far the fewest. The double dot (:) occurs 12 times in Matthew, 6 in John (excluding the first quire), 23 in Luke, and 11 in Mark (7 are in the first four chapters). It is used regularly at the end of each gospel, where it is accompanied by one or more line fillers (>); the majority of the remaining instances are found at the ends of paragraphs. It was therefore felt as a decidedly strong punctuation; for this reason it generally occurs at the ends of lines, or rather, nothing is written after it in the same line.

A substitute for punctuation is formed by leaving small blank spaces between the phrases. These occur frequently and regularly in all parts of the MS. It is difficult to determine the exact number in any portion because of the varying width of the spaces, which are often so narrow as to be hardly distinguishable. Also the spaces which fall at the ends of lines are seldom clear unless punctuated, which often happens.

The length of the phrases formed is quite even and approximates one and one-half lines of the MS. A count of the more carefully written pages in Matthew and John gives an average of $22\frac{1}{2}$ spaces per MS page. As there are 112 MS pages in Matthew, the total number of spaces would be about 2520. John, with 86 MS pages originally, would have had 1935 spaces. On the better written pages of Luke and Mark the number of spaces per page approximates 25; on the whole there seems rather more carelessness in the division. Yet the 116 pages of Luke indicate 2900 spaces, and the original 64 pages of Mark would have given 1600 spaces. These numbers correspond fairly well with the number of *στιχοι* or *ρηματα* enumerated in many MSS.[1] Omissions and additions to the text would have a tendency to make the totals vary in different MSS, and for that reason I have not attempted a more exact enumeration of totals. The approximate numbers obtained seem on the whole to come closer to the *ρηματα* than to the *στιχοι* as recorded in the various MSS, but these two are so nearly the same that they must represent merely variations of the same system. Because of the great age of W we are interested more in this original system, which doubtless gave the *στιχοι* counted by the scribe in determining the length of the MS. Of this earlier form Eustathius (fl. 326 A.D.) has left us information in the record that between John 9, 1 and 10, 31 there are 135 *στιχοι*.[2] A careful count of this portion of W gives 130 spaces and punctuations which are sure, though some of the spaces are rather narrow. There are two very narrow spaces not counted, as they seemed purely accidental. A survey of my results showed that some long phrases were left undivided, and by a comparison with D, Δ, and Syr cu[3] I was able to locate six more punctuation points which coincided with line ends in W. We may therefore assume that these space divisions in W are the original *στιχοι*, and that they have on the whole been rather carefully preserved. They doubtless coincided with the sense

[1] Cf. Scholz, N. T., p. xxviii; Harris, On Origin of Ferrar Group, p. 9:

	Matth.	*Mark*	*Luke*	*John*
ρηματα	2522	1675	(3083)	1938
στιχοι	2560	1616	2740	2024

[2] Cf. Scrivener, Introd. to Crit. of N. T., vol. 1, p. 52; Scholz, op. cit., p. xvii.

[3] Cf. Harris, Codex Sangallensis, p. 55, that there is related phrasing in these.

divisions used in reading. The subject seems worthy of a special treatment, including comparison with other MSS.

Still more interesting is the punctuation in the first quire of John. It is regularly a single dot in middle position (over 400 cases in the 16 pages). The double dot (:) occurs twice, and in 44 cases we find a space only without a dot. That this is not an ordinary system of punctuation is shown by the differences from the punctuation of the printed editions. There are 48 punctua tions in the MS, where not even a comma occurs in the editions, yet about 200 punctuations are omitted, of which 40 are full stops. The frequency of punctuation and spacing is greater than in any regular portion of the MS, averaging 28 per page as against 25 or less. It seems on the whole rather more careless and irregular than in the rest of the MS; cf. *νυμ·φιος* in 3, 28, *αυτω · αμην · αμην · λεγω* in 1, 52, and *· εδωκεν ·* in 3, 16. We must therefore allow for a certain number of mistakes or for the confusion of two systems at some points. Yet in spite of these defects it is apparent that the divisions correspond rather closely to those shown by capitals in Δ and to the punctuations in Syr cu and in some Old Latin MSS, as q and b. The short lines and punctuations of D show many agreements, but on the whole make shorter divisions. They perhaps arose from the union of two systems or a revision of the original one. W and Δ infrequently show equally short phrases. A comparison of all these MSS establishes one original system, of which W is the best representative. Δ and Syr cu show the closest agreement with W. Δ is hard to handle accurately, since there are all gradations in the size of capitals, especially *κ* of *και*. It seems to vary from W in less than 50 cases, of which 25 are additional divisions. Syr cu has only 16 punctuations not found in W, but has omitted more. The Old Latin MSS q and b have no punctuations not found in the others, but are very careless, often omitting the dots for long spaces.

The division into lines of varying length in D and the introduction of each phrase by a capital in Δ seem to indicate that we have to do with an ancient system of phrasing, used in reading the Scriptures in church service. If we are right in referring these widely separated MSS to the same system, its origin must have been as early as the second century.

4. Paragraphs

Closely allied with the punctuation is the system of paragraphing, shown by setting the first letter of the paragraph about its full size into the margin. These letters are generally a little enlarged, rarely even to double the regular size (cf. Matthew 1, 1; 17, 14; 23, 15; Luke 1, 1; 1, 5; 3, 7; 4, 8; 11, 24, etc.). The paragraph mark (—), standing at the end of the paragraph, sometimes just precedes the projecting letter of the next paragraph. In a few cases the paragraph mark stands alone. At Luke 1, 5 it has the form . It is noteworthy that it is always the first letter of the paragraph that projects into the margin. The vacant end of the previous line is never used for the beginning of the paragraph, as often happens in ancient MSS. Rather more numerous than the regular paragraphs are the cases where the line end is left vacant for quite a space, and yet the first letter of the next line does not project. These seem to mark rather more decided divisions than mere punctuation, yet one is hardly warranted in classing them as real paragraphs, though errors and interchanges between the two were doubtless easy. The numbers of these divisions are as follows:

	paragraphs	*marks*	*vacant line ends*
Matthew	195	14	310
Mark, 1 – 5, 30	0	3	23
Mark, 5, 30 to end	14	0	71
Luke, 1 – 8, 12	130	1	88
Luke, 8, 13 to end	117	12	212
John, 5, 12 to end	69	1	212
John, quire 1	28	3	2

The small number of paragraphs or quasi-paragraphs in the first quire of John is noteworthy. Furthermore, of this small number eight occur on the last page, where the scribe seems to be stretching the text to the utmost in order to finish the quire exactly with his copy or at some fixed point. It is possible that he thought of the paragraphs as a natural accompaniment of the vacant line ends, which are the characteristic means for stretching the text. Twice in this quire the paragraph mark has the form . Eleven times the paragraph projects practically two letters, and twice even three letters, into the margin. I have seen similar examples on papyrus, chiefly documents of the early centuries,[1] but in parchment MSS I know but one example. Coptic frag. 1 in the Freer collection has several instances of paragraphs projecting two full letters into the margin. This fragment, containing Psalm 44, is said to be from the same ruined monastery as W, and is one of the oldest Coptic fragments I have ever seen. There are no examples of the so-called Coptic μ and ν, and even more decisive the *schima* and *huri* still have the original Demotic forms unassimilated to the Greek.[2] I have dated it tentatively in the fourth century, but it may be older.

The remarkable variations in paragraphing in the different parts of the MS indicate quite plainly the care of the scribe in following his patchwork copy. As regards the affiliations of the different parts of that parent it is harder to speak with certainty. In no portion do the paragraphs agree with the Eusebian sections, with the κεφαλαια, or with any other system of numbering known to me, such as the shorter chapters of codex B. The paragraphs of Luke bear the most resemblance to the Eusebian sections, yet even here we find 27 disagreements out of 66 sections in the first part up to 8, 12, though W has 131 paragraphs. In the second part of Luke the difference increases, as chapters 8 to 14 show 59 disagreements in 114 Eusebian sections. The agreement is therefore but little more than could be expected from independent systems of dividing, where both are based on natural sense divisions. As the Eusebian sections agree closely with the paragraphs of codex Alexandrinus except for the addition of extra paragraphs, we can expect no agreement between W and A. In codex B there is a similar system of paragraphing by use of the mark (—) and by projecting letters. These are on the whole considerably more numerous: Matthew, 454, Mark, 208, Luke, 489, John, 351. The chapter numbers in B coincide with the beginnings of paragraphs except for a few errors; evidently one of the systems was based on

[1] Cf. Amherst Papyri, plates ix; xii; facs. 2 of Rev. Laws of Ptol. Phil.; also pl. i, a literary fragment, first century; Berlin. Klassikertext. vol. 3, Taf. 11, Ps. Hippokrates, Ep.

[2] Cf. Ralfs, Gött. Akad. 1900–1901, nro. 4, p. 13.

the other. Codex Sinaiticus has even more paragraphs, which are shown as in W, though the paragraph mark is regularly added in the earlier portion. I counted over 550 paragraphs in Matthew, yet there is little agreement with W. Codex D shows greater variation; the regular method is by projecting letter. Because of varying length of line the blank line end could not be used. The number of paragraphs is: Matthew, 590 (12 pages lost), John, 172 (omitting 18, 2–20, 1), Luke, 151, Mark, 161. In Matthew W shows quite a remarkable agreement with the paragraphs of D. Of its 209 paragraphs 20 are covered by lacunae in D; of the remaining 189 there is agreement with D in 168 cases, while the rest are paralleled by punctuation or line end in D. But this does not show the full extent of the agreement, for we consider the vacant line ends and space punctuations of W closely related to the paragraphs. Comparing these we find the following: the paragraphs of D are supported by W 168 times with paragraphs and 197 times with blank line ends, while the remaining 225 paragraphs agree almost perfectly with space punctuations in W. The disagreement with the paragraphs and chapters of ℵ, A, and B shows that this is not due to mere chance. As in punctuation so in paragraphing we have found a system in which W and D can be traced back to a common ancestor.

In John 5, 12 to end, there is almost as close an agreement between the paragraphs of W and D, though less numerous in both MSS. In this part the agreement with codex B is close; the paragraphs of W which find no support equal only about one-fourth of the whole number. Furthermore, nearly all the paragraphs of B are paralleled by paragraphs, line ends, or punctuations of W. It seems, however, more likely that the paragraphing of B was made on the basis of a punctuation like that of W and D, and that there is no relationship between the paragraphs.

In the first quire of John the agreement between the paragraphs of W and D is even more decided, though some of the paragraphs of D are paralleled by punctuations or spaces in W, or *vice versa*. It is noteworthy that all nine of the Eusebian sections in this portion, which are not supported by projecting paragraphs in D, find no support in W. The Eusebian sections are a later intrusion into the D tradition and have had no influence on the system of paragraphs.

In Mark the few paragraphs of W are less related to those of

D and in the first five chapters there is no other MS showing such an absence of divisions.

As I have stated above, the paragraphing in Luke is somewhat similar to the Eusebian sections, yet these do not present the closest parallel; that is found in codex B. Of the 131 paragraphs of W in Luke 1–8, 12, 81 are supported by the paragraph marks of B, 25 by space punctuations, and 7 by line ends, leaving only 18 unaccounted for. Of the 32 extra paragraphs in B, 19 equal vacant line ends, and 13 equal punctuation in W. In the remainder of Luke the same relationship exists, though more obscured. This system of paragraphing goes back to a common ancestor independent of the system in D. Considering the age of W and B, it seems quite certain that the Eusebian sections were influenced by this system, and not the reverse.

I have stated above that the paragraphs of W were sometimes introduced by decidedly enlarged letters. There are forty such cases in Matthew, once in the middle of a line, not counting of course the slightly enlarged letters, which are rather numerous. In the first quire of John the initial letters are even more enlarged, though the use here also is very irregular; less than one-third of the initial letters are enlarged. There are three of these enlarged letters in the middle of the line, but each time following punctuation. These are doubtless substitutes for paragraphs omitted through ignorance or the desire for condensation.

5. Diacritical and Other Marks

Accents are not found in W, and rough breathings (ͱ or ˪) occur only very rarely; these are mostly on monosyllables and especially to distinguish words liable to be confused, as ἑν from ἐν, ἑξ from ἐξ, and the relative pronoun from the article.[1] I counted 29 instances in Matthew; none in Mark 1–5, 30; 3 in the rest of Mark; 44 in Luke; and 4 in John 5, 12 to end. There are no mistakes in its use. In the first quire of John there are no breathings, but we find several instances of a curved stroke over initial vowels or successive vowels at the beginnings of words. The examples follow: οῠτος, 1, 2; 1, 30; 4, 47; ο̆νομα, 1, 6; ο̆ ο̆πισω, 1, 15; 1, 27; οῠ ο̆, 4, 46; ο̆ῠ for οὔ, 1, 21; 4, 9; οῠ for οὗ, 1, 27; ο̆ῠκ, 4, 17; ο̆ῠχ, 4, 35; οῠν, 1, 21; ο̆ for ὃ, 3, 11; 3, 32; 4, 22;

[1] The article never has the breathing; ὁταν, ἡμερα, ἡξει, ὁπως, ὡρα also occur.

ὃ for ὁ, 3, 21; 3, 36; ὅς, 4, 12; ὦ, 3, 26; ὅτι, 3, 21; ἤ for ἦ, 3, 2; ἤ for ἦ, 4, 27.

The mark is similar over χ in εχ̆θες, 4, 52. It seems clear that the mark has nothing to do with breathings, for it occurs over vowels having the rough breathing 17 times, the smooth 10 times. A comma-shaped mark is similarly used over initial vowels in the Psalms MS in the Freer collection, and in codex Alexandrinus a curved stroke is used to distinguish η in its various meanings as a word. The stroke over letters used as numerals in John, quire 1, is similar, but less curved.

An apostrophe may occur after any final consonant except ν,[1] ξ, ρ, ς, ψ. It is most frequent with foreign proper names, but may be used when a word has dropped a final vowel, as αλλ', κατ', απ', μεθ'. The apostrophe also occurs several times after ουχ' and is rarely inserted in the middle of a proper noun; cf. in Matthew, ματ'θαιος, 10, 3; βηθ'σαιδαν, 11, 21; βηθ'σφαγη, 21, 1; γεδ'σημανι, 26, 36; in Luke, ματ'θολομευν, 6, 15; βηθ'σαιδαν, 9, 10; in John, βηθ'σαιδα, 1, 45; 5, 2. The apostrophe is rare in Mark.

Dots may occur over ι and υ when initial or not to be pronounced with the preceding vowel. Exceptions are numerous, especially in the case of the initial vowel. In the main portion of the MS two dots are used over ϊ and one over υ̇; in the first quire of John two dots are used over ϋ also. Very rarely in both hands the two dots coalesce into a simple stroke; cf. Luke 18, 38; John 3, 7.

Quotations from the Old Testament are indicated by marks (⋚) in the left margin. There are seven cases in Matthew, covering the longer quotations in the earlier chapters. Some ten cases are not so marked. In Luke these marks are used but once (10, 27), while there are no instances in Mark and John.

6. Spelling, Grammatical Forms, Scribal Errors

Variations in spelling in the MS are noteworthy. In Matthew ι for ει occurs very frequently, yet the opposite mistake is found fully three-fourths as often. Rather more common still is αι for ε, while the opposite occurs about half as often. In Luke the frequency and proportion of these errors are about the same, except that the error ε for αι becomes rare. In John (except first quire)

[1] ενων' for αινων occurs, John 3, 23.

the cases of ει for ι become nearly twice as frequent as those of ι for ει; ϵ for αι is not found, and the instances of αι for ϵ increase accordingly. In Mark ει for ι remains the favorite misspelling, being nearly twice as frequent as the opposite mistake. On the other hand, the errors ϵ for αι and αι for ϵ are of almost equal frequency. Itacistic errors other than these are rare. We may note: συ for σοι,[1] Mark 1, 24; 5, 7; σοι for συ, John 13, 7; διανυχθητι[2] for διανοιχθητι in Mark 7, 34 (cf. D); ανυχθησεται and ανηχθησεται, Luke 11, 9–10; ανυγησεται, Matthew 7, 7; μιζον, Mark 9, 34; Luke 7, 28; John 13, 16, and elsewhere; ο for ω: σιδονι, Matthew 11, 21–22; Luke 10, 13–14; Mark 3, 8 (cf. Thackeray, p. 169); η for ει: ηασεν, Matthew 24, 43; ηα, Luke 4, 41; ηργασατο (= B D 28, 69, etc.), Matthew 26, 10; Mark 14, 6; a not infrequent interchange of η and ει in verbal endings is classed as change of mood, but is, I think, often only itacistic; ου for ω: οδυνουμενοι, Luke 2, 48 (= V, l. 47, l. 54); κατεγελουν, Matthew 9, 24 (= K, l. 185); ηρωτουν, John 4, 40 (= N). Here perhaps belongs ινα κατηγορησουσιν, Matthew 12, 10, though supported by D X 74, 259. θεωρουσιν man 1, John 17, 24, was corrected by the διορθωτής. The opposite mistake also occurs, cf. Matthew 24, 9, παραδωσωσιν (= Δ Σ Φ). ϵ for η: ω εαν βουλεται, Matthew 11, 27 (= Σ N 473); ϵ for α: χορεζειν, Luke 10, 13; α for η: της γλωσσας, Mark 7, 33; η had almost entirely replaced α pure in declension of nouns of the first declension. Yet the papyri rarely show forms like σπιρας (cf. Thackeray, p. 142). Our case is an instance of the opposite or corrective tendency, which often accompanies a dialect peculiarity. αυ for ω: επιφαυσκεν, Luke 23, 54; ο for οι: οκοδομησαι, Luke 14, 28; ο for ω: οφιλομεν, Luke 17, 10 (= B E G H K M, etc.); εχον, John 12, 6; ω for ο: το γεγονως, Luke 8, 34. εορακα and εωρακα are both used interchangeably, though εορακα is the more common, especially in John; cf. Blass, N. T. Gram., p. 39.

In the first quire of John the itacisms are as follows: ι for ει, 193 times; ει for ι, 17; ϵ for αι, 82; αι for ϵ, 16; ο for ω, 3; ι for ϵ, 3; οι for ω, οι for η, υ for οι, ι for η, and ϵ for υ occur once each. It is to be noted that the common words εἰς, εἱς, εἰ, ειπαν, ειδαν, ειχεν, και, μαθηται, αιωνιον, etc., are almost never misspelled, while

[1] Cf. MSS ℵ B A C, 28, l. 184 for similar errors. The interchange arose first in Egypt; cf. Thackeray, Gram. of O. T. Greek, p. 94.

[2] Cf. Thackeray, loc. cit., for examples in codices ℵ A B and papyri.

in most other cases of ει and αι the spelling is consistently wrong. Especially noteworthy is the regularity of the ending -τε for -ται in the verb forms. Odd, but probably itacistic, are the errors ελοιλεθας, 3, 2, and οδηποριας, 4, 6.

Certain spellings seem peculiar to a single gospel. Thus in Matthew we find δικαιωσυνη regularly; δικαιοσυνη occurs twice, 5, 20 and 21, 32, while in 5, 6 it was written by the first hand, but changed by the διορθωτής (ω over ο). ιηρεμιου appears in 27, 9, and κλαθμος for κλαυθμος is always used in Matthew except at 8, 12.[1] In Mark ω occurs for υ, cf. τρωμαλιας, 10, 25; and ου for υ, cf. λουτρον, 10, 45; ι occurs for η in Luke 23, 11, εξουθενισας. In Luke 1 – 8, 12, ναζαρετ occurs four times, ναζαρεθ once (4, 16). In the other gospels it is always ναζαρεθ except in Matthew 21, 11. Matthew has καπερναουμ except in 17, 24, but καφαρναουμ is found in the other gospels, except Luke 10, 15, which is the only occurrence in the part 8, 13 to end. Εαν occurs for αν after ος, οταν etc., in Matthew, less often so in Luke and John. In Mark we find regularly αν in this position.

In general, however, distinctions in spelling between the different gospels or parts of gospels cannot be sharply drawn.

Throughout the whole MS dissimilation of consonants is the rule, as might be expected in the Hellenistic period: — cf. in Matthew: ενπεση, 12, 11; ενβαντα, 13, 2; συνλεξωμεν, 13, 28, etc.; in Mark: ενβαντα, 4, 1; ενβενοντος, 5, 18; συνποσια, 6, 39, etc.; in Luke: συνκαλεσαμενος, 9, 1; ενβας, 8, 37; συνκυριαν, 10, 31, etc.; in John: ενκενια, 10, 22; ενποριου, 2, 16; ενγυς, 3, 23; συνμαθηταις, 11, 16; ενβριμων, 11, 38, etc. Yet the customary assimilation rarely occurs: cf. Matthew 13, 29, συλλεγοντες; Mark 14, 67, εμβλεψασα; 15, 1, συμβουλιον; Luke 20, 17, εμβλεψας; John 11, 50, συμφερει. Assimilation of preposition to noun occurs but once, Luke 24, 21, συμ πασιν.[2]

Variations in aspiration occur in Matthew: γεδ' σημανι, 26, 36; διδραγμα, 17, 24 (= D E F L H Σ); ραχα, 5, 22 (= ℵ D); in Mark: καθ ιδιαν, 4, 34; 9, 2 (= B D Δ); εξουθενηθη, 9, 12 (= N Σ Φ Ψ); σφεκουλατορα, 6, 27; εκχθρους, 12, 36; in Luke: εφειδεν, 1, 25 (= D W^{C} Δ 13, etc.); καθ ετος, 2, 41; καθ' ιδιαν, 10, 23; αυθοπται, 1, 2; ουχ ειδον, 10, 24; χειθωνας, 9, 3; εχχυννομενον, 22, 20 (= A

[1] Codex L reads κλαθμος seemingly only here; codex E has κλαθμος *passim*, *teste* Wetstein; cf. Moulton, p. 47.

[2] Cf. Thackeray, p. 131.

B E L T U Δ Π); *ουθενος*, 22, 35 (= A B Q T X Γ Δ Π, etc.); *ζαχχαιος*, 19, 2–8; *πατνης*, 13, 15; *λωθ*, 17, 29–32 (= D and Latin MSS); *φοβηθρα*, 21, 11 (= B D); *ουχ οψεσθαι*, 17, 22 (= A); in John: *εχ σχοινιων*, 2, 15 (cf. Thackeray, p. 103); *ουχ οψετε*, 3, 36 (= D Δ Λ 28 Ign); *ουκ εστηκεν*, 8, 44 (= B D L X Δ Λ 1, etc.); *βηδσαιδα*, 12, 21 (= D Lat. Cop.); *γεσσημανιν*, Mark 14, 32; *ουχ ειδον*, Luke 24, 24. Of the above peculiarities even those which lack New Testament support find good warrant in the papyri and older uncials; cf. Thackeray, p. 102 ff. W agrees with the older uncials in the spelling *μαθθεος*; there is only one exception, *ματθαιος*, Matthew 10, 3.

Omission of letters rarely occurs: Matthew 23, 13, *προφαει* for *προφασει*, cf. Thackeray, p. 114; Mark 6, 45, *βηθαιδαν*; Mark 12, 28, *προελθων* for *προσελθων*; Luke 24, 41, *τη χαρας*; John 6, 55, *σαξ* for *σαρξ*, cf. Thackeray, p. 116; Matthew 6, 6, *ταμιον* (= D, etc.); John 4, 9–10, *πιν* for *πιειν*; John 5, 11, *ποισας*, cf. Thackeray, p. 93; Luke 4, 19, *τεθραυμενους* (= D); Luke 10, 17, *ω* for *τω*; Matthew 21, 41, *απολει* for *απολεσει*; Matthew 14, 3, *ηρωιαδα*. *ν* omitted: John 4, 23, *προσκυνουτας*; Mark 14, 18, *υμω*; Luke 9, 58, *την κεφαλη*; John 1, 35, *παλι*; Matthew 27, 41, *φαρισαιω*; 12, 12, *ου* for *ουν*.

Rather more common are single consonants for double: *εριπισαν*, Matthew 26, 68; *διερηξεν*, Matthew 26, 65 (= Θ[b]); *εριπτε*, Luke 17, 2 (= Π*); *προσερηξεν*, Luke 6, 48 (= B D L); *συσημον*, Mark 14, 44; (= F L l. 184); *περισον*, John 10, 10; *γενηματος*, Mark 14, 25; Luke 12, 18 (= uncials); *ελεισαιου*, Luke 4, 27; *περισευματος*, Luke 6, 45; Matthew 12, 34; *πλημυρης*, Luke 6, 48; *παρησια*, John 11, 14 (= ℵ* X); *αιμοροουσα*, Matthew 9, 20 (= ℵ[c] L); *γομορων*, Matthew 10, 15; *μανασης*, Matthew 1, 10; *γενητοις*, Matthew 11, 11, etc. Most of these spellings have uncial support; cf. Thackeray, p. 119. Here we may note the regular spelling *κραβαττον* in W; *βαρραβαν* occurs (man 1) in John 18, 40.

There are a few cases of the insertion of an extra consonant: *μετα ρορκου*, Matthew 26, 72; *ιστραηλ*, Matthew 19, 28; Mark 12, 29 (= D and Old Latin MSS); *βηθ'σφαγη*, Matthew 21, 1 (= B F K M N, etc.); *κεκονιασμενοις*, Matthew 23, 27 (= 69, Eras., etc.).

The interchange of consonants is rare: *τε* for *δε*, Matthew 24, 49; *λ* for *σ*: *διελωθησαν*, Matthew 14, 36; *μ* for *β*: *μασανισταις*, Matthew 18, 34; *μαρθολομεος*, Mark 3, 18; *ματθολομεον*, Luke 6, 14; *β* for *λ*: *ταβιθα*, Mark 5, 41 (= D, 157, 225, 259, and O. L.

MSS); λ for ρ: καλφος, Luke 6, 41; λ for ν: λεφελη, Luke 9, 34; ζ for σ: ζμυρνα, Matthew 2, 11; John 19, 39 (cf. D Sah Bo and Moulton, N. T. Gr. p. 45).

In the verb the so-called Alexandrian first aorist forms are rather common, but not invariable. Those of most frequent occurrence are ειπαν, ηλθαν, ευραν, ειδαν, εφυγαν, επεσαν, ωνιδιζαν, and their compounds; cf. also σπειραντος, Matthew 13, 18; ελεγαν, Mark 3, 21; ειχαν, Mark 8, 7 (= ℵ B D Δ); εξεβαλαν, John 9, 34. Yet the change, α for ο, must at some time have been recognized as a fault, for we find the opposite error: απηγγειλον, Matthew 28, 11; Mark 6, 30; Luke 7, 18; 9, 36; ανηγγειλον, Mark 5, 14; ηυλησομεν, Matthew 11, 17; εμεινον, Matthew 11, 23 (= L X Δ); αποστιλοντα, Matthew 10, 40; 14, 35; Luke 10, 16; in Mark: οιδομεν, 11, 33; συνηκον, 6, 52; κρατησοντες, 14, 1; επλυνον, Luke 5, 2 (= B D 91); εσπειρες, Luke 19, 21; εωρακες, John 8, 57 (= B).

The temporal augment is more often retained: cf. in Matthew ηυδοκησα, ωμοιωθη, etc.; in Mark, ηυλογησεν, ηδυνηθησαν, ηπορειτο, etc.; in Luke, ηυφορησεν, ηυδοκησεν, ηυλογησεν, ημελλεν; in John cases are rare and I noted the exceptions εμελλεν and οικοδομηθη. Exceptions in Mark are ευλογει, 10, 16; εδυναντο, 5, 3. There are some cases of extra or misplaced augment in compound verbs: απεκατεσταθη, Matthew 12, 13 (= ℵ B C E F, etc.); επροεφητευσεν, Mark 7, 6 (= B**); επροφητευσεν, Luke 1, 67 (= ℵ A B C L 1, 33); Matthew 7, 22; ηνεστη, John 2, 22[1]; ηνεωχθησαν, John 9, 10 (= uncials); ηνεωξεν, John 9, 17–32 (= A B N X Δ 13, 33, etc.).

There are certain words which show the influence of the Atticists: γιγνωσκω is often used; γινωσκω occurs at John 7, 49; Luke 12, 39; 21, 31; Matthew 12, 33; Mark 13, 28–29 and elsewhere; αναγινωσκω is found in Mark 13, 14. γιγνομαι also occurs, though less often.

The form λημψομαι, characteristic of the κοινή, is regularly used; no exceptions were noted. In Mark 14, 10–11, παραδοι occurs twice (= B D C?) and in 5, 43, γνοι (= A B D L). John 16, 19 even has εγνοι, plainly an itacistic error, cf. Thackeray, p. 93. This may cause one to hesitate to explain all the other cases as special subjunctives, though they are so classified by Thackeray, p. 256, Moulton, p. 55. The perfect in -αν (τετηρηκαν, John 17, 6) is supported by B D L, and is a well established, though rare,

[1] Cf. Luke 9, 8, where codex D has this form.

form in N. T. Greek, cf. Moulton, p. 52. In Mark 14, 67 *ης* occurs for *ησθα* (=fam. 1, fam. 13, 565, 700); *εσχεν* for *ειχεν* occurs once or twice; *στηκω* replaces *ιστημι* rarely; cf. *στηκουσιν*, Mark 3, 32; *στηκον*, Mark 13, 14 (=fam. 1, fam. 13, 299); *στηκοτων*, Matthew 27, 47. Other odd verb spellings are *βατταλογειται*, Matthew 6, 7; *γονομενης*, Matthew 8, 16; *διακονησαι*, Matthew 27, 55; *λιθοβολησασα*, Matthew 23, 37; *θεωρουσαι*, Matthew 28, 1 (= 240); *αφιενται* for *αφεωνται*, Luke 7, 47–48; John 20, 23; *αφιομεν*, Matthew 6, 12; most of these have good support.

Of peculiar case forms I noted *χειραν*, Matthew 12, 10; John 20, 25; Luke 6, 8 (man 1); *τριχαν*, Matthew 5, 36; *απανταν*, Luke 19, 37; *φρονιμαι*, Matthew 25, 9 (man 2); *σαλους* for *σαλου*, Luke 21, 25; cf. Thackeray, p. 146, and Moulton, p. 48, for explanation and other authorities. Nominative for vocative is rare: *θυγατηρ*, Luke 8, 48; John 12, 15; Matthew 9, 22; Mark 5, 34; *υιος*, Matthew 9, 27; *π̅η̅ρ̅*, John 17, 21; cf. Moulton, p. 71. Nominative or indeclinable for accusative once: *σιμων*, Luke 6, 14. Luke 19, 29 has *ελεωνα* as an accusative for the regular *ελαιων*. It is noteworthy that Moulton, p. 69, suggests this form as an emendation to bring the passage into accord with Acts and Josephus.

Probably to be classed as archaising forms are: *πηχεων*, John 21, 8; *ορνιξ*, Luke 13, 34 (= D and cited by Photius), cf. Moulton, p. 45, for papyrus authority; *γλωσσοκομιον*, John 12, 6; 13, 29. Once *εαυτον* occurs for *σεαυτον* (Mark 1, 44); we may compare the development of the plural reflexives, Moulton, p. 87; Thackeray, p. 190. A few mistakes in gender or number occur: *λιθον μεγα*, Matthew 27, 60 (= M U 1, 28, 69, etc.); *λιμος μεγαλη*, Luke 4, 25 (=fam. 13, Latin MSS); *τα πασχα*, Matthew 26, 18; *το διδραγμα*, Matthew 17, 24.

Changes in voice are rare: *εποιουντο*, Mark 3, 6; *αρθηναι και βληθηναι* for *αρθητι και βληθητι*, Mark 11, 23 (=fam. 1, 28, 124 Latin); *δος* for *διδου*, Matthew 5, 42 (=א B D fam. 13); *παρετηρουν*, Luke 6, 7 (=א E K S U V Γ Λ, etc.).

Among the numerals *δεκα δυο* occurs several times: Matthew 26, 14; Luke 2, 42; 8, 1. Peculiar uses of the article are *το ἑν* six times in Mark 4, 8–20; *το πολυ* twice in Luke 12, 48; *το μεν* (= *ο μεν*), Mark 4, 4; *το εξ ολης*, Mark 12, 33.

Other noteworthy variations in construction are: *εσθιοντων* alone in gen. abs. Mark 14, 22, cf. Moulton, p. 74; *εκ παιδοθεν* for *παιδιοθεν*, Mark 9, 21 (= I N fam. 1); acc. *σε* for dative, Mark 10,

21 (=ℵ B C M, etc.); *σου* for *σοι*, John 17, 6 (a Latinism?); *μαλλον υπερ*, John 12, 43 (=ℵ L X, 1, 33, 69, etc.); *εως εις* Mark 8, 3; dative for accusative of duration of time: *τοσουτω χρονω*, John 14, 9 (=ℵ D L Q, cf. Blass, p. 121, Moulton, p. 75); *καταβαντος αυτου*, genitive absolute for dative, Matthew 8, 1 (=ℵ B C fam. 1, fam. 13); *εισελθοντος αυτου*, gen. abs. for acc., Mark 9, 28 (=ℵ B C L); *προς αυτους νομικους*, Luke 14, 3, is supported by G*, but I hesitate to consider *αυτους* a weak demonstrative, though *αυτη* for *ταυτη* occurs, Luke 17, 34; John 4, 11 *εστιν* for *εχεις* looks a little like a Latinism; so also *αυτω* (=ℵ B C* D L X, etc.) for *αυτου* and *αυτη* (= 300, r, Vulgates) for *αυτης*, Luke 1, 5.

In cases like *σαραπτα*, Luke 4, 26; *εκατονταρχης*, Luke 7, 6; *προβατια*, man 2, John 21, 17; *μωυσης* (always except Luke 16, 29); *μαριαμ*, as nominative, Luke 2, 19; 10, 39; John 20, 1; *σολομωνος*, Matthew 12, 42; *σαλομωντος*, John 10, 23; the spellings probably indicate age, as the best MSS support. *δαυειδ*, *νοσσους*, *αλα* (for ἅλας), *ουτως*, *ευθυς*, *αναπειρους* (Luke 14, 13–21), *ειλκωμενος* (Luke 16, 20), and *σινηπεως* (Luke 17, 6, an Ionic form) are likewise old.

The strange form *κα* for *και* occurs seven times: Matthew 3, 5; 12, 50; 24, 18; Mark 1, 3; 12, 33; 16, 1; John 20, 1; codex L has it, Mark 11, 8. Matthew 5, 36, has *μελαναν* for *μελαιναν*; Luke 10, 13, *ουα* for *ουαι*; these errors probably reflect careless pronunciation of the diphthong and are paralleled in Ptolemaic papyri, cf. Thackeray, p. 77. There are two cases of *ζων* for *ζωην*: John 3, 15 (corr. man. 2) and 4, 36. They may well be due to an error in writing, caused by the similarity of *η* and *ν*.

Αλλα for *αλλ'* is very frequent and occurs before all vowels; as Coptic uses only the full form the influence is apparent. W regularly has *ν ἐφελκυστικόν* after *εστι*, the third singular of verbs in *ε*, and the ending *σι*, both of verbs and dative plurals. I noted eleven omissions in Mark: *ειχε* and *ανετειλε*, 4, 5; *συνπνιγουσι*, 4, 19; *αλυσεσι*, 5, 4; *ηθελε*, 7, 24; *εφωνησε*, 9, 35; *εγραψε* 10, 5; *πασι* and *εθνεσι*, 11, 17; *αγρευσωσι*, 12, 13; *προσεκυλεισε*, 15, 46; in Luke, *ειπε*, 9, 50; *εστι* for *εσται*, 1, 34; cf. *ανωθε*, 1, 3; only one in Matthew, *εστι*, 14, 2, and one in John, *εορακε*, 6, 46.

In gathering these lists I have considered especially those examples which might throw light on the character, nationality, and age of the scribe; yet there is little that seems to offer decided evidence. The errors are all old and often agree remarkably with the papyri. A few cases look like Coptic or Latin influence, but can be otherwise explained.

I enumerate here a few odd errors, which I have not classified: —

In Luke: *πλησθησον* for *πληρωθησονται*, 1, 20; *η καρδια* for *μακαρια*, 1, 45; *περι σου περι σου*, 4, 10; *δε* for *δει*, 13, 33; *βδελυσμα*, 16, 15; *ου* for *ουαι*, 17, 1; *ποτε ποτε*, 17, 20; *οιδαμεν* · · · *οιδαμεν*, 20, 21; *ουκεντι*, 22, 16; *ετι* for *αιματι*, 22, 20; *εις αυτηνρου*, 13, 1; *τη οικουμενης*, 21, 26; *υποπταζη*, 18, 5; *και* for *κε̅*, 22, 38; *ον μεν* · · · *τον δε*, 23, 33; *υψεστρεψαν*, 24, 33.

In John: *γαλιδεαν*, 1, 44; *αυ|αυτοις*, 7, 45; *ος* for *ο θεος*, 4, 24; *βαλιν* for *λαβειν*, 6, 21; *εμειν*, 10, 40; *ιδα* for *ιουδα*, 13, 2; *κάϊκαι*, 19, 9.

In Matthew: *γαμων* for *μαγων*, 2, 16; *παταμω*, 3, 6; *του* for *τους*, 5, 44; *τε* for *τελει*, 17, 24; *το ναυιον*, 18, 27; *α* for *ο*, 21, 5; *ει* for *εις*, 25, 46; *τους* for *τουτους*, 26, 1; *μα* for *λαμα*, 27, 46; *εσχισθη* for *εσεισθη*, 27, 51.

In Mark: *ιακωβου και ιακωβου και*, 1, 29; *διαπερασαντες* (= -τος), 5, 21; *δαν* for *εαν*, 6, 22; *φαριοεων*, 8, 15; *απελογουντε*, 16, 14a.

In John 6, 56 there is a repetition of five whole lines not discovered by scribe or correctors. Omissions by carelessness or because of like endings, which can be definitely assigned to our scribe, are few: Matthew 4, 21–22; 15, 18; 16, 2–3; Mark 6, 23; 7, 13; 11, 15; Luke 8, 31; 15, 19; 15, 24; 17, 35[1]; John 5, 11–12 (perhaps from parent); 21, 4. The regular scribe is very free from such errors, if we consider the rapid style of his script and the length of the MS. Neither can the peculiarities of spelling, forms, and construction, as a rule, be referred to our scribe, but rather mark the character of the text tradition and its locality and age. Only in the case of those characteristics which run through the MS without change can we assume our scribe responsible. Among these I venture to draw deductions only from those pronounced characteristics which are rare or non-existent in other Biblical MSS. In this class we may enumerate: tendency towards aspirated consonants, *αλλα* before all vowels, *κα* for *και*, and the decided tendency towards Attic or other old forms. The most of these find their nearest parallels in the early papyri and the oldest uncials of Egyptian origin, thus confirming the supposed Egyptian origin and suggesting an early date.

[1] A most interesting case; the scribe himself corrected his mistake after writing three words.

III. CONTENTS

1. Order, Omissions, Crowded Writing

The ms once contained the whole of the four gospels in the order, Matthew, John, Luke, Mark. This is the order known as the Western, of which the best known examples have been the mss D X 594, Old Latin (a b e f ff_2 q), and Gothic. As noted above, there are two lacunae caused by the loss of leaves. These cover John 14, 25 (*ο δε παρακλητος*) to 16, 7 (including *ελευσεται προς υμας*) and Mark 15, 13 (*οι δε παλιν*) to 15, 38 (including *εσχισθη εις δυο*). The remainder of the ms is so perfect that there is rarely a letter missing or indistinct.

On the preceding page I have listed 12 cases of longer omissions by our scribe; 9 of these were due to like endings and 3 to like beginnings of successive phrases. We may assume that these omissions would more easily occur if the parallel parts stood at the beginnings or ends of neighboring lines, and thus may draw inferences as to the length of line in the parent ms. The three omissions in Matthew are respectively 214, 44, and 36 letters long, indicating a line of either 20 or 40 letters in the parent. As W has about 30, it seems quite certain that the parent did not agree. In Mark the three omissions are of 36, 30, and 14 letters each. These lengths might be consistent with a line length similar to W, but seem to point to a line of about half the length. In Luke, the lengths of the four omissions are 17, 27, 22, 65 letters, which would seem to suggest the short line attributed to the parent of Matthew. In John there are two omissions of this type; one comes between the first and second quires and is 69 letters long; the other, at 21, 4, is 49 letters long. We are also assisted by a repetition 139 letters long, covering five lines in the repeated form and five lines and eight letters in its first form. If we may unite the evidence of these three, the parent ms would seem to have had a line from 23 to 25 letters in length, *i.e.* again a different length, and so indicating a different parent.

The average amount of text written on a sixteen-page quire of the ms is ten and one-half pages of the Oxford 1880 edition. Yet the first quire of John has about eleven and one-half pages, and the last two full quires of Luke (crowded writing noted above, p. 7) contain nearly twelve pages of text each. It is easy enough to explain large quires toward the end of a gospel, if crowding would have saved an extra small quire, but such is not the case here, as Luke ends in a four-page quire. This looks like a hint that the parent MS had larger quires. The larger first quire of John suggests a similar guess for that gospel as well. We shall find this thought confirmed in our study of the text affiliations later.

2. Corrections

There seem to be four well-defined groups of corrections to the MS.

(1) *First Hand*

There are seventy-eight cases where the scribe corrected his own blunders. Only rarely is there doubt as to the author of the correction. The original scribe uses a full round dot above a letter to delete it. The dot is made as dark and heavy as his ink allowed. He erases only rarely, preferring to wash or wipe off the still moist ink. The example which makes the delete dot sure for the first hand is in Luke 17, 35, where we find κ̇α̇ι̇ α̇π̇ο̇κ̇ρ̇ι̇θ̇ε̇ν̇τ̇ε̇ς̇ λ̇ε̇γ̇ο̇υ̇ of verse 36 standing before verse 35, though it follows in its regular place; cf. above, p. 26. Similarly deleted errors are: Matthew 17, 25 ο̇ ι̇ς̇ (also deleted by second hand); Mark 10, 35 (see under third hand); 15, 43 ο̇; Luke 6, 26 υ̇μ̇ι̇ν̇; 17, 20 π̇ο̇τ̇ε̇; 19, 23 μ̇ο̇υ̇; 20, 1 α̇υ̇τ̇ω̇; 24, 14 π̇ε̇ρ̇ι̇ π̇α̇ν̇τ̇ω̇ν̇; John 10, 30 μ̇ο̇υ̇; 17, 22 δ̇εδωκας (δ also deleted by second hand); 19, 9 κ̇α̇ι̇.

A few of the corrections by the first hand give light on his language: Matthew 6, 20 *ουδε* corr. to *ουτε*; 16, 25 *απολεση* corr. to *απολεσει*; 17, 19 *υμεις* corr. to *ημεις*; 27, 46 *θε* corr. to *θεε*; Mark 6, 28 *φυλακει* corr. to *φυλακη*; 11, 15 *ετω ιερω* corr. to *εν τω ιερω*; Luke 4, 36 *δυναμε* corr. to *δυναμει*; 6, 8 *χειραν* corr. to *χειρα*; 7, 38 *αυτου* corr. to *αυτης*; 8, 7 *απεπνιξον* corr. to *απεπνιξαν*; 13, 35 *ηξοι* corr. to *ηξει*; 22, 39 *τω* . . . . corr. to *εις το ορος*; 23, 9 *αυτον* corr. to *αυτω*; John 6, 18 *διηγειριτο* corr. to *-ρετο*; 11, 24 *αναστησιται* corr. to *-σεται*; 18, 40 *βαρραβαν* corr. to *βαραββαν*.

A few of the corrections by the original scribe are well-established variant readings. Their appearance as corrections made by first hand seem to indicate that they stood in the parent MS as glosses either between the lines or in the margin, and so were not always seen by the copyist at first. The examples follow:

Matthew, 12, 31 *η δε του $\overline{\pi\nu\varsigma}$ βλασφημια ουκ αφε*, *i.e.* one line, stands in an erasure. The first writing was washed off immediately and erased very neatly so that hardly any traces remain. The first letter was taller or there was something over it, since the erasure extends rather high (cf. ὁς two lines below). There were no abbreviation marks to be erased. Two upsilons can be read near the end of the line, also *ον* near the middle. It all agrees fairly well with the supposition that the scribe omitted just one sentence, but if so he must have started *ος εαν ειπη*, etc., without *και* before it. It is evident that our MS must be related in some way to the MSS X 6, 113*, 234, 435, l. 25, l. 47; Old Latin (a g l), Vulgates (J R), and Victorinus, all of which omit the whole verse: "But the blasphemy against the Holy Ghost shall not be forgiven unto men." It seems quite clear that the parent of W omitted the sentence, but it had been supplied in a marginal gloss, which was not discovered by the copyist of W, until he had written the next following line. As this omission is almost certainly an error, we must accept a certain relationship between W and the above enumerated MSS.

Matthew 21, 19 *επ* corr. to *εν* or *vice versa; επ* is supported only by MSS 59, 66, 238, l. 22, l. 150*, l. 185. The confusion of *ν* and *π* is a common scribal error.

Matthew 21, 30 *απεκριθη*, which was written at first, is supported by Syr cu S, Sah Bo. The correction to agree with Greek MSS was only partial, so that *απεκριθεις* resulted.

Matthew 16, 24 *αυτον* corr. to *εαυτον*, which is attested by all Greek MSS, may be compared with OL MSS, r r_2, which have *se* for the regular *semet*.

Mark 8, 31 *απο* corr. to *υπο* which is the reading of ℵ B C D G K L N Π Σ Φ 11, 19, 20, 60, 114, 122**, 220, 238, 473, l. 48; all others have *απο*.

Mark 15, 43 *ο* before *απο* was written and deleted by the first hand. The authorities for omission are: D 13, 28, 219, 220, 472, 484, l. 49, Syr S, Bo (five MSS), Eth. All other Greek MSS have it.

Luke 5, 25 *παντων* was corrected at once to the regular reading, *αυτων*. Fam. 13, 157, l. 47 are the only other authorities I have found for *παντων*; 111, 124, Sah (111) have the conflate *αυτων παντων*.

Luke 6, 26 υμιν was written and deleted by first hand. It is found in D Δ fam 13,[1] 28, 472, 700, etc., also b Bo Sah Arm Eth Ir Chr. Most of the uncials omit.

Luke 8, 21 αυτοις corr. to προς αυτους man 1. The only authorities for the dative are D 127, 569, c e Basil.

Luke 11, 6 εξ απ corr. by erasing απ and writing οδου. This points to a gloss containing the reading of D d, απ αγρου.

Luke 18, 43 ηκολουθησεν, which was written at first, is supported by 252*, 254, 569, l. 48, l. 49, gat. The corrected form ηκολουθει is found in all other MSS.

Luke 19, 23 the scribe at first wrote μου το αργυριον with ℵ A B L Ψ 33, 157, l. 48, Sah Bo. He then corrected the order to το αργυριον μου as found in most MSS, especially the Antioch recension.

Luke 20, 1 + αυτω, which was first written, is supported by 472, Syr S cu g, Sah Eth. Its deletion brought the text into agreement with all other MSS.

Luke 23, 12 ο was added above and before ηρωδης by first hand. The authorities for omission are H U fam 13, 72, 74, 86, 90, 106, 234, 235, 245, 252*, 254, 330, 435, 565, 569, l. 47, l. 48, l. 49, l. 54.

Luke 8, 42 συνεθλιβον, which seems to have been written at first, is supported by C L U fam 13, 28, 33, 157, 243, 259, 472, l. 47, l. 49, l. 183. It seems an harmonistic insertion from Mark 5, 24. The corrected form συνεπνιγον is supported by all other MSS.

Luke 10, 11 υμιν written and corrected to ημιν by first hand; υμιν is found in ℵ* D Λ, 3, fam 13, 115, 242, 433, 478*, l. 184, Vulg D. All others have the corrected form ημιν.

Luke 6, 48 δια το καλως οικοδομησθαι αυτην is the reading of W, man 1, thus agreeing with ℵ B L Ξ, 33, 157, Syr h, Sah Bo. But δια το stands on an erasure and I seemed to read τε̣̣ · · as the original writing. We may feel certain that the scribe started to write τεθεμελιωτο, etc., of most MSS, but saw the correction mark or gloss in season to change without much erasing.

John 10, 18 απο erased and παρα written by first hand. There is no MS authority for απο but we may compare *a patre* of all Latin MSS and απο του πατρος of Justin. Dial. c. Tryph. 100.[2]

[1] Fam. 13, fam. 1, etc., indicate the testimony of the respective group whether all members agree or only a majority.

[2] Mr. Hoskier has found απο in MS 157. Through his kindness I am able to insert in proof readings from this interesting MS in other noteworthy passages.

John 10, 30 *μου* written and deleted by first hand. The authorities for *μου* are Δ 71, 247, l. 44, e δ Syr S g, Sah Bo Go Arm Eth Pers. All others omit.

John 17, 22 *δεδωκας* corr. to *εδωκας* by first hand. For *δεδωκας* the authorities are ℵ B C L X Y Γ Δ Λ unc. 6, etc.; for *εδωκας* A D N U Π 106, 157, 248, 482, l. 48, l. 49, al. 6, Clem Hipp Eus Chr Cyr.

Summing up this evidence we may note that in Matthew the first written forms agree in all four cases with the version tradition,[1] while the corrected form is each time the same as the Antioch and Hesychian [2] recensions.

Practically the same condition holds for Luke 8, 13 to end, for of the seven corrections six agree with the Antioch recension, usually supported by the Hesychian, while one agrees with the Hesychian alone. The forms first written agree with the version tradition. The Hesychian and Antioch recensions are found supporting these readings only once each.

Also in Luke 1 – 8, 12, both of the corrections are from the text found in bilinguals or lectionaries to the Hesychian and Antioch recensions.

In Mark one correction is from the Antioch recension supported by lectionaries and some versions to the Hesychian supported by part of the version tradition. The other is from the Hesychian and Antioch recensions to the version tradition.

In John two of the corrections are from the version tradition to the Hesychian and Antioch recensions, and one is the opposite. Even from this fragmentary evidence it seems likely that the different parts of the parent MS had been corrected to agree with different text traditions.

The remaining 33 corrections by first hand are mostly due to errors of eye or memory; all are given in the collation, so I shall omit them here.

(2) *Second Hand*

Corrections by the second hand (*διορθωτής*) number 71. His delete mark is to draw a line through the letters rejected; examples are found in Matthew 17, 25; 27, 55; Mark 2, 25; 3, 10; 10,

[1] I shall use the term version tradition to designate the type of text found in the bilinguals, versions, and Greek MSS allied to the versions.

[2] See v. Soden, Schriften d. N. T. p. 894 ff.

35; John 17, 22. Omissions are marked by the sign ·/., which is repeated in the margin with the words to be added. Examples are: Matthew 2, 17 ·/. *του προφητου*; 7, 17 ·/. *αγαθον*; 24, 24 ·/. *μεγαλα*; Luke 12, 30 ·/. *του κοσμου*; John 11, 9 ·/. *τουτου*. The mark (>) is used in similar fashion once: John 8, 12 >*λεγων*. This is not an addition but a substitute expression, and the change of sign may denote this fact.

The second hand generally shows the following differences from the first hand: the ink is lighter; letters are regularly somewhat smaller, especially when written between the lines or on the margin; the slope is less even; there is less difference between the light and heavy strokes, thus giving a rather heavy appearance to the writing; *ο*, *ε*, and *σ* are rounder; *ο* is smaller and *ε* has regularly a shorter middle stroke; *α*, *δ*, *λ*, *μ* seem to have rather straighter lines; *ν* is narrower and the cross stroke starts from the top of the first upright stroke; the cross stroke of *θ* projects less, while the perpendicular stroke of *ρ* regularly shows above the curve; *υ* has a shorter tail; *ω* is flatter and closes in more at the top.

Quite a number of the corrections by the second hand are either known or natural variants, yet the sum total of such variants is too small to suggest that the *διορθωτής* regularly compared a second MS. Matthew 15, 8, gives a hint as to the method of origin or the cause of these corrections. In this passage the first hand omitted *και τοις χειλεσιν με τιμα*, but left some space at the end of the line and the first half of the following line vacant. It is correctly supplied in the characteristic smaller letter of the second hand. This phrase is found unvaried in all the MSS known to me. It might be explained that the original scribe could not read his copy either because of illegibility or of damage to the parent MS. But if such were the fact, similar cases should have occurred. Also, as above noted, the second hand does not seem to have used another MS for purposes of comparison, so he must have read the passage in the parent. There is a more natural explanation. In W this correction is preceded by *εγγιζει μοι ο λαος ουτος τω στοματι αυτων*. All of this except *ο λαος ουτος* is omitted by ℵ B D L T[c] (1), 33, 124, Old Latin Vulg Syrr Bo Arm Eth, etc. We may be sure that *εγγιζει μοι τω στοματι αυτων* was not original in this passage. But it was regular in all MSS of the Antioch recension, to which this portion of W is related, as we shall see later. If, then, the parent of W was accommodated to the Antioch recension by correction, the whole matter becomes clear. The gloss inserted above και τοις χειλεσιν με τιμα was considered a substitute for it rather than an addition; therefore the scribe did not venture to write it, though he left a space for the διορθωτής to use, if he desired. Corrections and additions to the parent MS seem the proper source for the following products also of the second hand:

Matthew 6, 7 +οτι; οτι is omitted by minuscule 4, and we may note that Sah and Bo have the weaker conjunction ϫⲉ. Its omission thus seems due to Coptic influence.

Matthew 10, 14 τους λογους is corrected by second hand for των λογων, elsewhere found only in certain MSS of Chrysostom in his citation of this passage.

Matthew 19, 8 +υμιν. In addition to the first hand of W minuscule 11 and Chrys. omit.

Matthew 22, 22 απηλθαν is corrected to απηλθον by second hand. The form in α is characteristic of Egyptian texts and the older parts of W. The omicron forms are universal in the Antioch recension.

Matthew 24, 2 +ωδε; the first hand of W omits, supported by minuscule 241, and a few MSS transpose.

Mark 4, 31 μικροτερος is correction for μικροτερον of the first hand. The latter is supported by ℵ B D* L M Δ 13*, 28, 33, 131, 179, 235, 258, 482, 569, 700, while the great majority have μικροτερος.

Mark 6, 14 αυτου is corrected to αυτω. The regular reading is εν αυτω, which the corrector may have been trying to restore; αυτω is supported by 485*, l. 88, and the vulgates R T*; αυτου of the first hand seems to be supported by Syr S alone (possessive ending).

Mark 6, 16 ον is added before εγω ον. This was probably intended as a correction of order, though the second ον was not deleted. We may, however, note that before ον W reads οτι, which is omitted by ℵ B D L 1, 28, 33, 67, 124, 209, 565, Latin Syrr Arm Eth. The insertion of οτι at some time in an ancestor of W may have caused the displacement.

Mark 8, 25 ανεβλεπεν of first hand, supported by Δ 346, is corrected to ενεβλεπεν of ℵ[c] B L fam 13, 28, Syrr Sah Bo, etc. ανεβλεψε has some support, but most MSS have ενεβλεψε.

Mark 10, 36 *με* is added before *ποιησαι*, with א[cb] L (Sah Bo); (cf. א[c] B Arm = *με ποιησω*). The first hand omits *με*, as do Δ 282, 472, 569, l. 29, etc. Also most MSS reading *ποιησω* omit *με*. Most MSS read *ποιησαι με*.

Mark 13, 25 *τω ουρανω* of first hand is corrected to the plural. The singular is elsewhere found only in minuscules 38 and 700, while Syr S is indeterminate.

Mark 15, 40 *ιωση* is corrected by second hand from *ωση*. With this mistake of the first hand we may compare *ηωση* of minuscule 472 and *ωση* of 28 in Matthew 27, 56. For the cause of the error compare Sahidic N̄IⲰCH.

Luke 6, 37 *ινα* of first hand is supported only by D, the Latin MSS (a c d e ff_2 r_2 mol) Syr S Diatess Sah Eth and Basil. Tertul. Cypr.; *και ου* of the second hand is supported by all others.

Luke 8, 49 *απο* of the first hand is supported by A D fam. 1, 51, 251, 472, 700, a b l q Vulg (A), Syr cu g, Bo (F), Dam. All others support *παρα* of the second hand.

Luke 9, 52 *αυτου* of the first hand has by far the best authority, while *εαυτου* of the second is supported by A E G S V Λ and other representatives of the oldest Antiochian recension.

Luke 10, 11 *υμων* is added by the second hand; besides the first hand only Syr cu S seem to omit.

Luke 11, 49 *αποκτενουσιν* of the first hand is the regular reading. Only א* supports *αποκτεινουσιν* of the second hand.

Luke 11, 54 *κατηγορησουσιν* of the first hand is supported by A X Δ 69, 569, l. 19 only. All others agree with the second hand in having the subjunctive.

Luke 12, 17 *συναξαι* of the first hand is supported by Λ fam 13, 131 (*teste* Scholz). All others have *συναξω* with the second hand.

Luke 12, 30 *του κοσμου* is added by second hand; its omission by first hand is supported only by minuscules 12, 40, 53, 58, 59, 63, 67, 119, 248, 253, 259, 330, 482, and Old Latin l.

Luke 12, 47 *αυτου* of the first hand has the best and oldest support; *εαυτου* of the second hand belongs to the Antioch recension (= A E** G[sup] H M R S U V Γ Δ Λ, etc.).

Luke 12, 50 the first hand omits *ου*, as do MSS 53, f and i*. The second hand adds *οπου*, not elsewhere found, but which must stand for *οτου* of א A B D K L M R T U Π al (30), Origen, Dionys. This mistake tends to confirm the idea that the second hand was inserting hastily written or crowded glosses of the parent MS.

Luke 15, 30 σιτευτον of the first hand is correct; σιτιστον of the second hand has no support in this passage, but is borrowed from Matthew 22, 4. Therefore the glosses of the parent MS seem to have contained harmonistic additions or corrections.

Luke 20, 26 εσιωπησαν of the first hand has no other support. It is a synonym of the correct εσιγησαν, and may well have crept into the text under the influence of the early versions with which we find W allied so often. Another explanation may make it an harmonistic error, for while σιγαω occurs two or three times in Luke, σιωπαω occurs twice in Matthew and four times in Mark.

Luke 20, 35 της εκ νεκρων of the second hand is the regular reading; των νεκρων of the first hand is supported by 38, 59, 234, 435, l. 7, l. 13, c, Sah Bo.

Luke 21, 33 παρελευσονται (1) of the second hand is the best supported reading. The singular, given by man 1, is supported by C K Π fam 1, etc., and Old Latin a e q r r_2.

Luke 21, 34 first hand omits η before ημερα, as do D K V. The addition by the second hand is supported by all other MSS.

Luke 22, 37 πληρωθηναι of the first hand is found only in 56, 108, 124, 218, 262, 482; also in 66 τελεσθ stands in an erasure; τελεσθηναι of the second hand agrees with all other MSS. The error arose as a retranslation from one of the versions or through an harmonistic influence from Mark 15, 28.

Luke 24, 34 the omission of οντως by the first hand is supported by 258*, b e l and Cyril. The second hand inserts the word after $\overline{κς}$, as do A X Γ Δ Λ Π unc. (8), etc., of the Antioch recension. Other MSS and versions insert before $\overline{κς}$.

Luke 24, 50 for βηθανιας of the first hand I have found no support, though εις is omitted also by 237, l. 15, l. 253, Vulgate (C), and Augustine. The second hand correction, εις βηθανιαν, is supported by A C*** X Γ Δ Λ Π unc. (7), etc., as also by the Latin MSS.

John 8, 12 και ειπεν of the first hand is supported by Syrr Diatess Eth Pers, though it has no support in Greek MSS; λεγων is added in the margin, perhaps as a substitute, though και ειπεν is not deleted. It is the regular reading.

John 11, 18 omission of ως by the first hand agrees with D d Syr S Diatess Cyr. All others agree with the second hand in adding ως.

John 16, 22 εξεται of the first hand is supported by ℵ[c] A D L Ψ 33, 42, 122, 131, 145, 157, 249, 254, 481, 482, l. 15, l. 184, a b d e r Vulg Cop Chrys, etc. εχετε of the second hand occurs in ℵ* B C Y Γ Δ Λ Π unc. (7), etc.

Analyzing these cases we get results similar to those obtained for the first hand changes. In Matthew all of the second hand corrections agree with the Antioch recension, sometimes but not always supported by other MS groups. The first hand generally has weak support, but it always includes MSS, versions, or Church Fathers related to the version tradition. The same relationship to the Antioch recension prevails in the second hand corrections in Luke 8, 13 to end, though one case out of the seventeen points to a different influence. The first hand here also is always related to the version tradition. There is but one example in the first two quires of Luke and this gives a correction from the version tradition to the Antioch and Hesychian recensions. In Mark we find six cases of correction to the Hesychian recension, but usually supported by some branches of the version tradition, while one case is just the opposite. The fact that representatives of the version tradition are found on both sides in all except one case hinders us from assuming a definite accommodation to either of the great recensions. In John there are but three cases and all show corrections from the version form to the Hesychian supported by the Antioch recension. The remaining 33 cases of second hand are mostly corrections of simple errors. All are found in the collation.

(3) *Third Hand*

I have noted only the following eleven cases of correction by the third hand:

Matthew 24, 32 ευθυς for εγγυς; υθ is in an erasure and by a later, rougher hand; there is no variant recorded for the passage. Possibly the first hand wrote εγγυς.

Mark 5, 1 omitted ν of την before χωραν was added by the third hand.

Mark 10, 35 προσελθοντες of the first hand, corrected at once to προσελθοντες, was further corrected by the second hand, who crossed out ες. The third hand again crossed out these two letters, erased the first ε and wrote η. All other Greek MSS have προσπορευονται. The perfect tense of the Old Latin MSS c d f ff₂ r aur, Syr S Sah Bo gives some warrant for the first hand reading.

Mark 11, 33 οιδομεν of the first hand was corrected to οιδαμεν.

Luke 4, 19 the third hand corrected τεθρωμενους to the spelling, τεθραυμενους, of D[2]; τεθραυσμενους is the regular reading.

Luke 7, 3 third hand changes αυτω to αυτον after ερωτων.

Luke 7, 22 ειδατε of the first hand is corrected to ειδετε.

Luke 8, 2 of εξεληλυθη the letters ξεληλυθ are in an erasure and by the third hand. The letters are unduly spread, showing that the original writing was longer. The only recorded variant is the pluperfect in Syr cu, Cop.

John 5, 19 the third hand adds the omitted ν of αμην.

John 8, 46 διατι after λε|γω omitted by first hand is added by erasing γω, writing γω δι at end of previous line and ατι in the erasure.

John 11, 7 omitted α of αγωμεν is added by third hand.

These are all natural corrections made by an intelligent reader. The corrections at Matthew 24, 32 and Mark 10, 35 almost forbid our thinking that he had another text to use for comparison, while + διατι, John 8, 46, seems to imply knowledge of a corrected text. It is possible that this correction was made by the διορθωτής and that the awkwardness of the writing is due to the depth and roughness of the erasure. The omission of διατι is supported only by 28, (87), 250, Bo (two MSS), Syr g (nine MSS).

The third hand is written with large, awkward letters. Ornamental dots are heavier, especially on the middle stroke of ε and the cross stroke of θ; also υ and ν are ornamented. The ink is brown but rather darker than the regular hand. It is decidedly later than the original writing, but may be dated as early as the sixth century, possibly the end of the fifth.

(4) *Other Hands*

Of the fourth hand there are but four instances:

Luke 17, 1 ου for ουαι is corrected to ουε.

John 6, 53 omitted μη is added.

John 9, 6 omitted ο of του is added a little below and smaller.

John 9, 23 ειπον is changed to ειπαν.

These are all corrections by a reader and were not drawn from acquaintance with another MS. The letters are very awkward in shape: Coptic μ is used. The ink is jet black. The corrector was certainly not in the habit of writing in uncials, so it would be useless to attempt to date him on the basis of the forms of these few letters. We have, however, seen that black ink was used in the Deuteronomy-Joshua MS in the sixth century and later; so we may safely date this hand later than the third hand.

The first quire of John I have excluded from the discussion thus far, as the hands are all different. To avoid confusion I name them *a*, *b*, and *c*, instead of first, second, and third.

In this quire there are four cases of letters crossed out. The following three were certainly deleted by hand *a*: 2, 16 ο between μ and η of μη; 2, 24 ο before εαυτον; 4, 10 α between τ and ο of αυτον.

In 4, 22 οοκ for ουκ is corrected by crossing out the second ο and writing υ above it. This is surely not hand *a*. In 1, 33 the same hand corrected οτος to ουτος by writing υ above. In 3, 15 ζων is corrected to ζωην by changing ν to η and adding ν above. In 3, 22 ι is written above to change ες to εις.

These four changes I refer to hand *b*. The noticeable characteristics are the angularity and narrowness of the letters. The ink is of the same shade.

In 1, 13 the first two letters of σαρκος stand in an erasure; the ink is darker and the α both angular and broad. It was certainly not written by hand *b* and probably not by hand *a*, yet it is of the same general style and so not much later. The fact that none of the hands bear any resemblance to the hands in the remainder of the MS proves that all date from a time before the quire became a part of the MS, or that the whole quire is later than the fourth hand of the MS; I incline to the first alternative, for it does not seem likely that three different scribes would have busied themselves with the first quire of John and yet have left no mark in the rest of the MS.

I have above, on p. 2, referred to the three hands in which the subscription to Mark was written. These may now be numbered 5, 6, and 7; nos. 5 and 6 are semi-cursives of the fifth century and in light brown ink; no. 7 is a similar but ruder semi-cursive in jet black ink. An eighth hand wrote across the top of the same page (372 of the MS) certain words of which ··λλος ναως or ··λλου ναως is still legible. The ink is pale brown and the forms of the letters most crude. I have found no explanation for the note.

The regular subscriptions to the four gospels are ευαγγελιον κατα μαθθεον, κατα ιωαννην, ευαγγελιον κατα λουκαν, ευαγγελιον κατα μαρκον. All are preceded by a simple ornamental division, identical for Matthew, John, and Luke, but larger for Mark. The subscriptions are all by the first hand and of the regular size of letter.

At the beginnings of the Gospels, crowded near the top of the page, stand the usual titles, [ευ]αγγελιον κατα μαθθεον, ευαγγελιον κατα ιωαννην, ευαγγελιον κατα λουκαν, ευαγγελιον κατα μαρκον. In spite of slight variations it is manifest that the titles of Matthew, Luke, and Mark were written by the same hand, who was not the scribe of the MS, though there seems to be a tendency to imitate the regular hand in a few letters. The smaller size, varying slope, and characteristic forms of certain letters have caused me to assign these three titles to the second hand, though I recognize that the identification is somewhat doubtful. Those who accept this view must admit that the διορθωτής was consciously or unconsciously influenced by the forms of some letters on the page before him as he wrote. The writer of the title to John is even more doubtful. Yet we may venture the assertion that it was not by the scribe of the first quire nor by either of its correctors. I base this view not only on the style of writing, but still more on the lighter shade of the ink and its apparent escape from the severe wear which the ink on the two outside pages of this quire has suffered. It seems clearly later than the original writing of the quire. It bears, to be sure, a certain general resemblance to the regular hand of the quire, but one feels that it is only imitative and not very well done at that. The almost complete absence of ornamental dots on the letters distinguishes it sharply from the regular hand of the quire. In fact, in this regard it stands on a par with the regular hand of the whole MS. The variations in slope, smaller size, and shapes of ω, τ, ν, λ remind us of the διορθωτής. The title would be most easily explained by supposing it written in a hand striving to imitate the writing of that quire; as the other titles are rather imitative, this assumption would suggest the διορθωτής as the writer, a decision that we cannot accept until the question of relative age of the two parts of the MS has been settled. It may be of interest to note that the word ευαγγελιον, where it occurs in the text and subscription, measures approximately $1\frac{1}{4}$ inches in length each time, while in the titles it measures about an inch each time. In the title of John it measures $\frac{15}{16}$ of an inch, thus approximating the work of the διορθωτής.[1] We may also note that the last letters of ιωαννην in the title have offset or printed across on to the opposite page. This may have been caused by closing the book before the title was dry, or a little moisture or decay may have caused these letters to print across. The marks on the opposite page feel a little smoother than the ordinary offset.

The quire numbers are all by the regular hand except Θ, of the first quire of John. This is smaller and in paler ink. It is probably by the same hand as the title of John.

[1] Cf. Amer. Jour. of Arch. vol. 13, p. 130 ff., for plates and further discussion.

IV. THE PROBLEM OF THE TEXT

THE solution of the text problem of W has been much impeded by the inadequacy of the textual material in the critical editions and the impossibility of explaining its peculiarities on the basis of the text theories generally accepted. It was a common occurrence to find in the Tischendorf apparatus al 2, al 3, etc., as the chief authorities for noteworthy variants of W. This seemed at first much more disconcerting than to find no authorities cited, yet in the end I found that the two conditions were often not different, for Tischendorf might have taken from the older editions cursive MS authority for many readings, which he left unmentioned. The inadequacy of any one critical edition, and the danger in omitting from consideration the minuscule MSS and the variants in the versions, is well illustrated by the fact that a comparison of W with the apparatus of Tischendorf left unexplained nearly five hundred important variants in the gospel of Mark alone. Through the use of the minuscule MSS and the early versions this number of unsupported readings has been reduced by nearly three-fourths. Furthermore, a comparison of the readings of W with von Soden's results, as shown in his prolegomena, convinced me that Tischendorf and Westcott and Hort had built on a false foundation. Von Soden's earliest form of the Antioch recension (K^1) pointed so plainly in Matthew to W as its oldest and best representative, and his Hesychian recension (H) agreed so closely with W in Luke 1 – 8, 12, that I could not hesitate to accept his results, at least up to that point. The matter was made more certain by the fact that the corrections of first and second hands showed plainly that these recensions had been corrected into an older style of text in our MS or its parent (cf. pp. 31 and 36). That there was another, probably older, recension connected in some way with Origen is also likely, but that assumption does not seem sufficiently to explain all the divergences of the "Western Texts" of Westcott and Hort. Harris,[1] Chase,[2] and especially Hoskier[3] have, I be-

[1] Codex Sangallensis, Cambridge, 1891; Study of Codex Bezae, Cambridge, 1891.

[2] Old Syriac Element in the Text of the Codex Bezae, London, 1893; Syro-Latin Text of the Gospels, London, 1895.

[3] Genesis of the Versions, London, 1910–1911.

lieve, started on the right path here. Enough has been done so that it may be considered as settled that the peculiarities of the so-called Western text (von Soden's I) are closely allied to the early versions. My comparisons with the text of W, especially in Mark and the early part of John, establish this intimacy most clearly. Only rarely did I fail to find authority for W's "special" variants in some one of the versions, Syriac, Latin, Coptic, Gothic, Armenian, or Ethiopic. In the cases where I failed I generally attributed it to the inadequacy of the textual apparatus in the versions or to the insufficiency of my own acquaintance with all these languages. Harris (*op. cit.*) first showed the extent of Latin reaction on the Greek text in the bilinguals; Chase (*op. cit.*) followed with a more elaborate proof of the Syriac influence, which though adequate on the main theme claimed too exclusive an influence of Syriac. It remained for Hoskier to reconcile the conflicting ideas by assuming the early existence of trilinguals, in which there might be influence of more than one version on the Greek text at the same time. In my article in the Amer. Jour. of Phil. vol. 33, pp. 30 ff., I hesitated to accept this theory in full on the ground that it was barely possible to explain the textual conditions on the basis of bilinguals alone, and that no proof of the early existence of trilinguals was known to us. Yet even in the few weeks of study since that article new evidence has come to view, and doubtless more lies hid in the Church literature. We may note first Auxentius, 305–306 (Streitberg, Gotische Bibel, xvi), concerning Ulfilas: *Grecam et Latinam et Goticam linguam sine intermissione in una et sola eclesia Christi predicavit . . . qui et ipsis tribus linguis plures tractatus et multas interpretationes volentibus ad utilitatem et ad aedificationem sibi ad aeternam memoriam et mercedem post se dereliquit.* This does not state that Ulfilas completed or used a trilingual version, but that he used all three versions. That these were, however, combined in a trilingual may now be assumed, and I feel sure that with the new material available scholars will be able to prove that the Gothic version was made from a Greek-Latin bilingual and that it existed for a long time parallel to a Latin version at least, of which the best-preserved example is Old Latin f.

A much more decisive passage occurs in Ibn al-Assal's (1252 A.D.) introduction to his Arabic version of the Gospels.[1]

[1] My attention was called to this reference by Professor Worrell of the Hartford Theological Seminary.

I quote from Professor MacDonald's translation[1] in Estudios de Erudicion Oriental, 1904, p. 386: "I have seen in Cairo a codex of the Psalms in three columns, Coptic, Greek, and Arabic, and in Damascus also a codex of the Psalms in three columns, Syriac, a transliteration of Greek, and Arabic." On page 385 Ibn al-Assal mentions a Greek-Arabic bilingual of the Gospels, and on page 387 refers to a Coptic-Arabic Bible. On page 389 he states that his translation has a Coptic interlinear over all words which are doubtful or difficult. Furthermore, there is now on exhibition in the British Museum (Harl. 5786) a trilingual Psalter, Greek, Latin, and Arabic, of a date before 1153. Mr. Hoskier writes me that the Greek forms the first column and the Latin the middle, and that the two correspond line for line. This evidence does not, to be sure, prove that there were trilingual MSS of the Gospels; but the fact that a trilingual of the Psalms still exists and that such MSS were perhaps frequent in the thirteenth century, when they must have been relatively unnecessary, and that the known examples included Syriac-Greek as well as Greek-Latin columns, gives us a most convincing suggestion as to what must have been the condition in the earlier times when the peoples of the East were bilingual or even trilingual. We know that bilingual (Greek-Syriac) inscriptions were common in Syria (cf. Mommsen, Prov. Rom. Emp. vol. 2, p. 96), and Latin also must have gained a foothold in the larger cities and garrison towns. In Egypt the conditions are known to have been quite similar. The absolute necessity of having Syriac and Coptic versions of the New Testament in spreading Christianity among the peoples of those regions will be felt by any one who has ever observed the enthusiasm with which a speaker in their own tongue is greeted by the Germans in Wisconsin, the French in Quebec, and still more the common people in Wales, though all of these understand English.

We may be sure that the rapid spread of Christianity over the Roman world was caused by or accompanied by the translation of the Gospels into the chief languages of the Empire. Yet Pliny, Ep. 10, 96, tells us that Bithynia was overrun by it before 111 A.D., and Tacitus, Ann. 15, 44, that it was widespread in Rome before 65.

The question of the date of the earliest translations of the New

[1] From Brit. Mus. Orient. 3382.

Testament is still undecided, but I have no hesitation in taking the side of those who claim the earliest date. That the translations into Syriac and Latin were the earliest has been generally conceded, but some have tried to put the date late in the second century The real difficulty with such an assumption, aside from its incompatibility with the rapid spread of Christianity before that date, is the impossibility of explaining the age, frequency, and wide distribution of N. T. text corruptions, which are best assigned to bilingual or translation influences. Peculiarities characteristic of the bilinguals headed by codex D and by the Old Latin and Old Syriac MSS are now found in W, an old Greek MS of Egypt, and have long been known in Irenaeus and other church fathers of his time and earlier. The characteristic features of this type of text were well established and widespread before 150 A.D., and to those who find the most acceptable explanation in the use and influence of the versions, as I do, there can be no doubt about the early date of the first New Testament translations. Even in the case of the Coptic translations the trend is now towards the earlier date; cf. Bousset, Text. u. Untersuch. vol. 11, p. 95. On pages 903 ff. of his Prolegomena von Soden states that MSS ℵ and B show influence of the Sahidic translation and, while he assumes that the Bohairic version was made later, he notes instances where the Bohairic version shows variants plainly older than Sahidic and the related ℵ and B. Hoskier upholds the early date of both the Sahidic and Bohairic versions; cf. his Genesis of the Versions and Concerning the Date of the Bohairic Version, London, 1911.

The date of the Sahidic version has now been definitely placed before 300 by the discovery and publication of a MS of Acts in that version, which has been dated before 350 by Dr. Kenyon on the basis of a subscription in a cursive Greek hand of that date; cf. page lv in the introduction to Budge's Coptic Biblical Texts in the Dialect of Upper Egypt, London, 1912. Budge also notes that the version of Acts in question was not an original translation from the Greek, but because of transcription errors must be considered a later copy. We thus gain no definite date for the Sahidic version, but 300 may now be considered the *terminus ante quem*.

Another equally important and difficult question is the character and amount of influence of Tatian's Harmony of the Gospels. Did it influence or was it influenced by the Old Syriac version?

Of recent works Burkitt, Evangelion da Mepharreshe, von Soden, Die Schriften des Neuen Testaments, p. 1536, etc., and Vogels, Texte und Untersuchungen, vol. 36, 1a, have made the earliest Syriac translation dependent on Tatian's Diatessaron. Vogels even supposes a Latin version of Tatian, which influenced the Old Latin version or versions, and thus explains the close relationship of the Syriac and Latin translations. His work is able as well as elaborate and will be of value to scholars because of his long lists of "harmonistic" errors catalogued on pp. 63 to 106. To me he seems both to exaggerate the harmonistic influence and to err in his fundamental assumption that all harmonistic errors must be referred to the influence of Tatian's Diatessaron. Every one knows how easy it is for us to remember the Lord's prayer according to Matthew, while few can repeat the original form in Luke. The ancient Christians, both readers and scribes, knew their Gospels far better than we, yet they also would have remembered the words of Christ and the story of his life in a form which omitted or harmonized the differences in the accounts given in the four Gospels. Such a reader or such a scribe was sure to make corrections in his copy of the Gospels, especially in the period before the end of the second century, when the New Testament canon had not been formed and the written word was not yet so rigidly adhered to as in the Old Testament. The early established habit of collecting parallel passages for lectionary use aided this harmonistic tendency. There can be little doubt that Tatian's Harmony had an influence on the separate Gospels in those regions of Syria where it was used, but it certainly was not the cause of all harmonistic errors in MSS both east and west. Hoskier, Genesis of the Versions, chapters iv and xii, has gathered many examples showing that the first Syriac translation of the Gospels was prior to Tatian,[1] and I shall note a few others in the discussion below. If this view is correct, the excessive exaltation of Tatian's Harmony rests on a very insecure foundation.

This outline of the current controversies on matters affecting the New Testament text does not aim or hope to settle the questions under discussion, but has been introduced in order that terms to be used later may be intelligible and the evidence of W placed on the proper side in these various controversies.

As it has already been seen that there are noteworthy differ-

[1] Cf. also Amer. Jour. of Phil. vol. 33, p. 35.

ences in the different parts of W, I shall discuss the text of each Gospel separately. The proof that such a course was necessary will appear from the different results arrived at in the different Gospels.

1. Matthew

In the discussion of first and second hand corrections to Matthew, pp. 31 ff., we found that practically all of the corrections agreed with the Antioch recension, sometimes supported by the Hesychian, but that the first written forms were always found in the version tradition. We can add to this evidence of a revision in the parent of W.

1) In 2, 6 *τη ιουδα* stands for *γη ιουδα*. This might be a scribal error of *τ* for *γ*, but our scribe has no tendency in that direction. It seems more likely that the parent MS had *της ιουδαιας* with D 61, a b c f ff$_2$ g$_1$ q, which was corrected by delete marks to *της̇ ιουδαια̇ς̇*. With this form before the eye of the scribe it would make little difference if the *τ* had been corrected to *γ*, his tendency would be to write *τ*.

2) In 3, 6 +*παταμω* for *ποταμω* looks like a cursive gloss. Confusion of *α* and *ο* is not a natural fault of our scribe.[1] The addition belongs to the Hesychian recension, though it has support in the version tradition also.

3) In 8, 29 the conflate reading *απολεσαι ημας και προ καιρου βασανισαι* occurs. The regular reading is *προ καιρου βασανισαι ημας*, while only ℵ, Bo, Eustathius, Orosius, Augustine, and Ambrosius support *απολεσαι ημας*. Vulgate D shows this as an addition, but deleted. It seems that *προ καιρου βασανισαι* was written above *απολεσαι* as a correction in the parent of W; as the delete marks were not used, some reader, or our scribe, considered it an addition and inserted a *και*. The error *απολεσαι* was perhaps harmonistic in its origin; cf. Mark 1, 24; Luke 4, 35.

4) In 12, 16 W combines the regular reading *και επετιμησεν αυτοις* with the substitute *δε ους εθεραπευσεν επεπληξεν αυτοις* of D 1, a b c ff$_1$ h k. The same explanation applies as in example 3.

5) In 17, 9 W has *καταβενοντων* for *καταβαινοντων αυτων*. We may compare *καταβαινοντες* of D and *descendentes* of d; cf. also e. The correction of the parent of W was evidently careless, as *αυτων* was not inserted when the change was made requiring it. But

[1] Cf. above, pp. 20–26.

compare Mark 14, 22 εσθιοντων alone; the genitive absolute developed as ablative absolute in Latin; cf. Moulton, p. 74.

6) In 18, 7 W adds εκεινω of the Antioch recension before ουαι τω $\overline{\text{ανω}}$ instead of after it; εκεινω is omitted by ℵ D F L 1, 22, l. 184, d g_1 aur Vulg Syrr Bo Clementine Ep., Cyr. Basil. Aphr. Anast. Hier. It is clear that εκεινω was added to make the text conform to the Antioch recension, and the fact that it comes two words too early indicates that it was a gloss between the lines or in the margin of the parent. Old Latin r_2 has the order *vae huic homini*, which is indeed a Latin order, but no other Latin MS changes from the Greek order.

7) In 23, 25 W has ακρασιας αδικειας, where the scribe copied his original so accurately that he did not add the connective necessary to make a conflate reading, as was done in Syr g. As in examples 3 and 4, we find the Antioch reading αδικειας placed last, its natural position if the other reading stood on the line in the parent and this was added between the lines or in the margin. The reading ακρασιας is supported by both the Hesychian recension and the version tradition.

8) In 27, 41 W reads φαρισαιω (=φαρισαιων of D 63, 64, l. 2, l. 7, l. 9, l. 12, l. 36, l. 47, l. 183, l. 253, Syr S, Old Latin, and Cassiodorus). This has been explained on p. 22 as a possible scribal omission of ν, but the omission may also have been occasioned by a correction inserted between the lines or in the margin of the parent MS. At the end of a line ν was shown by an abbreviation mark, which was easily obscured by anything written above.

Cumulative evidence of this sort can never be quite conclusive, but we may, I think, assume that there was an ancestor of W, which had been corrected. It does not seem necessary to suppose more than one corrector, for all except one or two of the changes can be accounted for on the basis of accommodation to the Antioch recension. This conclusion does not force us to think previous readers incapable of making changes in their copies, but simply says that this plain evidence of recent correction points to a single corrector. Furthermore, the fact that most of this evidence is drawn from changes by first and second hands indicates that the corrections were made in the parent of W and not in some more remote ancestor. With a second or third copying many, if not all, of these inconsistencies would have been removed. That the corrector aimed to make the text conform to the Antioch recension is borne out by the study of the text.

To avoid evidence liable to deceive, variants which are purely orthographical or grammatical have been treated under a previous head and will be, so far as possible, excluded here, even in cases where W has notable support for its mistakes. It has seemed that these peculiarities indicate rather the date and nationality of the scribe, or even the character of Hellenistic Greek, but not direct MS affiliation.

With these deductions there remain 1505 notable variants in Matthew, of which 1205 belong to the Antioch recension. It is furthermore the oldest type of the Antioch recension, viz. the K^{I} type of von Soden, of which the best MSS previously known are Ω S V. The special peculiarities of the later or revised types of the Antioch recension are not found in W.

It remains to determine the text form on the basis of which this corrected type of text was produced, and the 300 text variants opposed to the Antioch recension may be supposed to contain evidence on this question. I cite first those variants which have good uncial support, giving in each case all the authorities known to me for the reading:

1, 22 — *του* before *κυριου* = א B C D Z Δ 1, 33, 127*;
2, 15 — *του* before *κυριου* = א B C D Z Γ Δ Π al;
2, 17 *δια* for *υπο* = א B C D Z, 33, 61, 71, 73, 125, 131, 157, l. 63, OL Vulg Syrr Chr;
2, 22 *του πατρος αυτου ηρωδου*[1] = א B C Eth;
3, 1 *δε* for *και* = א B C U Γ 1, 33, etc. OL Vulg Sah Bo (ten MSS) Syrr;
3, 3 *δια* for *υπο* = א B C D 1, 13, 33, 124, 157, 209, 700, OL Vulg Sah Bo;
3, 4 *ην αυτου* = א B C D 1, 209;
3, 10 — *και* (1) = א B C D^{sup} M Δ 4, 124, 314, 471, 700, d Syr cu g, Sah Bo Or Ir (OL Vg);
3, 11 *υμας βαπτιζω* = א B 1, 13, 33, 209, 700, ff_1 g_2 l m Vulg Just Clem Or Cyr Cyp Tert;
3, 12 (*αποθηκην*) + *αυτου* = B E L U 7, 9, 38, 52, 53, 58, 60, 157, 220, 224, 235, 236, 242, 253, 436, b ff_1 g_1 m Vulg (B T X* Z*) Syrr Arm Eth Sah (P. S.) Cyr Ambr;

[1] Variants cited without explanatory remarks are regularly transpositions, or variations in form or spelling.

3, 16 *ευθυς ανεβη* = ℵ B D^{sup} 1, 127, 243, 435, 700, OL Vulg Syr cu g, Sah Bo Eth Hipp Chr Hil Op;

4, 3 *ο πειραζων ειπεν αυτω* = ℵ B 1, 13, 33, 124, 157, 209, 700, ff$_1$ h k l Vulg Sah Bo Syr g Arm Eth Chr;

4, 9 *σοι παντα* = ℵ B C* Z 1, 21, 33, 209, 335, 435, l Vulg Or Chr;

4, 16 *σκοτια* = ℵ^b B D Or;

4, 16 *φως ειδεν* = ℵ B C 1, 13, 33, 124, 209, 238, 240, 250, OL Vulg Or Eus Chr Cyr;

5, 25 *μετ αυτου εν τω οδω* = ℵ B D L 1, 13, 28, 33, 124, 209, a b c d g$_1$ h q Syr cu g, Cop Arm Eth Ambr;

5, 32 *μοιχευθηναι* = ℵ B D 1, 13, 22, 33, 124, 209, 237, 238, 253, 259, 1071, Thphil Or Chr;

5, 36 *ποιησαι η μελα[ι]ναν* = ℵ B L a b c f ff$_1$ g$_{1,2}$ h l m Vulg Cop Arm Eth Chr Cyp Aug;

5, 39 *ραπιζει* = ℵ B Σ 33, 234, 476, 700, l. 48, (Tert);

5, 39 *εις* for *επι* = ℵ* B 4, 125, 169, 234, 235, 238, 245, 247, 253, 435, 473, 484, l. 184, Dial Eus Bas Chr;

5, 47 *το αυτο* for *ουτω* = ℵ B D M U Z Σ 1, 4, 13, 21, 28, 33, 44, 47, 61, 124, 209, 235, 299, 346, 471, 700, al l. 48, Syr g Arm Eth Go Cyp Lucif Aug;

6, 6 *ταμιον* = ℵ D, l. 47 (cf. B E L etc.);

6, 10 − *της* = ℵ B Z Δ 1, 22, 406, Clem Or Chr;

7, 6 *καταπατησουσιν* = B C L X 33, 485, δ;

7, 10 *αιτησει* = ℵ B C L Δ 33, 475, l. 184;

7, 24 *αυτου την οικιαν* = ℵ B C Z 1, 33, 471, Sah Bo Or;

7, 26 *αυτου την οικειαν* = ℵ B Z Σ 1, 700, Sah Bo;

7, 28 *ετελεσεν* = ℵ B C Z$^?$ Γ 1, 2, 33, 68, 73, 99, 122*, 124, 127, 470, 476, 482, 485, 700, l. 44, l. 183, Or Chr;

8, 13 − *και* (2) = ℵ B 99, 251, a b g$_{1,2}$ h k q Syr cu g, Sah Bo Ir Chr;

8, 27 *αυτω υπακουουσιν* = ℵ B 1, 33, Eus Chr;

8, 32 − *των χοιρων* (2) = ℵ B C* M Δ 1, 13, 33, 115, 118, 124, 142, 157, 299, 471*, OL Vulg Syrr Sah Arm Eth Go;

8, 34 *ινα* for *οπως* = B (cf. Latin Sah Bo);

9, 2 *σου αι αμαρτιαι* = ℵ B C Δ* 1, 4, 5, 6, 7, 8, 9, 14, 33, 38, 64, 209, l. 50, Or Chr;

9, 8 *εφοβηθησαν* = ℵ B D 1, 22, 33, 59, 118, OL Vulg Sah Bo Syr g Eth Hil Aug;

9, 11 *ελεγον* for *ειπον* = ℵ B C L 1, 21, 33, 115, 118, Cyr;

10, 12 (αυτην) + λεγοντες ειρηνη τω οικω τουτω = ℵ* D L Φ 1, 4, 22, 99, 209, 237, 259, l. 4, l. 7, l. 18, l. 19, l. 49, l. 184 al OL Vulg Arm Thphil Hil (cf. Luke 10, 5);
10, 13 εφ for προς = ℵ B 243, Syr S g Eth Chr (cf. Luke 10, 5);
10, 23 ετεραν for αλλην = ℵ B 33, 265, Or Petr Ath Cyr Chr Thdrt;
10, 28 αποκτεννοντων = ℵ C D U Γ Δ Π** 1, 72, 106, 247, 475, 476, 485, 700, l. 49 al;
10, 28 φοβεισθαι = ℵ B C 21;
10, 31 φοβεισθαι = ℵ B D L 1, 13, 33, 118, 157, 209, l. 36, l. 70, Or Cyr;
10, 33 καγω αυτον = ℵ B D Δ 1, 32, 33, 44, 73, 86, 127, 237, 300, l. 34, l. 60, al OL Vulg Syr cu S Arm Go Or Cyr Chr;
11, 2 δια for δυο = ℵ B C* D P Z Δ 33, 124, d q Syrr Arm Go;
11, 5 + και (3) = ℵ B D L P Z Δ 1, 13, 28, 122, 300, 478, a b d g_1 k l q Vulg (D J L) Syrr Arm Go;
11, 9 προφητην ιδειν = ℵ* B Z Or Chr;
11, 16 καθημενοις εν αγοραις = ℵ B C D L M Z Δ Σ Φ 33, 106, 124, 157, 238, 243**, 299, 300, 346, 700, l. 48, l. 49, l. 184, al OL Vulg Chr;
11, 19 εργων for τεκνων = ℵ B* 124, Sah (111) Bo Syr g h Arm Eth Pers Hier;
11, 23 μη · · · · υψωθηση = ℵ B C D L 1**, 22, 42, a b c d ff_1 g_2 k l Vulg Syr cu Bo Arm Eth Ir Hier;
11, 23 − του = ℵ B D Δ 157, 243, 478, l. 184, Bo Caes Chr;
11, 26 ευδοκεια εγενετο = ℵ B 1, 33, k Vulg (Wurz J P*) Bo Ir;
12, 10 − ην την = ℵ B C k l Vulg Bo Syr cu Eth;
12, 10 θεραπευσαι = ℵ D L 106;
12, 22 − και (4) = ℵ* B D 1, 77, 124, 201, 246*, 252*, 253, 262, 479, 480, l. 49, l. 184, OL Vulg Sah Bo Syr cu Arm;
12, 29 αρπασαι = B C* X 1, 238, l. 49, l. 184, a;
12, 32 τουτω τω αιωνι = ℵ B C D fam 1, fam 13, al mult Or;
13, 2 − το = ℵ B C L Z Σ 1, 4, 18, 33, 124, 237, 201, 241, 242, 248, 252, 253, 435, 479, 480, 700;
13, 3 σπειραι = ℵ D L M X fam 1, 4, fam 13, 28, 99, 237, 243, l. 49, l. 184, al Or Chr Thphil;
13, 34 ουδεν for ουκ = ℵ* B C M Δ 4, fam 13, 47, 50, 106, 131,

235, 238, 299, 300, l. 4, l. 18, l. 48, l. 49, l. 184, f Syr h Arm Clem Or Chr;

13, 55 ουχ = ℵ B C M Δ Σ 33, 237, 244, 299, 472, 700, Or Eus Bas Cyr;

14, 19 του χορτου = ℵ B C* I Σ Φ 1, 22, 33, 106, 124, 157, 245, 481, 700, l. 27, l. 44, Syr h Bo Arm Or;

14, 22 − ο ις = ℵ B C* D I P Δ Θ fam 1, 4, 33, 106, 124, 238, 472, al d e f ff_1 (Vulg) Syr cu g h j Bo Arm Eth Or;

14, 25 την θαλασσαν = ℵ B P T^c Δ Θ Φ 1, fam 13, 22, 238, 700, l. 27, Or;

14, 28 ελθειν προς σε = ℵ B C D Δ Θ Σ Φ 1, fam 13, 33, 157, 238, l. 47, OL (Vulg) Syrr Sah Bo Arm Eth Eus;

14, 34 επι for εις = ℵ B C D T^c Δ fam 13, 33, 157, 238, 245, Syr h Chr;

14, 34 + εις before γεννησαρετ = ℵ B D T^c Δ 33, Syr cu h Arm;

15, 5 τιμησει = ℵ B C D E** T^c Δ Θ Π** 1, 3, 9, fam 13, 33, 73, 225, 471*, 481, l. 184, Lat Cyr Or;

15, 31 + και before χωλους = ℵ B C D M P Δ 1, 4, fam 13, 157, l. 184, d f k Vg (J) Syrr Bo Eth;

16, 19 κλειδας = ℵ* B* L Or;

17, 3 συνλαλουντες μετ αυτου = ℵ B 1, $ff_{1,2}$ q Syr cu g Sah Bo Eth Or Cyr Chr;

17, 10 − αυτου = ℵ L Z 1, 33, 124, 700, OL Vulg Sah Bo Arm Or;

17, 11 − ις = ℵ B D L Z 1, 33, 237, l. 13, l. 15, l. 184, OL Vulg Syrr Sah Bo;

17, 11 − αυτοις = B D 33, 124, 700, a b c d e ff_2 Vulg (A H Q) Sah Bo;

17, 11 − πρωτον = ℵ B D 1, 22, 33, 435, 700, l. 184, OL Vulg Sah Bo Syr cu Arm Hil Aug;

18, 28 − μοι = ℵ B D L Π 1, 33, 114, 700, l. 184, OL Vulg Sah Bo Eth Or Dam Lcif;

19, 3 − οι = B C L M Δ Π Σ 1, 4, 33, 72, 237, 238, 242, 248, 253, 700, l. 184, Bo Dam;

19, 14 (ειπεν) + αυτοις = ℵ C D L M 77, 89, f $g_{1,2}$ l Vulg Syrr Sah (111) Bo Eth Chr;

22, 5 ος *bis* = ℵ B C* L Σ 1, 22, 33, 69, 124, 346, 238, 700, l. 15, Or;

22, 27 − και = ℵ B L U Δ Π* 1, 2, 71, 72, e Syr cu Sah Eth Vulg (T);

22, 32 – θεος (5) = ℵ B D L Δ 28, 33, 67, 122, l. 184, OL Vulg Syr cu g h Sah Bo Or Ir Hil Eus Chr;

23, 4 δε for γαρ = ℵ B L M Δ Π 1, 33, 71, 72, 106, 209, 237, 299, 473, l. 184, al a b c ff$_{1,2}$ g$_{1,2}$ l q (Vulg) Syr h Sah Bo Op;

23, 8 – ο $\overline{\chi\varsigma}$ = ℵ B D E** L Θ^{b} Π fam 1, 22, 71, 124, 253, 433, 474, l. 25, l. 29, al OL Vulg Syrr Sah Bo Arm Eth Pers Bas Chr Cyp;

23, 34 – και (3) = ℵ B M Δ Π fam 1, fam 13, 33, 72, 114, 157, 482, e q (Vulg) Syr S g Arm Or;

23, 37 αυτης = ℵ* B^{mg} D M Δ 33, 258, l. 48, Clem Or Cyr Eus Thdrt;

24, 31 – φωνης = ℵ L Δ fam 1, 56, 57, 58, 106, 700, l. 184, e Syr S g Bo Arm Eus Or Cyr Chr Thdrt Cyp;

24, 42 ημερα for ωρα = ℵ B D I Δ Σ 1, fam 13, 33, 115, 157, 238, d f ff$_{2}$ Syrr Sah (Bo) Arm Ir Hil Cyr Ath (cf. r$_{2}$ e Vulg D E R, etc. Eth);

24, 45 οικετιας for θεραπειας = B I L Δ Π* fam 13, 33, 42, 63, 114, 253;

25, 27 τα αργυρια = ℵ* B 700, Syr h Sah (8);

25, 32 αφοριζει = ℵ* L Δ fam 1, 157, 472, Cyr Thdrt;

26, 36 (μαθηταις) + αυτου = ℵ A C D fam 1, 237, 240, 253, 433, l. 44, l. 46, al OL Vulg Bo Syrr Eth Hil;

26, 38 – ο $\overline{\iota\varsigma}$ = ℵ A B C* D I L fam 1, fam 13, 33, 470, b c d ff$_{1,2}$ g$_{1,2}$ l q Vulg Syr g Sah Bo Arm Eth Chr;

26, 45 – το = B C L 2, 6, 102, 142*, 201, 482, 543, Chr;

27, 46 εβοησεν = B L Σ 33, 69, 124, 700, Vulg;

27, 51 απ for απο = B C Θ^{b} 102;

27, 56 ιωσηφ = ℵ* D L 59^{mg}, 69**, 157, l. 55, OL Vulg Syr S h Sah (4 MSS) Bo Eth Eus Or;

28, 4 ως for ωσει = ℵ A B D L Δ fam 1;

28, 9 – ως ···· αυτου = ℵ B D 33, 69, 142*, 237, 435, 700, l. 15, l. 17, l. 184, al a b c d e ff$_{1,2}$ g$_{1,2}$ h l n mol Vulg Sah Bo Syrr Arm Pers Or;

28, 15 – τα = ℵ B*;

28, 19 + ουν = B Δ Π Σ Φ fam 1, fam 13, 33, l. 184, etc. c e f ff$_{1,2}$ g$_{1}$ q Vulg Syrr Sah Bo (12 MSS) Arm Eth;

28, 20 – αμην = ℵ A* B D 1, 22, 33, 102, 240, 244, l. 53, d e ff$_{1,2}$ g$_{1,2}$ h n q Vulg Sah Bo Chr.

The great majority of these ninety-nine readings are quite probably correct, and so have less weight in proving MS affiliation. Yet I have gathered these in one group because they seem to point somewhat toward the Hesychian recension. It will be noted that one or more accepted members of the Hesychian group (ℵ B C L Z Δ 33) are found in support of each of these readings. But the total of one hundred variants in the whole of Matthew is not very imposing, and we can increase the number only by adding readings which belong also to the Antioch recension, a most questionable assignment in view of the excessive number of undoubted Antioch readings in Matthew. But the case for the Hesychian influence on our MS in Matthew is still weaker, for examination shows that some 90 of these 99 variants have good non-Hesychian support, such as D, fam 1, fam 13, 157, 700, the lectionaries and versions. There are few cases left and the variants involved are not striking enough to countenance our assuming direct Hesychian influence, though some scribe or reader may have incidentally inserted a correction of that type. The MSS (omitting the Hesychian) and versions to which W shows the most similarity are the following: fam 1, D, fam 13, OL, Syr, Bo, Sah, 700, Eth, l. 184, Arm, 238, 22, 157, 4, 106, 299, 245, 435, 28. We shall find that these closely parallel the relatives of W in that larger group of variants, which find neither Antioch nor Hesychian support. The 201 cases follow:

1, 3 *εζρωμ bis* = Syr S;
1, 14 *σαδδωκ bis* = Δ e c f Vulgates (A B ℈ F H R T U X Y Z*** Θ);
1, 14 *αχειν bis* = Δ D (in Luke) Syrr Bo Arm (= *αχιν* in Σ fam 1);
1, 18 − *χριστου* = 74, Pers^p et cod^ Max^dial^ Cyr^com in matth^;
1, 20 *εφανη κατ οναρ* = g_2 (Vulg) Hier Anianus^chr in matth^ (cf. r_2 g_1 aur Sah Bo R^vg^);
2, 13 *φαινεται τω ιωσηφ κατ οναρ* = l. 184, f Bo (Chr);
3, 17 *εκ του ουρανου* = Hebr Evan (Resch Agrapha ap. 4; 47) T^vg^ Syr S cu Diatess Ambr Vig-Tapf Hil and Mark, 1, 11, in W l. 184 b c Epiph;
4, 6 *ειπεν* for *λεγει* = ℵ^b^ Z 157, OL Vulg Sah Bo;
4, 13 *παρα θαλασσαν* = ℵ* 517; cf. Δ *παρα θαλασσιαν* separated, Hier^in Ez^ Diatess;

4, 15 −γη (2) = D 71, 230, 478, 485, l. 44, d Vulgates (A F Y);
4, 16 +τη before σκοτι = D;
4, 20 (δικτυα) + αυτων = K Π 252, 253, a b c g_1 h m R^{vg} Syrr Sah Bo Eth;
5, 11 διωξουσιν = ℵ Δ Σ (D) 543; cf. Luke 6, 22;
5, 13 −ετι = D OL Vulgates (D E L), Syrr Sah Bo (two MSS) Cyp;
5, 19 −ος δ' αν ····· ουρανων = ℵ* D 12, 15, d g_2 r_2 Vulgates (D Turon. 25, S. John Ox. 194) Bo (3 MSS) $Chr^{in\ mt\ 6}$;
5, 21 φονευσης = 477, l. 184 Clem;
5, 26 ου for αν = L 10, 11, 56, 58, 74, 84, 86, 89, 90, 234, 235, 243, 471, 483, 484, l. 49, Colb evg 12, Sah (P.S.);
5, 29 +την before γεενναν = L 18, 21, 243, 435, l. 13, l. 48, l. 184, Sah Bo;
5, 30 κοψον = Δ 21, Syr cu S, Tert;
5, 33 αποδωσης = a b d k (*reddas*) Cypr (*exsolvas*);
5, 33 −δε = Sah (108) Bo (two MSS);
5, 39 −σου (1) = ℵ fam 1, 33, 127, 157, 201, 237, 238, 243, 252, 435, 482, l. 48, l. 49, l. 184, al a f h Vulgates (B* em) Dial Amb Adimant Bas Chr Dam Or;
5, 43 μισησης = Σ l. 52;
6, 6 αποδωση = Σ l. 183, Syr cu S;
6, 20 −ουδε κλεπτουσιν = k Clem Procop;
6, 23 εστιν σκοτος = k;
6, 23 tr. η before ο οφθαλμος = ℵ*;
6, 25 +η τι πιηται = B 27, 61, 62, 118, 124, 235, 240, 242, 244, 259*, 435, c f g_1 h m q gat lux Arm Sah (108, 118) Bo (Or Eus Ath) Mc^{mon} Max;
6, 29 −οτι = 235, 248, g_1 Basil Theodrt;
7, 9 επιδωση = k Syr cu Cypr;
7, 21 +αυτος ··· ουρανων = C** Φ 33, 471, OL Vulg Syr cu Cyp Hier Hilar Lup;
7, 25 προσεκρουσαν = Philo, enarr, in cant, 54, 234, and MS 243 at 7, 27;
7, 29 +και οι φαρισαιοι = C** 17, 21, 33, 471* a c ff_1 $g_{1,2}$ h l q (k) Vulg Syrr Eus Hil;
8, 10 παρ ουδενι τοσαυτην πιστιν εν τω ισραηλ = B 1, 4, 22, 118*, 209, a k q (g_1) gat** dimma Vg (D L) Syr cu S h (Sah) Bo Eth Marcion Ambr Aug;

8, 13 ημερα for ωρα = 700;
8, 17 + οτι = a b c g_1 h q mol gat** dimma Vg (D L Q Wurz J, etc.) Syr cu S Sah Bo;
8, 18 οχλον πολυν = c g_1 Syr cu S Sah (4 MSS) Arm; cf. B 12, 119, 120, 243, Sah (3 MSS);
8, 27 (ουτος) + ο ανος = Chr Hil Theodrt;
8, 29 εκραζον = 489, Bas Macar Epiph (Cyr Athan Eus Chr);
8, 30 βοσκομενων = X 243, 472, OL Vg (D E Ƿ^{mg} L Wurz J) Bo;
9, 1 ιουδαιαν for ιδιαν = F a g_1;
9, 10 τελωναι πολλοι = 157; (Bo Arm om. πολλοι);
9, 13 δικαιους καλεσαι = C* 517, k Pist-Soph Nilus;
9, 15 νηστευειν for πενθειν = D 61*, a b c d f ff_1 g_1 h l q Syr g h Sah Bo (2 MSS) Chr Hil (Arn Aug);
9, 27 τω ιυ εκειθεν = 106, T^{vg} Go Diatess;
9, 34 − εν = ℵ*;
10, 8 δαιμονια εκβαλλεται νεκρους εγειρεται = P Δ 28, l. 37, l. 60, Syr h Chr;
10, 19 παραδωσουσιν = D G L X 33, 99, 124, 157, 251, 299, 346, l. 13, l. 15, l. 44, etc. (OL) Chr Hil Ambr (= Mark 13, 9);
10, 21 τεκνα = 49, 64, Or;
10, 22 − ουτος = Syr S Diatess;
10, 24 (διδασκαλον) + αυτου = ℵ F M 4, fam 13, 106, 235, 299, 473, 476, 485, l. 13, l. 19, l. 184, al Syrr Sah Bo Arm Eth;
10, 31 (φοβεισθαι) + αυτους = M fam 13, 478, a g_1 dimma Vg (D E L Q R);
10, 33 και οστις = Syr cu S;
11, 4 ιωαννει = D Δ;
11, 9 εξεληλυθατε = F (cf. second perfect in Sah);
11, 11 εστιν αυτου = C OL Vulg;
11, 17 εκλαυσασθαι for εκοψασθε = k d Syr cu S Sah Bo;
11, 20 + ο ις = C K L Π fam 1, 4, fam 13, 72, 99, 201, 238, 253, 485, al g_1 h Vg (B H) Syrr Sah Eth Chr;
11, 23 καταβηση = B D OL Vulg Sah Arm Eth Go Ir Caes;
12, 1 + εν before τοις = 238 (Syr cu S) Sah Bo;
12, 1 + τους before σταχυας = D U 28, 99, 108, 235, 251, 253, 435, 700, l. 15, l. 17, l. 49, Sah Bo;
12, 4 ο for ους = B D 13, 124, a b d k q aur Z^{vg} Syr cu g Arm;

12, 5 + εν before τοις = C D 157, l. 48, d Sah Bo Cyr;
12, 14 − εξελθοντες = Δ 77, 123, 225, 245, l. 184, ff_2 q;
12, 20 ($ου_1$) + μη = (D* adds to $ου_2$);
12, 21 επι for εν = 4, 157, 262, Syr cu S (Sah) Eus Chr;
12, 22 κωφον και τυφλον = L X Δ Σ 1, 4, fam 13, 76, 99, 238, 247, 700, l. 48, l. 184, Syr g Juv;
12, 29 διαρπαση = ℵ D G K Π* 1, fam 13, 28, 72, 106, 157, 201, 253, 472, 700, al Chr;
12, 40 (εσται) + και = D E F L (4), 27, 76, 142, 182, 236, 243, 245, 247, 253, 470, 473, 482, al OL Syr cu Bo Or Ir Eus Chr Cyr (cf. Luke 11, 30);
12, 48 − τω λεγοντι αυτω = X dimma E^{vg};
12, 48 η for και = D a d $ff_{1,2}$ h k q T^{vg} Bo Arm Tert Aug;
12, 48 − εισιν = Σ l. 184, c k Tert Aug Ambr;
13, 8 επεσαν = C 2, 33, 243, all versions;
13, 19 σπειρομενον = D d Sah (Diatess); cf. Mark 4, 16–18;
13, 20 (λογον) + μου = X Δ 245, f* Syr h;
13, 22 ($λογον_1$) + μου = q (cf. 301);
13, 23 (λογον) + μου = q 245, Syr g;
13, 26 − και (2) = D fam 13, 248, OL Vulg (10 MSS) Syr cu S Sah (Bo);
13, 30 μεχρις = Φ;
13, 52 εκβαλει = E G L (472), etc. Probably error of single consonant for double, p. 22;
13, 54 (τουτω) + ταυτα και τις = 242 (cf. Diatess);
13, 55 ιωσης = K L Δ Π fam 13, 28, 157, 237, 238, 240, 243, 245, 253, etc., k q** Sah (Bo) Syr g h Arm Eth Bas;
13, 57 επ for εν (1) = 247;
14, 6 − της = 517 (D) Sah Bo (Chr);
14, 7 δουναι αυτη = K Π 1, 4, 72, 157, 238, 243, 245, 248, 253, 300, 474, 482, l. 53, colb unus of Wets. ff_1 Syr cu S Sah Bo;
14, 8 (αυτης) + ειπεν = (D OL Vg (D Q dim) Syrr Eth); but W conflates with the regular reading φησιν, as also g_2 l and Vulgates E Þ O^{gl} T Z*;
14, 19 και λαβων = ℵ C* I X 14, 99, 245, 246, 472, 485, l. 184, ff_1 h Bo Arm;
14, 21 − ωσει = Θ 241, 247, OL Vulg Syrr Bo Or;
15, 2 εσθιουσιν = 9, 248, 346, l. 184, OL Vulg Cyr;
15, 4 ($\overline{πρα}_1$) + σου = C** K L M N U Π Σ Φ (E*) 4, 71, 75**,

237, 239, 242, 247, 248, 249, 251, 253, 474, 482, al OL (Vulg) Syr cu g h Sah Bo Arm Or Ptol;

15, 4 (μητερα$_1$) + σου = N 4, 75**, 99, 237, 251, 299, l. 13, l. 48, OL Syrr Sah Bo Or Ptol;

15, 14 εμπεσουνται = D F Σ Φ 99, 238, 240, 242, 244, 248, 251**, 253, 480, l. 184, etc. d Cyr Bas Chr;

15, 19 πον·πορ·μοιχ·φον·κλο·ψευδ·βλασ· = L (l. 184) q Cyr (catech x app);

15, 23 εμπροσθεν for οπισθεν = 245;

15, 30 κωφ·χωλ·τυφλ·κυλ· = L M Δ 4, 61, 262, 299, (474, l. 184) q (Vulg) Syr h;

15, 32 φαγειν = q Diates (a b c Ambr);

15, 32 – αυτου = ℵ 700, Hil Chr;

15, 39 μαγδαλαν = C M 33, 42, 106, 122**, (238, 253), 299, 482, l. 2, l. 48, q Bo;

16, 3 – υποκριται = C* D L Δ 1, 11, 22, 23, 33, 76, 115, 262, 471, l. 34, l. 36, OL Vulg Syr h Eth Chr Aug;

16, 13 εξελθων = H G 61, 68, 106, 346, al Syr h Chr;

16, 13 λεγουσιν με = C Or; (cf. Syr cu S Diatess Athan);

16, 14 – οι μεν = D a b d e ff$_{1,2}$ g$_1$ Vg (E L); cf. Luke 9, 19;

17, 4 – ο = H 71, 244, Sah Bo;

17, 4 – ει = 1, 33, 131, 301, Sah Bo;

17, 4 ηλια··· μωυσι = l. 184;

17, 8 – αυτων = 235, l. 44, e dimma;

17, 8 – τον = ℵ B* Sah Bo;

17, 9 αναστη εκ νεκρων = Syr cu Sah Bo Diatess;

17, 12 – εν = ℵ D F U (Γ) 13, 28, 106, 127, 131, 237, 299, 435, l. 48, al OL Just; cf. Mark 9, 13;

17, 15 – πολλακις (2) = 238, Hil;

18, 4 γαρ for ουν = g$_1$ Syr cu S Aphr;

18, 15 αμαρτη = 33, 127, 201, 235, 242, 243, 244, 248, 253, l. 49, al Or Bas Chr;

18, 19 (παλιν) + δε = M Δ l. 47, Syr g (15 MSS) Eth Chr;

18, 21 αμαρτηση = E H Δ 41, 253, 483, 485;

18, 29 + παντα = ℵ^c C** L Γ Π (K) 1, 33, 474, 475, 482, l. 184, OL Vulg Syr g h Sah Bo Eth Chr;

19, 5 ($\overline{μρα}$) + αυτου = E Γ 66, 69, 237, 243, 244, 247, 253, 262, 471, 543, Sah Bo Syrr Eth Or Dam Ath;

19, 9 γαμων = C* I N Δ Π Σ Φ fam 1, fam 13, 33, 72, 238, 245, 248, 474, l. 184 al;

19, 16 ζωην εχω αιωνιον = J^{vg};

19, 18 – το = D M l. 184, (versions);

19, 19 ($\overline{\pi\rho\alpha}$) + σου = C** fam 13, 33, 237, 242, 243, 245, 248, 251, 252, 482, al a b f $ff_{1,2}$ h r (Vulg) Syr cu g Sah Bo Eth Aug Ephr;

19, 24 εισελθειν δια τρυπ·ραφ· = Or, Cels in Or, Chr;

19, 30 ($\epsilon\sigma\chi\alpha\tau o\iota_2$) + εσονται = Syr cu S Pist-Soph; cf. Luke 13, 30;

20, 23 (εμον) + τουτο = C D Δ Π 33, 72, 106, 346, l. 48, al q h Syr h Bo;

20, 25 (ειπεν) + αυτοις = D 238, d e Vg (B O) Syr cu g Sah Bo Eth;

20, 27 πρωτος ειναι = OL Vulg Arm; cf. 28;

21, 1 ηλθεν = ℵ* C*** E U V^{mg} Δ 28, 238, l. 6, l. 21, l. 44, l. 47, l. 50, l. 183, al e q ff_2 gat E^{vg} Syr cu g j Or Chr;

21, 7 εκαθεισεν = N Π Σ 4, 71, 72, 243, l. 6, l. 11, l. 53, al OL Vulg (cf. ℵ 16, 57, 61);

21, 8 αυτων = D L Δ Φ 13, 106, 122, 157, 237, 238, 243, 251, 471, 700, al (cf. Mark 11, 17; Luke 19, 36);

21, 8 – απο των δενδρων = 6;

21, 9 – οι (3) = Δ q Or;

21, 19 αυτης for αυτην = L 157, 238;

21, 19 επ for εν = 59, 66, 238, l. 22, l. 150*, l. 185;

21, 21 και for καν = (D) 472, l. 48 (59, 69, l. 5);

21, 27 υμιν λεγω = M Δ Π fam 13, 71, 238, 470, 474, l. 48, OL (Vulg) Or;

22, 1 – παλιν = F 243, r_2 Bo;

22, 4 (σιτιστα) + μου = X 60, 61, 243, 258, 574, 700, ff_2 g_1 h q R^{vg} Syrr Arm Eth Chr;

22, 6 – αυτου = L Ir Or Eus (Hil);

22, 17 κηνσον δουναι = Δ** a ff_2 g_1 q aur Vulg;

22, 18 τας πονηριας = r_2 T^{vg} (Syr);

22, 24 επιγαμβρευση = l. 184;

22, 30 γαμισκονται = 33, 124, 157, 700, (69), Or Meth Epiph Chr;

22, 32 – ο (4) = ℵ D 28, 67, 33, 122, Eus Chr;

22, 37 $\overline{\iota\varsigma}$ ειπεν = fam 13, 66, 506, 517, q Syrr Arm Eth;

22, 38 η πρωτη και η μεγαλη = (L) Sah Bo;

22, 46 ωρας for ημερας = D E* 1*, 118, 131, 209, 70, 76, 247, 252*, 472, a d q Q^{vg} Syrr Bo Or Cyr Op;

23, 1 — ο = B V 251, Sah Bo;

23, 9 ο εν ουρανοις = D Δ Σ fam 1, 435, l. 184, Dam;

23, 10 — υμων = K Π* 71, 72, 114, 236, 243, 245, 252*, 253, 259, 433, 474;

24, 3 (μαθηται) + αυτου = C U Γ Δ Π 73, 80, 122, 127, 235, 299**, 258, 417, l. 5, l. 20, l. 44, l. 47, l. 49, l. 183, al c h r δ Syr S g Vulg (10 MSS) Sah Bo;

24, 7 λοιμοι και λιμοι = L 33, 225, l. 32, c f ff$_1$ g$_{1,2}$ l q r aur gat Vulg Oros;

24, 8 ταυτα δε παντα = fam 1, 6, 9, fam 13, 243, 244, l. 24, l. 63, c e f ff$_{1,2}$ g$_{1,2}$ l Vulg Syr S g Sah Bo Arm Eth Or Chr;

24, 11 αναστησονται = Σ 4, 262, Didasc vi 13, Just Theodrt;

24, 13 — ουτος = Syr S Diatess;

24, 14 — πασι = Γ Bo (J$_1$) Or Chr; cf. Matth. 10, 18;

24, 20 υμων η φυγη = Sah Bo Or Eus;

24, 21 ουδεμη = D U Δ 44, 72, 470, 472, 482, 700, l. 5, l. 16, l. 20, l. 48, l. 184, Bo (F$_1$) Eus Chr Theodrt;

24, 27 (εσται) + και = M Δ Φ fam 13, 118, 157, 209, 245, 472, l. 183, etc. OL Vulg Syr h Eth Hipp Cyr Chr Dam Cyp;

24, 31 (και$_1$) + τοτε = F^{vg} Chr; cf. Mark 13, 27;

24, 32 εκφυει = 251, 258, l. 47, l. 184;

24, 33 ταυτα παντα = ℵ D K H U V* Σ Φ fam 1, fam 13, 28, 33, 157, 243, 472, 700, l. 184, etc. OL Vg Syr g Sah Bo Arm Or Chr;

24, 43 τον οικον = L l. 47, l. 183;

24, 45 — αυτοις = q (e);

24, 49 εσθιειν ··· πινειν = G Π* 28, 238, 243, 245, 251, l. 47, l. 49, etc. a Sah Bo Ephr Dam;

25, 11 ηλθον for ερχονται = D c d f r$_2$ mol (Vulg) Syr S g Sah Bo Eth Or;

25, 14 — γαρ = D l. 222 d Vg (Ƿ** L R) Bo (ℵ) Arm;

25, 20 — ταλαντα (2) = Δ l. 184, h r δ mol R^{vg} Syr g Eth;

25, 24 οπου for οθεν = D 56, OL Vulg Chr;

25, 26 (οτι) + εγω $\overline{\text{ανος}}$ αυστηρος ειμει = Syr g (18 MSS) Sah (l. 34);

25, 27 + τω = Δ Σ l. 6 Sah Bo;

25, 29 — παντι = D 77, l. 18, l. 24, l. 31, l. 49, d Syr g Chr Tert Hier Philas;

25, 35 + και before εδιψησα = Δ c* Syr g h Diatess Clem Ps-Nil;
26, 2 μεθ ημερας δυο = Sah Bo;
26, 15 παραδω = d (*trado*); cf. Syr S;
26, 17 λεγοντες τω ιυ = M** Σ fam 1;
26, 17 (θελεις) + απελθοντες = fam 13; cf. Arm;
26, 23 εκεινος for ουτος = Pers[walt] Or;
26, 26 – και (1) = 245, 472, mol Sah; cf. Luke 22, 19;
26, 33 (ει) + και = ℵ[c] F K Π 28?, 71, 201, 241, 248, 252, 482, etc. (OL) Vulg Syrr Arm Eth Or Chr Bas;
26, 36 ο ις μετ αυτων = D 238, OL Vulg Arm;
26, 36 αν for ου = D K L M** Γ Δ fam 1, fam 13, 42, 49, 71, 238, 248, 470, 471, 474, 483*, 484, 487, l. 183, l. 184, Chr;
26, 44 προσηυξατο παλιν = A K Δ Π 12, 14, 71, 72, 142, 157, 235, 238, 474, 482, q Syr h;
26, 49 προσηλθεν ···· και = r_2 Syr S Diatess; cf. Bo;
26, 60 (δυο) + τινες = N Σ 61, 157, 238, l. 23, l. 48;
26, 63 (θυ₂) + του ζωντος = C* N Δ Θ[f] Σ Φ 5, 47, 54, 59, 61, 121, 157, l. 6, l. 23, l. 44, l. 184, ff_2 r_2 (Vg) Syr h j Sah Bo Eth Diatess Cyr Chr;
27, 6 εστιν for εξεστι = Eus;
27, 10 εδωκα = ℵ 122, 476, l. 24, l. 31, Syrr Pers Eus;
27, 11 – ο ηγεμων = Syr S Or; cf. – *dicens*, r_2 R* Sah (m[l]) Hil;
27, 29 εθηκαν = K N Δ Π fam 1, fam 13, 42, 68, 71, 157, 229*, 235, 482, l. 23, Latin (Syr Cop);
27, 33 λεγομενον = ℵ* N Σ 6, 115, 201, 240, 244, 252**, 301, 433, 479, 480, l. 23, l. 52, l. 54, al;
27, 41 – δε και = ℵ A L Π* 71, 114, b J[vg] Bo (10 MSS);
27, 43 + του (θυ) = l. 47, l. 185, Sah Bo;
27, 45 εγενετο σκοτος = U Γ Δ Σ 127, 472, l. 47, l. 183, Syrr Go;
27, 49 σωζων = g_1 aur Vulg (cf. g_2 D E Ᵽ* mol gat = *liberare*);
27, 50 κραξας παλιν = dimma Sah Eth Ambr;
27, 52 ανεωχθη = A Π* (C*) 42, 71, 72, 252*, 470, 482, l. 22;
27, 55 – απο (1) = A K Δ Π 15, 68, 248, 472, 474, al Sah Chr;
27, 60 ω for ο = L Z 28;
28, 2 κατεβη ··· και = (472, 482) OL Vulg Syrr (Sah Bo) Eth;

28, 5 — δε (1) = C 59, Syr S Sah (111) Bo (4 MSS) Arm;
28, 9 + ο = D L S Γ fam 1, fam 13, etc., Or;
28, 14 ποιησωμεν = ℵ E* F G H M fam 13, 33, 157, 242, 245, 248, 300, 433, 435, 472, 475*, 483, 484, 485, 700, l. 6, l. 184, Chr.

In this list of special readings, which are in the main errors, W agrees with each nearly related version and MS the following number of times: Old Latin, 93; Sahidic, 54; Bohairic, 54; Syr cu S, 48; D, 44; Syr g, 42; Δ, 32; fam 13, 29; l. 184, L, fam 1, and Eth, 22 each; MS 157, Arm, and ℵ, 18 each; Σ and 243, 17 each; MSS 245, 238, and 33, 15 each; MSS 28, 253, and M, 13 each; MS 4, Diatess, l. 48, 71, and 482, 11 each; MS 700, 10 times.

It is interesting to note that we find in this list primarily the versions, the bilinguals, and those cursive MSS and groups of MSS which Hoskier in his Genesis of the Versions has shown were related to the versions. The entrance of l. 184 and l. 48 into the group merely indicates that the lectionaries show similar relationship to the versions. The other MSS in the list, as L ℵ Σ, are old or Egyptian and probably go back to a similar base. It is manifest that all of these are related to what I have chosen to call the version tradition. In the case of W it is quite evident that its parent before correction was a MS most closely related to the three older versions and to the bilinguals. This ought to be considered proof that somewhere in its early history there was a bilingual or trilingual MS.

To make our picture of the text of W in Matthew complete, I add the noteworthy variants for which no satisfactory parallels have been found:

6, 18 + αυτος before αποδωσι;
6, 26 ουχει (cf. ουχ' in Φ 440, 477, 489, l. 150, l. 181, l. 185);
6, 30 (σημερον) + εν αγρω (harmonistic, cf. Luke 12, 18);
8, 28 — εις την χωραν (is regular text harmonistic? cf. Mark 5, 1; Luke 8, 26);
9, 6 αφιεναι επι της γης αμαρτιας (harmonistic, cf. Mark 2, 10, which Chrys. de fut. vit. delic. 5, probably quotes);
9, 9 καλουμενον for λεγομενον (cf. 28, which has a lacuna here, but makes the same interchange at 4, 18; 10, 2; 17, 21; cf. k, which has *qui M. vocabatur*);
9, 15 αφερεθη for απαρθη;

10, 5 *εξαπεστιλεν* (for this use of the compound, cf. Gal. 4, 4; 24, 6);

10, 17 − *αυτων* = Mark 13, 9; Luke 21, 12; Acts 22, 19; Hil; the error is harmonistic;

12, 4 *ως* for *πως*;

12, 27 *κριται εσονται αυτοι υμων* (cf. k and ℵ B D 157, 517, l. 49, l. 184, OL);

12, 33 *ποιησηται* for *ποιησατε*;

13, 20 (*ευθυς*) + *και* (not harmonistic, cf. Mark 4, 16);

13, 41 *και* before *αποστελει*;

14, 25 *ουν* for *δε*;

14, 30 (*ισχυρον*) + *σφοδρα* (cf. quotation of Matthew 8, 26 in Cyril. Alex.);

14, 30 (*εφοβηθη*) + *ελθειν*;

16, 3 (*δυνασθαι*) + *δοκιμασαι* (cf. + *δοκιμαζειν* (= Luke 12, 26) in G M U Z 33, al OL Vg Syr g);

16, 24 *αυτον* (man 1) for *εαυτον* (cf. b c ff$_2$ g$_1$ r r$_2$ Ir Lucif, *se* for *semet*);

18, 3 *γενεσθαι* for *γενησθε*;

18, 8 − *εισελθειν* (transposition in K Π al OL Vg);

18, 15 *ελεγξε* for *ελεγξον* (247 has *ελεγξαι*);

18, 17 − *ο* before *εθνικος*;

18, 19 *υμιν λεγω* (cf. 21, 27, where this order has support of the version tradition);

19, 8 *επετρεψεν υμιν* before *προς*;

19, 9 − *και* (1);

21, 18 *υπαγων* for *επαναγων* (cf. *παραγων* in D, etc.);

21, 23 *προσηλθεν*;

21, 26 *ανθρωπου* for *ανθρωπων* (confusion in number looks like Syriac influence);

21, 32 *τω πιστευσαι*;

24, 11 *υμας* for *πολλους*;

24, 38 *εκγαμισκοντες* (cf. B and l. 184); cf. Luke 20, 34, where W again interchanges these verbs;

24, 39 (*εως*) + *αν*;

24, 49 *μεθυστων* for *μεθυοντων* (cf. different words used in Old Latin MSS);

25, 19 *τινα* for *πολυν*;

25, 24 *ουκ εσκορπισας* (cf. uncompounded verb in Old Latin and Vulgate MSS);

25, 32 *παντα τα εθνη εμπροσθεν αυτου* (similar order in Ethiopic only);
25, 41 *εξ ευωνυμοις* (cf. *a sinistris* of Latin);
26, 3 *φαρισαιοι* for *γραμματεις* (harmonistic, cf. Mark 14, 1; Luke 22, 2; John 11, 47);
26, 19 *ουν* for *και* (1);
26, 52 *αυτοις* for *αυτω*;
27, 39 *αυτων τας κεφαλας* (cf. prefix used in Coptic to replace pronoun);
27, 60 + *εν* before *τη θυρα* (cf. *επι* of A, 242, 243, OL Vg Or; also Syr S = a stone one great);
27, 61 *επι* for *απεναντι*.

It is probable that the majority of these 44 cases would find their parallels in the versions and related cursives, if the material for comparison were more complete. In general character the errors are very similar to those in the preceding list. The smallness of the number of unique variants is accounted for by the fact that I have treated above the pure scribal errors as well as the mistakes in spelling and grammar.

By examining the previous lists the reader will find that the variants enumerated are distributed fairly evenly throughout Matthew. The same is true of the Antioch readings not enumerated. The same type of text therefore extends throughout the whole of this gospel.

2. Mark

The text problem in Mark is both more difficult and more interesting. Even the first survey convinced me that there could be no extensive Antioch or Hesychian influence in this most erratic part of W, though the text did not seem homogeneous throughout. The true character and approximate point of break came to light through comparison with the Old Latin MSS, especially e. In 750 weakly supported, and so probably erroneous, readings there are the following agreements with the Old Latin in the different chapters:

chap.	1	2	3	4	5	6	7	8	9	10	11	12	13	14	15	16
agree	46	49	43	47	18	13	14	18	26	29	14	19	18	33	7	11
disag.	11	9	10	11	18	33	19	28	44	24	16	30	23	45	13	10

The change in type of text is thus shown to fall in chapter five, and as all except two of the eighteen agreements with Old Latin MSS in that chapter come before verse 30, the break or text change of the parent MS can be placed at that point.

(a) Mark 1 – 5, 30

The most striking characteristic of this portion of the text is its relationship to the Old Latin, and this is best seen by cataloging the readings where W and the Old Latin MSS stand alone together. The cases follow:

1) 1, 3 + Isaiah 40, 4–6 = c;
2) 1, 26 – το ακαθαρτον = e r;
3) 1, 26 ανεκραγεν · · · · και for κραξαν = e (cf. Bo);
4) 1, 26 απηλθεν for εξηλθεν = e f r (*discessit*);
5) 1, 27 εθαυμαζον for εθαμβηθησαν = Latin (*mirati sunt*), yet with change of tense, as often in other passages;
6) 1, 27 και συνεζητουν = b d e ff$_2$ q r (*et exquirebant*);
7) 1, 27 η εξουσιαστικη αυτου added before και οτι = e (*inpotentabilis*); cf. ff$_2$ r and Gr. D;
8) 1, 27 – και (2) = c e g$_1$ (cf. Bo);
9) 1, 31 αυτω for αυτοις = d e (*ei*) = 579;
10) 1, 35 – πρωι = a b c d e ff$_2$ q (δ); cf. Syr S;
11) 1, 35 – εξηλθεν = b d e ff$_2$ q r (cf. some Bohairic MSS);
12) 1, 37 – και ευροντες αυτον = b c;
13) 1, 37 – οτι = c e;
14) 1, 38 κηρυσσιν for ινα κακει κηρυξω = b c e (*praedicare*) (ff$_2$ q r G^{vg});
15) 1, 42 – και εκαθαρισθη = b c e, cf. Gr. M*, which omitted much more;
16) 1, 43 – και · · · · αυτον = b c aur (e);
17) 2, 1 ερχεται for εισηλθεν = b e q (*venit*);
18) 2, 3 – φεροντες = b c e f;
19) 2, 4 προσελθειν for προσεγγισαι = a c e ff$_2$ g$_{1,2}$ r b (*accedere*);
20) 2, 8 – εν εαυτοις = c e;
21) 2, 12 ο δε εγερθεις for και ηγερθη = c ff$_2$ (*ille vero surgens*) a e (*et . . . surgens*);
22) 2, 12 – ευθεως = b c e ff$_2$ q;

23) 2, 12 *εμπροσθεν παντων απηλθεν* = e (*coram omnibus abiit*), cf. other Latin MSS;
24) 2, 12 *θαυμαζειν αυτους* for *εξιστασθαι παντας* = all Latin MSS (*admirarentur*);
25) 2, 12 *ειδον* for *ειδομεν* = b (*viderant*);
26) 2, 16 – *ιδοντες* ··· *αμαρτωλων* = e; cf r_2;
27) 2, 21 (*αιρει*) + *απ αυτου* = l; cf. 157, 579;
28) 2, 22 (*παλαιους*) + *αλλ εις καινους* = a b c;
29) 2, 22 *διαρρησσονται οι ασκοι* for *ρησσει* ··· *ασκους* = a, Hegemonius, acta Archelai, 21, 1 (*rumpentur*);
30) 2, 23 *εσπαρμενων* for *σποριμων* = c d g_1 r aur Vg (*sata*);
31) 2, 25 *ουδε τουτο* for *ουδεποτε* = c e ff_2 i q t G (*nec hoc*), b (*non hoc*); from Luke 6, 3;
32) 2, 26 *εισελθων* for *εισηλθεν* ··· *και* = Hier. ep. 57, 9 (*ingressus*);
33) 2, 26 *εφαγεν τους αρτους της προθεσεως* = ff_2;
34) 2, 27 + *οτι* = a c e ff_2 i;
35) 3, 1 *ερχεται ανθρωπος προς αυτον* for *και ην εκει ανθ.* = b c e i (*venit ad illum homo*);
36) 3, 1 *εχων ξηραν την χειρα* = a (*habens aridam manum*);
37) 3, 4 *η ου* for *η κακοποιησαι* = f (*an male*); for the parallel passage, Luke 6, 9, Tert has *annon;* cf. also Luke 14, 3, where ℵ B D L fam 1, fam 13, 157 and some versions add *η ου* after *θεραπευσαι*;
38) 3, 5 – *συλλυπουμενος* = b c; cf. d (*cum ira indignationis*);
39) 3, 8 *ηκολουθουν αυτω* after *σιδονα* for *ηκολουθησαν αυτω* of verse 7 = b c; many omit;
40) 3, 8 – *ηλθον προς αυτον* = b c; cf. transposition in e;
41) 3, 12 – *πολλα* = b c e ff_2 g_1 i q r;
42) 3, 13 *αναβας* for *αναβαινει* ··· *και* = Old Latin Vulg;
43) 3, 15 (*δαιμονια*) + *και περιαγοντας κηρυσσιν το ευαγγελιον* = a c e g_2 gat Vg (D E L Q T);
44) 3, 17 – *και ιακωβον* ····· *ιακωβου* = e; cf. c;
45) 3, 17 *κοινως δε αυτους εκαλεσεν βοανανηργε* = b c e q (*communiter autem vocavit eos* (*boanerges*); cf. Z* *boanaerges;*
46) 3, 18 *ανδρεας φιλιππος*, etc. nom. for acc. is found also in c and e (suggested by Syr);
47) 3, 18 – *και θαδδαιος* = e;

48) 3, 22 — και οτι = c e q (και added later, see next line; 255 and 700 omit οτι);

49) 3, 22 τον αρχοντα (for εν τω αρχοντι) ..... + και δι αυτου = c e q (*principem ... et per eum*);

50) 3, 25 — η οικια εκεινη = e;

51) 3, 27 διαρπασαι εισελθων εις την οικειαν = b c e (*diripere ingressus in domum*);

52) 3, 28 τα αμαρτηματα αφεθησεται = e f Cypr. iii, 3, 28; 16, 2 (*peccata remittentur*);

53) 3, 28 — οσας αν βλασφημησωσιν = a b c e ff_2 g_1 i q r Cypr Ambrst;

54) 3, 30 εχειν αυτον for εχει = a b c e ff_2 g_1 q d (*habere eum*);

55) 3, 33 — μου (1) = Ambr;

56) 3, 35 και ος for ος γαρ = a c Aug (*et qui*); e = *quicumque;*

57) 4, 1 παρα τον αιγιαλον for εν τη θαλασση = a b c e ff_2 r (*ad litus*); Bo conflates;

58) 4, 2 — πολλα = b c e;

59) 4, 2 λεγων for και ελεγεν = b c e (*dicens*); 28 = λεγων και ελεγεν;

60) 4, 4 τα ορνεα for τα πετεινα = b c ff_2 (*aves*);

61) 4, 5 — και = e i q r;

62) 4, 5 — δια το μη εχειν βαθος γης = b c e; cf. Syr S;

63) 4, 17 (λογον) + και = ff_2;

64) 4, 20 πιπτοντες for σπαρεντες = e (*qui cadunt*) ff_2 r (*qui ceciderunt*);

65) 4, 21 αλλ for ουχ = b c e q (*sed*);

66) 4, 29 — ευθυς = c e;

67) 4, 30 δωμεν for παραβαλωμεν (θωμεν in ℵ B C* L Δ 28, 63, 579, and conflate in fam 13) = e (*damus*);

68) 4, 32 αυξει for αναβαινει = b e r (*crescit*);

69) 4, 36 αμα πολλοι ησαν for αλλα δε πλοιαρια ην = e r* (*simul multi erant*);

70) 4, 39 — σιωπα = b c e ff_2;

71) 4, 39 — μεγαλη = e;

72) 4, 40 — πως ουκ = e q; cf. 579;

73) 5, 4 + ετι before δαμασαι = e (*iam domare*); c d ff_2 i l q (r) = *amplius vincere;*

74) 5, 6 προσεδραμεν for εδραμε = c d e (*adcucurrit*);

75) 5, 22 προσπιπτι for πιπτει = b c d f ff_2 q r Vg (*procidit*).

These 75 cases of special agreement within four and one half chapters show the closeness of relationship which must have existed between the parents of W and of these Latin MSS. The best representative of that Latin parent is e with its 10 special agreements with W, yet even e is by no means an unadulterated source, for we find it again and again agreeing with the Vulgate, where other Old Latin MSS, like c b q r a f, reproduce the reading parallel to W. Mss e and c are rather closely united and four times agree with W otherwise unsupported; six more times b joins this group, and four times b c alone support W. The fact that c has two special agreements with W, one of which is the long addition, 1, 3, inclines me to rank c or rather the parent of c next to e in nearness of relationship to W. Yet we must recognize that c has been corrected to the Vulgate form far more extensively than e. In fact, none of the Old Latin MSS seem to have entirely escaped Vulgate influence, to which quite as much as to the peculiarities of provincial or individual development are due the wide variations in this group of MSS. That all go back to a single original translation closely related to this portion of W is now perfectly clear.[1] Far more difficult is the question of the exact nature of this relationship. Does W represent the original Greek from which the North African translation was made, or is it a retranslation from the North African Latin, or can we find an intermediate explanation?

The first of these suggestions will perhaps appeal more strongly to most scholars and it is in fact supported by so many proofs that I open the discussion with the admission that many of these peculiarities are Greek in origin, or at least not Latin. A good illustration is no. 67 of the above list, δωμεν of W equal *damus* of e. The best MSS have θωμεν, which is paralleled by *ponemus* of Old Latin b, while the common Greek reading παραβαλωμεν is copied by the Vulgate *comparabimus*. A part of this confusion arose in the Greek, for δωμεν and θωμεν represent an easy sound interchange. *Ponemus* and *damus* could not have been confused so easily in Latin, and so must be considered independent translations or imitations from the Greek. But Greek errors would ordinarily perpetuate themselves in Greek MSS, so that we usually find other Greek support for this class of errors. Further examples are, however, unnecessary, for the essentially Greek character of the

[1] Note the special agreements between W and a f ff_2 l q and r as shown in the table.

text of W as a whole is sufficiently established by the following table of agreements with the chief Greek uncials; all important variants being counted:

Chap.	ℵ	A	B	D	L
1	50	64	50	79	51
2	38	33	37	43	41
3	45	37	43	55	42
4	34	35	37	60	43

The slight preponderance of D was to be expected because of its Latin relatives. Yet the mass of agreements with the other pure Greek MSS is sufficient to prove the essentially Greek character of the text tradition in this part of W.

Proof that W was in turn under Latin influence is the more necessary, since mere agreement with OL MSS proves little and besides the assumption is opposed to the Greek character of the text as a whole. Yet the evidence seems sufficient. Of the special agreements cited above nos. 7, 13, 14, 21, 32, 42, 54, 59, and perhaps 6 and 29 are changes due to Latin or late Latin construction; nos. 17, 35, and 68 (*crescit* and *crescet*) are tense changes due to the double force of the Latin perfect, or to confusion of Latin forms; nos. 12 (cf. e = *et ven* · · · *et dic* · · as explanation of omission in b c), 38 (cf. e = *cum ira tristis*, Vg = *cum ira contristatus*, and b = *cum iracundia*), 40 (cf. insertion of *ut viderent eum* at this point in e; because of this *venerunt in eum* fell out, but was replaced in e by *qui venerunt* earlier in the sentence), 58 (the e text had *in parabola multa* before omission of *multa*), 70 (*tace obmutesce*), and 71 (e alone has *malacia* and would have had *malacia magna* or *magna malacia* before omission) are omissions due to like endings in Latin, which are not present in the Greek; nos. 4, 5, 24, 30, 45, 60, 64, 65, 74, and 75 are retranslations, where the Latin word, though a passable translation for the original Greek, yet more naturally suggests a different Greek word; nos. 23, 36, and 52 are cases of order change to conform to the regular Latin order. We may further call attention to the fact that most of the cases cited have considerable Old Latin support, while in each case W is the only Greek MS showing the variant. The combination of this circumstance with the numerous agreements with Latin alone is enough to establish the indebtedness of W to the Old Latin. Yet, as we have seen, not only has the most of the text of W escaped this influence, but there are many perfect agreements between Old Latin and W, which are not due to Latin influence. It has plainly been a case of action and reaction, which is most naturally explained on the basis that W and an early form of the Old Latin (that of North Africa) were at one time parallel columns of the same Bible and mutually influenced each other. That this was actually the Bible of North Africa is amply proved by the agreement with Old Latin e, which von Soden (Texte und Untersuchungen, vol. 33) has shown to be nearly identical with the Bible text used by St. Cyprian. The striking variations even from the bilingual D indicate how thoroughly these Greek and Latin texts had become assimilated and suggest that the development had been a bilingual one for a considerable time. Yet back of this Greek-Latin bilingual lies the influence of other versions or of an old trilingual. We note the following examples of Syriac influence or affiliation:

1, 20 *μετα των μισθωτων εν τω πλοιω* = Syr S; this change in order caused b to omit *in navi;*

1, 31 + *και επιλαβομενος* = Syr S; d, r have similar participle in acc.;

2, 27 − *ουχ ο ανθρωπος δια το σαββατον* = Syr S; longer omission in D a c e ff_2 i, *quia* to *quia;*

3, 26 − *ανεστη* = Syr S;

4, 12 − *βλεπωσι και* = Syr S.

In addition to these cases, where W and Syr S stand alone together, I add a few in which the Syriac influence has spread a little further in the version tradition:

1, 25 *και ειπεν* for *λεγων* = Syr S g, OL (b c e); a common Syriac change;

1, 32 − *και τους δαιμονιζομενους* = Syr S and Vulgates X* Z*, OL r;

2, 15 − *αυτου* (1) = Syr g and OL b c;

2, 18 − *οι* (4) = Syr g and Δ b;

3, 8 − *πληθος πολυ* = Syr S and OL a b c; the order is changed in Sah and Bo;

3, 27 *τα σκευη* for *την οικιαν* (2) = Syr S and OL e;

3, 31 + *αυτου* before *η μητηρ* = Syr S Sah Bo; most MSS have *αυτου* but once, after *μητηρ*;

3, 32 στηκουσιν ζητουντες for ζητουσι = Syr S Arm Eth and e; cf. c f r;

3, 33 και ειπεν αυτοις for αυτοις λεγων = (Syr S) Syr g Arm and Gr. 33; cf. 700, and e;

4, 2 – αυτοις εν τη διδαχη αυτου = Syr g, Gr. L, Or, and OL b c e;

5, 22 ω ονομα for ονοματι = Syr S and Gr. 565, 700; not Greek but Syriac construction.

I do not attempt to make these examples exhaustive but merely illustrate the presence of the influence.

Less marked, but unquestionable, is the Coptic influence, showing that the Greek-Latin bilingual of North Africa traveled to its home by way of Egypt. In four cases W is supported by Sahidic alone; 2, 9 (τι) + γαρ; 4, 16 δε for και; 5, 4 δεδεσθαι και πεδες και αλυσεσι (this order is supported by D d, but with changed construction); 5, 4 δε for και (2). To these may be added the following cases, in which there is some slight support from other sources:

1, 37 ζητουσιν σε παντες = Sah Bo and OL b c e; this is Coptic, not Latin order;

1, 41 λεγων for και λεγει = Sah and fam 13, 565; a common Coptic change;

2, 3 (και) + ιδου ανδρες = Sah and Gr. 28, 565; often a Syriac trait, but Syr. MSS omit here;

3, 1 – παλιν = Sah (1 MS) Bo (4 MSS) and OL b c e i;

3, 16 – τω before σιμωνι = D Sah Bo; Coptic often omits article before proper nouns;

3, 23 ειπεν αυτοις εν παραβολαις = Sah Bo Gr. U 565, and OL e; cf. c;

4, 29 – δε = Bo (3 MSS) and OL b e; omission of conjunctions is old in Coptic:

5, 27 + και at beginning = Eth and OL e; Sah and Bo have ⲇⲉ, used to mean "and" as well as "but" in early Coptic.

The relative strength of these various influences on the text of W is well illustrated by a study of 258 noteworthy readings, which have such weak support that they may with reasonable certainty be assumed to be errors. In this number the agreements of W with the various text traditions are as follows: Old Latin, 202; Greek D, 85; Sah, 40; Bo, 34; Syr S, 33; Gr. 700, 24; Syr g, 21; Eth, 21; Gr. 565, 18; Arm, 17; fam 13 and 28, 16 each; fam 1, 15. It may be noted that Sah and Bo are very often in agreement, so that the entire Coptic affiliation does not much exceed 50 cases, a number nearly equaled by the Syriac, some of the instances of which are rather more striking.

To complete the study of the text of this portion of W I add the readings for which I have found no other support:

1, 9 + *και* before *ηλθεν*;

1, 10 (*καταβαινον*) + *απο του ουρανου*; crept in from verse 11;

1, 17 − *ο* before ι̅ς̅; due to Coptic influence;

1, 24 (*απολεσαι*) + *ωδε*; harmonistic from Matthew 8, 29, cf. also 75**;

1, 39 − *και τα δαιμονια εκβαλλων*; a most interesting omission, perhaps original;

1, 44 *καθαρσιου* for *καθαρισμου*; not a N. T. word, but common even in early Greek;

2, 2 − *μηδε τα προς την θυραν*; cf. OL e; Matthew and Luke omit in the parallel passages;

2, 4 *εις ον* for *εφ ω*; perhaps due to retranslation; an easy change in late Greek, cf. Moulton, p. 68;

2, 7 *αφειναι* for *αφιεναι*; perhaps from Luke 5, 21, or translation tense change;

2, 14 *επι του τελωνιου* for *επι το τελωνιον*; a late Greek change, cf. Moulton, p. 107;

2, 15 *ανακειμενων αυτων* for *εν τω κατακεισθαι αυτον*; harmonistic from Matthew 9, 10; D a b c ff_2 are also harmonistic, but from Luke, 5, 29; e agrees better with W;

2, 19 *νυμφιοι* for *υιοι*; due to Old Latin influence, cf. *filii sponsi;* the latter was considered a nominative plural and caused loss of *filii;*

3, 1 *εισελθοντος αυτου* for *εισηλθε*; perhaps a Latinism, cf. *cum introisset* of b c e i;

3, 3 *εκ του μεσου* for *εις το μεσον*; this seems an intentional correction;

3, 5 *δε* for *και*(1); perhaps an earlier Coptic had ⲇⲉ;

3, 10 *επεπιπτον* for *επιπιπτειν*; the indicative with *ωστε* emphasizes the actuality; also cf. OL, especially r_2 (*inruerunt*);

3, 11 δε for και (1); see above;

3, 11 ιδον for εθεωρει; cf. *viderent* of OL; this seems to be a translation change;

3, 14 αποστιλη for αποστελλη; a tense change, cf. Latin *mitteret;*

3, 19 ο παραδους for ος παρεδωκεν; harmonistic from Matthew, 10, 4;

3, 21 εξηρτηνται αυτου for εξεστη; a change in the thought = "they were attached to him"; unfortunately OL e omits the verse;

3, 22 γραμματις after καταβαντες for οι γραμματεις; a stylistic change;

3, 25 καν for και εαν; a rather rare form in N. T.;

3, 33 ος δε for και; an error for ο δε of Matthew 12, 48; Luke 8, 21; similar errors noted pp. 24; 26; 83;

3, 34 κυκλω αυτου for τους περι αυτου; cf. D a;

4, 4 — εγενετο εν τω σπειρειν; W had σπειραι as D, hence omission due to like ending;

4, 5 ανετειλε for εξανετειλε; adapted to the versions, cf. e (*fructificaverunt*) Syr Eth, etc.

4, 8 εδιδει for εδιδου; shows ignorance of μι forms;

4, 16 οιτινες for οι; οιτινες οταν looks like a conflate caused by the Latin *qui cum*, which suggested *quicumque;*

4, 22 ουδεν for ου; harmonistic from Matthew 10, 26; Luke 12, 2;

4, 30 την παραβολην for παραβολη; adaptation to error δωμεν for θωμεν, perhaps aided by *parabolam* in Old Latin; cf. c e;

4, 30 — αυτην; further accommodation to the same error;

4, 31 οποταν for ος οταν; intentional change of construction, but cf. Sah;

4, 32 αυτου υπο την σκιαν; hardly due to Sahidic order;

4, 37 εισεβαλλεν for επεβαλλεν; cf. Sah, Bo, and OL e, though connection is not close;

5, 1 γεργυστηνων is a scribal error for γεργεσηνων of $\aleph^{ca}$ L U Δ fam 1, 28, 33, 251, 517, 565, 700, l. 49, l. 184, Syr S, etc.

5, 3 εδυναντο for ουδεις εδυνατο; either ουκετι crowded out

ουδεις in W or ℵ B C* D L Δ fam 13, 28, etc., have a conflate reading;

5, 3 αυτον transferred before ουκετι; cf. D and some Latin MSS;

5, 4 μηδενα δε for και ουδεις; cf. και μηδενα of D 700, d e;

5, 7 – του (1); bilingual influence or carelessness;

5, 19 ηλεηκεν for ηλεησεν; Sah has second perfect; Latin MSS have the perfect;

5, 21 του ιυ transposed after πλοιω; because of error διαπερασαντες (see above, p. 26) no construction was left for του ιυ; it is therefore an editorial change;

5, 27 – ελθουσα; fam 1 omits the following εν τω οχλω; perhaps the errors are related;

5, 27 – του ιματιου; cf. Luke 8, 45–47, harmonistic?

5, 28 αυτον transposed after αψωμαι; either Syriac influence or wrongly inserted correction.

Some of these variations are rather remarkable and seem to indicate intentional changes, as already noted. The cases are not, however, numerous enough to prove a definite editorial revision.

(*b*) Mark 5, 31 to end

In the second part of Mark there is still a decidedly close relationship between W and the Old Latin MSS, but the special Latinisms and the peculiar agreements with MS e have mostly disappeared. To illustrate the characteristics of the text, I have made a study of all (490) the readings weakly supported by other Greek MSS or lacking that support. In these 490 readings W agrees the following number of times with the various versions, MSS, or groups of MSS: Old Latin, 186; fam 13, 170; fam 1, 122; MS 565, 120; MS 28, 118; D, 115; Syr S, 101; Sah, 101; Bo, 71; MS 700, 70; Arm, 58; Syr g, 55; MS 299, 38; MS 472, 32; L, 30; ℵ, 24; Eth, 19; lect. 184, 18; C, 18; B, 16; Goth., 16; Δ, 15.

The most interesting feature of this table is the increase in the number of agreements with fam 13 (Ferrar group) and the other Syriacising MSS, fam 1, 565, and 28. With this naturally goes the closer alliance with Syr S, while the close bond of union of all the early versions is shown by Sahidic also maintaining an equal relationship. The larger number of agreements with Old Latin is in a measure deceptive, for we have far better evidence for Old Latin than for early Syriac or Coptic. If we confine our comparison to a single Old Latin MS, we find that k now stands nearest, with just under 75 agreements or partial agreements; MSS ff_2 and c stand next in order of relationship.

In the case of fam 13 it is interesting to note that of the 170 agreements 43 are with MS 124 against the rest of the family; in like manner 13 are with MS 69 alone, 7 with MS 346, and 5 with MS 13. Thus only 102 out of the 170 agreements are attested by a fair proportion of the group; yet we may, I think, on the evidence of W assign the remaining agreements to the ancestor of the group; therefore the often expressed opinion that sometimes MS 124 alone preserves the original reading may now be considered as established.

A comparison with von Soden's classification shows that the MSS and groups of MSS most closely affiliated with W are placed by him in different sub-groups of the I recension. D, 565, 28, and 700 all belong to the oldest branch, I^a, while fam 13 is the sub-group J, fam 1 is the sub-group H^r, MS 472 is related to the sub-group Φ, and to sub-group Σ are assigned cursives 157 and 245; with these two W has several notable agreements, though the number does not run high.[1] The general conclusion that W stands back of all these groups is easily made but deceptive, if we leave out of consideration the equally remarkable relationship to the versions, Latin, Syriac, Coptic, and even Armenian, Ethiopic, and Gothic. The only adequate explanation, it seems to me, is to refer all to the version tradition. W will then represent the Greek column of a trilingual, which had come to Egypt in the form Greek-Latin-Syriac, but the Syriac column had then been replaced by a Coptic (Sahidic) version. Under such circumstances we might expect the Sahidic influence to be even stronger, as W was evidently written in Coptic territory, and so under Coptic influence, if not by a Coptic scribe. We must, however, remember that both Sahidic and Bohairic have been accommodated to the Hesychian recension, so that only the remnants of the original Coptic version are preserved.

At the risk of being wearisome, I append a list of the more notable readings of W as illustrative of the conclusions reached. Readings supported by not more than two MS groups or versions have been chosen.

[1] Mr. Hoskier writes me that his new collation of MS 157 shows the former publication quite inadequate; the relationship to W is probably nearer than my comparisons show.

5, 31 − αυτου = Arm;
5, 32 − ιδειν = 259 (in Vulgate Q *videre* stands in an erasure);
5, 32 πεποιηκυιαν for ποιησασαν = fam 1, 28, Sah;
5, 33 (αυτω) + εμπροσθεν παντων = fam 13, Sah; cf. Luke 8, 47;
5, 37 αυτω ουδενα = l. 49, l. 184, cf. e (*secum quemquam*);
5, 37 (ει μη) + μονον = Arm;
5, 40 ($αυτου_1$) + ειδοτες οτι απεθανεν = fam 13, Sah; from Luke 8, 53;
6, 1 − εκειθεν = 473; W omits και ερχεται also = 13, 131, 238, Sah Bo Arm;
6, 2 ηρξαντο for ηρξατο = 346, 435;
6, 11 ακουση for ακουσωσιν = fam 1; cf. ακουσει of 28 and fam 13 (?);
6, 13 εξεπεμπον for εξεβαλλον = Sah Bo; a sure case of re-translation from Coptic;
6, 18 − την before γυναικα = 472;
6, 18 γυναικα εχειν = fam 1;
6, 23 − μου = ff_2; cf. Eth, which has "his" for "my";
6, 29 κηδευσαι for και ηραν = 28;
6, 29 αυτον for αυτο = ℵ, 346; cf. Matthew 14, 12 in ℵ* B Θ a ff_1;
6, 30 εποιησεν for εποιησαν = Δ Syr S; this is a characteristic error in Syriac;
6, 30 εδιδασκεν for εδιδαξαν = Syr S;
6, 33 αυτον for αυτους (1) = 108, 700, Arm^{cdd}; an error natural to Syriac;
6, 34 ηρξαντο for ηρξατο = 59, 253;
6, 37 ($φαγειν_2$) + ινα εκαστος αυτων βραχυ τι λαβη = fam 13; from John 6, 7;
6, 41 + πεντε before αρτους (2) = D b c d ff_2 g_2 r;
6, 45 − εις το περαν = fam 1, q Syr S;
6, 48 − προς αυτους = D 565, a b c d ff_2 i r;
6, 49 φαντασμα εδοξαν = fam 1, 28;
6, 51 αυτοις for εαυτοις = L 485;
6, 55 + εις before ολην = fam 13, Syr S; change arose in Syriac, since different verb was used;
6, 55 εστιν εκει = fam 1, 28, 700;
6, 56 οποταν for οπου αν = fam 1;
7, 1 τινες for τινας (+ τινας after αυτου) = ℵ;

7, 5 ερωτωσιν for επερωτωσιν = 28, 124, 271; Syriac has no compound verbs;

7, 5 + ταις before χερσιν = D 28; Syr S g Sah have "their" hands; Bo has the indefinite article;

7, 6 αγαπα for τιμα = D a b c; Eth conflates;

7, 13 (τον λογον) + την εντολην = (fam 1); a conflate which crept into W from gloss in parent; no connective;

7, 19 χωρει for εκπορευεται = i h Ir (Or); from Matthew 15, 17;

7, 23 – ταυτα = Syr S; cf. changed order in many MSS;

7, 24 – εκειθεν = a b c i n Syr S;

7, 28 ψιχων for ψιχιων = D (from ψιξ, regular reading is from the diminutive);

7, 33 πτυσας εις τα ωτα αυτου και = fam 13, 28, Syr S;

7, 36 οσω for οσον = 44, 700, Vulg (*quanto*);

7, 37 πεποιηκεν for ποιει = 472, q δ aur Vg (*fecit*); Sah and Bo have first perfect;

7, 37 – αλαλους = 28, Syr S;

8, 1 – αυτοις = Vulgates L and R;

8, 2 επι τω οχλω for επι τον οχλον = a f T^{vg} gat (*turbae huic*) h r_2 $Vg^{6\ MSS}$ (*super turba*); cf. D and other Old Latin MSS;

8, 4 – αυτου = Bo (8 MSS);

8, 4 ωδε δυνασαι αυτους = Syr S Arm; cf. fam 1, 28, a f l;

8, 5 (ποσους) + ωδε = Sah;

8, 8 – κλασματων = Δ Cypr;

8, 10 προς το ορος for εις τα μερη = 28, Syr S; cf. ℵ D Σ c f i Arm Eth;

8, 11 εκ for απο = fam 13 (except 124), Sah Bo;

8, 12 – υμιν = B L; W omits λεγω also;

8, 12 ταυτη τη γενεα = Sah Bo (regular Coptic order);

8, 14 ενα μονον εχοντες αρτον = 28, 69; fam 1, fam 13, 565, 700, agree except for order;

8, 18 – και (2) = Sah (except MS 18); και (1) omitted by several;

8, 20 – κλασματων = 346, k Vg (X**) Bo (one MS);

8, 23 επ αυτω ηρωτα for αυτω επηρωτα = Sah Bo; 245 and 251 conflate;

8, 25 ανεβλεπεν παντα τηλαυγως = f Sah Diatess (normal Arabic order);

8, 27 *τους μαθητας αυτου επηρωτα* = 28, Syr S;
8, 28 (*απεκριθησαν*) + *λεγοντες* = 579, 1071, f q Bo Arm;
8, 29 − *ειναι* = Sah Bo (omission of copula common in Coptic);
8, 29 ($\overline{\chi\varsigma}$) + *ο υιος του* $\overline{\theta\upsilon}$ *του ζωντος* = fam 13, (b) Syr g j Pers; from Matthew 16, 16;
8, 30 *λεγουσιν* for *λεγωσι* = 245, 251;
8, 31 (*και*$_1$) + *απο τοτε* ≐ fam 13, Sah (8 and 64) Bo (א);
8, 38 − *λογους* = k* D^{vg} Sah;
8, 38 *και* for *μετα* = Syr S (Sah Bo use *μεν* = with, but which is used for "and" with persons);
8, 38 − *ταυτη* = a Or;
9, 1 − *αν* = F;
9, 2 (*και*$_5$) + *εν τω προσευχεσθαι αυτους* = fam 13, Diatess[1]; also 28,[2] 472, 565, Or, but *αυτον* for *αυτους*; from Luke 9, 29;
9, 2 (*μετεμορφωθη*) + *ο* $\overline{\iota\varsigma}$ = fam 13, Diatess[1]; made necessary by change of person above;
9, 3 *ως* for *οια* = D; yet W has rest of comparison like א B C L, etc.;
9, 5 *ωδε ημας* = Vulg (10 MSS) Syr S;
9, 6 *λαλει* for *λαληση* = Syr S g Sah;
9, 7 − *εγενετο* (*ηλθεν*) = fam 1, k Syr g;
9, 8 *περιβλεπομενοι* = b c d f ff$_2$ q r aur Vulg (*circumspicientes*);
9, 13 *ηδη ελιας ηλθεν* for *και ελιας εληλυθε* = Go; also C fam 1, 700, f i gat, except order; cf. Matthew 17, 12;
9, 14 − *πολυν* = fam 1, 28, Arm Bo(Θ);
9, 18 *ηδυνηθησαν* for *ισχυσαν* = 700; Latin influence;
9, 19 *απιστε* for *απιστος* = D.
9, 20 − *και* (2) = ff$_2$ (a lacuna before *cum vidisset*, but compare enlarged C) Arm;
9, 20 − *αυτον* (4) = 435, gat; fam 13, 28, 565, OL substitute *το παιδιον*;
9, 21 *αυτου τον* $\overline{\pi\rho\alpha}$ = Sah Bo;
9, 23 *τουτο* for *το* = Sah Bo; Latin MSS do not show the expected *hic* or *iste;*

[1] This change has been used to prove that fam 13 was indebted to the Diatessaron, but the true explanation is now clear. Tatian is quoting Mark 9, 2, not Luke 9, 29, which nowhere shows these changes; he drew from the version tradition, which had already inserted the harmonistic error modeled on Luke.

[2] Thus Hoskier in his new collation of 28.

9, 24 *ειπεν* for *ελεγε* = fam 13, a f k q;
9, 27 – *και ανεστη* = 63, k Syr S g Diatess;
9, 28 – *αυτου* (2) = Vulg (2 MSS) Bo (3 MSS) Arm;
9, 31 *εγειρεται* for *αναστησεται* = 28; cf. *εγερθησεται* in fam 1, fam 13, etc. (= Matthew 17, 23);
9, 32 *ερωτησαι* for *επερωτησαι* = 1, fam 13, Chr; Syriac influence;
9, 33 *διελεχθητε* for *διελογιζεσθε* = fam 1, 28;
9, 36 – *εν* = 66;
9, 38 *ηκολουθει* for *ακολουθει* = 565;
9, 39 *με κακολογησαι* = fam 1, 28, 565, Sah; cf. Syr S;
9, 42 *εβληθη* for *βεβληται* = D; cf. *mitteretur* of Latin MSS;
9, 43 *εις την ζωην εισελθειν κυλλον* = 472; from Matthew 18, 8;
9, 45 *σκανδαλιση* = 90*, g_2 L^{vg}; cf. L;
9, 45 *κοψον* for *αποκοψον* = a ff_2 q r A^{vg} (*amputa*); cf. Syr;
9, 45 *απελθειν* for *βληθηναι* = fam 1, 28, Syr S;
9, 47 *ει* for *εαν* = D;
9, 47 – *σοι* = 565, Vg (D*); many transpose or change *σοι* to *σε*;
9, 47 – *βληθηναι* = L^{vg};
9, 50 *αρτυσηται* = Δ fam 13, 28; cf. K fam 1, Syr;
9, 50 + *υμεις ουν* before *εν εαυτοις εχεται* = fam 13, (28), 565;
10, 2 *οι δε φαρισαιοι προσελθοντες* = 406, 565, Arm; many omit participle;
10, 10 *επηρωτησαν οι μαθηται αυτου* = c k Syr S Sah;
10, 10 – *αυτον* = M L^{vg};
10, 11–12 verse 12 transposed before 11 = Syr S g Clem; cf. fam 1; from I Cor. 7, 10?
10, 12 – *και* (1) = fam 1;
10, 14 *αυτοις ειπεν* = fam 13;
10, 14 *εμε* for *με* = N;
10, 21 *ουρανοις* for *ουρανω* = E* 238; cf. Syr;
10, 24 (*εισελθειν*) + *πλουσιον* = c; cf. verse 25;
10, 25 tr. *πλουσιον* before *εισελθειν* = 1, 299; cf. 28;
10, 27 – *παρα* (3) = 10, 579, Clem;
10, 28 *αυτω λεγειν ο πετρος* = 1, 124; cf. 28, 565, Syr S Bo Arm;
10, 32 (*ακολουθουντες*) + *αυτω* = c k Sah;
10, 32 – *και* and *εφοβουντο* = c k ff_2; cf. D K 28, 157, 474, 700;

10, 33 – αυτον (2) = c r_2;
10, 37 τη βασιλεια της δοξης for τη δοξη σου = fam 13; cf. Sah "in the glory of thy kingdom";
10, 42 ο δε for ο δε ις = 238, Go; Syr S has "and he";
10, 43 οστις for ος = 485, OL Vulg (*quicumque*);
10, 46 – βαρτιμαιος = k, which omits ο υιος τιμαιου likewise;
10, 48 whole verse omitted because of like endings = 14, 477* colb^{wets} (= 22?) Syr g (36);
10, 49 – αυτω = c k;
10, 49 θαρρων for θαρσει = 28, (fam 1, fam 13);
11, 2 – υμων = ℵ* k;
11, 3 – ποιειτε τουτο = fam 1, 299, Syr S; more omit τουτο; cf. Matthew 21, 3;
11, 8 – αυτων = L i;
11, 8 – αλλοι · · · οδον = Syr S and OL i;
11, 9 – ωσαννα = D l. 184, b d ff_2;
11, 10 ειρηνη for ωσαννα = 28, 700, Syr S Or; fam 1, 299 have conflate;
11, 12 εις βηθανιαν for απο βηθανιας = r_2 Syr g (36) Bo (6 MSS);
11, 13 απο μακροθεν συκην = D 472, OL Vulg Or;
11, 14 καρπον μηδεις = fam 1, 299, Vg^{cl};
11, 22 του θυ for θυ = D Sah Bo (as always in Coptic);
11, 28 – ινα ταυτα ποιης = 28, 565, a b ff_2 i r aur (k) Syr S Arm;
11, 29 επερωτω for επερωτησω = b c f ff_2 i k ϻт;
11, 30 απ for εξ (1) = fam 1; OL and Vulg have *de;*
11, 31 αυτους for εαυτους = 157;
11, 31 (λεγοντες) + οτι = Sah Bo; cf. 69 and 346, which insert it two words later;
12, 1 – και (3) = Sah (except 73*);
12, 3 (εδιραν) + και απεκτιναν = 346; addition came from Latin doublette *ceciderunt occiderunt*, cf. OL MSS;
12, 6 – ετι ουν = 565, c k; many omit one of the words;
12, 19 – αυτου (1) = b;
12, 21 – και απεθανε = l. 184, Sah Syr S (in lacuna, but not sufficient space);
12, 25 + οι before αγγελοι = B Or Sah Bo (26 MSS); plain case of Coptic influence;
12, 26 ο θς λεγων αυτω = Syr S Sah (1 MS) Bo (1 MS);
12, 26 – ο (2) (3) (4) = D Or; B omits nos. (3) and (4) only;

12, 30 αυτη πρωτη for αυτη πρωτη εντολη = 28, 565, k Mcell^{Eus}; the Hesychian recension omits whole phrase;

12, 34 (ειπεν αυτω) + οτι = 157, 565, Sah;

12, 34 ετολμα αυτον ουκετι = ff$_2$ Vulg (K Z) cor-vat; cf. Diatess;

12, 35 – ο ι̅ς̅ = 700, aur;

12, 35 λεγει for ελεγε = colb^{wets} (= 22?) c ff$_2$;

12, 35 – ο before χ̅ς̅ = Barn;

12, 40 – τας, – των = D 229;

12, 40 οιτινες for ουτοι = fam 13, 28;

12, 40 περισσον for περισσοτερον = Δ δ Sah;

12, 43 – αυτου = Arm^{cdd};

12, 43 – οτι = ff$_2$; properly omitted in Latin;

13, 1 – ιδε = 59*;

13, 2 – ο ι̅ς̅ = 565, 700, a b e g$_2$ i Vulg (K V);

13, 2 at end + και δια τριων ημερων αλλος αναστησεται ανευ χειρων = D OL Cypr;

13, 3 δε for και (1) = al pauc^{tisch} 579, Sah Bo (2 MSS); Coptic influence;

13, 8 (λιμοι) + ταραχαι = 299; many add και ταραχαι;

13, 8 – αρχαι οδινων ταυτα = c; W omits next phrase also with D fam 1, 28, 124, 565, 700, etc.;

13, 13 – ουτος = 59* Syr S; cf. above to Matthew 10, 22;

13, 16 τα ιματια for το ιματιον = 61, 435;

13, 19 – κτισεως = 28, 299, Arm;

13, 22 (γαρ) + πολλοι = Sah (55, 74, 86) (Just); cf. Matthew 24, 11;

13, 25 τω ουρανω for τοις ουρανοις = 38, 700; cf. Syr;

13, 27 επισυνστρεψουσιν for επισυναξει = 28, (e g$_2$); regular verb occurs in plural also;

13, 27 ακρων ουρανων for ακρου ουρανου = fam 1, OL; from Matthew 24, 31;

13, 30 (αμην) + δε = L;

13, 30 εως for μεχρις ου = 259, 565; εως αν and εως ου also occur;

13, 33 – εστιν = D a c Syr S;

13, 35 μεσανυκτιον for μεσονυκτιον = B*;

13, 37 – λεγω (2) = D d 565; E ff$_2$ i k r$_2$ Vg omit more;

14, 3 προσηλθεν for ηλθε = fam 13, which changes order and adds αυτω; cf. Matthew 26, 7;

14, 4 (τινες) + των μαθητων = fam 13, Syr g Pers;

14, 5 – τουτο = ℵ k Syr S g;

14, 6 κοπον for κοπους = k (*taedium facitis*);
14, 13 των μαθητων αυτου δυο = fam 13 (except 124);
14, 13 (και$_3$) + εισελθοντων υμων = Sah; fam 13, 28, 299, 565, Arm Or add εις την πολιν also; cf. Luke 22, 10;
14, 14 – και (1) = 579, ff$_2$ r (Syr S) Sah (m[l]);
14, 18 με παραδωσει = f h i l q Vulg; natural Latin order;
14, 22 εδιδου for εδωκεν = fam 1, fam 13;
14, 22 – εστι = Syr S;
14, 30 αρνηση for απαρνηση = Or; cf. Syr and Latin (*negabis*);
14, 31 ο δε πετρος μαλλον = fam 1, fam 13; cf. Syr. S; others add in different order;
14, 31 (ελεγεν) + οτι = fam 13, Sah Bo;
14, 36 (σοι) + εστιν = fam 13, Arm; cf. D, which adds plural verb with OL;
14, 46 τας χειρας αυτων (– επ αυτον) = ℵ* C (Δ) Φ; many partially support;
14, 56–57 – και ισαι ··· αυτου· = 435, 440, 472;
14, 60 οτι for τι = B L;
14, 61 – ο αρχιερευς = c ff$_2$;
14, 63 (αρχιερευς) + ευθυς = 124, Sah (4 MSS); others add in different order;
14, 64 φαινεται υμιν = Sah Bo;
14, 65 (προφητευσον) + νυν χ̅ε̅ τις εστιν ο πεσας σε = fam 13, (1071); cf. Matthew 26, 68; Luke 22, 64, which many MSS copy without νυν χ̅ε̅;
14, 66 – του (1) = 700, Sah Bo; regular omission in Coptic;
14, 70 περιεστηκοτες for παρεστωτες = (D 124) (G 1);
15, 7 (ην δε) + τοτε = fam 13, Sah (6 MSS); cf. Matthew 27, 16;
15, 11 βαρναβαν for βαραββαν = Sah (73*);
15, 39 – ουτως = 565, Bo Arm Or;
15, 41 – αι (2) = Ψ;
15, 43 ιωσης for ιωσηφ = k; cf. D^{vg};
15, 44 ηδη τεθνηκεν for παλαι απεθανε = 472; cf. OL Vulg (*iam mortuus esset*) and other versions;
15, 45 ιωση for ιωσηφ = B; cf. k;
15, 47 (ιωση) + μ̅η̅ρ̅ = fam 13, 565 Syr j;
16, 1 εισελθουσαι for ελθουσαι = Goth (*atgaggandeins*);
16, 2 – τη before μια = B 1; cf. Syr and Lat;
16, 3 αποκυλιση for – σει = 483, l. 183, Goth Eus;
16, 5 θεωρουσιν for ειδον = L^{vg} (*vident*);

16, 6 *φοβεισθαι* for *εκθαμβεισθε* = D 565, d n Euseb;
16, 6 (*φοβεισθαι*) + *οιδα γαρ οτι* = Greek-Sahidic lectionary published in Oriens Christianus, Neue Serie, II; cf. Matthew 28, 5;
16, 6 *τον ναζαρηνον ζητιται* = c ff_2 (k);
16, 6 *ειδετε* for *ιδε* = D c ff_2 k^r n q aur; from Matthew 28, 6;
16, 6 (*ειδετε*) + *εκει* = D 565; cf. *ecce* in d^{supp} ff_2 k n q aur;
16, 7 *προαγω* for *προαγει* = D k;
16, 8 *ακουσασαι εξηλθον και* for *εξελθουσαι* = Syrr Sah (108) Bo Arm Gr. frg. in Paris MS Copt. 129^8 (order change);
16, 9 − *πρωτον* = Arm Eus Vict;
16, 14 long addition, see coll. = Hier. adv. Pelag. (quotes first verse only);
16, 19 ($\overline{\kappa\varsigma}$) + $\overline{\iota\varsigma}$ $\overline{\chi\varsigma}$ = Old Latin o Bohairic B Γ.

A comparison of all the readings of this portion of Mark with the chief uncials gave no decided results. ℵ A B C D L N varied in proportion of agreements slightly from chapter to chapter, but the totals showed no definite preference for any one or for any group. It is quite apparent that neither the Hesychian nor the Antioch recension had any influence on this part of W. What agreements exist are due to the fact, that these recensions drew from the same sources as W.

As in the previous sections, I add the readings of this part of Mark, for which there seems no other support; those discussed in previous sections are not included.

5, 31 *συντριβοντα* for *συνθλιβοντα*; a stronger word and common in N. T.;
5, 40 *εαυτου* for *μετ αυτου*; cf. *των αυτου* in the subscription to Mark in W;
5, 41 − *αυτη*;
6, 5 *ουκετι* for *εκει ουδεμιαν*; a milder denial;
6, 8 *πηραν* for *ζωνην*; careless repetition from first half of verse;
6, 10 − *αυτοις*; cf. Syr S which omits more;
6, 11 *αυτων* for *αυτοις*; Syr S has the possessive suffix;
6, 20 *ηπορειτο* for *εποιει* (*ηπορει*); the middle voice gives better meaning here;

6, 22 — της (2) after αυτης; many others omit, changing αυτου for αυτης;

6, 24 (ειπεν) + αιτησε; cf. 28 (+ αυτη); therefore scribal error occasioned by gloss;

6, 25 δωσης for δως; cf. 3d future in Sah, often used with conjunction like subjunctive;

6, 31 λοιπον for ολιγον; a scribal error, the change could hardly be intentional;

6, 33 υπαγοντες for -τας; accommodated to construction of other changes;

6, 40 ανδρες for ανα;

6, 45 (εως) + αν; influence of following subjunctive;

6, 50 μη φοβεισθαι εγω ειμι; order change to bring two imperatives together;

6, 55 οτι for οπου, a change to avoid two expressions of place in succession;

7, 10 αθετων for κακολογων; means "reject," therefore a weakened expression;

7, 13 παρεδοτε for παρεδωκατε; looks like a translation change;

7, 19 διανοιαν for καρδιαν; ditto;

7, 31 εις την δεκαπολιν for δεκαπολεως; looks like a Latinism, but not found in MSS;

7, 33 προσλαβομενος for απολαβομενος; cf. Latin MSS (*accipiens, apprehendens, adsumens*);

7, 33 — τους;

7, 34 εφεθθα for εφφαθα; an interchange of double consonants on form in ℵ[c] D c l r (Sah), etc.;

8, 5 ο δε for και; cf. early Coptic preference for δε;

8, 5 ηρωτησεν for επηρωτα; influence of the versions;

8, 6 αυτοις for τοις μαθηταις αυτου; an intentional change to lighten the expression;

8, 10 δαλμουναι; an error perhaps influenced by Syriac;

8, 11 απ for παρ; cf. Latin *ab;*

8, 12 — λεγω; cf. omission in B L;

8, 14 απελθοντες for επελαθοντο; scribal error;

8, 16 οι δε for και; cf. above;

8, 18 βλεπουσιν for βλεπετε; an odd change, evidently making "eyes" the subject;

8, 23 ενπτυσας for πτυσας; cf. Latin *expuens;*

8, 23 –τι;
8, 33 ιδως for ιδων;
8, 34 αρας for αρατω ··· και; a more natural Latin construction, but cf. Or. protr. 13;
8, 34 –αυτου (2);
8, 36 την εαυτου ψυχην; natural Coptic order;
9, 4 αυτος for αυτοις; scribal error;
9, 5 ειπεν πετρος for ο πετρος λεγει;
9, 24 το $\overline{\pi\nu\alpha}$ του παιδαριου for ο $\overline{\pi\eta\rho}$ του παιδιου; due to confusion of abbreviations;
9, 31 λεγει for ελεγεν; cf. λεγων l. 26, k (*dicens*) Sah;
9, 35 –και (1);
9, 37 των τοιουτων παιδιον; adjustment to a conflate, εκ and εν.
9, 39 δυνησονται for –εται; r_2 and D^{vg} read *posuit*, perhaps for *posint*;
9, 41 ος αν γαρ; transposed because the first two words were considered one;
9, 42 (μικρων) + μου; cf. k (+ *vestros*), a (+ *vestris*);
9, 42 μυλον ονικον for λιθος μυλικος; a change in gender from form in ℵ B C D L etc.
9, 47 σκανδαλιση for –ζη; cf. same change in verse 45, supported by 90* g_2 L^{vg};
9, 49 αλις γηθησεται for αλισθησεται; Latin influence; *salietur* was read *satietur;*
9, 50 μωρανθη for αναλον γενηται; (= MS 579); from Matthew 5, 13; Luke 14, 34;
9, 50 εν εαυτοις εχεται; Latin order;
10, 7 εκαστος for ανθρωπος; cf. ανθρωπων in ℵ, which might have been gloss on εκαστος;
10, 21 –ο δε;
10, 22 απο του λογου for επι τω λογω; looks like Latin change, but not found in MSS;
10, 22 (απηλθε) + απ αυτου;
10, 28 –ιδου ημεις; l. 185 and Sah omit "we";
10, 28 παντα αφηκαμεν; Latin order;
10, 30 –και αδελφους; D d and 700 transpose;
10, 35 αιτησωμεθα for αιτησωμεν; intentional change; middle voice means "ask for ourselves";
10, 38 αυτω for αυτοις;
10, 39 –ο δε $\overline{\iota\varsigma}$ ειπεν αυτοις;

10, 42 ου for οι (2); scribal error; it may indicate defective parent;

10, 42 –αυτων (3); an error in correction; αυτων (2) is omitted by ℵ N Σ fam 1, 28, 299, k, etc.;

11, 2 κατεναντι κωμην for κωμην την κατεναντι; from Luke 19, 30;

11, 2 ω for εφ ον; l. 48 = εφ ω; W points to same text in parent;

11, 2 επικεκαθεικεν for κεκαθικε; preposition joined to verb, cf. preceding example;

11, 12 αυριον for επαυριον; both words common in N. T. and Hellenistic Greek;

11, 13 εις αυτην for εν αυτη; copied from previous phrase, where supported by many;

11, 14 (αυτη) + ο ις̅; Antioch recension adds, but in different order;

11, 25 ανη for αφη; αφιημι does not seem to mean "forgive" in N. T. yet easy change, cf. OL Vulg;

12, 1 εξωρυξεν for ωρυξεν; probably Latin influence, *et fodit* read as *ecfodit;*

12, 2 –προς τους γεωργους; note the transposition in c k r;

12, 5 –κακεινον απεκτειναν; note addition of this verb in verse 3, discussed above;

12, 5 δε for μεν; cf. Syr g;

12, 10 ανεγνωκατε for ανεγωτε; cf. perfect tense in Syr Lat Sah;

12, 12 –και αφεντες αυτον απηλθον; perhaps accommodated to Matthew and Luke;

12, 14 –ου (1);

12, 21 –και (1);

12, 21 –και (4); for all such omissions cf. lack of conjunctions in early Coptic;

12, 23 αυτων τινος; cf. omission of αυτων in Δ 579, c k δ.

12, 26 ει for οτι; an editorial change; cf. I Cor. 15, 16;

12, 26 ανεγνωκατε for ανεγνωτε; cf. verse 10;

12, 29 –εις; crowded out by a correction; F 259, l. 183, Syr S a b k r_2, etc. omit κυριος (2);

12, 31 ομοιως for ομοια; cf. omission in Coptic and change of construction in other versions;

12, 32 θς̅ εστιν; θς̅ omitted by many, accounts for the change in order;

12, 38 +ταις before στολαις; cf. the indefinite article in Sahidic;

12, 41 (εθεωρι)+παντας; from vv. 43–4; cf. also Or. John Com. 19, 7, 42;

12, 44 –παντα οσα ειχεν; the appositive, ολον τον βιον αυτης, is omitted by ff₂ g₂ aur Syr S and Diatess; the regular reading seems a conflate, cf. Luke 21, 4; Diatess borrowed from Lat-Syr tradition, not *vice versa;*

13, 2 αφεθη ουδε διαλυθησεται for καταλυθη; cf. καταλυθησεται in ℵ* L fam 13, 106, from Matthew and Luke; αφεθη is a repetition from the previous phrase;

13, 9 δωσουσιν for παραδωσουσι; Syriac influence;

13, 12 αναστησονται for επαναστησονται; cf. Syriac and the different compounds in OL;

13, 15 τι after αυτου; a different transposition in B K L Π* 72, 253;

13, 17 –ταις (2);

13, 21 $\overline{κς}$ for $\overline{χς}$;

13, 33 (γαρ)+ει μη ο $\overline{πηρ}$ και ο υιος; cf. verse 32, which this contradicts;

14, 1 φαρισαιοι for γραμματεις; from John 11, 47; l. 185 combines the two readings;

14, 13 αποστιλας for αποστελλει··· και; good Latin, but not found in MSS;

14, 23 τοις μαθηταις for αυτοις; 69, 124, 235, and Syr S make same change in verse 22;

14, 27 σκορπισθησεται for διασκορπισθησεται; cf. Latin (*scandalizabimini*) and Syriac;

14, 28 (εγερθηναι με)+εκ νεκρων; a common addition, cf. John 12, 9 (where εκ νεκρων is omitted by W);

14, 30 –σοι; omitted to avoid succession σοι··συ; or regular text adds σοι from Matthew 26, 35; Luke 22, 34;

14, 32 εξερχονται for ερχονται; cf. Sahidic;

14, 41 (ωρα)+και; insertion due to change in order;

14, 47 παρεστωτων for παρεστηκοτων;

14, 53 συνπορευονται for συνερχονται; translation change, cf. Syr S and Sah;

14, 60 –ουκ αποκρινη ουδεν;

14, 62 της δυναμεως for των νεφελων; due to similar appearance of words in Syriac;

15, 4 σου ποσα; cf. order in Sahidic and Bohairic;
15, 7 βαρναβας for βαραββας; cf. Sah 73* in verse 11;
15, 39 −ο (2); cf. Sah;
15, 39 παρεστως for παρεστηκως; cf. 14, 47;
15, 41 διηκονουσαν for διηκονουν; cf. 28 (διακονησαι);
15, 46 (σινδονα) + ευθεως ηνεγκεν;
16, 2 −και λιαν; many omit λιαν;
16, 4 σφοδρα μεγας;
16, 6 (τοπος) + αυτου εστιν; added to give construction to the nom. independent;
16, 10 −και κλαιουσι; like ending of previous phrase caused omission;
16, 15 αλλα for και ειπεν αυτοις; change made necessary by long addition preceding;
16, 16 κατακριθεις ου σωθησεται for κατακριθησεται.

In this long list there are comparatively few harmonistic errors; rather more, especially towards the end, are the deliberate changes of a reader or editor, possibly showing the influence of a lost source; by far the larger number are of the same character as those given in the previous list, for which there was in general adequate authority found in the version tradition. Doubtless many of these errors arose in the same tradition, but other evidence of their presence there has perished.

3. Luke

In the study of the text of Luke also a decided change in character between the earlier and later portions was found. Here, however, a comparison with the four chief uncials sufficed to show the point of change. The following table gives the number of agreements of those uncials with W in each chapter. All important variants were counted.

Chap.	א	A	B	D
1	55	30	62	43
2	59	37	61	35
3	26	25	26	13
4	58	24	54	40
5	55	46	63	43
6	89	42	83	54
7	66	40	65	39

Chap.	ℵ	A	B	D
8	56	77	49	49
9	38	81	42	53
10	29	62	22	26
11	42	74	42	45
12	31	57	35	32
13	33	48	26	25
14	14	35	16	19
15	20	30	19	22
16	8	26	6	14
17	29	53	27	26
18	20	44	18	28
19	8	51	12	30
20	26	51	25	29
21	17	38	16	20
22	25	70	21	35
23	29	71	19	43
24	30	63	23	36

It is plain that early in chapter eight W definitely parted company with the ℵ B text and went over to a text closely allied to A. We can mark the point of change even more exactly, for there are but 5 agreements between A and W in the first 12 verses of chapter eight, while from that point on the agreements are numerous and in every section.

(*a*) Luke 1 – 8, 12

Out of 678 important variants in this section of Luke W agrees with the Hesychian recension (ℵ B L 33) 488 times, to which may be added 59 more cases, where the authorities for this recension are divided, but the added testimony of W seems sufficient to determine the text form. Only the four following cases point towards the Antioch recension:

3, 19 + φιλιππου before του αδελφου = A C K X Π Ψ 118, 209, 238, 247, 248, 249, 252**, 253, 259, 282, 474, 481, 579, l. 47, l. 48, l. 49, l. 50, l. 183, l. 184, Syrr Sah (73) Bo Arm^cdd Eth;

3, 20 + τη before φυλακη = A C E F G H S U V X Γ Δ Ψ fam 1, fam 13, 28, 157, 579, etc.

6, 9 προς αυτους ο ις̅ = K Π 72, 74, 89, 90, 130, 133, 134,

248, 252, 253, 300, 473, 482, 483, 484, 565, OL Vg Syr g j Eth Arm;

6, 10 (αυτου) + υγιης = E M S V Γ Λ 28, 240, 245, 248, 299, 435, 472, 474, 482, 579, etc.

The original home of these readings is seen from the minuscule authority, which points to the version recension. This is least clear in the first example, but there the lectionaries suffice, especially as the Antioch authority is not very strong. The explanation of the relationship is that the Antioch recension or some branch of it adopted readings from the version tradition. To the same text tradition belong the following 126 readings, though they were in some cases adopted into other families. I add in each case the MS authority for the reading, but where only the Hesychian recension is opposed, I state the MS authority in that way. Scribal peculiarities previously treated are not included.

1, 1 — εν = F 28, 54, 71, 74, 89, 127, 132, 234, 235, 237, 244, 248, 255, l. 32, l. 47, l. 60, l. 184;

1, 6 ενωπιον for εναντιον; against Hesych. rec.;

1, 15 εν κοιλια for εκ κοιλιας = K* c e l r Syr S Sah Go Cypr Ambr Vig-Tap;

1, 17 προελευσεται for προσελευσεται; ag. B* C L V 482, l. 47;

1, 32 αυτος for ουτος = X;

1, 35 διοτι for διο = A* Ir (*qua propter*); cf. c q r, etc. (*ideoque et*);

1, 41 ηκουσεν η ελισαβετ; ag. Hesych. rec. + D fam 1, fam 13, 565, Latin Arm;

1, 65 (ιουδαιας) + και = b c e (r) Bo;

1, 66 ταις καρδιαις for τη καρδια = D L 49, 254, 579, e d Syr S Arm;

1, 68 — $\overline{κς}$ = a b c ff$_2$ g$_1$ l r Vg (9 MSS) Syr S Sah Eus;

1, 68 του λαου for τω λαω = c b ff$_2$ q r r$_2$ aur Vg (12 MSS) Ambr (*plebis suae*); many Latin MSS have *plebi suae;*

1, 70 αυτου προφητων = e b aur Sah Bo; Coptic prefix seems to have influenced order;

1, 77 αυτου for αυτων = 130^{gr}, 565; cf. e (*suorum*);

2, 5 απογραφεσθαι for απογραψασθαι = ℵ* A D 33, 59, 73, 245, 472, etc., Chr;

2, 9 (*μεγαν*) + *σφοδρα* = Bo; B has *σφοδρα* in place of *φοβον μεγαν*;

2, 11 κ̅ς̅ χ̅ς̅ = Syr S Diatess; cf. e d Cypr Ir (X̅P̅S̅ I̅H̅S̅) through which the error arose;

2, 16 *ευρον* for *ανευρον* = D L^{scholz} fam 1, fam 13, 53, 61, 71, 106, (472), 565, 579, colb^{wets} (= 22 r);

2, 26 − *η αν* = fam 13, 118, 218, 472, l. 47, etc. OL Vg;

2, 26 − *τον* before χ̅ν̅ = 482, Sah Bo; regular Coptic usage;

2, 27 *εισαγειν* for *εισαγαγειν* = A 15, 53, 69, 473, Ps-Ath;

2, 37 (*και*$_1$) + *ην* = (579) r gat Q^{vg} Syr S Sah;

2, 37 *ως* against *εως* of Hesych. rec. + A f ff$_2$ g$_{1,2}$ Vg;

2, 49 *ζητειτε* for *εζητειτε* = א* 346, b ƎP* Syr cu Sah Bo;

2, 49 *οιδατε* for *ηδειτε* = D 225, 282, l. 49, OL Syr cu Sah Ir Thdrt Tert Cyr;

2, 49 − *μου* = Syr S cu;

2, 49 *με ειναι* = D fam 1, fam 13, l. 253, OL Vg Ir Or Did Cyr Epiph Thdrt Dial;

2, 51 *ετηρει* for *διετηρει* = 435, ƎP Syr cu S Sah Bo;

2, 52 + *ο* before ι̅ς̅ = א* Λ 59, 122, 131, 237, 248, 472, Or;

3, 1 *ιουδαιας* for *ιτουραιας* = l. 60*; cf. Sah *ιδουραια* as probable cause;

3, 8 *καρπον αξιον* for *καρπους αξιους* = D 106, e d r Syr h Bo Arm^{edd} Eth Go; from Matthew 3, 8;

3, 10 *επηρωτησαν* for *επηρωτων* = D 244, OL Syr cu S Sah Bo (L) Eth;

3, 11 *ειπεν* for *λεγει* = a b d e g$_1$ q Syrr Bo Arm Eth Diatess; Hesych. has *ελεγεν*;

3, 14 *προς αυτους* against *αυτοις* of Hesych. + D 700 and Latin;

3, 19 *πονηρων ων εποιησεν* = א* a b c f ff$_2$ g$_{1,2}$ l q Vg Syr cu S Sah Lucif;

3, 20 (*πασιν*) + *και*; against Hesych. + D b d e;

3, 21 *παντα* for *απαντα* = א, l. 49 al pauc;

3, 24–38 genealogy omitted = (579), Diatess; cf. D d (partly from Matthew); lectionaries 47, 50, 51, 52, and 53, omit, but later ones have it; Cyr. com. in Luke, omits;

4, 4 − *μονω* = Syr g (13) Eth Tert;

4, 5 + *εις ορος* before *εδειξεν* = e Sah (107); most MSS add *εις ορος υψηλον*;

4, 6 *πασαν ταυτην* = 247, 482; some MSS omit *πασαν*;

4, 7 *παντα* for *πασα* = 517, 579, 672, l. 183, al pauc OL Vg;

4, 9 (εστησεν) + αυτον; against Hesych.;
4, 12 γεγραπται for ειρηται = D 472, a b c d e f ff_2 g_1 l q r mol Pers Or; cf. Matthew 4, 7;
4, 12 − οτι = ℵ[a] D b c d e f (ff_2) g_1 l q r mol Vg Syr S g Arm;
4, 20 (βιβλιον) + και = moling Syr S Go;
4, 21 − οτι = D d mol Syr S Or;
4, 24 εαυτου for αυτου = ℵ D;
4, 38 η πενθερα δε = 1, 238, 243, 245, 247, 249, 470, 472, 481, l. 47, l. 183, etc.;
4, 40 ηγον for ηγαγον = Or (4, 171); cf. D (εφερον = Mark 1, 32) and OL Vg (*ducebant*);
4, 41 − απο = ℵ fam 1, 215;
4, 41 κραυγαζοντα for κραζοντα = A D E G H Q U V Γ Δ fam 13, 248, 700, al (50) Or;
4, 44 των ιουδαιων for της γαλιλαιας = l. 18; cf. l. 7, l. 13 (τοις ιουδαιοις), l. 34, l. 48 (αυτων); many MSS have της ιουδαιας;
5, 3 εδιδασκεν εκ του πλοιου; against ℵ B D e;
5, 4 επαναγαγεται for επαναγαγε = 106, X*[vg] Syr S g Pers (Diatess);
5, 5 + ο before σιμων; against Hesych.;
5, 5 σω ρηματι for ρηματι σου = 579; cf. Coptic prefix;
5, 6 διερρησσοντο for διερρηγνυντο = f r mol Syr S g Sah Bo; cf. διερρησσετο of Hesych.;
5, 7 επλησθησαν for επλησαν = B* Ψ 143, 225, 240, 244, 579, l. 47, al Arm; B* is doubtful, but Tischendorf's explanation can hardly be right; the erasure in B should be examined again;
5, 8 − πετρος = D fam 13, a b c d e r mol Syr S;
5, 11 απαντα against παντα of Hesych. + D;
5, 14 − αυτος = e Syr g Eth;
5, 20 (ειπεν) + αυτω; against Hesych.;
5, 20 σου αι αμαρτιαι for σοι αι αμαρτιαι σου = ℵ D F[w] 40, 142*, 409, 579; cf. Mark 2, 5; Matthew 9, 2;
5, 23 same change = ℵ D 142* 225, l. 48;
5, 26 − και εκστασις · · · $\overline{θν}$ (due to like endings) = D M S X 12, fam 13, 45, 70, 86, 90, 112, 120, 122*, 157, 243, 247, 406*, 435, 483, 484, 579, l. 184, d e Bo(B);
5, 29 αμαρτωλων for αλλων = X 239, 299, al; cf. Eth; from Mark 2, 16 (Matthew 9, 10);

5, 31 — ο $\overline{\iota\varsigma}$ = 44; B omits ο;

6, 4 — ελαβε και = ℵ D K Π fam 1, fam 13, 157, 243, 253, 254, 474, 482, 700, l. 47, l. 50, al d Syr j Arm Eth Ir;

6, 7 + κατ before αυτου = $ℵ^{c}$ F^{w} K L R Π 4, 33, 72, 124, 243, 299, 300, 472, 474, 579, al Syr h Bo Arm;

6, 8 ανθρωπω against ανδρι of Hesych. fam 1, etc.;

6, 10 — αυτους = Vg Syr j; order of words in version tradition differs from recensions;

6, 10 και εξετινεν for ο δε εποιησεν ουτω = ℵ D X 1, fam 13, l. 48, al OL Vg Syrr Sah Bo Arm Eth Go; from Matthew 12, 13; Mark 3, 5;

6, 11 ποιησειεν for ποιησειαν = ℵ A fam 13?, 33, 157, 254, 262, 299; cf. B L, etc.;

6, 16 ισκαριωτην; against Hesych. + D and Latin;

6, 17 (ιερουσαλημ) + και της περεας = ℵ*; cf. OL and Syr;

6, 18 οχλουμενοι against ενοχλουμενοι of ℵ A B L 1, 157;

6, 20 αυτων for υμετερα = ff_2 Syr S Sah Bo (F) Eth Tert; from Matthew 5, 3;

6, 21 γελασουσιν for γελασετε = e g_1 Syr S Sah Arm Eth Tert (marc) Eus; cf. Matthew 5, 4; Isaiah 61, 3; Psalms 126, 5;

6, 22 — οταν (2) = 68, 108, Sah Bo Go Tert; Eras and other early editors;

6, 22 ενεκεν for ενεκα = D F^{w} P Γ 28, 237, 239, 248, Bas Chr;

6, 26 υμας ειπωσιν = (D) E K M P Q R S U V X Γ Δ Λ Ξ Π al a c d f (Vg) Go Chr;

6, 27 (ακουουσιν) + μου = Sah (except 86) Eth;

6, 27 + και before καλως = mol Ꝑ^{mg} Syr S g Bo (4 MSS) Eth;

6, 28 + και before προσευχεσθαι = 238, 249, 251, 471, 472, 485, 506, 517, l. 183, al ff_2 Vg^{cl} Syr S g Eth Just Tert Adiman Hier Ambr;

6, 29 εις for επι = ℵ* D 700, OL Vg Sah (ε 111) Clem Or Tert;

6, 34 χαρις εστιν υμιν = a b ff_2 $g_{1,2}$ l q r mol Vg aur Arm Tert;

6, 37 ινα for και ου (1) = A D Λ Ψ 483*, 484, OL Syr S Sah Bo (7 MSS) Go Eth Diatess Tert Cypr Ambr; Diatess is surely indebted to the version tradition here;

6, 38 σεσαλευμενον πεπιεσμενον = D fam 1, 157, d Or Dial Eus;

6, 39 μη for μητι = X 60, 157, 251, Sah Bo (F*);

6, 41 — το before εν τω = D al OL Vg Sah (114) Bo Arm;

6, 45 — το (1) = D Sah (Arm);

6, 45 (πονηρος) + ανθρωπος; against Hesych. + D a b d g_1 l;
6, 45 − το (2) = l. 184, Sah (Arm);
6, 49 οικοδομουντι for οικοδομησαντι = C fam 13, 53, 245, 472, al OL Vg;
6, 49 και . . αυτη for η = Syr S g (Sah OL);
6, 49 επεσεν for συνεπεσεν; against Hesych. + D R fam 1, fam 13, al (10) b d e l q Vg (10 MSS);
7, 4 παρεκαλουν against ηρωτων of Hesych. + D 1, fam 13, 700;
7, 6 εχοντος απο for απεχοντος απο = l. 47, Syr S OL Vg; ℵ D fam 1, fam 13, etc., omit απο; the regular reading is a conflate;
7, 9 − ακολουθουντι αυτω = Bo (A*CH), which also omit οχλω; cf. transposition in D d e Bo Syrr Eth;
7, 11 − εν = D 254, c d e;
7, 12 ηγγειζεν for ηγγισε = D a b c d e ff_2 l q;
7, 12 − ην (after ικανος); against Hesych. + S V 1 al (15) OL Vg Syrr Arm;
7, 13 ι̅ς̅ for κ̅ς̅ = D fam 1, 142, 253, 300, 435, 700, al d f gat Vg (D J Q Ꝑ) Syr S g Bo Arm^{cdd};
7, 16 εγηγερται against ηγερθη of Hesych. + A (D) 1, 13; cf. Matthew 11, 11;
7, 21 + το before βλεπειν = ℵ^{a} F L U Λ 1, 28, 33, 71, 124, 157, 238, 241–244, 246, 248, 249, 251, 252, 259, 474, 475, 483*, l. 47, l. 48, Bas Cyr;
7, 22 + και before χωλοι = Ψ fam 13, 157, 229**, 235, 258, 435, l. 49, l. 184, e Vg (Q W) Syr S g h Arm (Sah) Diatess;
7, 26 εξεληλυθατε against εξηλθατε of Hesych. + D 69, l. 183;
7, 28 (λεγω) + δε = D fam 13, OL (Vg);
7, 28 (υμιν) + οτι = D c d e mol (Sah Bo);
7, 32 αγοραις for αγορα = F^{w} Δ Bo (2 MSS) Arm; cf. Matthew 11, 16;
7, 32 λεγοντα for και λεγουσιν = ℵ^{c} Ξ 157; cf. D L fam 13, a b d e ff_2 l q r Bo;
7, 33 μηδε for μητε = ℵ 157, Sah Bo; always so spelled in Coptic;
7, 33 + ο before ιωαννης = Or (4, 130);
7, 36 ανεκλιθη against κατεκλιθη of Hesych. + D X fam. 1, Epiph;

7, 39 — λεγων = D X 38, 69, 76, 106, d e r Syr h Arm Sah Or Amphil Aug;
7, 40 ειπεν ο ις = Ξ Syr S cu;
7, 40 διδασκαλε φησιν ειπε = 700; cf. order in Hesych.;
7, 43 ο δε σιμων (— αποκριθεις) = I, fam 1, 700, Syr cu S Arm;
7, 43 (ο δε) + ις = M 71, 129, 157, 245, 543, 565, 569, ff_2 mol Syr cu S g Diatess;
7, 46 — μου τους ποδας = D I 49, 63, 133, a b c d e ff_2 l q Arm;
7, 47 αυτης αι αμαρτιαι = ℵ A F K Π 69, 248, 253, 300, 481, 482, a b c e f g_1 Vg Sah Bo Or Ambr;
8, 2 ζ δαιμονια = D d ff_2 g_1 Vg^{cl} Syr cu S Sah Bo;
8, 5 — του (1) = D K Π 253, 472, 482, al (3);
8, 5 — του ουρανου = D OL Syr cu S g;
8, 8 επι for εις = D 71, 237, 238, 242, 243, 247–249, 251, 253, 258, 478, 483–485, l. 184, al a c d mol Sah Bo;
8, 9 — αυτου = R 700, a b c ff_2 Arm;
8, 10 — της βασιλειας = 50*, 258, 579, ff_2; cf. I Corinth. 4, 1; Just. dial. 121; Epiph. ad diogn. 11, 2.

In this list the agreements with W number as follows: Old Latin, 58; D, 35; Syr cu S, 31; Sahidic, 28; Bohairic, 19; fam 13, Arm, ℵ, 17; Eth, 11; fam 1, 472, 579, 9 each; MS 157, 11; Goth, 6; MSS 700 and X, 7 each. To the Syriac testimony we can add six cases supported by the other Syriac recensions, but not by Syr cu S, so that the two nearest relatives to the uncorrected base of W were the two earliest versions. ℵ, as well as D and fam 13, is found closely related to this tradition in places. Mss 472 and 157 (von Soden's Σ) are nearer here than they have been found elsewhere.

There remain to be noted the 32 variants, for which no other authority has been found; as usual, scribal errors previously treated are not included.

1, 20 — ης; D and OL transpose;
1, 32 δωση for δωσει; an itacism, though it involves change of mood;
1, 34 εστι for εσται;
1, 43 — μου;
1, 65 — και (2); asyndeton is a Coptic trait;

1, 77 – του (1); infinitive is regularly without the article in Coptic;

2, 7 – τον πρωτοτοκον; cf. Matthew 1, 23;

2, 37 + τε before και (2); cf. Syr S, which adds "and" to connect a following verb;

3, 1 – και (3);

3, 7 – φυγειν } either the parent MS was defective here or an ed-

3, 7 – οργης } itor was accommodating text to belief; cf. 579;

4, 5 γης for οικουμενης; cf. *orbis terrae* of many Latin MSS; Fort-Vig. has *terrae;*

4, 6 παραδιδωμι for διδωμι; copied from preceding verb;

4, 41 λαλειν αυτα; cf. Mark 1, 34, λαλειν τα δαιμονια; αυτα is omitted in e ff$_2$;

5, 8 ο σιμων; cf. ο δε σιμων in D fam 13;

5, 11 (πλοια) + και; cf. coördinate construction in Syrr Eth Diatess;

5, 17 χωρας for κωμης; looks like a translation change;

5, 37 μη for μηγε; cf. Mark 2, 21;

5, 38 βαλληται for βλητεον; cf. βαλλουσιν in ℵ* D OL Syrr Eth = Matthew 9, 17;

6, 34 απολαμβανωσιν for απολαβωσι; cf. *recipiant* of OL and Vg^{cl};

6, 35 εσται for εσεσθε; a tense change;

6, 43 κακον for σαπρον; interchange of synonyms; cf. Latin (*malos*); Epiph haer 66, 6;

7, 5 εποιησεν for ωκοδομησεν;

7, 6 αυτους for αυτον; ℵ B Sah omit;

7, 28 και ο for ο δε; cf. a (*et qui*) Eth;

7, 30 (αυτου) + το βαπτισμα ιωαννου; a repetition from end of previous verse;

7, 44 τον οικον for την οικιαν;

7, 44 υπο ποδας for επι τους ποδας; cf. suꝑ in δ, perhaps abbreviation read as *sub;*

7, 44 επεδωκας for εδωκας;

7, 49 προς εαυτους for εν εαυτοις; cf. *apud se*, *intra se*, *secum*, of Latin MSS;

8, 4 εισπορευομενων for επιπορευομενων; influence of a version.

These readings as a whole are not very important, but they are of the same general character as the variants which have previously been assigned to the version tradition; they consist in the main of slight omissions or additions, synonyms, and changes in number and tense. Harmonistic changes are few.

(*b*) Luke 8, 13 to end

As suggested by the relationship to codex A, this part of Luke belongs to the Antioch recension. Out of 1399 readings considered, 1112 agree with that recension. Furthermore, while W differs often from the derived forms of the Antioch recension (noted by von Soden as K^a, K^i, etc.), it does not agree with these against the original type of the recension, as shown in the MSS S V Ω, etc. (K^I of von Soden).

There remain 287 special readings of W to be accounted for; these are in the main to be referred to the original base, as it has been shown above (pp. 31 ff.) that in Luke just as in Matthew the corrections by first and second hands indicate that the parent MS had been revised from the version tradition form to the Antioch recension. Of these special readings in W the following 189 may be definitely assigned to the version tradition, though a few have been adopted by later Antioch types also:

8, 17 −γαρ = Bo (F_1, while C and H have δε), Aug Hier;
8, 20 απηγγελθη for απηγγελη = 47, 56, 58, 61, 476, Eras;
8, 22 +το before πλοιον = H M V fam 13, 71, 242, 253, 472;
8, 28 (ειπεν) + αυτω = l. 47;
8, 32 −εκει = Basil-Seleuc (Migne, 85, p. 277);
8, 33 εισηλθεν for εισηλθον = S U fam 1, fam 13, 237, 238, 243, 251, 253, 472, 474, 482, l. 47, l. 183, l. 184, al;
8, 35 τον ανθρωπον καθημενον = P fam 1, 124, 157, 243, OL (exc. a δ) Vg Sah Bo;
8, 37 παν for απαν = א;
8, 47 πως for ως = 579, Sah; cf. *quem ad modum, quo modo, quia, sicut* in OL MSS;
8, 55 δοθηναι αυτη = D R fam 1, fam 13, 33, 106, 245, 251, 254, 508, 565, l. 253, a d r r_2 Vg (FRQW) Syrr Sah Bo Arm Eth; cf. Mark 5, 43;
9, 2 ειασασθαι for ιασθαι = F 226*, 235; cf. Syr cu S Goth;
9, 8 +λεγοντων before οτι = Syr cu S g (Eth) Goth;
9, 12 −δε (2) = e c b ff_2 g_1 q aur Vg Syr cu S (Sah);

9, 17 περισσευμα for περισσευσαν = D 5, fam 13, 61**, (e);
9, 17 αυτων for αυτοις = 579;
9, 17 + των before κλασματων = D 5, fam 13, 61**;
9, 17 κοφινους for κοφινοι = 157, b f ff_2 q Vg (B B= G Y) Syr cu S Sah;
9, 18 (μαθηται) + αυτου = M U fam 1, 11, fam 13, 22, 60, 71, 106, 237, 242, 251, 435, 579, l. 18, l. 19, l. 48, l. 49, l. 184, a f Syrr Sah Bo (7 MSS) Arm Eth Go;
9, 24 απολεσει for απολεση = X Λ 28, 69, 157, l. 234;
9, 31 + τη before δοξη = A 579, Sah (91) Epiph;
9, 38 επιβλεψον for επιβλεψαι = ℵ D E W^a X Λ 28, 157, al; cf. Latin and Syriac; Mark 9, 22 has βοηθησον;
9, 39 μολις for μογις = B R fam 1, 157, 254, 274**, 471, 474, 700;
9, 46 − εν = H 53, 259, 700;
9, 59 − πρωτον = Theodoret; cf. change of order in ℵ B D, etc.;
9, 60 νεκρους εαυτων = c b d e q r aur Vg Syr cu S Ir Tert Cypr Hier;
9, 62 επιβαλλων for επιβαλων = A D L 474, b c e g_2 q r gat Vg Syr cu S Sah (Bo) Clem Ir Tert Cypr;
10, 4 ασπασασθαι for ασπασησθε = 472;
10, 8 δεχονται for δεχωνται = E* K L* M R U X Γ Λ 28, 245, 247, 251, 254, (472), 482, 700, l. 48, l. 49, l. 184 al;
10, 13 − ει = 1 (*teste* Wets not Lake), 72, 471*;
10, 19 − του (1) = fam 1, Constit. Apost. (8, 7, 5) Just (dial 76) Clem (strom 4, 6, 26) Test. xii patr (Levi, 18) Or Eus Bas Cyr Epiph Thdrt Caes Macar Euseb-Alex Procop, etc.;
10, 22 βουλεται for βουληται = AW^aXΛ 69, 124, 472, 579, l. 184;
10, 31 καταβαινων for κατεβαινεν = D e d Syr S Bo (ℵ J) Eth;
10, 32 − δε (1) = 240, 244, 700, c b ff_2 g_2 q r Vg (Syr cu S) Sah;
10, 37 − αυτω = D X d Bo (J) cat^{ox};
11, 2 προσευχεσθαι for προσευχησθε = A C H M P Γ Δ Λ Π* 1, 33, 69, 124, 157, l. 183, l. 184;
11, 5 ερει for ειπη = A D K M P R Π Ψ 4, fam 13, 71, 106, 251, 253, 472, 482, 569, l. 48, l. 49, l. 184 al OL Vg;
11, 7 εστιν for εισιν = D 57, 254, 472;
11, 8 φιλος for φιλον = fam 13, (OL) (Sah Bo) Chr;

11, 11 *ο υιος αιτησει* = D 243, 485, 700, d Sah Bo Or;
11, 12 *επιδωση* for *επιδωσει* = X 245;
11, 17 *μερισθεισα* for *διαμερισθεισα* = C F M X Γ Ψ 44, 61, 71, 106, 124, 235, 248, 258, 259, 433, 435, 579, 700, al;
11, 18 *εμερισθη* for *διεμερισθη* = ℵ C Λ 28, 61, 80, 108, 124, 127, 236, 259, 433, 472, 485, 579, l. 184, etc.
11, 18 *εκβαλλει* for *εκβαλλειν* = 130, Eth; cf. *εκβαλλω* in 218, 220, OL Syrr Bo;
11, 18 − *με* = F 69, 130, (218, 220), 239, l. 184, Vg (ꝺ D O dimma) Eth;
11, 19 − *ει δε ··· δαιμονια* = 69, 346, r_2 Vg (R); due to like endings;
11, 19 *εκβαλουσιν* for *εκβαλλουσι* = M R X Λ Γ** 248, 254, 478, (700), l. 48, l. 49, a_2 d l dimma;
11, 19 *αυτοι κριται υμων* = A C K L M U Π Ψ 71, 157, 251, 253, 472, 482, (700), l. 48, l. 49, l. 184, ff_2 Vg;
11, 22 *νεικησει* for *νικηση* = E H M R X Γ Δ 28, 219, 220, 251, 433, 472, 474, 475, l. 184;
11, 24 (*οταν*) | *δε* = D U X fam 1 (teste Wets. not Lake), 106, 157, 247, 472, l. 48, l. 184, b d r_2 aur (cf. i l) Vg (D) Bo (5 MSS) Sah Syr h;
11, 36 *μερος τι* = A B G K M X Π fam 1, fam 13, 71, 248, 251, 253, 254, 472, 474, 482, 579, l. 48, l. 184, f;
11, 37 *αριστησει* for *αριστηση* = 28, 59, 245, 472, l. 184;
12, 1 *πρωτον* with *προσεχετε* = G L Δ 28, 472, al mult c f i l q Syr cu g Eth;
12, 5 *βαλιν* for *εμβαλειν* = D 243, 245, 253, OL Vg Mcion Thdot;
12, 6 *δυο ασσαριων* = l (*duo assibus*) Vg (R Y[mg]); cf. *dipondio* of OL Vg;
12, 11 *απολογησεσθαι* for *απολογησησθε* = 18, 51, 57, 90, 66*, 106, 209, 240, 243, 244, 246, 247, 254, 470, 476, 478, 479, 480, 672*, Vg (R);
12, 15 *αυτων* (*bis*) for *αυτου* = 11, 38, c; cf. 118, 209 (*αυτου* in an erasure); *αυτω* in many MSS;
12, 18 − *μου* (1) = a c d ff_2 Hier Aug Ambr;
12, 36 *αυτων* for *εαυτων* = D fam 1, fam 13, 33, 49, 240, 244, 579, 700, l. 20, l. 47, l. 184, Clem Or Meth;
12, 38 (*και*$_2$) + *εαν* = P** 157, 254, 472, 481, al f ff_2 g_2 i q aur;

12, 42 δουναι for διδοναι = (ℵ*) Ψ 28, 63, 122, 253, 259, 700, l. 184;
12, 42 − του = D L Q X l. 60, l. 63, Or;
12, 44 − οτι = 59, b ff_2 i;
12, 44 αυτω for αυτου = M P T^{woi} Γ Λ 49, 157, 470, 475, l. 63, c e Syr S (Sah);
12, 47 − μηδε ποιησας = L fam 13, (59), 330, OL Syr cu S g Diatess Arm;
12, 55 ερχεται for εσται = ℵ* 157, l;
13, 5 μετανοειτε for μετανοητε = H 28, 251, 433, 472, 474;
13, 11 ην γυνη = 254, 700, Syr cu S; some omit ην;
13, 15 υποκριτα for υποκριται = D V X 106, 157, 482, 579, al mult d f l Syr cu g j Sah Arm;
13, 15 + εν before σαββατω = A T^{woi} al Syr cu S Sah Bo;
13, 21 ζυμωθη for εζυμωθη = D e r;
13, 21 ολη for ολον = 64;
13, 22 ποριας for πορειαν = 9, 11;
13, 24 − λεγω υμιν = Bo (F_1) Faust. Man. in Aug 8, 464; changed order in OL Syrr Diat;
13, 31 ταυτη for αυτη = D K M T^{woi} Π 63, 71, 116, 157, 481, 579, al Vg (E $\supset E^{mg}$ R) Sah Bo;
13, 31 σε θελει = aur*;
14, 5 + ο ῑς̄ before ειπεν = X 251;
14, 21 εαυτου for αυτου (1) = Γ 69, 124, 243;
14, 24 γευσηται for γευσεται = fam 1, 472; cf. l. 183;
14, 33 − ουν = Λ 237, gat Syr cu S g Bo;
14, 33 αυτου for εαυτου = 471; cf. D K M Π 15, 29, 42, 71, 248, αυτου, but in different order;
15, 1 − παντες = 237, 251, b c l q mol 130^{lat} Vg Syr cu S g Sah (90) Eth Go;
15, 20 επεσεν for επεπεσεν = fam 1, 69, 122, 234, 235, 243, 248, 253, 473, 484, l. 48, l. 184, al OL (Vg);
15, 22 (δοτε) + αυτω = 472;
15, 27 − οτι = c ff_2 aur Vg Syr cu S;
15, 29 σου εντολην = D Sah;
15, 32 − και (4) = Sah (due to omission of verb);
16, 3 δε αυτω for δε εν εαυτω = e (*sibi*);
16, 6 − αυτω = fam 1, Vg (D*) Syr S Bo;
16, 14 − και (2) = L^{wets} Λ 2, 53, 59, 67, 71, 245, 253, 472, Syr S Sah Eth Pers;

16, 17 *παρελθειν* for *πεσειν* = 472, a Syr S g; repeated from first half of sentence;

16, 22 + *του* before *αβρααμ* = fam 13, 28, 66, 71, 201, 479, 480, 517, l. 184, Epiph;

16, 26 *υμων και ημων* = N 130, 157, colb^{wets} (− aa) b c h m δ dimma mol Vg (12 MSS) Chr Eustath;

16, 26 − *εντευθεν* = D c d e m;

16, 27 − *ουν* = 579, e f l r Bo Eth; order changed in many;

16, 31 *απελθη* for *αναστη* = 237^{scol} b c e g (*abierit*) Dial; D d r Ir and Sah (114) combine the two; cf. *πορευθη* of 225, 245, *ierit* of a ff$_2$ i l Syr S;

16, 31 *εκ νεκρων απελθη* (− *προς αυτους*) = Syr S; yet the simple verb in Syr S agrees better with *πορευθη* (*ierit*) than with the compound *απελθη*;

16, 31 *πιστευουσιν* for *πεισθησονται* = f Vg (Z*); cf. D 157, OL Vg Syr S Ir Ephr Aug;

17, 2 *λιθος ονικος* for *μυλος ονικος* = 157; cf. *λιθος μυλικος* of the Hesych recens;

17, 10 − *οτι* (1) = A X fam 1, 42, 67, OL Vg Syr cu S Eth Or Bas Cypr;

17, 11 *διερχεται* for *διηρχετο* = Sah (γ^{l}); cf. Δ* (*διερχετο*);

17, 23 − *και* (*η*) = D K L X Π* 28, 33, 69, 131, 245, 247, 253, 258, 299, 435, 471, 472, 482, l. 48, l. 49, l. 184, e q Vg;

17, 29 *θειον και πυρ* = A D K M Π fam 13, 71, 106, 245, 248, 251, 254, 472, 482, d Syr h Go;

17, 31 *εστιν* for *εσται* = 245, 254, Syr cu S Sah Bo;

17, 33 *απολεση* for *απολεσει* = E H 28, 66*, 244, 473, 478, l. 49, l. 184, Vg (D);

17, 34 *δυο εσονται* = A K M R U Π fam 13, 71, 201, 239, 241, 245, 246*, 248, 251, 254, 472, 479, 480, 482, 483**, l. 49, l. 184, al q Syrr Eth Go Bas;

18, 2 $\overline{\textit{ανους}}$ for *ανθρωπον* = Syr cu Bo cor-vat^{mg};

18, 5 − *μοι* = Diatess;

18, 14 − *γαρ* (*παρ*) = 69, 118*, 473 (OL), Syr cu S Sah Arm Eth Antioch;

18, 26 *ακουοντες* for *ακουσαντες* = D L fam 1, 254, 569, 579, l δ; cf. other OL MSS;

18, 27 − *τω* = D P 157, 475, Just Thphl; cf. Matthew 19, 26;

18, 29 *υμιν λεγω* = Clem (quis div sal 4);

18, 33 αποκτινουσιν for αποκτενουσιν = D i;
18, 42 – αυτω = Ψ* Adamantius (858 d);
19, 2 – και (3) = 108, 157, Syr (g) h; (D d e omit *et ipse*);
19, 4 συκομωραιαν for συκομορεαν = E* G K U Π 40, 71, 124, 470, 473, 482, 484, 485**, l. 183, Cyr; (συκομωρεαν) = D Q fam 1, 237, 239, 242, 245, 433, l. 3, l. 24;
19, 8 το ημισυ for τα ημιση = 433, l. 19, OL Vg Syr cu S Sah Bo; cf. A R Δ 28, 69, 71, l. 251;
19, 11 μελλει after θεου = 59; cf. 131 OL Vg;
19, 12 (τις) + ην ··· και = a b c e f i l q r Lucifer (Ambr); cf. Sah Bo;
19, 13 πραγματευεσθαι for πραγματευσασθε = D Λ fam 1, 71, 472, 474, 579, OL Vg;
19, 15 – αυτω = Δ 579, OL (except a d) Vg Sah (114) Bo Arm Eth Lcif;
19, 15 πεπραγματευσατο for διεπραγματευσατο = OL Vg Syrr;
19, 21 ει αυστηρος = D 251, (d) e f Syr cu S; cf. Sah Bo;
19, 25 – και ··· μνας = D 16, 60*, 69, l. 18, l. 19, l. 36, l. 49, l. 251, l. 260, b d e ff_2 g_2 Syr cu S Bo (A*) Lcif;
19, 36 εαυτων for αυτων = A B K R U Π fam 1, (251), l. 49, al;
19, 38 – βασιλευς = Λ* 15, 16, 59, 142*, 475*, 579, l. 18, l. 48, Vg (D E R) Bo (ℵ) Eth Meth Tit Eulog; cf. D a c d ff_2 i s;
19, 39 φαρισαιοι for των φαρισαιων = Epiph (haer 2, 66, 43);
19, 40 – οτι = B* 48, 57, 69, 235, 240, 244, 470, 472, a c (e) ff_2 i l r r_2 s Vg (K) Or;
19, 43 – και συνεξουσι σε = c e i l q Eus;
19, 46 (γεγραπται) + οτι = A C D K M Π Ψ 33, 71, 106, 235, 248, 251, l. 18, l. 19, l. 48, l. 49, al d f $g_{1,2}$ s Vg Syr cu g j Go; cf. Mark 11, 17;
19, 48 ποιησουσιν for ποιησωσιν = K L S 59, 66, 71, 201, 234, 242, 253, 435, 470, 480–5, 672, al Or;
20, 5 συνελογιζοντο for συνελογισαντο = ℵ C D (56, 61) 157, 254, OL Vg Syrr; cf. Matthew 21, 25; Mark 11, 31;
20, 9 ($\overline{ανος}$) + τις = A fam 13, 28, 241**, 252**, 473, 517, l. 183, l. 184, al r Vg (G Θ*) cor-vat Syrr Arm;
20, 14 – δευτε = A B K M Q Π Ψ fam 1, 29, 42, 80, 470, 472, 475*, 482, l. 48, 130^{lat} OL Vg Arm Go;

20, 19 οχλον for λαον = 76, 145, l. 48, colb^{wets} (= 22 ?) Syr h; cf. Mark 12, 12;
20, 24 – δε = D Γ fam 1, 239, OL Vg;
20, 28 εξαναστησει = A E H P Γ Δ fam 13, 245, 248, 251, 254, 474, 475*, 476*, 481, l. 184;
20, 34 εκγαμιζονται for – σκονται = A K M P U Γ Δ Π al (50); cf. Matthew 24, 38;
20, 36 – ετι = fam 1, 575, c e ff$_2$ i l q Syrr Bo (6 MSS) Cypr;
20, 36 μελλουσιν for δυνανται = D a e Syr h Cypr;
20, 37 εδηλωσεν for εμηνυσεν = D 122 (a e d Syr cu S) Cypr;
20, 38 + ο before θεος = 60, 124, 475, l. 48, l. 184, Sah Bo;
20, 42 + των before ψαλμων = D P fam 13, 64, 71, 106, 157, 247, 569, l. 18, l. 19, l. 49, l. 184, l. 251, l. 260;
21, 2 – δε = S 124, 127, 262, 472, a Sah (111) Bo (8 MSS) Arm;
21, 3 πλιω for πλειον = D X Q Ψ 51, 106, 157, 235, 239, 483, 484;
21, 5 αναθεμασιν = ℵ A D X Ψ 1, 579, al;
21, 6 λιθον for λιθω = ℵ^c L X Ψ fam 1, fam 13, 33, 44, 66, 122, 157, 201, 237, 242, 472, 480, 485, al;
21, 7 μελλει for μελλη = Γ fam 1, fam 13, 157, 245, 470, (472), 484;
21, 16 συγγενεων = A 1;
21, 20 γινωσκεται for γνωτε = R fam 1, Sah Eus; cf. Syr;
21, 23 – ταις (2) = 251; (346 omits ταις$_1$);
21, 28 ανακαλυψατε for ανακυψατε = fam 1; cf. OL Vg Tert;
21, 30 απ αυτων for αφ εαυτων = ℵ^{ca} L fam 13, 157, Syr g j Bo Arm;
21, 34 αι καρδιαι υμων = A B X fam 13, 25, 251, l. 53, OL Vg;
21, 36 παντα ταυτα = A C* M 235, 471, a e i r Syr h j Eth Tert; many omit one;
21, 36 – τα = U al pauc;
21, 37 – εξερχομενος = q (D d Tert Tit-Bost);
22, 4 + τοις before στρατηγοις = C S U Λ fam 13, 28, 157, 131, 299, 473, 475, 476, 481, 506, 517, 579, l. 184, Sah Bo Eus;
22, 12 αναγεον for ανωγεον = C 1, 471, 478, 510, 575, 700; cf. Hesych;
22, 15 – με = Or^{semel}; cf. Ol Vg;
22, 17 + το before ποτηριον = A D K M U Π 38, 71, 73, 86, 127, 435, 472, 482, and 12 lect;

22, 18 + *νυν* before *γενηματος* = b f E^{vg} cor-vat* (*vitis huius*); cf. ℵ B L K M Π, etc. (+ *απο του νυν*) + DG 1, etc.;
22, 23 – *αυτοι* = c Vg (W);
22, 23 *ηρξατο* for *ηρξαντο* = 66*;
22, 25 *εξουσιαζουσιν* for *οι εξουσιαζοντες* = (ℵ*) Syr cu S;
22, 27 – *δε* = l. 150* Syr cu S Or Eph-Syr Sedul;
22, 37 *ελογισθην* for *ελογισθη* = b Vg (D) Syr cu Diatess Pers;
22, 49 *επιταξομεν* for *ει παταξομεν* = l (b) Syr cu S (Sah);
22, 51 *εασατε* for *εατε* = fam 13, 57, 157, Sah;
22, 59 *διαστησασης* = 579; cf. *διαστασης* of regular text and *διαστησας* of D; probably an attempted correction from D form to regular; both deleted and added letters were copied by scribe;
22, 66 *εαυτων* for *αυτων* = A Λ fam 1, fam 13, 157, etc.;
22, 70 *ουν* for *δε* = A K M Π fam 1, 69, 124, Vg (E);
23, 3 *αυτος εφη* for *ο δε αποκριθεις αυτω εφη* = Syr cu S Tert;
23, 8 (*ικανου*) + *χρονου* = H M X Π fam 1, fam 13, 71, 239, 248, 299, 470, 475, 482, l. 14, l. 184, al OL Vg Syr cu g Bo Eth; cf. ℵ B D L T 157, 579, etc.;
23, 11 – *ο* (1) = 240, 244, 472, l. 260; cf. Coptic;
23, 11 – *τω* = A M Π 472, 482;
23, 19 + *την* before *φυλακην* = fam 1, 237, 240, 242, 248, 475, 478, l. 48, l. 49, l. 63, l. 251, Sah Bo;
23, 21 – *σταυρου* (*σταυρωσον*) (2) = U** 157, a b e f ff_2 l Vg (E) Bo (N) Arm Eth;
23, 25 *εν τη φυλακη* for *εις την φυλακην* = 235, 579, l. 184, Vg (C H) (Syr cu S);
23, 33 *τον* for *ον* (2) = 157, l. 48;
23, 35 + *εν οις* before *και* (1); copied incorrectly from Syr cu S g Sah Bo (all add "for them" at end of previous phrase);
23, 40 *εσμεν* for *ει* = C* Syr cu S j Sah Bo Eth Chr (r?); cf. D;
23, 48 *αυτων* for *εαυτων* = U X P Γ Ψ fam 13, 258, 472, 476, l. 6, l. 47, l. 48, l. 49, l. 54, l. 183, l. 184;
23, 53 – *αυτο* (2) = H X Γ fam 1, 25, 475, 482, 506, l. 7, l. 9, l. 12, l. 13, l. 14, l. 48, l. 49, l. 184, OL Vg Arm;
23, 53 *ουδεις ουδεπω* = ℵ C K M P U Π fam 13, 33, 116, 131, 157, 251, 482, l. 48, l. 49;
24, 10 – *ησαν δε* = A D Γ fam 13, 28, 71, 106, 243, 247, 248, 254, 258, 435, l. 47, l. 48, l. 49, al d Syr cu S Bo Eth;

24, 20 αυτον παρεδωκαν = A D K P Π 1, fam 13, 157, 247, 1071, l. 253, OL Vg Aug;
24, 27 διερμηνευειν for διηρμηνευεν = א*; cf. D (ερμηνευειν) OL Vg Eth;
24, 37 φοβηθεντες for πτοηθεντες = א;
24, 39 – μου (2) = L 1, 13, 33, 53, 300, 579, c e f Vg Syr h Arm Eus Hil Tert Thdrt;
24, 39 – με = D OL Vg 130[lat] Syr cu S j Aug Ambr Hier Hilar Vig-Tap;
24, 49 και εγω ιδου = 1; א D L 33 OL Vg, etc., omit ιδου;
24, 50 – αυτου = D ff$_2$.

A comparison of these readings shows that the base was not only of the version tradition, but closely allied to that branch of it exhibited by W in the latter part of Mark. The various versions and MSS agree with W as follows: Old Latin, 77; fam 13 and Syr cu S, 43 each; D, 39; fam 1, 36; MS 472, 33; Sah and l. 184, 30 each; MS 157, 26; Bo and A, 25 each; X, 23; 579, Syr g and Eth, 19 each; MS 254, 13; MSS 700, 245, and Arm, 12 each.

To complete our total of 1399 readings studied there remains the following list related to the Hesychian recension:

8, 20 – λεγοντων = א B D L Δ Ξ fam 1, 22, 33, 157, OL Vg Syr cu g j Sah Bo Eth Go;
8, 21 – αυτον = א A B D L Δ Ξ Π Ψ 34, 36, 39, 63, 72, 240, 243, 244, 249, 253, 259, 470, 472, 478, 479, 700, al (10) OL Vg Syr S h Arm Eth Go Bas Tit;
8, 22 δε for και (1) = א A B D K L M U Π fam 1, fam 13, 33, 157, 253, 472, 482, 700, al OL Vg Syrr Bo Go;
8, 25 – εστιν (1) = א A B L X Ψ fam 1, 42, 63, 72, 251, 253, 254, 300, 472, 482, 700, al Eth;
8, 27 – αυτω (2) = א B E Ξ Ψ fam 1, 33, 74, 89, 90, 157, 483, 484, 700, al Arm Ps-Ath;
8, 28 – και (1) = א B L X Ξ (D) 33, 61, 157, 259, l. 47, OL Vg Syr cu S g j (Sah Bo);
8, 39 σοι εποιησεν = א B C* D L P R X Ψ 1, 131, 251, 435, OL Vg Tit Vict Cyr:
8, 45 συν αυτω for μετ αυτου = א A C D L P R U Ξ fam 1, fam 13, 33, 67, 106, 157, 251, 254, 472, l. 18, l. 19, l. 36, l. 48, l. 49;
8, 47 – αυτω (2) = א A B C** D L X Ξ Π Ψ fam 1, fam 13,

33, 42, 63, 72, 157, 253, 474, 482, 700, al OL Vg Syr cu g j Bo Arm Eth;

8, 52 *ου γαρ* for *ουκ* = ℵ B C D F L X Δ fam 1, fam 13, 16, 33, 64, 71, 157, 251, 254, l. 48, l. 49, al a c d f ff$_2$ g$_{1,2}$ l q em Syr cu S g j Sah Bo Arm Go Cyr;

9, 3 *ραβδον* for *ραβδους* = ℵ B C* D E* F L M (X) Ξ Ψ 1, 11, fam 13, 22, 33, 106, 157, 247, 253, 254, al OL Vg Syrr Sah Bo Arm Eth;

9, 5 *δεχωνται* for *δεξωνται* = ℵ A B C* K L M U Ξ Π Ψ 1, 33, 63, 71, 86, 116, 157, 209, 253, 254, al Go;

9, 5 − *και* (2) = ℵ B C* D L X Ξ Ψ 1, 33, 124, a c d f Sah Bo Arm Eth;

9, 21 *λεγειν* for *ειπειν* = ℵ A B C D K L M Ξ Π fam 1, fam 13, 28, 33, 71, 72, 157, 253, 300, 474, 482, 700, l. 18, l. 19, l. 48, l. 49, l. 184, Or;

9, 23 *ερχεσθαι* for *ελθειν* = ℵ* A B C* D K L Ξ Π fam 1, fam 13, 33, 42, 63, 72, 157, 253, 300, l. 49, l. 184, al Latin Or;

9, 23 *καθ ημεραν* = ℵ* A B K L M R Ξ Π fam 1, fam 13, 33, 72, 251, 253, 470, 482, l. 48, l. 183, f g$_{1,2}$ Vg Syrr Sah Bo Arm Go Hier;

9, 36 + *ο* before *ι̅ς̅* = C*** K L M X Δ fam 1, fam 13, 157, 243, 245, 253, 472, al;

9, 37 − *εν* = ℵ B L S fam 1, fam 13, q r (Sah);

9, 49 − *ο* = B C* D fam 13, 28, 50, 243, 251, 474, Sah Bo;

9, 50 *υμων* for *ημων* (*bis*) = ℵ^{cb} B C D K L M Ξ Π Ψ 11, fam 13, 22, 33, 71, 72, 244, 251, 254, 470, 472, 476, 482, 484, 700, l. 49, l. 184, al OL Vg Syrr Arm Eth Go;

10, 19 *δεδωκα* for *διδωμι* = ℵ B C* L X 1, 700, l. 48, OL (exc. c d) Vg Syr g j h Sah Bo Arm Eth Or Caes Bas Cyr Epiph Antioch Thdrt Hil Lcif;

10, 19 *αδικησει* for − *σῃ* = ℵ A D E H L M Γ Λ 1, fam 13, 33, l. 184, al Or;

10, 30 *εκδυσαντες* against *εξεδυσαν* of E G H S V Δ Λ fam 1, 433, 472, 475, 478, 481, 483, 484, al b e f g$_1$ i l q Vg Go;

10, 41 *θορυβαζῃ* for *τυρβαζῃ* = ℵ B C D L 1, 33, Bas Evagr;

11, 2 − *της* = ℵ*^{cb} A C D M P Δ 69, 254, 482, l. 48;

11, 6 (*φιλος*) + *μου* = ℵ A B L X fam 1, fam 13, 71, 157, 253, 254, 470, (472), 482, l. 48, l. 49, l. 184, OL Vg Syr cu h Arm Eth Or;

11, 8 οσων = ℵ* A B C K M R Π al mult OL Bo Or Bas Chr;

11, 11 + εξ before υμων = ℵ A B C D K L M R X Π fam 13, 33, 71, 106, 157, 299, 474, 700, al OL Vg Dial Or Epiph;

11, 15 + τω before αρχοντι = ℵ A B C K L M Π Ψ 33, 42, 71, 106, 157, 253, 482, 700, l. 18, l. 19, l. 48, l. 49, l. 184, al Arm;

11, 26 εισελθοντα for ελθοντα = ℵ A B C D H K L M R X Ξ Π fam 1, fam 13, 33, 71, 157, 241, 245, 246, 259, 472, 481, 482, 484, al mult;

11, 28 – γε = ℵ A B* L Δ Ξ al;

11, 28 – αυτον = ℵ[a] A B C D L Δ Ξ 3, 9, 33, 42, 87, 114, 122*, 123, 145, 219, 226*, 476, 478, 481, OL (Vg) Syr h Arm Eth Tert;

11, 32 νινευειται against νινευι of E* H K S V Δ al mult Syr cu h Bo;

11, 34 – ουν = ℵ B D L Λ 435, OL Vg Sah Bo Arm Eth;

11, 34 (οφθαλμος) (1) + σου = ℵ* A B C D M 18, 25, al OL Vg Bo Syr g h Eth;

12, 5 εχοντα εξουσιαν = ℵ A B D K L R X Π Ψ 1, fam 13, 33, 157, 209, 251, 253, 254, 471, 482, l. 32, l. 47, l. 48, l. 49, l. 184, OL Vg Syr h Sah Bo Arm Or Epiph;

12, 9 ενωπιον (1) for εμπροσθεν = ℵ B L R X Γ Δ Λ fam 1, fam 13, 28, 33, 71, 157, 472, etc.

12, 15 πασης for της = ℵ A B D K L M Q R T U X Π fam 1, fam 13, 33, 71, 106, 157, 248, 251, 254, 472, al OL Vg Syrr Sah Bo Arm Eth Clem Bas Antioch;

12, 22 – υμων = ℵ A B D L Q 1, 42, 108, 124, 157, 229**, 700, l. 48, al (OL) am fu for em Syr S h Arm Ambr;

12, 28 – τω before αγρω against E K S V Γ Δ Π Ψ al mult Sah Bo Arm;

12, 49 επι for εις = ℵ A B K L M T U X Π Ψ fam 1, fam 13, 33, 157, 240, 248, 483, l. 48, al Sah (Bo) Clem Or Archel Eus Ath Cyr Chr Bas Antioch Hil;

12, 59 το εσχατον λεπτον = ℵ* B M T Γ fam 1, fam 13, etc.

13, 4 αυτοι for ουτοι = ℵ A B K L T X Π 4, 33, 69, 157, 251, 254, 300, 482, l. 48, OL Vg Syr h Chr;

13, 6 πεφυτευμενην εν τω αμπελωνι αυτου = ℵ B D L X Ψ

fam 1, 106, 251, 253, 259, 346, OL Vg Syr g h Sah Bo Arm Petr Bas Cyr;

13, 11 — *και* (2) = ℵ B T Ψ fam 1, 46, 52, 472, Sah Bo; cf. D b d e;

13, 14 *αυταις* for *ταυταις* = ℵ A B L T X Π fam 1, fam 13, 42, 157, 251, 254, 300, 472;

13, 35 *ιδητε με* = ℵ A B K M R Π 69, 106, 114, 248, 251, 254, 300, 472, 482, l. 48, a f i l Vg;

14, 5 *πεσειται* for *εμπεσειται* = ℵ A B L Π Ψ fam 1, fam 13, 157, 251, 253, 254, 259, 471, 472, 481, 482, OL Vg;

14, 21 — *εκεινος* = ℵ A B D K L P R Π Ψ fam 1, 27, 63, 69, 130^{lat}, 157, 254, 472, 482, OL Vg Sah Bo Arm Eth Go Bas;

14, 21 *τυφλους και χωλους* = ℵ B D F K L M P U Π 33, 71, 106, 157, 241, 252, 254, 346, 472, 479, 480, 482, l. 48, al OL Vg Syr h Sah Bo Eth Go Eus Bas;

14, 27 *εαυτου* for *αυτου* = A B L** M** Δ 106, 251, 472, l. 48, l. 49, l. 184;

14, 28 *εις* for *τα προς* = B D L R Ψ 20*, (28, 71 al), 225, 240, 244, 245, 248, 251, 472, 474, 475, 476, 478, l. 48, b c d ff_2 l q r Vg;

14, 29 *αυτω ενπεζειν* = ℵ A B K L R U X Π fam 1, 106, 248, 251, 253, 259, 482, l. 48, l. 49, l. 184, al Bas Eph;

14, 32 *αυτου πορρω* = ℵ B D L X fam 1, fam 13, 157, 474, l. 183, al mult OL Vg;

15, 1 *αυτω εγγιζοντες* = ℵ A B K M U Π Ψ fam 1, fam 13, 71, 89, 248, 251, 254, 482, Go Bas;

15, 4 *εξ αυτων ἐν* = ℵ B D fam 1, fam 13, 157, e;

15, 22 — *την* (1) = ℵ A B D* K* L P Q Π Ψ 254, 482, al;

15, 32 — *ην* (2) = A B D L R X Ψ fam 1, fam 13, 33, l. 184, Arm Go Const;

16, 2 *δυνη* for *δυνησῃ* = ℵ B D P fam 13, 254, 470, 475, l. 18, l. 19, l. 48, l. 49, l. 184, d e ff_2 Syr cu S g Go;

16, 6 *βαδους* for *βατους* = ℵ L X Ψ 36, 40**, 44, 48, 57, 59, 127, 237, 239, 299, r_2 Q^{vg} Or;

17, 3 — *εις σε* = ℵ A B L fam 1, 42, 254, 346, a b f ff_2 $g_{1,2}$ i l m (Vg) Sah Bo Syrr Arm Go Clem Dam Tert;

17, 4 *αμαρτησῃ* for *αμαρτῃ* = A B D L X Δ Ψ 16, 61**, 80, 90, (124**), 130, 131, 157, 229*, 346, 473, 475*, 483, 484, l. 17, l. 21, l. 22, l. 47, l. 184, OL Vg Antioch Dam;

17, 17 ουχ for ουχι = B L S 71, 131**;
17, 24 −η (2) = ℵ B L X Γ fam 1, fam 13, 106, 157, 235, 254, 472, 475, 482, l. 184, al;
17, 24 υπο τον for υπ = ℵ A B D K R Π Ψ 245, (251), 472, al;
18, 4 ηθελεν for ηθελησεν = ℵ A B D L Q R X Λ Ψ 1, fam 13, 157, 201, 243, 246, 252, 253, 254, 472, 475, 480, al OL Vg Syrr Bo Arm Hipp Bas Chr Dam;
18, 20 −σου (2) = A B D I K L M P X Π Ψ fam 1, 25, 29, 33, 42, 49, 67, 71, 86, 157, 245, 248, 251, 300, 382, 472, 473, 475, l. 22, d e f ff_2 i l q Vg Syr h Arm Go;
18, 27 παρα $\overline{\theta\omega}$ εστιν = ℵ B D L Ψ fam 1, 28, 157, 248, l. 49, a e (d) Syr cu S g j;
18, 39 σειγηση for σιωπηση = B D L P X Ψ 245, 254, 382, Or;
19, 13 εν ω for εως = ℵ A B D K L R Π Ψ fam 1, 25, 42, 142, 145, 157, 254, 382, (472, 482), 475, l. 36, l. 48, l. 49, l. 184, Or;
19, 34 (ειπον) + οτι = ℵ A B D K L M Π Ψ fam 1, fam 13, 42, 71, 86, 106, 157, 245, 251, 254, 472, 473, 482, l. 6, l. 19, l. 48, l. 49, al a d f q Vg Syr cu g h Bo Or;
19, 41 αυτην for αυτη = ℵ A B D H L R Γ Δ Π fam 1, fam 13, 42, 49, 56, 58, 60, 61, 66, 67, 71, 73, 106, 157, 240, 244, 248, 255, 472, 481, l. 6, l. 48, l. 184, Ir Or Bas;
20, 3 −ενα = ℵ B L R fam 1, (fam 13,) 33, 157, c q mol durm Vg (C J K R T V X) Syr S g;
20, 19 γραμματις και οι αρχιερεις = A B C K L M U Π fam 1, fam 13, 33, 71, 251, 254, 472, 475, e Syr h Bo Arm Eth Go;
20, 24 δειξατε for επιδειξατε = ℵ A B D L M P fam 13, 33, 71, 86, 106, 157, 240, 244, 245, 248, 254, 435, 470, 475, l. 48, l. 49, l. 184, al Bas;
21, 4 −ταυτα λεγων, etc., against E G H M S V Γ Λ fam 13, 71**, 245**, 435, 470, 471, l. 48, l. 49, etc.
21, 14 θετε for θεσθε = ℵ A B* D L M R X Π Ψ 33, 482;
21, 17 υπο παντων δια το ονομα μου = ℵ A B D E G H L R X fam 1, fam 13, 33, 71, 106, 157, 245, 254, 435, 472, 482, 700, etc., OL Vg Syrr Sah Bo, etc.
21, 20 −την = ℵ B D R Or Eus;
21, 33 παρελευσονται for παρελθωσι = ℵ B D L 13, 33, 157, d e c aur Vg Syr cu S Sah Bo;

22, 3 καλουμενον for επικαλουμενον = ℵ B D L X 57, 66, 69, 243, 258 (OL Vg) Bo Arm;

22, 30 καθησεσθαι for καθισησθε = ℵ A B*** G L Q Π* Ψ 25, 254, 258, 299, 472, 478, 481, 700, l. 184;

22, 30 + εν τη βασιλεια μου against E F G H S V Γ Λ 235, 237, 243, 245, al mult;

22, 37 − ετι = ℵ A B D H L Q T X 1, 12, 59, 157, 247, 258, 579, b d f r Syr j Sah Bo Eth;

22, 37 το for τα = ℵ B D L Q T fam 1, 157, b d Syr cu h j Sah Bo;

22, 39 − αυτου = ℵ A B D L M** T Δ** Ψ fam 1, 13, 67, al q Vg Syr h Sah Bo Arm;

22, 43–44 omit both verses = ℵ[a] A B R T fam 13, 473, 481, 1071*, f Syr S h Sah Bo Arm[cdd] Ath Cyr Ambr Dam;

22, 47 − δε (1) = ℵ A B G L M R T U X Λ Π Ψ 1, fam 13, 49, 68, 80, 142, 157, 239, 262, 470, 482, l. 6, l. 184, al l q Vg Sah Bo;

22, 51 − αυτου = ℵ B L R T fam 1, Arm;

22, 53 εστιν υμων = ℵ[c] B D G K L M R T X Π Ψ 22, 116, 124, 248, 252, 253, 259, 435, 482, l. 49, l. 184, a Syr cu S g Sah Arm Eth;

23, 34 − ο δε ις̅ ⋯ ποιουσιν = ℵ[a] B D* 38, 82, 435, 579, 597, a b** d Syr S Sah Bo (12 MSS);

23, 35 του θυ̅ ο = ℵ B L fam 1;

23, 46 παρατιθεμαι for παραθησομαι = ℵ A B C K M P Q U X Π Ψ 4, 6, 22, 33, 42, 67, 68, 71, 78, 127, 131, 251, 252*, 470, (472), 482, l. 18, l. 19, l. 48, (l. 184), Or Tert, etc.;

23, 46 τουτο δε for και ταυτα = ℵ B C* D 71, 248, c r Bo;

24, 9 ταυτα παντα = A B G L M S fam 1, fam 13, 33, 71, 157, 472, 482, etc., OL Vg;

24, 12 − κειμενα = ℵ B 243, l. 44, l. 47, Syr cu S Sah Bo Eus;

24, 42 − και απο μελισσιου κηριου = ℵ A B D L Π d e Syr S Sah (Bo) Clem Or Eus Epiph Cyr Ath Diatess;

24, 53 − αμην = ℵ C* D L Π 1, 22, 33, 130, 240, 244, a b d e ff_2 l Vg (14 MSS) Syr S j Sah Bo Arm.

This is the whole evidence for a partial or preliminary Hesychian revision of W in this part of Luke, and while the readings make an imposing array, the proof cannot be considered adequate; there are too many of the readings which are undoubtedly correct, and most of the others are simply instances, where the Hesychian recension has adopted the form of the version tradition; all such cases must be added to our evidence of the basic text, which stood in the parent of W before correction. A little further light can be thrown on the question of that base by an analysis of the variants in the above list.

The chief support of W outside of the Hesychian MSS is as follows: fam 1, 58; MS D, 56; fam 13, 53; OL, 50; MS 157, 43; MS X, 37; Bo, 34; MS M, 32; Sah, 30; MS 254, 29; MS 472, 29; MS R, 26; Arm, 25; MS 71, 23; MS 251, 22; Syr cu S, 22; l. 48, 22; l. 184, 19; Syr g, 18; Syr h, 18; MS 253, 18; MS 106, 15; Eth, 14. Many of these readings were taken over by one of the types of the Antioch recension (K^a type of von Soden), so that we find agreements with the chief members of that group as follows: MS A, 48 times; MS Π, 37; MS K, 28; MS 482, 28; MS 72, 8, etc. If we omit this group along with the Hesychian, the supporting MSS and versions are in the main the same as for the previous list, though fam 1 and MS 157 are more closely related. The really notable fact is that there are no readings having Hesychian support only; there are always some members of the version tradition in agreement, so that W, the Hesychian recension, and the K^a type of the Antioch may all be considered indebted to that text form.

For the following readings of W no other support has been found:

8, 31 — και παρεκαλουν αυτον; due to like endings;
8, 32 (ορι) + τουτω;
8, 38 — εδεετο δε ···· συν αυτω; απελυσε changed to εδιδασκεν; editorial change, perhaps from a lost source;
8, 47 εναντιον for ενωπιον;
9, 13 αρτων for αρτοι;
9, 24 — αυτου (1);
9, 51 αυτου after εστηριξεν;
9, 52 + τους before αγγελους;
9, 53 εξεδεξαντο for εδεξαντο;
10, 6 επαναπαυσηται for επαναπαυσεται;
10, 7 — και πινοντες; due to like endings, not to the temperance movement;
10, 10 πλατιους for πλατειας;
10, 39 ταυτη for τηδε; cf. 579 αυτηδε;

10, 40 ενκατελιψεν for κατελιπε; cf. εγκατελειπε in l. 253; *dereliquet* in d r_2;

11, 44 – τα (1);

11, 49 – και (4);

12, 19 συ for ψυχη (2); editorial change; cf. omission in OL (Bo);

12, 29 μετεωριζεται for μετεωριζεσθε;

12, 31 – ταυτα;

12, 46 – των;

12, 53 – και θυγατηρ επι μητρι; omission due to like endings;

13, 2 – ειπεν αυτοις; some MSS omit ο ιησους, so the error here may be due to an attempted correction crowding out the words over which it was written;

13, 15 – τω; perhaps displaced by inserted εν, perhaps Coptic influence;

13, 21 – ου;

15, 3 – την;

15, 16 – αυτου;

15, 16 W alone combines Antioch reading with older text; another proof of correction;

15, 17 μισθιου for μισθιοι; cf. *quanti mercenarii* of OL MSS; wrong translation;

15, 28 – αυτου;

16, 5 χρεωστων for χρεωφειλετων; a synonym, but rare; cited from Plut. and Lucian;

16, 29 + ο before αβρααμ;

17, 8 διπνωσω for δειπνησω;

17, 12 πορρω for πορρωθεν;

18, 11 προσευχεται for προσηυχετο; cf. present participle of Sah;

18, 13 ηδυνατο for ηθελεν; cf. Syr cu (was daring) = g_1 Aug; this looks like the original text of some gospel; but the eulogistic form prevailed;

18, 16 εμε for με; ημας was written at first;

19, 15 – τι; omitted in one early edition, I think, but am not able to verify;

19, 23 + τω before τοκω;

19, 42 απ for απο;

20, 6 ανθρωπου for ανθρωπων; not harmonistic, cf. Matthew 21, 25–6 (same error in W); Mark 11, 27–33; Syriac influence?;

20, 14 *διελογιζοντες* for *διελογιζοντο*; note error in form and long succession of participles; it seems to be the mistake of a Coptic scribe;

20, 18 *πεσειτε* for *πεση*; itacistic spelling of future indicative; cf. Sah Bo;

20, 20 *υποχωρησαντες* for *παρατηρησαντες*;

20, 32 *υστερα* for *υστερον*;

20, 37 −*και τον θεον ιακωβ*; cf. like beginning of preceding phrase;

20, 38 *αυτου ουτοι* for *αυτω ζωσιν*; Latin interchange of *ei* and *illi* may explain the demonstrative;

21, 21 −*οι* (3); =579;

21, 24 *μαχαιραις* for *μαχαιρας*;

21, 25 (*απορεια*)+*η ως*; cf. f Syr cu S Arm;

21, 36 *κατισχυσατε* for *καταξιωθητε*; cf. *κατισχυσητε* of ℵ B L X Ψ 1, 33, 36, 57, 131, 157, 209, 579, Sah Bo Syr j Eth;

22, 23 *αυτους* for *εαυτους*;

22, 33 −*ετοιμος*;

22, 36 −*ο* (2);

22, 36 −*το*;

22, 47 *αυτου* for *αυτων*; cf. *αυτους* of the best MSS;

22, 53 *αλλ η* for *αλλ*;

22, 54 *συνηγαγον* for *εισηγαγον*;

23, 11 −*ο* (1);

23, 18 *ουν* for *δε* (1); much variation in MSS and versions;

23, 36 *προσευχομενοι* for *προσερχομενοι*; mere scribal error but most strange;

23, 39 *και αυτον* for *σεαυτον*; cf. Act. Pil. 10, 6 (p. 308); as W was hardly influenced by this work, both may go back to an earlier source;

24, 6 *ανεστη* for *ηγερθη*; cf. Mark 8, 31; 9, 9; Luke 9, 8; 9, 19; 16, 31; 24, 7; 24, 46; John 20, 9; Ephesians 5, 14; I Thessalonians 4, 14;

24, 29 *εσπερας* for *εσπεραν*;

24, 30 *κατακεισθαι* for *κατακλιθηναι*;

24, 30 −*λαβων τον αρτον*; scribal error;

24, 35 *το* for *τα*;

24, 36 *αυτοις* for *αυτος*; sentence reads like a Semitic translation;

24, 36 + εγω ειμει μη φοβεισθαι before ειρηνη; in 28 there is a faint /. over ειρηνη, but the addition, which once stood on the margin, has been trimmed off; cf. G P 88, 127, 130, (579), l. 253, c f $g_{1,2}$ Vg Syrr Bo Arm Eth Aug Ambr for same addition in different order; it was an insertion in W text, perhaps from Bohairic scribe;

24, 39 με for εμε; cf. above, 18, 16.

These variants are of the same character as those previously discussed and referred to the version tradition and so have received briefer treatment. They consist mainly of interchange of synonyms, numbers, tenses, and voices, and the omission or addition of the article. The influence of the versions is a sufficient explanation.

4. JOHN 5, 12 TO END

As the first quire of John (1 – 5, 11) is in a different hand and on a different kind of parchment, it is fair to assume that it is textually independent; it will be treated in a separate section.

The text of the remainder of John shows a decided Hesychian trend. Not counting the previously excluded variations in orthography and grammar, out of 1307 readings considered there are 840 certain and 147 possible Hesychian variants in this part of John, while but 8 variants point toward the Antioch recension.

6, 10 (ειπεν) + δε = A Γ Δ Λ Π unc (8) fam 1, fam 13, 28, 33, 157, 435, 472, 579, al b f q r Syr h Go;

6, 15 – παλιν = E F G H M S U V Γ Δ Ψ fam 13, 22, 28, 142, 229*, 299, 433, 435, 472, al (90) Syr S g Sah Bo Eth Diatess Cyr Nonn;

6, 36 (πιστευεται) + μοι = A Π** Chr Bo (B);

6, 39 αυτον for αυτο = E G H L* N S V Γ Δ Λ 13, 28, 131, 299, 433, 435, 474, 579, l. 48, l. 184, al a b f e q (Vg) Sah (13) Bo Cyr;

6, 57 ζησεται for ζησει = Γ Δ Λ unc (7) fam 1, 28, 108, 157, 433, 472, 486, al mult Cyr;

6, 65 – οτι = K Π 42, a Chr Cypr;

9, 31 (οιδαμεν) + δε = A X Γ Δ Λ unc (6) fam 13, 28, 157, 472, 579, al mult f Syr g j h Vg Eth Go Chr;

12, 40 επιστρεψωσιν for επιστραφωσι = K L M X Π 42, 62, 157, 474, 482, Eus Did; cf. X fam 13.

All of these except nos. 2, 4, and 5 are related to von Soden's K^a type (= A K Π, etc.). Nos. 1, 2, 5, and 7 are seen to be related to the version tradition also. No. 6 has only OL a and no. 3, only Bo (B) to indicate the same relationship, which is however now probable, since supported by W. No. 8 is an error which was rather widespread in earlier MSS, as it appears in Eusebius and Didymus, as well as in L M X W. In these cases therefore one finds the source from which the Antioch sub-recensions drew their material instead of Antioch influence on W. It is to be noted further that most of the cases fall in chapter six and none later than chapter twelve. That is not the only indication, that there is a variation in the type of text within the Gospel of John. In the latter half of the Gospel the variants show a decided trend toward ℵ and away from B. This is well seen in the following table, giving the number of agreements between W and the chief uncials:

Chap.	ℵ	A	B	D	L
5	29	33	41	26	38
6	63	67	101	72	98
7	35	lac	69	51	75
8	26	lac	46	23	35
9	55	31	61	19	50
10	48	36	50	27	59
11	51	37	47	30	49
12	46	36	43	36	44
13	44	43	43	36	45
14	24	20	15	21	12
15		lacuna in W			
16	23	17	22	26	19
17	34	23	29	27	30
18	49	36	39	25	38
19	46	26	42	30	49
20	33	24	27	25	27
21	42	34	35	32	27

The increase in agreements with ℵ seems to begin in chapter nine, but the closeness of relationship is most apparent from chapter fourteen on, at which point the drift away from B and L becomes evident. Some part of this variation may be due to changes in the type of text of ℵ, B, or L, especially the change in

ℵ at chapter nine, but the change in relationship towards all near chapter fourteen is best ascribed to variation in the text of W from the latter part of chapter thirteen on. Whether this change is due to a difference in the parent MS for the two parts, or to increasing carelessness on the part of the Hesychian corrector, cannot be absolutely decided. The two types of text are certainly not very different, whether we call them both Hesychian, or the first Hesychian and the second Egyptian.

The 313 readings opposed to the Hesychian recension, and so presumably showing the original base, give some light on the question. It is necessary first to exclude from consideration 72 instances in which the corrector failed to insert Hesychian readings; almost all seem editorial changes without original authority, so that the opposing text of W has overwhelming support. To include these in our calculations would tend to confuse the point at issue. As the MS authority is in each case the Hesychian against practically all the rest, the enumeration of authorities is omitted. The list is as follows; in each case the W reading supported by most MSS is given first, the Hesychian, second: 5, 19 *ειπεν* (*ελεγεν*); 6, 17 *το πλοιον* (*πλοιον*); 6, 23 *αλλα δε* (*αλλα*); 6, 29 *ι̅ς̅* (*ο ι̅ς̅*); 6, 29 *πιστευσητε* (*πιστευητε*); 6, 43 *ουν* (—); *ο ι̅ς̅* (*ι̅ς̅*); 7, 4 *εν κρυπτω τι* (*τι εν κρυπτω*); 7, 14 *ο ι̅ς̅* (*ι̅ς̅*); 8, 39 *ητε* (*εστε*); 9, 6 *του τυφλου* (—); 9, 11 *ανθρωπος* (*ο ανθρωπος ο*); *υπαγε* (*οτι υπαγε*); 9, 17 *συ τι* (*τι συ*); 9, 30 *θαυμαστον* (*το θαυμαστον*); 10, 17 *ο πατηρ με* (*με ο πατηρ*); 10, 28 *ουχ αρπασει* (*ου μη αρπαση*); 10, 29 *πατρος μου* (*πατρος*); 10, 32 *λιθαζετε με* (*εμε λιθαζετε*); 11, 21 *τον ι̅ν̅* (*ι̅ν̅*); 11, 24 *μαρθα* (*η μαρθα*); 11, 32 *ο ι̅ς̅* (*ι̅ς̅*); 11, 44 *και εξηλθεν* (*εξηλθεν*); *υπαγειν* (*αυτὸν υπαγειν*); 11, 46 *ο ι̅ς̅* (*ι̅ς̅*); 12, 2 — *εκ* (*εκ*); 12, 22 *και παλιν* (*ερχεται*··· *και*); 12, 36 *ο ι̅ς̅* (*ι̅ς̅*); 13, 18 *ους* (*τινας*); 13, 19 *οταν γενηται πιστευσητε* (*πιστευσητε οταν γενηται*); 13, 21 *ο ι̅ς̅* (*ι̅ς̅*); 13, 24 *πυθεσθαι τις αν ειη* (*και λεγω αυτω ειπε τις εστιν*); 13, 25 *επιπεσων* (*αναπεσων*); 13, 26 — (*ουν*); *και ενβαψας* (*βαψας ουν*); — (*λαμβανει και*); *ισκαριωτη* (*ισκαριωτου*); 13, 31 *ο ι̅ς̅* (*ι̅ς̅*); 13, 38 *ο ι̅ς̅* (*ις*); 14, 3 *ετοιμασω* (*και ετοιμασω*); *υμιν τοπον* (*τοπον υμιν*); 14, 6 *ο ι̅ς̅* (*ι̅ς̅*); 14, 7 *και απαρτι* (*απαρτι*); *εωρακατε αυτον* (*εωρακατε*); 14, 10 *λαλω* (*λεγω*); *ο εν εμοι* (*εν εμοι*); 14, 14 *εγω* (*τουτο*); 14, 15 *τηρησατε* (*τηρησετε*); 14, 16 *και εγω* (*καγω*); *μενη μεθ υμων* (*μεθ υμων η*); 14, 20 *γνωσεσθε υμεις* (*υμεις γνωσεσθε*); 16, 12 *λεγειν υμιν* (*υμιν λεγειν*); 16, 23 *εν τω ονοματι μου δωσει υμιν* (*δωσει υμιν εν τω ονοματι μου*); 16, 27 *θεου* (*πατρος*); 16, 29 *λεγου-*

σιν αυτω (λεγουσιν); 16, 32 και εμε (καμε); 17, 11 και εγω (καλω); 18, 1 ο ις (ις); 18, 2 ο ις (ις); 18, 3 φαρισαιων (εκ των φαρισαιων); 18, 7 αυτους επηρωτησεν (επηρωτησεν αυτους); 18, 16 ος ην···τω αρχιερει (ο···του αρχιερεως); 18, 20 ο ις (ις); ελαλησα (λελαληκα); 20, 10 εαυτους (αυτους); 21, 6 ισχυσαν (ισχυον); 21, 15 πλειον (πλεον); 21, 21 τουτον (τουτον ουν); 21, 25 οσα (α); ουδε (ουδ); χωρησαι (χωρησειν).

The remaining non-Hesychian readings have less support and may help to establish the relationships of the basic text in this part of W.

5, 14 τι σοι = ℵ D E K Π fam 1, fam 13, 28, 157, 245, al mult a b d e f l q Syr h Arm Or Bas Chr Ir Cypr;
5, 15 (ιουδαιοις) + και ειπεν αυτοις = Syr cu S Diatess Cyr (but these omit ανηγγειλεν); cf. ℵ C L, etc.;
5, 16 + τω before σαββατω = 237, 251, 264, Sah Bo;
5, 17 απεκριθη for απεκρινατο = D;
5, 18 αποκτειναι οι ιουδαιοι = 107, Ambr Epiph (haer. 3, 6);
5, 19 απεκριθη for απεκρινατο = D N 33, 53, 68, l. 47, al;
5, 19 ο for α = Epiph (haer. 2, 74) Diatess; cf. Syr;
5, 19 αφ εαυτου ποιειν = 7, fam 13, 215, 355, 357, 482, 579, a b f g r Vg Syr cu S Hil Or;
5, 19 − τι = 245, 472, a d e q Tert Nonn; cf. Syr cu S;
5, 20 δειξη for δειξει = 66**, 472, 474;
5, 26 ως for ωσπερ = ℵ* D Eus;
5, 26 και τω υιω ζωην εδωκεν = N Or:
5, 29 εξελευσονται for εκπορευσονται = D e l q r Sah Bo (Syr cu) Ir Tycon Hier;
5, 29 και οι for οι δε = m Syr cu g Bo Arm Ir;
5, 35 προς ωραν αγαλλ− = A 19, 472, 476, 485, a ff_2 aur** gat Vg^cl^ Chr Hil Aug Maxim;
5, 36 μειζων for μειζω = A B E G M Λ 472, 579, l. 48, l. 184, al;
5, 37 − αυτου (2) = b r* r_2 Athan;
5, 39 αυται for εκειναι = b r Bo (Sah);
5, 47 πιστευσητε for − σετε = D G S Δ fam 1, fam 13, 28, 157, 248, 253, 433, 579, l. 49, l. 184, al a Go Or Chr;
6, 2 θεωρουντες for οτι εωρων = Chr (hom. in joan. com.) Nonn;
6, 3 ουν for δε = D fam 1, fam 13, 25, 565, OL Vg Sah (13);
6, 7 + ο before φιλιππος = ℵ L N 239, 258, 1071;

6, 10 — οι before ανδρες = D L N Ψ fam 1, 25, 33, 157, 579, l. 184, al Cyr;

6, 13 επερισσευσαν for — σεν = B D Θ^{g} 67, l. 60; all versions have the plural;

6, 14 — οτι = א 242, 249, 476, l. 53, a b q r Vg Syr cu S Arm Cyr;

6, 23 — εγγυς του τοπου = Syr cu S;

6, 28 ποιησωμεν for ποιουμεν = (D) G fam 13, (OL Vg) Syr cu S;

6, 30 — συ = fam 13, 66, 71, 201, 234, 240, 254, 472, 483*, 484, al l aur fos P Arm Chr Cyr;

6, 31 δεδωκεν for εδωκεν = א fam 13, Eus; cf. Latin and Coptic;

6, 42 — και την μητερα = א* b Syr cu S Arm Quaest;

6, 44 (αυτον (1)) + προς με = e Bo Georgian Hilar Hier Vigil-Tap (Epiph);

6, 46 αυτος for ουτος = Syr cu S g Eth (Go);

6, 51 — δε = א^{*c} D Γ 28, 108, 125, 218, 219, 220, 225, 433, 486, c d ff$_2$ m Vg Syr cu S g j Bo Arm Eth Clem Amm;

6, 58 ζηση for ζησει (ζησεται) = Chrys (4 MSS);

6, 58 τον αρτον τουτον = e q;

6, 62 ειδηται for θεωρητε = 28 (ιδητε) Chr Epiph Eus^{mcell} Thdrt; cf. Latin *videritis;*

7, 1 ειχεν εξουσιαν for ηθελεν = 142**, 240, 244, 249, a b ff$_2$ l r Syr cu Bo(B) Eth Chr;

7, 3 και for ουν = Syr cu S Eth; cf. c ff$_2$ Vg (*autem*);

7, 5 επιστευσαν for επιστευον = D L d q Syr cu S Arm Eth;

7, 6 ουδεπω for ουπω = Vg (Z*) = *necdum;*

7, 6 — ουν = א* D* 57, 106, 579, l. 19, l. 60, e fos Syr cu S g Arm Georg Pers Cyr;

7, 17 ποιη for θελη (· · ·) ποιειν = 254, Bo Georg Chr Cyr;

7, 28 — και (1) = 28, a ff$_2$ aur Vg (D E) Sah Bo (8 MSS);

7, 30 τας χειρας for την χειρα = N G fam 1, 14, 22, 44, 53, 242, 565, 1071, OL Vg Syr cu S g Bo Arm Ir Nonn;

7, 31 (εκ του) ουν for δε = 299, 482, 486; cf. K Π fam 1, etc.;

7, 37 — τη μεγαλη = 12, 17, 229*, Vg (J); cf. Syr and OL;

7, 37 ει for εαν = Did; cf. Coptic and Latin constructions;

7, 40 (λογων) + αυτου = (א* D 124) K Π 122**, 127, 229**, 473, 482, 486, c d ff$_2$ g l Vg Syr cu S h Pers Arab;

7, 41 (ελεγον$_1$) + οτι = D L X 24, 69, 157, 406, d g Syr h Cyr (Sah Bo);

7, 46 (απεκριθησαν) + αυτοις = (c) foss Syr cu S g Eth;

7, 48 − εκ (1) = K fam 13, 15, 240, 244, 248 Go;

7, 52 (εραυνησον) + τας γραφας = (D 229*) OL Vg (14 MSS) Syr g Sah Bo;

8, 16 − και (1) = 29, 71, 248, b r Vg (D K) Syr cu S g (14) Bo (g$_2$) Eth Arm Georg;

8, 19 + ο before ις = ℵ N fam 13, 33, 71, 472, al Or Cyr;

8, 23 τουτου του κοσμου (2) = fam 13, OL Vg Sah Bo;

8, 24 − οτι (1) = Syr S g Eth Pers;

8, 25 ειπον for ελεγον = 245, Vg (E); cf. Syr Eth, etc.

8, 26 ειπειν for λαλειν = b (*dicere*); cf. Sah Syr g Eth;

8, 28 − ο πατηρ = Tert Eus;

8, 33 − οτι = 1, 69, al b c ff$_2$ l r aur Vg Syr S Arm Eth Go;

8, 36 − ο υιος = 472, r$_2$;

8, 38 απο του πατρος for παρα τω πατρι = Vg (J); cf. 131, Sah;

8, 38 − ουν = 96, 97, 248, 251, 435, 472, l. 19, f ff$_2$ g l m Vg Syr S g Sah (c) Bo Arm Tert Chr;

8, 38 + ταυτα before λαλω = D 33, 229** b c d q (Sah) Bo Cyr Chr;

8, 42 (εμαυτου) + ουκ = Chr Athan Eus; D fam 13, OL have ου instead of ουδε; cf. Syrr Sah Bo;

8, 46 − υμεις = 71, 157, a r Vg (Z) Sah (75, 86) Bo (3 MSS) Arm Eth Go; cf. 28, 87, 250 (− υμεις ου);

8, 53 − πατρος ημων = D a b c d e ff$_2$ l Syr S;

8, 54 − μου (2) = Syr S j Arm Or Tert Chr;

9, 9 − οτι (1) = ℵ 470, a b c e ff$_2$ l r Eth Pers Cyr Ps-Ath;

9, 16 σημια τοιαυτα = Sah Bo Georg Arab;

9, 19 − λεγοντες = ℵ* a b c ff$_2$ l Syr g (S) Sah (4 MSS) Pers;

9, 21 − αυτον ερωτησατε = ℵ* b Syr S Sah Eth Chr;

9, 22 συνεθεντο for συνετεθειντο = 47, 54, 116 (Sah Bo), Cyr Thphil;

9, 35 (ηκουσεν) + δε = fam 13, 474, b c f ff$_2$ l Vg (Q) Sah Bo; cf. ℵ* D Syr S g Eth;

9, 38–39 − ο δε εφη ··· ειπεν ο ις = ℵ* b (l*);

10, 2 εκεινος εστιν ο ποιμην for ποιμην εστι = 22$^?$; Wetstein cites *colb unus i.e.* one of the MSS 22 to 26; 22 has elsewhere shown some relationship to W;

10, 7 — παλιν before αυτοις = ℵ[ca] fam 1, 63, 69, 124, 253, 565, e ff₂ r aur*; ℵ* omits both; B omits αυτοις;
10, 9 — και εισελευσεται = Δ 579, a e δ Lucif;
10, 15 διδωμι for τιθημι = ℵ* D d (Eth Pers Arab);
10, 18 + και before εξουσιαν (1) = Vg[hent sixt cl] Hier; cf. a, Syr S g, Diatess, etc.;
10, 21 + δε = fam 13, d Syr S Sah (m[l]); order varies in different authorities;
10, 31 — οι ιουδαιοι = Syr S Sah (m[l]) Athan; note change of order in others;
10, 32 — καλα = 220, l. 54, b Syr S Thdrt; change of order in many;
10, 32 (ποιον) + ουν = Bo;
10, 32 — αυτων = Λ** 69, 157, 435, l. 44, e Vg (T) Bo Ath;
10, 36 — του = ℵ D E G 28, 69, 124, 218, 258, 330, 472, etc.;
10, 41 ουδε εν for ουδεν = fam 1, fam 13, 60, Syr g j h Go Or;
10, 41 — ιωαννης (2) = 248, Syr S Bo Arab[walt];
11, 12 αυτω οι μαθηται = ℵ D K Π 13, 42, 145, 481, 482, 489, 579, al b d ff₂ r Sah Arm;
11, 14 — ουν = A 157, 249, 565, 579, a dimma Syr S g j Bo Arm Eth Georg;
11, 14 λεγει for ειπεν = c ff₂ l r Vg (E G); cf. Syr S;
11, 17 εν τω μνημιω εχοντα = D L Ψ b c d l r aur Vg;
11, 22 αιτησης for αιτηση = Syr S;
11, 26 — εις εμε = Nonn;
11, 28 (ειπουσα) + οτι = D d Sah Bo;
11, 30 — η = D 249, 472, l. 47, Sah Bo, etc.;
11, 43 εκραξεν for εκραυγασε = C* Chr;
11, 48 την πολιν for τον τοπον = Syr S (Chr);
11, 49 — ων = l. 184, d f Syr S Eth; cf. X;
11, 51 αρχων for αρχιερευς = d (*princeps*); *princeps sacerdotum* regular in OL;
11, 51 αποθνησκειν ις̅ = 579; order only;
11, 54 και εκει for κακει = L Γ 33, 69, 157, 249, 251, 252, Or;
12, 2 (διηκονει) + αυτω = c; cf. gat Syr g;
12, 2 των συνανακειμενων αυτω = 28, 71, 157, 330, 565, 569, l. 253, al; cf. 33, 76;
12, 3 — εκ = a c e dimma deer Vg (R) Go; cf. Hier trans. of Or cant 11, 12;

12, 9 — εκ (1) = 157, 258, 579, l. 184, e Bo Eth Georg Pers Go Vigil;
12, 16 + ο before $\overline{\iota\varsigma}$ = D H Λ fam 13, 33, 66, 157, 472, 474, 579, etc.
12, 16 — τοτε = b c e ff$_2$ l Syr S g Diatess Georg Pers;
12, 18 — ο = ℵ 69, 157, 234, 251, l. 47, al (2) Bo (P); cf. D c Syr g, etc.
12, 20 αναβαντων for αναβαινοντων = Syr S Sah Bo (OL Vg);
12, 21 + τω before φιλιππω = D;
12, 25 φυλαξει αυτην εις ζωην αιωνιον = Syr S Sah Bo Eth Arab;
12, 26 εγω ειμι = D a b c d e r Syr g Sah Eth;
12, 29 δε for ουν = Syr g Sah (Bo) Eth Go Slav;
12, 29 εστηκως for εστως = A D G K M X Π Ψ fam 13, 15, 22, 33, 131, 157, 249, 251, 254, 435, 482, l. 48, l. 184, al;
12, 29 (αλλοι) + δε = 56, 58, 61, l. 253, e l Syr g j Sah (76) Bo Georg Arab; cf. Syr S Eth;
12, 31 — τουτου (1) = D L 6, 71, 248, 482, 569, b d g ff$_2$ l r Vg Sah (munt) Bo (K) Syr S g;
12, 35 λαβη for καταλαβη = Or (joan. com. frg. 91); cf. Syr;
12, 40 επηρωσεν for πεπωρωκεν = ℵ Π 482**, l. 48, Did;
12, 42 — και = c e ff$_2$ f l gig mol gat Vg (10 MSS) Sah Bo Eth;
12, 42 πολλοι των αρχοντων = Chr (ioan. com.) Diatess (Bo) Eth Arm Arab;
12, 44 εκραξεν δε ο $\overline{\iota\varsigma}$ = Eth^{walt} Arab^{walt} (69, 346, l. 260);
12, 47 (μου) + μη = 579, e Syr j Pers Aug Chr;
12, 49 εντολην μοι = fam 1, 565, Bo;
13, 11 παραδιδουντα for — δοντα = 28, 475, l. 181, l. 183, l. 184, l. 185;
13, 18 επηρκεν for επηρεν = ℵ A U Π 1; cf. Latin Syr;
13, 23 — αυτου = aur Pers^{walt};
13, 25 — ουτως = ℵ A D Π 1, 69, 124, 201, 473, 479, 480, 482, 579, l. 183, l. 184, etc. OL Vg Syr S Or;
13, 32 — και ευθυς δοξασει αυτον = 245, 251, Nonn; cf. 157, 579, l;
13, 33 — οτι = ℵ* D 59, 249, 250, 579, l. 13, al b c d e ff$_2$ l Vg Eth Pers Cyr;
13, 33 — εγω = 477, 579, Syr g (4 MSS);

13, 37 υπερ σου την ψυχην μου = ℵ X 579;
14, 2 – αν = ℵ X* 579;
14, 3 εγω ειμει = b c d f ff_2 q aur Sah Bo Ambr;
14, 3 – και (2) = A E G K Γ Δ 36, 72, 131, 248, 250, 473, 475, 476, 481, al (20); cf. D M, etc.
14, 4 – εγω = D L X 1, fam 13, 71, 254, 470, 565, a b d e ff_2 q aur Syr S g Arm Eth Chr;
14, 7 γνωσεσθαι for εγνωκειτε (2) = ℵ D* 579, d Syr S Ir Vict;
14, 10 ποιει τα εργα αυτος = L X 579, 33, Cyr;
14, 11 μηγε for μη = D 69, 579;
14, 17 αυτον for αυτο (3) = D* G** L 579; cf. versions;
14, 20 – εν (1) = a Eth Vict Hilar;
14, 22 μελλεις ημιν = D d e Vg Or;
16, 13 – δε = D 473, 579, l. 19, l. 28, l. 184, d e r Sah Arm Pers Or Tert Cyr Hil;
16, 17 ουκετι for ου = D 33, 124;
16, 17 + εγω before υπαγω = D Y Γ Δ unc (6) fam 1, 28, 157, 248, 251, 472, etc., d f Syr S Go;
16, 18 – ο λεγει = ℵ* D* 1, 3, fam 13, 71, 95, 248, 251**, 565, 579, a b d e ff_2 Syr j Sah Arm Georg;
16, 19 ημελλον for ηθελον = ℵ 69, (579), c ff_2 Sah (85, 92); cf. Syr S;
16, 23 – οσα = A 145*;
16, 24 αιτησασθε for αιτειτε = ℵ* 579, l. 185;
16, 24 πεπληρωμενη ην = d Vg(H);
16, 26 αιτησ– εν τω ονοματι μου = ℵ 1, 565, 579, Syr S g Sah Bo Eth;
16, 26 αιτησασθαι for -σεσθε = ℵ 1, l. 184, a Bo;
16, 28 – εξηλθον παρα του πατρος = D 63, 249, b d ff_2 Syr S;
16, 29 – αυτου = ℵ* 63, 73, 106, 249, 253, 259, 475*, 478, 565, 579, a fos Sah (57) Arm;
17, 1 λελαληκεν for ελαλησεν = ℵ 579, l. 184;
17, 2 δως for δωση = L 394, (Bo^{fr});
17, 2 αυτω for αυτοις = ℵ* 1, 22, 38, c e ff_2 f Vg (C) Syr S g Vict Hil;
17, 3 – σε and απεστιλεν for απεστειλας = Epiph (anc. 2) Or (ioan. com. frg. 95);
17, 4 εδωκας for δεδωκας = C D K Π l. 53, ($colb^{mill}$, a lectionary) Chr Bas Ign Const;

17, 7 εγνωκα for εγνωκαν = A$^?$ 7, 118, 579, l. 32, l. 36, l. 44, l. 60, a b c e f ff_2 q Syrr Sah Go Theophil (Chr); cf. ℵ;

17, 8 – και εγνωσαν = ℵ* A D a d e q Vg (R) Go;

17, 9 εδωκας for δεδωκας = D N 579; cf. versions;

17, 12 εδωκας for δεδωκας = C N 579, Chr;

17, 14 εδωκα for δεδωκα = 251, 254, 579; cf. D (δεεδωκα);

17, 19 – εγω = ℵ A 71, 248, 579, 700, b c e q r mol dimma fos Vg (D P M) Syr S Sah Eth Did Ath Chr Vict Ambrst;

17, 20 μονων ερωτω = a c dimma ℈ Eth Pers Arm Georg;

17, 20 υπερ for περι (2) = 579;

17, 23 – ινα$_2$ (+ και) = ℵ 1, 579, b c Vg Sah Arm Eth Syr j;

17, 23 καμε for εμε = (OL) Vg (exc. a few);

17, 24 και εκεινοι for κακεινοι = A K U Π* N 157, 482, 489 Thdrt;

17, 25 εγνων σε = 579, Vg (E ℈ MT O) Syr S (Sah Bo) Eth Arab;

18, 1 του κεδρου for των κεδρων = ℵ* D a b d r Sah (Bo) Eth;

18, 16 τω for τη (2) = 486; cf. Syr S;

18, 18 (ην δε) + και = fam 13, 579, a b c q Vg Syr S h Sah Bo Arm;

18, 23 ειπον for ελαλησα = ℵ* 579, Aug; cf. Sah Bo;

18, 29 προς αυτους ο πειλατος = ℵ Sah Bo;

18, 31 – αυτον (2) = ℵ* Θ^c fam 1, 28, 477, 565, 579, l. 251, c Arm Cyr;

18, 32 πληρωθη before ο λογος = Sah Syr g Eth^{walt};

18, 34 + και at beginning = D^{sup} a c d ff_2 g Vg Eth;

18, 34 απεκρινατο for απεκριθη = A D^{sup} N U Θ^c Π Ψ 1, 33, 157, 254, 299, 470, 482, 700;

18, 35 μη for μητι = ℵ* fam 1, 565, l. 253, Bo (Syr Eth);

18, 36 ην before εκ (2) = Or (jerem. hom. 14, 17);

18, 37 – ο before ῑς̄ = L X Γ Δ Λ Ψ 3, 27, 28, 33, 71, 157, 245, 435, 565, etc. (Sah);

18, 39 (ουν) + ινα = ℵ K U Y Π 12, 15, 27, 245, 258, 299, 475, 700;

19, 4 – παλιν = 17*, 258*, 346, 477, l. 47, b ff_2 Pers^{walt};

19, 4 (εξηλθεν) + ουν = E G H M S U Y Δ Λ 28, 245, 472, 579, fam 13, al mult b ff_2 Vg;

19, 4 αιτιαν · · · ουχ = (ℵ*) 78, 127, (579), l. 63, l. 253, r Arm;

19, 6 υμεις αυτον = D^{sup} L Y Ψ e q r;

19, 7 — *αυτω* (1) = ℵ fam 1, 579, a b c e f ff$_2$ MT Bo(N) Eth Georg Pers Or;

19, 12 *αυτον απολυσαι* = M 33, Syr g Cyr;

19, 12 *εκραυγαζον* for *εκραζον* = A I L M Y Π fam 1, fam 13, 22, 106, 235, 245, 248, 579, etc.

19, 12 *ποιων εαυτον* = M Y 579, l. 26, b ff$_2$ Sah Arm Eth;

19, 13 *τον ιν̅ εξω* = Bo; cf. Syr Eth;

19, 13 + *του* before *βηματος* = E H K M S U Γ Δ Λ fam 13, 22, 28, 106, 435, 472, 700, etc.;

19, 14 *ελεγεν* for *λεγει* = 579, f q foss Sah Bo (Syr Eth Pers Arab)^{walt};

19, 15 *ελεγον* for *εκραυγασαν* = ℵ* 579; cf. + *λεγοντες* in many;

19, 16 *οι δε παραλαβοντες* for *παρελαβον δε* = ℵ* M fam 1, fam 13, 61**, 78, 239, 299, 565, 579, l. 1, l. 7, l. 14, l. 15, l. 17, l. 47–50, l. 54, l. 251, l. 253, Sah Arm;

19, 16 (*ιν̅*) + *απηγαγον* = ℵ*^{c} M N U Π** fam 1, 127, 239, 246, 565, 579, 700, l. 54, etc. Sah Arm;

19, 17 *εαυτω τον σταυρον* = ℵ L Π (1), 489, (579), l. 185^{semel}, OL Vg Cyr Or; cf. B X 33, etc.;

19, 20 *ανεγνωσαν πολλοι* = 579, Diatess Arab^{walt};

19, 20 *της πολεως ο τοπος* = 1, fam 13, 239, 565, 579, l. 253, OL Vg Syr g j Sah Bo Arm;

19, 24 — *εαυτοις* = Λ* 579, b Pers^{walt};

19, 25 — *του ιν̅* = l. 150* Georg Nonn Chr;

19, 26 — *παρεστωτα* = Λ* 477, l. 54, g$_2$ cor-vat^{mg} P Book of Margaret; Syr g j Arm Eth, etc., change order;

19, 27 *αυτην ο μαθητης* = ℵ D^{sup} T^{d} U Γ 1, fam 13, 247, 471, 565, al OL Vg Bo;

19, 28 — *ηδη* = Y 1, 51, 71, 86, 249, 473, 486, 565, 579, 700, l. 47–50, al (15), a b c e g$_2$ n r mol Vg Syr g (j) Sah Eth Eus Did Chr Hil;

19, 31 — *η* = ℵ A E Γ 71, 248, 250, 435, 470, 472, 473, 475, 579, l. 253, al;

19, 38 *ηλθον ··· ηραν* for *ηλθεν ··· ηρε* = ℵ* N a b c e ff$_2$ fos Syr j Sah Arm;

19, 38 *αυτον* for *το σωμα του ιν̅* (2) = ℵ* a b c e ff$_2$ fos Syr j Arm;

19, 39 *ωσει* (against *ως*) = A N U X Y fam 1, fam 13, 59, 66**, 157, 470, 506, 672, al Cyr;

19, 40 *ην* for *εστι* = ℵ* Syr g (36) Arm (OL e) Nyss;

20, 1 — *πρωι* = a b c;

20, 1 (ηρμενον) + απο της θυρας = ℵ 579; cf. + της θυρας = fam 1, 19**, 22, 157, 565, etc.; cf. + εκ της θυρας = X 37, 69, 229, 258, etc.;
20, 14 ειδεν for θεωρει = 579, c q δ aur Vg (16 MSS) Sah Bo (Syr S);
20, 15 αρω αυτον = Syr S Sah Bo Eth[walt] Arab[walt];
20, 17 – μου (3) = ℵ* D d e Syr S Or Ir;
20, 18 αναγγελλουσα for απαγγ– = E G S Δ** 33, 122, 127*, OL Vg;
20, 20 ταυτα for τουτο = ff_2 dimma mol (a);
20, 21 παλιν αυτοις = e Sah Eth Pers Slav; cf. Syr S;
20, 22 αυτοις και λεγει = Arm Georg Pers; a peculiar inversion which transfers the dative to preceding clause; cf. Syrr Eth Arab;
20, 26 – αυτου = ℵ 1, 56, 58, 69, 122, 124, 472, a b c e Syr S g j Sah Bo (8 MSS) Arm;
20, 26 – ο before ις = (Sah Bo);
20, 29 ειπεν δε for λεγει = ℵ* fam 13, q (c e); cf. Sah Bo;
20, 29 ειδοτες for ιδοντες = Chr (psal. 110, 4);
20, 31 ο χς εστιν = b (c) f Syr S Sah Bo Arm Pers[walt] Ir;
21, 1 ο ις παλιν = Ψ 19, 69, 435, Vg (K);
21, 3 ουδε εν for ουδεν = C*;
21, 5 και for ουν = Syr S g Eth Pers Slav;
21, 5 – ις = A* a Syr S Pers;
21, 5 – τι = ℵ* a;
21, 6 λεγει for ο δε ειπεν = ℵ*cb 239, b c r g aur dimma Vg (5 MSS) Syr S g j Bo;
21, 6 οι δε for ουν = ℵ* D Syrr Sah (132) Bo Eth Arab;
21, 6 ισχυσαν ελκυσαι = 127, c f Sah; cf. Vg, etc.;
21, 8 πλοιω for πλοιαριω = P OL (exc. a e) Vg Sah Bo;
21, 9 ανεβησαν for απεβησαν = ℵ* H 299, Syr S g;
21, 14 – ο ις = S 234, (ff_2) Vg (E);
21, 17 – ο ις = ℵ D fam 1, 33, 120, 565, OL Vg Syr S Bo Eth Arab;
21, 18 αποισουσιν for οισει = ℵ[c] Π 1, 19, 22, 565, Cyr;
21, 18 (οπου) + συ = D* b d c e f ff_2 aur Vg (D E G) Syr S Nonn;
21, 19 ελεγεν for ειπε = fam 1, 565, Chr; cf. variation in Latin MSS;
21, 20 – ακολουθουντα = ℵ* ff_2 (Bo); order varies in OL;

21, 21 ειπεν for λεγει = ℵ f g r deer Vg (4 MSS sixt cl) Syr g Sah Bo (Eth Pers[walt]);

As has been found in the other gospels, these variants are supported primarily by the versions and allied MSS. In chapters 5 to 13 inclusive (132 readings) those showing the largest number of agreements with W are as follows: OL, 65; Syr cu S, 39; Bo, 36; MS D, 31; Sah, 29; fam 13, 27; MS ℵ, 24; Eth, 21; Arm., 18; Syr g, 17; MS 579, 16; MS 157, 16; fam 1, 14; MS 472, 12; MS 28, 11; Go, 10; lect. 184, 8; MS 482, 8; MS Π, 7; 565, 251, and Syr j, 6 each.

In chapters 14 to 21 (108 readings) the agreements are OL, 56; MS ℵ, 44; MS 579, 38; Sah, 30; Bo, 24; MS D, 23; fam 1, 23; Syr cu S, and Eth, 20 each; Syr g, fam 13, 17 each; Arm, 16; MS 565, 15; MS A, 11; MS Π, 8; N and L, 7 each.

There seems to be a decided Egyptian trend in the later chapters, as shown not only by the greater number of agreements with Sahidic and ℵ, but with all other older MSS of Egyptian origin, whatever the text affiliation. Old Latin leads in number as usual because of our better knowledge of it, but its supremacy is diminished. Most noteworthy is the decrease in agreements with the older Syriac and the syriacising MSS. This does not include fam 1, which runs closely with ℵ in the second part of John as likewise in most of Luke. The remarkable increase in agreements with MS 579 begins at 13, 25 and is even greater than the figures show, since MS 579 fails after 20, 14. It seems quite clear that there was a difference in base between the two parts of John in W, but that both were corrected to the Hesychian form of text. The fact that the dividing point is less clearly marked than in the other cases may be due to the greater degree of similarity in the basic texts or to an earlier union with consequent opportunity for assimilation. The union cannot therefore be assigned to the parent of W with any degree of certainty, and it may have occurred much earlier. The small number of agreements with the Diatessaron is noteworthy, especially in the earlier part, where the Syriac trend is strong. W certainly shows no direct indebtedness; the similarities come from the version tradition, to which the Diatessaron is also indebted.

The variants in this part of John for which W is the only known authority follow:

5, 15 (απηλθεν) + δε; "and" is added by some MSS and versions;
5, 15 W has both Syriac and regular expressions for "he said"; see above;
5, 21 τους νεκρους εγειρει ο $\overline{\pi\eta\rho}$;
5, 24 ουκ ερχεται εις κρισιν; cf. Sah;
5, 36 μαρτυρουσιν for μαρτυρει; cf. versions;
6, 16 − οι μαθηται αυτου;
6, 21 αυτον βαλιν for λαβειν αυτον; scribal error;
6, 28 αυτω for προς αυτον; cf. Syriac;
6, 60 − εστιν; cf. Sah Bo;
7, 14 μεσης ουσης for μεσουσης;
7, 39 ελαμβανον for εμελλον λαμβανειν; cf. Latin and Sah;
10, 13 − ο δε μισθωτος φευγει οτι μισθωτος εστι; the phrase may well be suspected; ℵ B D L, etc., omit first half; 579 omits part;
10, 21 ελεγον δε αλλοι; the order is the only special peculiarity; see previous list;
10, 25 − τω;
10, 25 αυτα ταυτα τα εργα; ταυτα is the regular reading; αυτα is found in D OL Bo Syr Arm; τα εργα appears only here; it seems an explanatory gloss on the conflate;
10, 25 μαρτυρησει for μαρτυρει; cf. *testimonium perhibent* of Latin mistaken for future;
10, 38 αναγνωτε for ινα γνωτε; cf. *et scitote* in OL.
10, 42 (πολλοι) + ουν;
11, 10 − το;
11, 19 + την before μαριαν;
11, 20 εκαθητο for εκαθεζετο; cf. Syr S;
11, 32 − ην; cf. Syriac Eth;
11, 32 (ιδουσα) + δε; note addition of "and" in b ff$_2$ fos Syr S Sah Bo Eth Arm;
11, 38 ενβριμων for εμβριμωμενος; cf. *fremens* of OL and Vg;
12, 9 (οχλος) + ο;
12, 9 − εκ νεκρων; cf. Matthew 26, 32; Mark 14, 28, where W adds the words;
12, 22 + ο before φιλιππος (2); an Hesychian correction, but belongs to first occurrence of name; cf. 157;
12, 41 επει for οτε; ℵ A B L M X 1, 33, 97, 252, 472, e Sah

Bo Arm Epiph Nonn Cyr Or have *οτι*; W seems to have been influenced by the Syriac or Old Latin;

12, 47 *μηδε* for *και μη*;

12, 48 — *τη*;

13, 2 *ισκαριωτη*; a mistake for the Hesychian form;

13, 7 *τι* for *αρτι*;

13, 26 *δωσω ενβαψας το ψωμιον*; only the order is peculiar;

13, 38 *συ με απαρνηση* for *απαρνηση με*; cf. ff$_2$ Syr g;

14, 7 *εγνωκεται* for *εγνωκειτε* (1); cf. ℵ D* 330, Bo;

16, 17 — *οτι*; cf. ℵ* Sah Diatess;

16, 22 *αφερει* for *αιρει*; cf. *aufert* of e f q (a r Cypr);

16, 23 — *εν* (1); = 579; OL MSS omit the preposition with this phrase in other passages;

17, 4 (*εργον*) + *σου*;

17, 8 *εδωκα* for *δεδωκα*; cf. above John, 17, 9–14;

17, 8 *αυτο* for *αυτοι*; cf. Arm Arab Eth;

17, 22 (*δοξαν*) + *μου*;

17, 26 *και εγω* for *καγω*;

18, 1 *εισεληλυθεν* for *εισηλθεν*; cf. perfect of Bo Latin, etc.

18, 16 *εισηνεγκεν* for *εισηγαγε*;

18, 17 (*ουν*) + *αυτω*; cf. the conflate in Syr S;

18, 18 — *ο*;

18, 30 *παραδεδωκειμεν* for *παρεδωκαμεν*;

18, 39 *απολυω* for *απολυσω* (1); note the conjunctive in Bo while Sah has third future;

19, 7 + *του* before *θεου*; Beza, Elzevir, Mill, Wetstein have it, but there seems no other MS authority in spite of Tisch (*c. minusc. pauc.*); a few may be inferred from failure to mention by Wetstein and Scrivener;

19, 20 *τοτε* for *τουτον*;

19, 20 *εβραειστι* for *ελληνιστι*; due to different order in Hesych. and careless correction;

19, 30 *παραδεδωκεν* for *παρεδωκε*;

20, 1 *επι* for *εις*;

20, 4 *επι* for *εις*;

20, 5 *μεντοις* for *μεντοι*; cf. *μεντοιγε* of L X Ψ 1, 579, etc.;

20, 6 + *ο* before *σιμων*;

20, 13 *τεθεικασιν* for *εθηκαν*;

20, 19 *μιας σαββατων* for *τη μια των σαββατων*; cf. ℵ* Syr S;

20, 26 *μετα* for *μεθ*;

20, 30 πεποιηκεν for εποιησεν;
21, 4 a long omission due to like endings in sound (*i.e.* itacistic error assumed); see collation;
21, 12 αριστατε for αριστησατε;
21, 15 (πλειον) + παντων;
21, 17 αγαπας for φιλεις (1); from verse 16.

The changes above enumerated are similar to those which characterize the version tradition; compare the chapter on Mark for the discussion of each type of variant.

5. The First Quire of John

In the text of this part of John there is somewhat the same puzzle to be solved as in Mark. Out of 225 important variants of W, 90 agree or partially agree with the Hesychian recension, though there is generally other and older support. There are 41 agreements with the Antioch recension, but these always have other support, especially from the MS group Γ Λ, etc. In 65 cases W finds its only support in the descendants of the version tradition, and for 28 readings there is no other support.

It is evident that there has been no adaptation to either of the recensions, which have been corrected into other parts of the MS. The agreements indicate rather that those recensions drew many of their readings from a text form allied to W. The closer relationship to the Hesychian suggests that this type of text was of Egyptian origin. That it belongs to the version tradition is shown by the following readings, which have no adequate Hesychian or Antioch support:

1, 1 + ο before θεος = L Nyss;
1, 15 (ειπον) + υμιν = D** X f Vg Eth Epiph;
1, 15 + ος before εμπροσθεν = ℵ* l. 184, c Ƥ dimma Eth Chr;
1, 16 + ζωην before ελαβομεν = Sah;
1, 17 + δε before χαρις = l. 253, a b c f ff$_2$ l q r deer Syr (g) h Bo Eth Georg Ambr;
1, 18 + ει μη before ο μονογενης = OL Vg (10 MSS) Arm Ir Hilar Ambr;
1, 18 (εξηγησατο) + ημιν = c Syr cu Adimant;
1, 19 ερωτησουσιν for ερωτησωσιν = L Δ 33, 579; note **ⲬⲈⲔⲀⲤ** in Sah with future but Bo uses conjunctive;

1, 20 – *και* (3) = C** L fam 1, 33, b f ff$_2$ r Bo (B F M) Arm^{cdd} Georg;
1, 21 (*αυτον*) + *παλιν* = ℵ^c a b e ff$_2$ l r Vg (D R) Syr g Pers; cf. ℵ* c;
1, 21 + *τι ουν* before *ο προφητης* = a b c e (r);
1, 23 ($\overline{κυ}$) + *ευθιας ποιειτε τας τριβους αυτου* = e Or Ambr; cf. l. 47, b;
1, 27 *ουκ ιμι εγω* = B T^b X Ψ fam 13, 118, 579, Or Aug;
1, 29 *τας αμαρτιας* for *την αμαρτιαν* = e l aur cor-vat Vg (4) Did Cypr Eus;
1, 30 (*ειπον*) + *υμιν* = fam 13, 248, l. 47, l. 52, l. 184, Eth;
1, 30 + *οτι* before *οπισω* = X Vg (O) Syr cu S g h j Sah Bo;
1, 31 *βαπτιζιν* for *βαπτιζων* = e q Sah (109) Arm Georg; cf. Syr cu S;
1, 32 *μενον* for *εμεινεν* = ℵ b e q r Vg (R) Chr Ambr Hier;
1, 36 (*θεου*) + *ο ερων τας αμαρτιας του κοσμου* = C* 59, 235, a ff$_2$ aur Vg (Γ ꟾꞇ foss) Eth Cyr; yet all have *την αμαρτιαν* except foss (*peccata*);
1, 43 + *και* before *εμβλεψας* (for *δε*) = 46, 117, l. 15, a e q Syrr Eth Chr; many omit conjunction;
1, 45 – *ο* before *φιλιππος* = ℵ* F* fam 13, 17, 24, 122, 248, 471, 472, 565, Sah Bo Epiph;
1, 48 (*ειδεν*) + *δε* = 157, e (*iesus autem*) Bo Chr (1 MS); 124, a b ff$_2$ l aur foss and Epiph also add but with participial construction;
1, 51 – *σε* = Arm;
2, 2 ($\overline{ις}$) + *εκι* = 131, Vg (A B Δ ℈ F G H Θ M O Q S X Y foss deer);
2, 7 + *και* before *λεγι* = ℵ X (e ff$_2$ l foss) deer ℈ Eth Georg;
2, 12 – *εκει* = 66, Chron-Alex;
2, 15 + *ως* before *φραγελλιον* = Oxy. Pap. 847, G L X 1, 19, 22, 33, 565, l. 253, OL (exc. e l δ) Vg Syr h j Or Cyr;
2, 16 *πωλουσιν τας περιστερας* = a b ff$_2$ r δ Syr S Sah Bo;
2, 17 *και* for *δε* = e f ff$_2$ l q aur foss Syr g j Bo (Γ) Eth Georg Arab Epiph;
2, 17 (*εστιν*) + *οτι* = X 486, Pers Or Epiph (Sah Bo);
2, 20 *ο ναος ουτος οικοδομηθη* = Clem-Al Diatess;
2, 21 *αυτος* for *εκεινος* = Syr S Sah Bo Diatess;
3, 2 *τα σημια ταυτα* = ff$_2$ Sah Bo Slav Or;

3, 13 (ουδις) + εστιν ος = Eth Arm; a common Latin paraphrase, but not found in MSS here;

3, 14 δι υψωθηνε = A l. 26, a Syr cu S Sah (pap 109) Bo Eth Arab Slav Lucif.;

3, 20 αυτου τα εργα = A K Π 1, 72, 74, 59, 90, 209, 470, 476, 482, 484, 569, 672, Sah Bo Chr; this reading was taken by the K[a] type of the Antioch; it does not belong to the original Antioch recension;

3, 21 εισιν for εστιν = Ψ 2, 28, 67, 72, 254, 472, Syrr Latin, etc.;

3, 23 + ο before ιωαννης = B l. 44, Sah;

3, 28 − εγω = D 245, a d ff_2 l aur Syr cu Cypr Firm;

3, 31 − εκ της γης εστι και = g l aur Vg (D E) Or Tert Hier;

4, 6 (ωρα) + δε = b cor-vat Vg (D) Sah (γ^1) Bo Cyr; cf. e (*et*) Syr h;

4, 7 + και before ερχεται = 64, 258, OL Vg (HΘ) Syr S cu g j Eth Arab; cf. f (*autem*) Sah (3 MSS);

4, 23 (αυτον) + εν $\overline{πνι}$ = 124*, a b Vg (R); cf. 131, 229* which seem to add; due to omission;

4, 25 αναγγελλι for αναγγελει = ℵ* D;

4, 27 (μεντοι) + γε = Or; cf. above, John 20, 5;

4, 27 λαλει for ελαλει = 486, 579, Syr g Bo;

4, 29 − μοι = ff_2 Bo (O);

4, 30 (εξηλθον) + ουν = ℵ N Λ fam 1, fam 13, 28, 71, 330, 474, 478, 481, 483–5, 565, 569, l. 184, al e f ff_2 l q aur Vg (cl MT) Sah Cyr;

4, 31 και for δε = Syr g Arm Eth Aug;

4, 35 τετραμηνον (against τετραμηνος) = H 28, 254, 482, e q Chr;

4, 38 − ο = D* L d e;

4, 42 − ὅτι (1) = B 80, l. 53, b f r Syr cu g Eth Or Ir;

4, 42 − αληθως = K* Π 42, 71, ff_2 r mol Vg (D K*) Pers Or Vict Heracl;

4, 45 + τοις before (ιεροσολυμοις) = Or; cf. Sah;

4, 45 − αυτοι = Cyr Chr;

4, 51 υπηντησαν αυτω οι δουλοι αυτου = e Syr cu;

4, 52 − αυτω = a b dimma Sah Chr (1 MS);

4, 54 (τουτο) + δε = B C* G fam 13, 71, 485, l. 253, Bo (7 MSS) Or;

4, 54 εποιησεν σημιον = ℵ Chr (a b Eth);

5, 2 τη επιλεγομενη = d b (c δ);

5, 9 − ευθεως = ℵ* D d l aur Arm; 28, 245, 254, etc., omit more;

5, 10 *αριν* for *αραι* = OL Vg (*tollere*) Sah Bo;

5, 11 *ο δε απεκρινατο* for *απεκριθη* = ℵ* Syr g j h Sah (91) Bo (2 MSS) Georg Slav; cf. ℵ C* G, etc.;

5, 11 *υγιην* for *υγιη* = ℵ* 579.

5, 11–12 – *κραβαττον* · · · *αρον τον* = Γ Λ* 54*, 57, 64, 68, 357, b Syr S;

The number of agreements of W with each of the versions and various MSS in question is as follows: OL, 35; Bo, 17; Sah, 15 (total Coptic agreements, 25); Syr cu S, 14; Eth, 13; later Syriac, 13; MS ℵ, 9; Arm, 6; fam 1 and fam 13, 5 each; 579, 33 and X, 4 each; D, 28, L, 565, and lect. 184 and 253, 3 each. From this it is clear that the type of text is related to the base found for the later portion of John. The Old Latin agreements are rather more numerous and striking, reminding one of the text of Mark 1 – 5, 30. Coptic, and even ℵ, maintain the expected relationship, though the majority of agreements was removed by the rigidness with which possible Hesychian readings were excluded in making the above list. The small number of agreements with D is due in large part to the lacuna in D. Conclusions should not be based on so brief a portion of text. The two cases where the Diatessaron is found in the support are of less account since Semitic construction is involved.

The following table of all the agreements between W and the six chief uncials will correct any errors in impression obtained from the above:

Chap.	ℵ	A	B	C	D	L
1	31	34	38	42	lac	41
2	8	12	16	lac	lac	13
3	18	18	30	lac	lac	25
4	35	44	49	55	39	51
5	12	6	10	12	10	8

The list of readings for which W seems the only authority follows:

1, 4 – *ην* (1); note variation in tense in best MSS; cf. 1, 6 for style of John;

1, 6 *απο* for *παρα*; cf. John 10, 18, where scribe corrects same error;

1, 21 *συ ει ηλιας*; cf. B e foss which differ only slightly;
1, 29 − *προς αυτον*;
1, 33 *επ αυτω* for *επ αυτον*; cf. OL e (*in eo*);
1, 37 *κηκουσαν* for *και ηκουσαν*;
1, 46 *τον τω* for *τον υιον του*; not a late Greek construction, perhaps from Latin;
1, 51 *τουτων μιζω*;
2, 1 *εγινετο* for *εγενετο*; it appears to be an imperfect for aorist; perhaps an itacism;
2, 12 − *εις καφαρναουμ*; perhaps due to the change of order noted below;
2, 12 *οι μαθητε αυτου* before *και η* $\overline{\mu\eta\rho}$; other MSS show change of order or omission;
2, 12 − *αυτου* after *μητηρ*;
2, 14 *κολλυβιστας* for *κερματιστας*; cf. verse 15; Latin uses the same word both times;
2, 20 *γιρις* for *εγερεις*; cf. l. 47 (*εγιρεις*), therefore present for future;
2, 22 *ηνεστη* for *ηγερθη*; *ανεστη* in Chr 134 E; 135 B; Nemesus, nat. hom. 576 B; cf. Matthew 17, 9; Luke 9, 8; on augment see p. 23;
2, 22 *αυτω* for *οι μαθηται αυτου*;
3, 13 *ανεβη* for *αναβεβηκεν*; cf. perfect tense in the versions;
3, 22 *κακι* for *και εκει*;
4, 11 *και ουτε αντλημα εχις* after *βαθυ*;
4, 11 *και* for *ουν*;
4, 11 *εστιν* for *εχεις*; see above on grammatical peculiarities;
4, 12 (*φρεαρ*) + *το ζων*; from verse 11;
4, 14 (*δ αν*) + *δε*; the combination arose from correction in parent; scribe copied both;
4, 17 − *ο* before $\overline{\iota\varsigma}$;
4, 47 *ηκεν* for *ηκει*;
4, 48 − *ο* before $\overline{\iota\varsigma}$;
5, 5 $\overline{\mu}$ *και* $\overline{\eta}$ for *τριακονταοκτω*; seems to imply misuse of letters as numerals;
5, 7 *εν οσω* for *εν ω*; cf. Sah (ϩⲟⲥⲟⲛ).

The peculiarities are in the main similar to those found in the rest of the MS, which have been assigned to the influence of the version tradition. The individual cases here point to Latin and Coptic, particularly Sahidic, influence.

6. Summary

By far the most decided evidence gathered in this long study has to do with the parent or parents of W. It was made up out of six separate parts: (1) Matthew, (2) John 5, 12 to end, (3) Luke 1–8, 12, (4) Luke 8, 13 to end, (5) Mark 1–5, 30, (6) Mark 5, 31 to end. We do not know whether it originally contained John 1–5, 11, or not, but it may be assumed. At some earlier date portion 2 seems to have been combined from two separate MSS. The dividing point is near the end of chapter 13. Portions 1 and 4 had been previously corrected to agree with the Antioch recension; portions 2 and 3, with the Hesychian; portion 5 was from a Greek-Latin bilingual; portion 6, from a trilingual with decided Latin-Syriac and less Coptic tendencies. The basic text (*i.e.* before correction) of portions 1, 3, and 4 must have been closely allied to this type of text. The first half of portion 2 had the same base, but the second half shows more Coptic affiliation. It may be noted that Mark 1–5, 30 is slightly more than a quire, and Luke 1–8, 12 about five MS pages more than two quires. The MSS, or parts of MSS, which made up the parent of W presumably had somewhat larger quires.

The first quire of John, though really an independent MS, has a text closely related to the text of the latter part of John, before correction to the Hesychian standard. In some respects this is like the text found in Mark 1–5, 30, but there is less Latin and more Coptic influence.

V. DATE

THE discussion of the date of W has been postponed to this point in the study, partly because of its difficulty and uncertainty, and partly because I wished the MS to exhibit its great worth, unaided by the prepossession which attaches to hoary age. In the preliminary notice about the MSS in the Freer Collection (Amer. Jour. of Arch. vol. 12 (1908), p. 52) I assigned the MS tentatively to the fifth or sixth century; in the same journal, vol. 13, p. 132, I dated it more exactly in the fifth century, and Dr. Kenyon, in the English Paleographical Society Publications (Plate 201 of the new series) gives the same date. Professor Grenfell, both by letter and in conversation at Oxford, dated the MS as "probably fourth century." But in a MS of such importance it is well to give all the evidence bearing on the date, rather than to rely on the general acceptance of any date.

Even in antiquity this MS was exhibited as an object of interest or peculiar sanctity, presumably because of its great age. On the first page of each gospel there are several large blots, twenty on Matthew 1, sixteen on John 1, five on Luke 1, and four on Mark 1. The blots on the first page of John are much the largest; there are no similar blots elsewhere in the MS except three small ones on page 326. Though these blots were dried and hardened, so that no semblance of the original material remained, they were still thick enough so that small bits could be cleaved off. These were analyzed by Professor Gomberg of the University of Michigan. He found slight traces of iron, but only to the extent that was expected from the ink, which cleaved off with the bits of blot material. The MS was written with an iron ink, but the blots were not ink. The rest of the material was readily combustible, leaving only a scanty ash. The blots were therefore of vegetable or animal matter and we may with safety assume that they came from the dripping of candles or lamps, probably the former, if one may judge from the thickness of the blots. As a flock of wool was found between two leaves, evidently used as a book mark, sheep were probably kept in the neighborhood of the monastery which

PLATE II

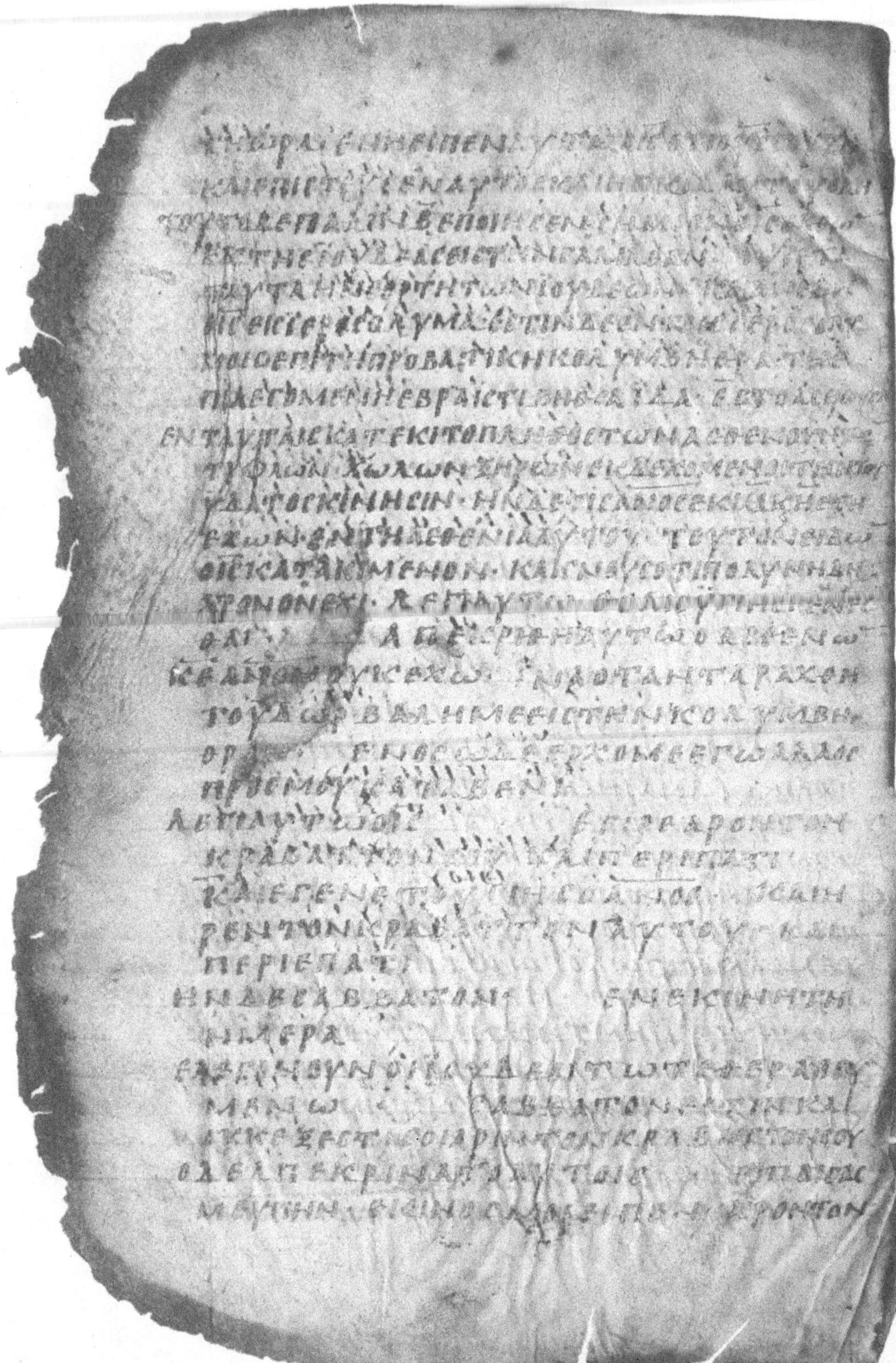

JOHN iv. 53 - v. 11.

possessed the MS. The inference that the candles used were of tallow is an easy one. The blots did not come from any natural use in reading, as they would then have been found in other parts of the MS. It seems that this Bible must have been kept in some dark part of the monastery and, when shown to visitors, usually only the first pages of Matthew and John were looked at, but the more curious or distinguished visitors may have been shown the first page of each gospel. No similar blots appear in the other Biblical MSS found with this one, so they were evidently not considered equal objects of interest. That they were all younger is not thereby proved, but is at least suggested.

On page 35 of the Deuteronomy–Joshua MS there is a cursive note in black ink, which from the style of writing has been dated at the end of the sixth century. The same shade of black ink was used by the third hand in W, and also by the last corrector of the subscription to Mark. As a crude Coptic μ is found in one of these corrections and none of them show much familiarity with Greek or Greek Bible MSS, it is probable that all four of the MSS were in a Coptic monastery during the sixth century.

An earlier terminus *ante quem* for the MS is given by the subscription to Mark (Facsimile, p. 372; Amer. Jour. Arch. vol. 13, Plate iii). As has been stated above (p. 2), the two lines of this were written by two fifth century semi-cursive hands and indicate two successive owners of the MS. The second of these was the head of a monastery. We may thus with safety date the whole MS as not later than the early part of the fifth century. But does this apply also to the first quire of John? Dr. Kenyon (op. cit.) thinks not and dates it tentatively in the seventh or eighth century, on the basis of the writing, which he classes as a Slavonic sloping uncial. It seems impossible to separate so far the two parts of the MS, and fortunately we do not have to rely entirely on the comparison of styles of writing. It is certain that this strange quire was written to fill a gap, to supply a lost quire. On the last page of it the text is stretched and ends of lines left vacant after each sentence, so as to come out just even; cf. Plate II. The three preceding pages were just as plainly crowded, an extra line even being added on each page. It must be admitted that the writer was both inexperienced and had before him a copy quite different in size of page. Yet with all his care to make his quire come out even he omitted nearly a verse at the end. This not only emphasizes the difference in form of the MSS from which and for which he was copying, but proves conclusively that one was not the parent of the other. In other words, he was not copying an injured or wornout quire, but was restoring a lost one; he was not copying a definite quire, but was striving to arrange in a quire a certain amount of text. His task was to copy as far as the words κραβαττον σου και περιπατει of 5, 12, but he stopped with the same words in verse 11. This might have been an omission in the parent text and be explained as due to like endings, but the fact that the omission falls exactly at the end of the quire seems sufficient proof that it was first made in copying this inserted quire. Exactly the same omission is noted by Tischendorf with the words "*Ceterum* Γ Λ* *al*[6] *b om versum* 12, *quippe transilientes a* και περιπατει *ad* και περιπατει." This explanation is, of course, possible, but exactly the same words are omitted by the jump from κραβαττον to κραβαττον, which we know took place in W. I can not avoid the conclusion that the error had a common origin, and therefore all others having it are indebted to W, or rather to the first quire of John in W. The omitting MSS are Γ Λ* 54*, 57, 64, 68, 357, Old Latin b, and Syr S. Of these we have seen above (p. 128), that Γ and Λ were related to W in the first quire of John at least, while the fifth century MSS b Syr S show a closer relationship to all the uncorrected parts of the W text. Yet if the mistake was original in W, the date of this quire must be before the fifth century, while the whole MS would have to be still earlier, if a lost quire of it was replaced by the quire under discussion. A date for the whole MS earlier than the second half of the fourth century seems impossible. Furthermore the fact that Γ and Λ show a closer affiliation to W in the first quire of John than in the rest of the MS implies that the parts were not yet united when the ancestor of Γ and Λ did the borrowing.

Another proof may be drawn from the condition of the writing. The superscription ευαγγελιον κατα ιωαννην and the quire number θ are less worn than the rest of the writing on the first page and without losing much in brightness have nevertheless printed across on to the opposite page very decidedly. This feels less rough and is more easily legible than the offprints due to age, which are so common in the MS. It seems to be a case of blotting and not an offprint. If so, the quire was bound in the MS when the title and quire number were added. This would be final on the greater

Plate III

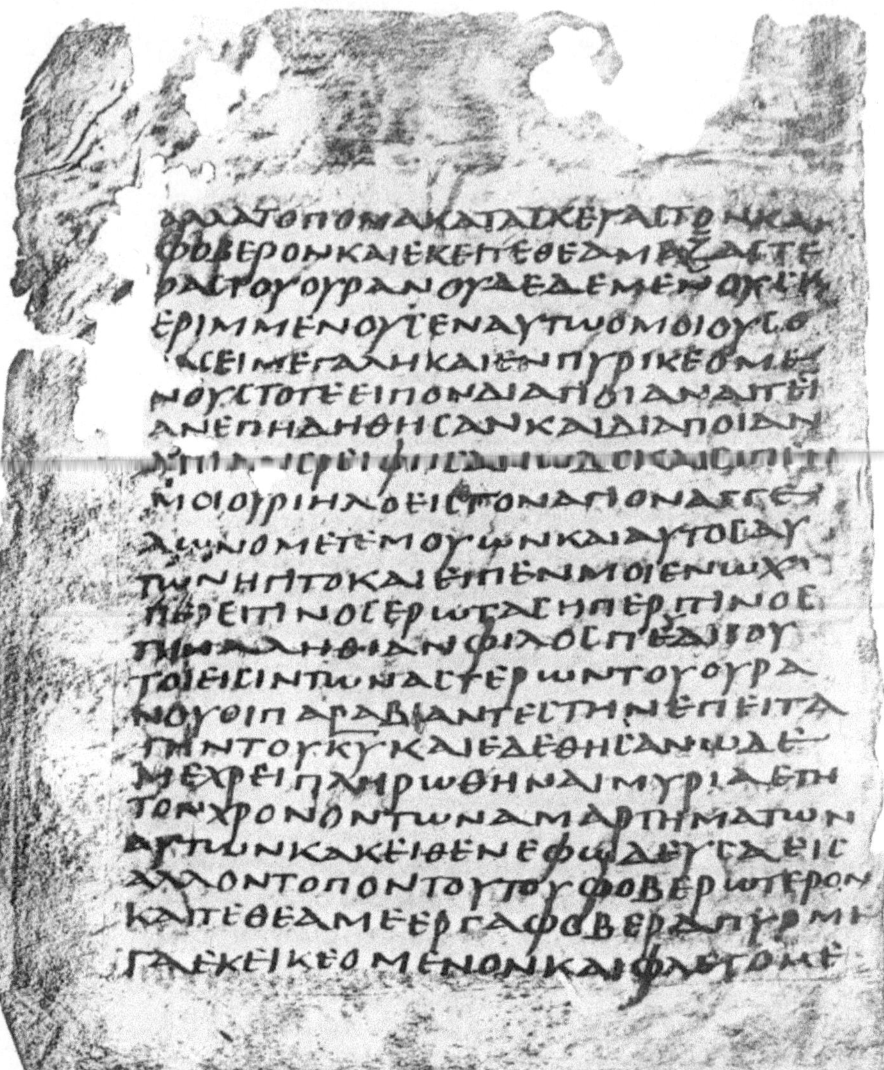

PLATE IV

ΚΕΚΑΙΕΛΑΒΕΤΑΙΕΑΥΤΟΙϹΓΥΝΑΙΚΑϹΩϹΠΕΡ
ΥΙΟΙΤΗϹΓΗϹΕΠΟΙΗϹΑΤΕΚΑΙΕΓΕΝΝΗϹΑ
ΤΕΕΑΥΤΟΙϹΤΕΚΝΑΥΙΟΥϹΓΙΓΑΝΤΑϹΚΑΙ
ΥΜΕΙϹΗΤΕΑΓΙΟΙΚΑΙΠΝΕΥΜΑΖΩΝΤΑ
ΑΙΩΝΙΑΕΝΤΩΑΙΜΑΤΙΤΩΝΓΥΝΑΙΚΩΝ
ΕΜΙΑΝΘΗΤΑΙΚΑΙΕΝΑΙΜΑΤΙϹΑΡΚΟϹΕΓΕ
ΝΝΗϹΑΤΕΚΑΙΕΝΑΙΜΑΤΙΑΝΘΡΩΠΩΝΕΠΕ
ΘΥΜΗϹΑΤΕΚΑΘΩϹΚΑΙΑΥΤΟΙΠΟΙΟΥϹΙΝ
ϹΑΡΚΑΚΑΙΑΙΜΑΟΙΤΙΝΕϹΑΠΟΘΝΗϹΚΟΥ
ϹΙΝΚΑΙΑΠΟΛΛΥΝΤΕΔΙΑΤΟΥΤΟΕΔΩΚΑ
ΑΥΤΟΙϹΘΗΛΕΙΑϹΙΝΑϹΠΕΡΜΑΤΙΖΟΥϹΙΝ
ΕΙϹΑΥΤΑϹΚΑΙΤΕΚΝΩϹΟΥϹΙΝΕΝΑΥΤΟΙϹ
ΤΕΚΝΑΟΥΤΩϹΙΝΑΜΗΕΚΛΕΙΠΕΙΑΥΤΟΙϹ
ΠΑΝΕΡΓΟΝΕΠΙΤΗϹΓΗϹΥΜΕΙϹΔΕΥΠΗΡ
ΧΕΤΕΠΝΕΥΜΑΖΩΝΤΑΑΙΩΝΙΑΚΑΙΟΥΚΑ
ΠΟΘΝΗϹΚΟΝΤΑΕΙϹΠΑϹΑϹΤΑϹΓΕΝΕΑϹ
ΤΟΥΑΙΩΝΟϹΚΑΙΔΙΑΤΟΥΤΟΟΥΚΕΠΟΙΗϹΑ
ΕΝΥΜΕΙΝΘΗΛΕΙΑϹΤΑΠΝΕΥΜΑΤΑΤΟΥΟΥΡΑΝΟΥ
ΕΝΤΩΟΥΡΑΝΩΗΚΑΤΟΙΚΗϹΙϹΑΥΤΩΝΚΑΙ
ΝΥΝΟΙΓΙΓΑΝΤΕϹΟΙΓΕΝΝΗΘΕΝΤΕϹΑΠΟ
ΤΩΝΠΝΕΥΜΑΤΩΝΚΑΙϹΑΡΚΟϹΠΝΕΥΜΑ
ΙϹΧΥΡΑΕΠΙΤΗϹΓΗϹΚΑΙΕΝΤΗΓΗΗΚΑ
ΤΟΙΚΗϹΙϹΑΥΤΩΝΕϹΤΑΙΠΝΕΥΜΑΤΑΠΟΝΗ
ΡΑΕΞΕΛΘΩΝΑΠΟΤΟΥϹΩΜΑΤΟϹΑΥΤΩ
ΔΙΟΤΙΑΠΟΤΩΝΑΝΩΤΕΡΩΝΕΓΕΝΟΝΤΟ

age of the first quire of John, if we were certain that these additions were written by the διορθωτής (cf. above, p. 39), but we do not need that assumption. The quire number θ is written exceptionally low for this MS and a careful examination with a good lens revealed the reason. In the place above the quire number the parchment, though badly decayed, shows plain signs of an erasure. I have not been able to read an erased quire number on this spot, even with the aid of hydro-sulphide of ammonium, and the decayed state of the parchment prevents further attempts. However, on an excellent negative of this page, secured four years ago, both Professor Bonner and I have read independently a small angular alpha under the erasure. This accords exactly with all the other points noted. The quire was once the first quire of a MS and so suffered more severely from wear. The MS probably did not include Matthew and may have contained only John. After the original first quire had been lost or worn out, the present quire was written to complete it. The MS seems not to have been well bound, for the last page of the quire has suffered from wear almost as much as the first page; cf. Plate II. Yet the quire as a whole was in such good condition, when W was copied, that it was taken over into the new MS.[1] Presumably it is not much older than the rest of the MS.

Examples of the early, sloping uncial of W are not very frequent on parchment. The closest parallel known to me is the Enoch fragment found at Akhmin in 1886. The first two quires of this (Plates xi–xxv in Mem. de la Miss. Arch. fran. au Caire, vol. ix, fasc. 3, Paris, 1893) are in a small rough uncial hand, having a decided slope to the right and, though written carelessly with a broad pointed pen, bearing considerable resemblance in forms of letters to the first hand of W.[2] Plate III gives a facsimile of page 22. We may note further that the plural abbreviations $\overline{\pi\nu\alpha\tau\alpha}$, etc., are used, as once in W, and also there is agreement in two noteworthy misspellings, εκχθρους (cf. above, p. 21) and οκ (οοκ) for ουκ (cf. p. 38).

The third and last quire of the Enoch fragment (Plates xxvi–xxxiii) bears a much closer resemblance to the hands of W. Plate IV shows page 52. The ease, grace, and slope of the hand

[1] This is not an impossibility in ancient MSS. Sometimes MSS were repaired when the newly added portion equaled the old in amount, as codex Aesinus of the Agricola of Tacitus, tenth and fifteenth centuries.

[2] Cf. Plate I.

remind one strongly of the first hand of W, but the shapes of many of the letters, notably *γ ε κ μ σ* and *ω*, are far closer to hand *a* (first quire of John). I see no reason for not considering the two hands of the Enoch fragment contemporary. It has been dated in the sixth century, but, though both hands are somewhat more developed types than the hands of W, I should not place the date later than the end of the fifth.

Another interesting parallel is the Sappho fragment (Berlin, P. 9722; facs. in Sitzungsber. d. kgl. Preus. Akad. d. Wissen. 1902, p. 195 ff.). Though much blurred and disfigured, the writing both in slope and forms of letters is a close parallel to hand 1 of W. The ornamental dots on such letters as *κ γ τ υ* are, however, much more pronounced and frequent, thus approximating hand *a* of W. The editor, Professor Schubart, dated this fragment in the sixth or seventh century in spite of the fact that it was a part of a parchment roll, and found in a mass of papyrus fragments. The entire absence of accents and punctuation and the fact that the iota adscript is regularly written speak for a relatively early date. Because of the roll form I should date the fragment in the transition period from papyrus to parchment (third or fourth century).

Another sloping uncial hand on parchment has been published by Professor Hunt (Cat. of Gr. Pap. in John Rylands Libr. Manchester, vol. 1, no. 53). This is the remnant of a vellum book which once contained the whole Odyssey. Because of its close similarity to papyrus hands it has been dated in the third or possibly fourth century. It bears no close resemblance to any of the hands above discussed, though it approximates the first hand of the Enoch fragment in its roughness and inelegance. I believe we can assert with confidence that all of these sloping uncial hands have no connection with the later Slavonic uncial, but are parallels to or imitations of the sloping papyrus hand of the second to fifth centuries.

Dr. Kenyon (op. cit.) has called attention to Pap. 46 of the British Museum as a very close parallel to the first hand of W. This is a magical papyrus of the fourth century. See Plate V b. Another interesting parallel is no. 108 in Papiri Greco-Egizi, vol. 2, Milan, 1908, a fragment of the Iliad (Plate V a). The appearance of a letter from Sarapammon to Eroninus on the verso gives a perfect date *ante quem*. All the dated examples of the rather extensive correspondence of these men fall in the years 255–266.

PLATE V

A

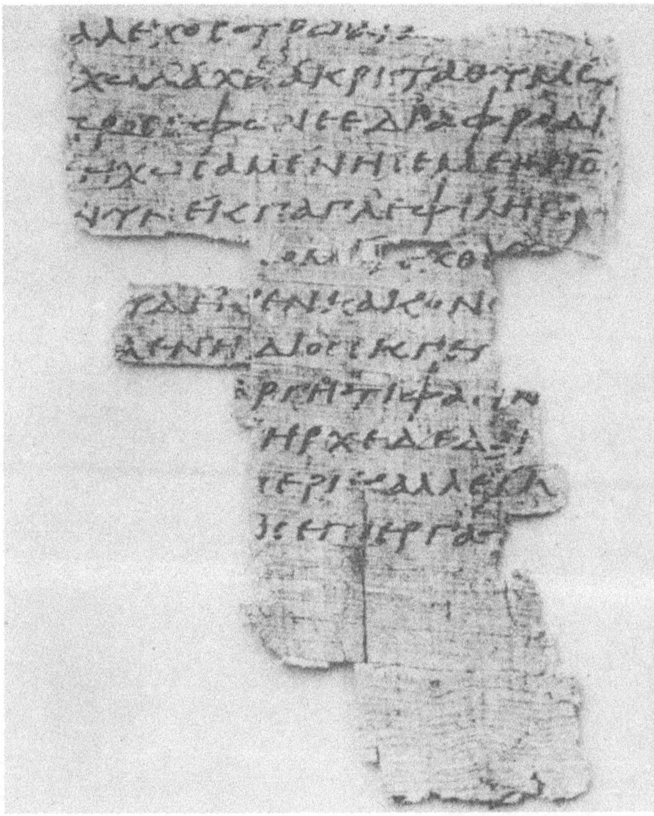

B

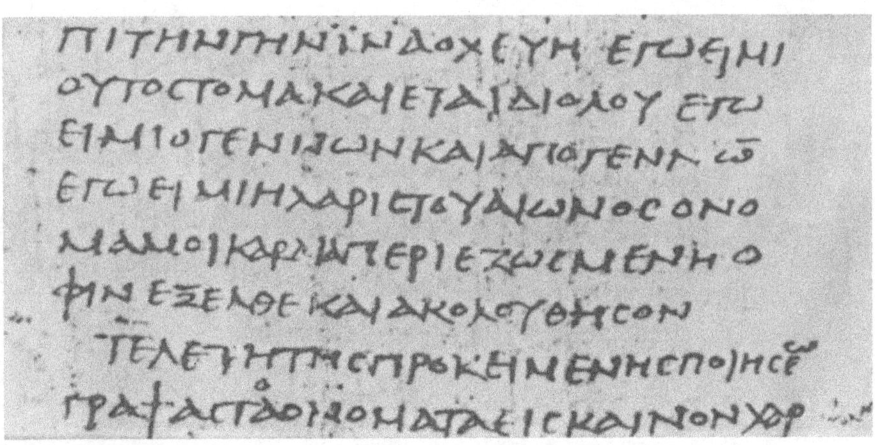

The letters were found at Harît in the Fayûm. The MS of the Iliad, which was torn up to use for correspondence, must have been materially older. The writing is the characteristic sloping uncial, which we have been discussing, and is even more noteworthy since it has heavy ornamental dots on the letters *γ χ υ* and rarely *τ* as in hand *a* of W. Also the *ξ* and *ω* have similar, decidedly early forms. Heavy ornamental dots are no more a mark of late date than the sloping hand. Both are early, if not frequently combined. Cf. Ox. Pap. nos. 844, 406, and 447. For early sloping uncials compare O. P. 23, 26, 403, 655, 223, 232; Rylands Libr. Gr. Pap. 57; Berlin. Klassikertexte, vol. 5, Plate ii; vol. 3, Plate i. Uncials with ornamental dots are fairly common and early; cf. O. P. 25, 20, 661; Rylands, Gr. Pap. 20, 16, 44, 51, 55; Berlin. Klassikertexte, vol. 5, no. 46 D, Taf. i.

In determining the date of W most of the evidence thus seems to point to the fourth century, though the beginning of the fifth must still be admitted as a possibility. The first quire of John is slightly older than the rest of the MS. The two parts can not be separated far in date, for most of the peculiarities of hand *a* appear infrequently in the rest of the MS. Enlarged letters, punctuation, and ornamental dots are more frequent in hand *a*, but occur throughout the MS. On the other hand, the slope of hand *a* is less pronounced and the presence of old forms of *μ ξ* and *ω* is more regular than in the rest of the MS. The peculiarities of text, absence of titles by first hand, and the presence in one case of the shorter subscription, *κατα ιωαννην*, point to an early date. The patchwork character of the parent MS plainly indicates origin in a time when Biblical MSS came near extinction in certain regions at least. As the last great persecution, in which we are expressly told that the sacred books were ordered destroyed, was begun by Diocletian in 303, we are probably justified in dating the parent of W soon after that date. Just how complete a MS of the gospels was gathered for that parent and how much the scribe of W had to add from other MSS we can not determine. Certainly some one had to send to North Africa for the beginning of Mark, and the Hesychian recension, which should have been the favorite one in Egypt at this time, seems to have been in large part inaccessible. Matthew and the later part of Luke, which are of the Antioch recension, were quite probably added by the scribe of W to fill the gaps in the more ancient MS, which he was copying.

VI. THE TEXT OF W AND THE EARLY CHURCH FATHERS

INDIVIDUAL agreements are often more instructive than mere numbers when many authorities support. For this reason the following brief lists of readings are repeated, in which W finds almost its only support in the early church fathers.

1. W AND CLEMENT OF ALEXANDRIA

Matthew 5, 21 *φονευσης* for *φονευσεις* (Strom. 7, 60, 4); 6, 20 − *ουδε κλεπτουσιν*[1]; 25, 35 (*φαγειν*) + *και* (also in Ps. Nil.); Mark 10, 27 − *παρα* (3); Luke 18, 29 the inverted order *υμιν λεγω* (Clement combined with Mark 10, 29); John 2, 20 *ο ναος ουτος οικοδομηθη* (inverted order).

Of these the last is by far the most noteworthy, for the Arabic Diatessaron also agrees. As this is not the normal Arabic order the agreement can not be accidental. Furthermore the citation in Clement is literal and three verses long (cf. Stahlin's edit. vol. 3, p. 219). It seems almost equally inconceivable that any one of these three authorities should have copied from one of the others. Furthermore the change in order was not called for by Syriac, but rather suggests Latin influence. The Diatessaron can not have originated the change but all drew eventually from the same source. As the transposition is entirely possible in Greek, though not called for by a rigid rule of order, I do not venture to refer the change to a bilingual MS.

2. W AND ORIGEN

Matthew 10, 21 *τεκνα* for *τεκνον*; 16, 13 *λεγουσιν με* (inverted order); 19, 24 *εισελθειν δια τρυπηματος ραφιδος* (order change, Chr agrees); 21, 9 − *οι* (3); 22, 6 − *αυτου* (Ir and Eus also omit); 24, 14 − *πασιν* (Chr agrees); 24, 20 *υμων η φυγη* (a Coptic order also found in Eus); 26, 23 *εκεινος* for *ουτος*; 27, 11 − *ο ηγεμων*;

[1] *Quis dives salvetur*, 13; Strom. 3, 12, 86; 3, 6, 56 support; Strom. 4, 6, 33, supported by Protr. 10, 93; 105; Paed. 3, 6, 34, does not omit.

Mark 4, 12 − ακουωσιν; 8, 38 − ταυτη; 11, 10 ειρηνη for ωσαννα; 12, 25 + οι; 12, 26 − ο (2 3 4); 14, 30 αρνηση for απαρνηση;

Luke 4, 40 ηγον for ηγαγον; 7, 33 + ο before ιωαννης; 19, 37 απανταν for απαν; 22, 15 − με;

John 5, 26 τω υιω ζωην εδωκεν (change of order); 12, 35 λαβη for καταληβη; 17, 3 − σε and απεστιλεν for απεστειλας (also in Epiph); 18, 36 ην before εκ;

John 1, 23 ($\overline{κυ}$) + ευθιας ποιειτε τας τριβους αυτου (also in Ambr); 2, 17 + οτι (also Epiph); 3, 2 τα σημια ταυτα (order change); 4, 27 (μεντοι) + γε; 4, 45 + τοις before ιεροσολυμοις.

The length and striking character of this list is impressive enough without further comment, but a word should perhaps be added on Luke 19, 37. The variant απανταν involves not only a mistake in gender but a transfer in declension of a well-known word. Such an error would probably not arise twice independently and certainly not in the same passage. Neither could it long survive in any text tradition, for almost any scribe or reader would know enough Greek to correct it. Koetschau, Texte u. Unter. vol. 28, pt. 2, p. 26, assures us that this is the reading of the best MS of Origen, John Comm. 10, 21, 127, though the error has been silently corrected by the editors. The passage of Origen is a literal citation covering twelve verses, and the variations from W are practically all due to the Antioch corrections inserted in the W text. The parent before correction must have been very closely related to the MS used by Origen or his secretary.

3. W and Other Early Fathers

Matthew 7, 25 προσεκρουσαν for προσεπεσον = Philo; 8, 27 + ο ανθρωπος = Hil Chr Thdrt; 8, 29 εκραζον for εκραξαν = Bas Macar Epiph; 10, 14 των λογων (man 1) = Chr; 10, 17 − αυτων = Hil; 12, 21 επι for εν = Eus Chr; 12, 48 − εισιν = Aug Ambr; 15, 19 πορνιαι μοιχιαι φονοι (order change) = Cyr; 15, 32 − αυτου = Hil Chr; 18, 4 γαρ for ουν = Aphraates; 19, 8 − υμιν (man 1) = Chr; 19, 30 + εσονται = Pistis Sophia; 24, 31 + τοτε = Chr; 27, 6 εστιν for εξεστι = Eus;

Mark 1, 11 του ουρανου for των ουρανων = Epiph; 1, 15 των ουρανων for του θεου = Justin; 2, 26 εισελθων for εισηλθεν ··· και = Hier; 3, 33 − μου = Ambr; 12, 35 − ο before $\overline{χς}$ = Barnabas;

Luke 1, 35 διοτι for διο = Ir; 8, 17 − γαρ = Aug Hier; 8, 32 − εκει = Basil-Seleuc; 9, 31 + τη before δοξη = Epiph; 9, 59 − πρωτον = Thdrt; 13, 24 − λεγω υμιν = Faust-Man; 16, 31 απελθη for αναστη = Dial. c. Marc.; 18, 42 − αυτω = Adamant;

John 5, 18 αποκτειναι οι ιουδαιοι (order change) = Ambr Epiph; 5, 19 ο for α = Epiph; 6, 2 θεωρουντες for οτι εωρων = Chr Nonn; 6, 44 + προς με = Hil Hier Vig-Tap; 6, 58 ζηση for ζησεται = Chr; 6, 62 ειδηται for θεωρητε = Chr Epiph Eus Thdrt; 7, 17 ποιη for θελη·· ποιειν = Chr Cyr; 8, 28 − ο πατηρ = Tert Eus; 8, 42 + ουκ = Chr Athan; 9, 22 συνεθεντο for συνετεθειντο = Cyr Thphil; 10, 31 − οι ιουδαιοι = Athan; 11, 26 − εις εμε = Nonn; 11, 43 εκραξεν for εκραυγασε = Chr; 12, 42 πολλοι των αρχοντων for εκ τ·αρ·πολ = Chr; 12, 47 + μη = Chr Aug; 14, 20 − εν = Hil Vict; 20, 29 ειδοτες for ιδοντες = Chr;

John 1, 1 + ο before $\overline{\theta\varsigma}$ = Nyss; 1, 18 + ημιν = Adamant; 2, 12 − εκει = Chron-Alex; 4, 45 − αυτοι = Cyr Chr; 4, 54 εποιησεν σημιον (order change) = Chr.

In the above list there are 17 agreements with Chrysostom, who thus ranks next to Origen in nearness to the text of W; yet it must be noted that none of these agreements come in Mark or Luke. The agreements with Hilarius, Epiphanius, Cyril, and Eusebius are also noteworthy. In general we must conclude that the citations in the early Church Fathers are more apt to represent Biblical texts current in their time, than has been sometimes assumed.

VII. COLLATION

THE collation is based on the Oxford 1880 edition of the Textus Receptus, which is designated as *iuxta exemplar Millianum.* The edition of Mill is a reprint of Stephen 1550. The following table shows the variations of these editions (variations in accent and breathings are not included):

		Oxford 1880	*Mill*	*Stephen 1550*
Matthew	8, 4	αλλ'	αλλα	αλλ'
	9, 3	—	οτι	οτι
	15, 32	τοεις	τρεις	τρεις
	20, 15	η ο οφθ.	η ο cφθ.	ει ο οφθ.
	20, 22	δε ο	δε ο	ο δε
	21, 15	ιδοντες	ιδοντος	ιδοντες
	23, 13–14		has same order of verses	verse 14 before 13
	24, 15	εστως	εστως	εστος
Mark	6, 53	Γεννησαρετ	Γενησαρετ	Γενησαρετ
	10, 32	ηρξατο	ηρξατα	ηρξατο
	11, 22	ο Ιησους	ο Ιησους	Ιησους
	15, 7	γενομενος	λεγομενος	λεγομενος
	15, 29	ουαι	ουαι	ουα
Luke	7, 12	χηρα	χηρα	ην χηρα
	7, 12	ικανος ην	ικανος ην	ικανος
	10, 6	ο υιος	ο υιος	υιος
	13, 15	ακεκριθη	απεκριθη	απεκριθη
	17, 1	μη	μη	του μη
	21, 38	ωρθριζε	ωθριζε	ωρθριζε
	22, 45	μαθητας αυτου	μαθητας	μαθητας
	22, 47	εγγισε	ηγγισε	ηγγισε
	24, 10	Ιακωβου	η Ιακωβου	Ιακωβου
John	3, 23	Σαλεμ	Σαλειμ	Σαλειμ
	8, 4	κατεληφθη	κατεληφθη	κατειληφθη
	8, 39	ειπεν	ειπον	ειπον
	13, 31	—	ουν	—
	18, 16	ον	ος	ος
	19, 7	του θεου	του θεου	θεου

For ease in using the collation each variant is printed in a line by itself; these are distinguished as follows: + for "add"; – for "omit"; < for "transpose to read"; † to call attention to an important variation in spelling; all other variants worthy of any consideration are preceded by the sign *. It has been deemed wise to include minor variations in spelling, mostly itacistic, but there is no distinguishing mark placed before them; they can be easily disregarded by any one not interested. I have omitted the cases of addition of *ν ἐφελκυστικόν*, as it is regularly added; see p. 25 for the rule and exceptions.

The paragraph sign (¶) indicates a paragraph division of the MS. In case a paragraph does not coincide with the beginning of a verse, the first words are given.

Words or letters illegible or missing are inclosed in square brackets. Letters only partially legible are distinguished by a dot placed below.

Abbreviations, punctuations, and apostrophes are given in so far as they occur in the variants, but none besides. Colon and Greek colon are used in the MS; commas are used to represent the punctuation by vacant space. Line ends within the variants are indicated by a light upright line. Variants are printed as they occur in the MS without accents, breathings, or capitals. Word division has been introduced. The extent of longer omissions is sometimes shown by giving the first and last words only.

The different hands are designated by figures or letters on the line following the word *man*. Repeated occurrences of a word in the same paragraph are marked by a numeral placed above and to the right. All erasures and corrections, even by the first hand, are given.

The Latin abbreviations are those commonly used or are easily intelligible.

I. SECUNDUM MATTHAEUM

Inscr ⳩ [ευ]αγγελιον κατα μαθθαιου̣ man 2

CAPUT I

1. † *δα[νε]ιδ|*
2. *εγεννησεν̣ [τον]|*
ιακ̣|ωβ'[1]
ιουδα[ν]|
3. † *εζρωμ* bis
5. *ειεσσαι,*
6. † *δαυειδ'* bis
¶ ante *δαυειδ*[2]
8. *οζειαν,*
9. *οζειας*
εγεννη|σεν[1] (*γ* sup man 2)
10. † *μανασης*
11. *|[ι]εχο̣[νι]αν*
|[ε]π̣ι
12. ¶ 13. *ελιακιμ'* bis
14. † *σαδδωκ'* bis
† *αχειν* bis
17. † *δαυειδ'* bis
ι̅δ̅| pro *δεκατεσσαρες* bis
|κα[ι][2]
18. — *χριστου*
* *γενεσεις* pro *γεννησις*
¶ ante *μνηστευθεισης*
19. *παραδιγματισαι|*
20. ¶ *[ι]δο̣[υ]|*
< *εφανη κατ οναρ*
† *δαυειδ'*
21. *καλεσις|*
22. — *του* ante *κ̅υ̅*
24. ¶

CAPUT II

1. ¶ † *ιερουσαλημ'|* pro *ιεροσολυμα*
2. *ιδομεν*
|[κα]ι
3. *|[ακο]υ̣σας*
4. *γραμματις*
5. *ουτως*
6. * *τη* pro *γη*
ελαχειστη
7. ¶ 8. *ευρηται|*
απαγγειλαται
11. *οικειαν*
* *ιδον* pro *ευρον*
† *ζμυρναν,* pro *σμυρναν* man 1, corr man 2 (*σ* sup *ζ*)
13. < *τω ιωσηφ κατ οναρ|*
εισθει
15. — *του* ante *κ̅υ̅*
16. ¶ *ενεπεχθη*
* *γαμων* pro *μαγων*[1]
αποστιλας
17. * *δια* pro *υπο*
† *ιηρεμιου*
— *του προφητου* man 1, ·/. sup et in marg *του προφητου* man 2
18. † *|κλαθμος*
|κλεουσα
19. ¶ 22. ¶ < *του πατρος αυ|του ηρωδου*
23. † *ναζαρεθ,*
ναζωρεος

CAPUT III

1. ¶ *παραγει|νεται*
2. *μετανοειται·*
ηγγεικε̄|

3. * δια pro υπο

ποιειται

4. < ην αυτου

με|λει

5. † κα pro και^{2}

6. + παταμω| post ιορδανη

7. ¶ |σαδδουκεων

8. * καρπον| αξιον pro καρπους αξιους

9. δοξη|ται

εγειρε

10. — και^{1}

11. < υμας βαπτιζω

12. πτοιον pro πτυον

\+ αυτου post αποθηκην

† ασβεστω·| ($σ^{1}$ sup man 2 ?)

13. παραγεινεται

14. χριαν

15. ¶ † δικαιωσυνην·|

16. < ευθυς ανεβη

ιδεν pro ειδε

17. * του ουρανου pro των ουρανων

† ηυδοκησα·|

Caput IV

1. πιρασθηναι

2. |επινασεν,

3. < ο πειρα|ζων ειπεν αυτω,

4. + ο ante ανθρωπος

6. * ειπεν pro λεγει

8. δικνυ|σιν

9. < σοι παντα

10. λατρευσις,

13. † ναζαρεθ'

† |παραθαλασσαν

|νεφθαλιμ'

15. — γη^{2}

νεφθαλιμ',

16. * τη σκοτια pro σκοτει

< φως ειδεν

ανετιλεν

17. ¶ κηρυσσιν

ηγγεικεν

18. ¶ — ο ιησους

20. + αυτων,| post δικτυα

21–22. — και προβας εκειθεν ···· ηκολουθησαν αυτω

23. ¶ 24. ποι|κειλαις

Caput V

1. καθεισαντος

6. πινωντες|

† δικαιοσυνην| man 1, ω sup ο scr man 2

7. ¶ 9. ¶ 10. δικαιωσυνης

11. ¶ εσται

ονιδισωσιν

* διωξουσιν, pro διωξωσι

12. χαιρεται

αγαλλιασθαι·|

|ουτως

13. εσται

† αλα pro αλας bis

— ετι

καταπατισθαι

14. εσται

15. οικεια·

16. ουτως

17. νομισηται

18. ¶ 19. ουτως

— ος δ' αν ποιηση ···· βασιλεια των ουρανων

20. ¶ < |υμων η δικαιοσυνη

† πλεον pro πλειον

εισελθη|ται

21. * |φονευσης, pro φονευσεις

22. † ραχα

† δα pro δ' αν^{2}

23. ¶ 24. διαλλα|γηθει

25. < |μετ αυτου εν τη οδω,
26. * ου pro αν
27. – τοις αρχαιοις
28. * αυτην pro αυτης
29. ¶ + την ante γεενναν,|
30. * |κοψον pro εκκοψον
31. † εαν pro αν
32. * πας ο απολυων| pro ος αν απολυση
|πορνιας
* μοιχευθηναι| pro μοιχασθαι
μοι|χατε,
33. † απο|δωσης
– δε
36. † τρι|χαν
< ποιησαι η μελαναν· (sic)
39. ¶ 39. * ραπιζει εις pro ραπισει επι
– σου
40. χει|τωνα
41. † ανγαρευση
42. * δος, pro διδου
δα|νισασθαι
43. αγαπησις
† μισησης
44. † του εχθρους|
ευλογειται
ποιειται
* τοις μι|σουσιν pro τους μισουντας
– και[1]
προσευχεσθαι
45. γενησθαι
46. ¶ αγαπησηται
εχεται,
47. ασπασησθαι
* φιλους pro αδελφους
ποιειται,
* το αυτο pro ουτω
48. |εσεσθαι
τελιοι
* ουρανιος pro εν τοις ουρανοις
τελιος

Caput VI

1. εχεται
2. υ|ποκριτε
4. αποδωσι
5. πλατιων
6. † |ταμιον pro ταμιειον
κλισας
προσευξε
† αποδωση
7. * βατταλογειται pro βαττολογησητε
– οτι man 1, add sup man 2
8. ομοιω|θηται
εχεται
9. προσευχεσθαι|
10. † ελθατω
– της
12. οφιληματα
† αφιομεν
οφιλεταις|
13. δυναμεις
14. αφηται
† αυτων, in ras man 1 (υτων prim scr)
15. αφηται
16. νηστευηται
γινεσθαι
17. |αλιψε
νιψε
18. + αυτος post κρυπτω[2]
αποδωσι
– εν τω φανερω
19. ¶ θησαυριζεται
20. θησαυριζεται

† ουτε[1]| (τε in ras man 1; ουδε prim scr)
— ουδε κλεπτουσιν
22. < η ο οφθαλμος σου απλους|
φωτινον
23. < η ο οφθαλμος σου πονηρος·|
σκοτινον
< εστιν σκοτος|
24. μεισησει
δυνασθαι
† μαμωνα,
25. μεριμναται|
φαγηται
* η pro και[1]
πιηται|
ενδυ|σησθαι,
26. πετινα
σπιρουσιν
† ουχει| pro ουχ
διαφερεται
27. ¶ ηλικειαν
28. |μεριμναται· καταμαθεται
29. — οτι
30. + εν αγρω post σημερον|
κλειβα|νον
31. μεριμνησηται|
32. χρηζεται|
33. |ζητειται
† δικαιωσυνην
34. ¶ μεριμνησηται
— τα ante εαυτης·|
κακεια

Caput VII

1. κρινεται
κριθηται,
2. κρινεται
κριθησεσθαι,
μετριται
* μετρηθησεται| pro αντιμετρηθησεται
3. ¶ 6. |βαληται
* κα|ταπατησουσιν pro καταπατησωσιν
7. αιτιτε
ευρησεται,
κρου|εται
ανυγησεται
8. * αιτων pro ζητων man 1 (αι del et ζη superscr man 2)
9. † ε|πιδωση
10. † αιτη|σει
12. † εαν pro αν
θεληται
ουτως
ποι|ειται
13. † |εισελθατε
|πλατια
14. * τι pro οτι
ολει|γοι
15. |προσεχεται
16. επιγνωσεσθαι
¶ ante μητι
17. |ουτως
— αγαθον man 1 (·/. sup et in marg ·/. αγαθον scr man 2)
20. επιγνωσεσθ(αι)|
21. ¶ + αυτος εισελευσεται| εις την βασιλειαν των ουρανων,|post ουρανοις,
22. † επροφη|τευσαμεν,
23. αποχωριται|
24. ¶ < αυτου την οικιαν
25. * προσεκρουσαν pro προσεπεσον
οικεια
26. < αυτου την οικειαν

27. οικεια
28. ¶ * ετελεσεν pro συνετελεσεν
29. + αυτων κ(αι) οι φαρισαιοι·| post γραμματεις

Caput VIII

1. ¶ * |καταβαντος δε αυτου pro καταβαντι δε αυτω
3. εκτινας
4. ¶ † αλ|λα
διξον
† |μωυσης
5. ¶ * αυτω pro τω ιησου
† εκατονταρχης
6. οικεια
|δινως
7. ¶ 8. ιμει pro ειμι
* λογω pro λογον
9. ειμει
10. ¶ * παρ ου|δενι pro ουδε
< τοσαυτην πιστιν εν τω ισραηλ'
11. ¶ ανακλειθη|σονται
13. ¶ † εκατονταρχη
— και[2]
* ἡμερα pro ωρα
14. ¶ οικειαν
15. διηκονι
* αυτω·| pro αυτοις
16. ¶ |οψειας
† γονομενης pro γενομενης
$\overline{\text{πντα}}$ (prim scr πν(α) et corr man 1)
17. + οτι post λεγοντος·
ασθενιας
18. ¶ * οχλον πολυν pro πολλους οχλους
19. † |αν pro εαν
20. ¶ φωλαι|ους
πετινα

κλεινη·|
22. ¶ 23. ενβαντι
24. σισμος
26. ¶ εσται
27. ¶ + ο $\overline{\text{ανος}}$ post ουτος
< αυτω υπακουουσῑ·|
28. ¶ — εις την χωραν
μνημιων
29. * εκραζον pro εκραξαν
+ απολεσαι| ημας και post ωδε
— ημας
30. * βοσκομενων, pro βοσκομενη
32. υπαγεται,|
— των χοιρων[2]
33. † απηγγειλō|
34. * ινα pro οπως

Caput IX

1. ¶ ενβας
* ιουδαιαν pro ιδιαν
2. κλεινης
— σοι
< σου αι αμαρτιαι,|
3. ¶ 4. ¶ ενθυμισθαι
5. αφαιων|ται
* σου pro σοι
εγειρε|
6. ειδηται
< αφιεναι| επι της γης
κλεινην
8. ¶ * εφοβηθησαν pro εθαυμασαν
9. ¶ * μαθ|θεον καλουμενον, pro ματθαιον λεγομενον
10. ¶ οικεια,
< τελωναι πολλοι|
συνανε|κιντο
11. * ελεγον pro ειπον

12. ¶ † αλλα
13. μαθε|ται
< δικαιους καλεσαι
† αλλα|
— εις μετανοιαν
14. ¶ 15. ¶ * νηστευειν pro πενθειν
* αφερε|θη pro απαρθη
16. ¶ † |αγναφους (σ sup man 2) pro αγναφου
ερει pro αιρει
γεινεται,|
17. * αμφο|τεροι pro αμφοτερα
18. ¶ * εισελθων pro ελθων
20. ¶ † αιμοροουσα
22. ¶ * θυγατηρ pro θυγατερ
23. ¶ οικειαν
24. |αναχωρειται
|κατεγε|λουν pro κατεγελων
25. ¶ 27. ¶ < τω ῑῡ εκειθεν
* υιος δαυ|ειδ', pro υιε δαβιδ
28. οικειαν|
¶ ante και λεγει
πιστευεται
32. ¶ 34. ¶ — εν
35. ¶ — εν τω λαω
36. * εσκυλ|μενοι pro εκλελυμενοι
37. ¶ εργατε
ολειγοι|
38. |δεηθηται

Caput X

1. εκβαλλιν
|μαλακειαν,
2. ¶ ζεβαιδεου,
3. † ματ'θαιος|
5. ¶ * εξαπεστιλεν| pro απεστειλεν
απελθηται·
σαμάριτων
εισελθηται·|
6. πορευεσθαι
7. κηρυσσεται
ηγγεικεν
8. θεραπευεται,
|καθαριζεται,
< δαιμονια εκβαλλε|ται, νεκρους εγειρεται,
δωραιαν bis
|ελαβεται
δοται,|
9. κτησησθαι
10. * ραβδους| pro ραβδον
11. |εισελθηται
μειναται
εξελ|θηται
12. οικει|αν
ασπασασθαι
+ λεγοντες,| ειρηνη τω οικω τουτω, post αυτην
13. οικεια
† ελθατω
* εφ pro προς
14. † αν pro εαν
* των λογων pro τους λογους (corr sup man 2 — ους — ους)
οικειας
|εκτιναξαται
15. ¶ † γομορων
16. ¶ γινεσθαι
17. προσεχεται
* παραδωσωσιν pro παραδωσουσι
— αυτων
18. αχθησεσθ(αι)|
19. ¶ * παραδωσουσιν pro παραδιδωσιν
με|ριμνησηται

λαλησηται,|
* λαλησηται, pro λαλησετε
20. εσται|
21. * τεκνα, pro τεκνον
22. εσεσθαι
— ουτος
23. ¶ φευγεται
* ετεραν,| pro αλλην
τελεσηται|
24. + αυτου, post διδασκα|λον
25. * επε|καλεσαν pro εκαλεσαν
οικεια|κους
26. φοβηθηται
27. |σκοτεια
ακουεται
κηρυξαται
28. φοβηθηται[1]
* αποκτεννοντων pro αποκτεινοντων
αποκτιναι·|
* φοβεισθαι pro φοβηθητε[2]
+ την ante ψυχην[2]
+ το ante σωμα[2]
31. * φοβεισθαι αυτους pro φοβηθητε
διαφερεται
33. + και ante οστις
— δ' αν
< καγω αυτον
34. νομεισηται
βαλιν bis
36. οικειακοι
40. † αποστι|λοντα
41. † λημψεται, bis

Caput XI

1. ¶ |κηρυσσιν
2. * δια| pro δυο
4. † ιωαννει
ακουεται
βλε|πεται
5. + |και ante νεκροι
7. † εξηλθα|τε
8. † εξηλθατε ειδειν
9. * εξεληλυθατε pro εξηλθετε
< προφητην ιδειν,|
11. ¶ † γε|νητοις
* μιζον pro μειζων
μεικροτερος|
μιζω̅|
< εστιν αυτου,|
12. ¶ 14. θελεται
16. ¶ * παιδιοις pro παιδαριοις
< καθημενοις εν| αγοραις·
† ετε|ροις
17. † ηυλησομε̅|
ωρχησασθαι,
* εκλαυσασθαι,| pro εκοψασθε
19. * εργων pro τεκνων
20. ¶ + ο ι̅ς̅ post ηρξατο
ονιδιζειν
21. χοραζειν,
βηθ' σαιδα̅|
† σιδονι
22. † |σιδονει,
23. * μη pro η
— του
* |υψωθηση, pro υψωθεισα
* καταβηση,| pro καταβιβασθηση
† εμεινον
25. ¶ 26. < ευδοκεια εγενετο
27. † επιγιγνωσκει bis
* βουλεται pro βουληται
28. ¶ 29. μαθεται
|ειμει
ταπινος
ευρη|σεται

Caput XII

1. + ε̅| ante τοις σαββασιν
επινασαν
τιλλιν
+ τους ante σταχυας
3. ανεγνωται
† δαυειδ',
επινασεν
− αυτος
4. * ως pro πως
* ο pro ους
5. ανεγνωται
+ εν| ante τοις
6. † |μιζον
8. − και
10. * |χειραν pro ην την χειρα
* θεραπευσαι pro θεραπευειν
* κατηγορησουσιν| pro κατηγορησωσιν
11. ενπεση
12. * ου pro ουν
13. |εκτινον
εξετινε̅|
† απεκατεσταθη
14. ¶ − εξελθοντες
15. + δε| ους εθεραπευσεν επεπληξεν αυτοις| post ,παντας
18. † ηυδοκη|σεν
19. πλατιαις
20. + μη post ου[1]
21. * επι pro εν
22. ¶ < κωφον και τυ|φλον
− και ante λαλιν
24. ¶ 25. ¶ |ιδως
οικεια
27. < κριται| εσονται αυτοι υμων,|
28. < εν πν̅ι̅ θ̅υ̅ εγω
29. οικειαν[1]
* αρπασαι, pro διαρπασαι
* διαρπαση, pro διαρπασει
31. ¶ * |η δε του πν̅ς̅ βλασφημια ουκ αφε| in ras man 1
32. † εαν pro αν[1]
33. ¶ * ποιησηται pro ποιησατε[1]
34. αιχιδνων
δυνασθ(αι)|
λαλιν
† περισευματος
35. − της καρδιας
− τα ante αγαθα,
36. ¶ * αποδω|σωσιν pro αποδωσουσι
38. φαρι|σεων
σημιον
39. ¶ σημιον ter
40. τρις quater
+ και post εσται
41. ¶ νινευειται
πλιον
42. † σολομωνος bis
πλιον
45. γεινεται
46. ¶ ι|στηκεισαν
* εξω in ras man 1
48. ¶ − τω ειποντι αυτω
* η pro και
− εισιν
49. εκτινας
50. † κα pro και[2]

Caput XIII

1. ¶ οικειας
2. − το ante |πλοιον
ενβαντα
εγειαλον ιστηκει,|
3. * σπειραι| pro σπειρειν
4. σπιρειν
5. εξα|νετιλεν

6. ανατιλαντος
8. * επεσαν pro επεσεν
10. ¶ 11. ¶ 14. — επ
προφητια
* ακουσητε pro ακουσετε
* βλεψηται pro βλεψετε
15. * |επιστρεψουσιν pro επιστρεψωσι
* ιασομαι pro ιασωμαι
16. ¶ 17. ειδειν
βλεπεται,
ακουεται,
18. ακουσαται
† σπειραντος
19. * σπει|ρομενον pro εσπαρμενον
σπαρις|
20. + μου post λογον
+ και post |ευθυς
22. ¶ + μου post λογον[1]
συνπνι|γει
γεινεται|
23. ¶ + μου post λογον
καρποφορι
24. ¶ † ομοιωθη
σπειραν|τι
26. — και[2]
27. † εσπειρες
— τα
28. ¶ ante οι δε δουλοι
συνλεξωμεν
29. εκριζωσηται
30. † μεχρις
— τω ante καιρω
συναγαγεται
31. ¶ 32. μεικροτερον
μιζον
γεινεται
πετινα
33. ¶ 34. * ουδεν pro ουκ
ελαλι
36. |οικειαν
37. ¶ σπιρω̄|
38. * εισῑ|[2] in ras man 1 (εστῑ prim scr)
40. * καιεται pro κατακαιεται
41. + |και ante αποστελει
42. † κλα|θμος
44. ¶ 45. ¶ μαργαρειτας,
46. † πο|λυτιμιον
48. |εγιαλον
καθεισαντες
αγγια,
49. |συντελια
50. † κλαθμος
51. ¶ 52. * τη βασιλεια pro εις την βασιλειαν
* εκβαλει pro εκβαλλει
54. † εκπλησσεσθαι|
+ ταυτα, και τις post τουτω|
55. † ουχ' pro ουχι
56. < παντα ταυτα
57. * επ pro εν[1]
¶ ante ο δε ις̄
οικεια

Caput XIV

1. ¶ 2. εστι
3. ¶ † ηρωιαδα
6. ¶ — της
7. < δου|ναι αυτη
8. + ειπεν, post |αυτης
πινακει
11. πι|νακει
12. ¶ 14. ιδεν
* αυτοις, pro αυτους
18. φερεται
19. * του χορτον, pro τους χορτους
† ηυλογη|σεν,

21. — ωσει
|πεντακισχειλιοι
22. ¶ — ο ιησους
— αυτου
|ενβηναι
23. ειδιαν|
οψειας
24. * βασανιζομε|νον (βασα in ras man 2)
25. * ουν pro δε
— ο ιησους
* την θαλασσαν, pro της θαλασσης
27. θαρσειται
|ειμει
φοβισθαι,|
28. ¶ < ελθειν προς σε|
30. + σφοδρα post ισχυρον
+ ελθει̅| post εψυβηθη
31. εκτινας
32. ενβαν|των
34. * επι pro εις
+ εις ante γεννησαρετ'|
35. † απεστιλον|
36. † διελωθησαν·| pro διεσωθησαν

Caput XV

1. ¶ γραμματις
2. * εσ|θιουσιν,| pro εσθιωσιν
3. ¶ παραβαινεται
4. ενετιλατο
+ σου| post μητερα[1]
5. λεγεται|
† εαν pro αν
† αν pro εαν
† |τιμησει
8. * τοις χειλεσιν με τιμα man 2; om man 1, spatio tamen relicto
10. ¶ ακουεται
συνιεται,
12. ¶ 13. φυτια
14. |αφεται
* εμ|πεσουνται,| pro πεσουνται
15. ¶ 16. ¶ εσται,
17. νοειται,
18. * εξερχεται man 1, corr man 2 εξερχονται (ν sup)
18–19. — κακεινα κοινοι τον ανθρωπον. εκ γαρ της καρδιας εξερχονται
19. < πορνιαι, μοιχι|αι, φονοι, κλοπαι,
22. * υιος |δαυειδ', pro υιε δαβιδ
23. * εμ|προσθεν pro οπισθεν
24. ¶ 25. * προσεκυνησεν pro προσεκυνει
26. ¶ 28. ¶ 29. ¶
30. < κωφους, χωλους| τυφλους, κυλλους,
31. + και post |υγιεις,
32. ¶ — αυτου
σπλαγχνιζομε
* ημεραι τρις pro ημερας τοεις (error edit Oxon)
* φαγειν·| pro φαγωσι
νηστις
34. ¶ εχετ(αι)|
35. αναπεσι̅|
38. τετρακισχειλιοι
39. * ανεβη pro ενεβη
† μα|γδαλαν,

Caput XVI

1. σαδδουκεοι
σημιον
2. λεγεται
2–3. — πυρραζει γαρ ο ουρανος.

και πρωι, σημερον χειμων
3. πυρα|ζει
— υποκριται
† γιγνωσκε|ται
σημια
+ δοκιμασαι,| post δυνασθαι
4. σημιον ter
6. ¶ σαδδουκεων,
8. — αυτοις
διαλογιζεσθαι
ελαβεται,
9. † ουτε pro ουδε
μνημονευεται
πεντακισχειλιων,|
ελαβεται,
10. τετρακισ|χειλιων,
ελαβεται|
11. νοειται
σαδδουκεων,|
12. † αλλα|
|σαδδουκεων·|
13. ¶ * |εξελθων pro ελθων
κεσαριας|
< λεγουσιν με
14. — οι μεν
15. λεγεται
17. ¶ 19. † κλειδας pro κλεις
† αν pro εαν[1]
20. ¶ διεστιλατο
21. δικνυ|ειν
δι pro δει
22. ειλε|ως
23. φρονις
24. ¶ * εαυτον, (ε sup man 2)
ακολουθιτω
25. † |απολεσει[2] man 2 corr ex
απολεση man 1
27. † αποδωση pro αποδωσει
28. ¶ — των
* εστω|τες pro εστηκοτων

Caput XVII

3. † μωυσης|
< συνλαλουντες μετ αυτου·|
4. — ο ante πετρος
— ει
τρις
< και ηλια μιαν, και μωυσι μιᾱ|
5. φω|τινη
† |ηυδοκησα
ακουεται,|
6. † επεσαν|
7. εγερθηται
φοβεισθαι,
8. — αυτων
— τον
9. καταβενοντων
— αυτων
* εκ| pro απο
ενετιλατο
ειπηται
< αναστη εκ νεκρων|
10. — αυτου
γραμματις|
11. — ιησους
— αυτοις
— πρωτον
12. † αλλα
— εν
ουτως
14. ¶ * |αυτον pro αυτω[2]
15. — πολλακις[2]
17. ¶ φερεται
19. ¶ * διατι ημεις (ιη in ras man 1; υμεις prim scr)
20. |εχηται
ερειται
ορι
μεταβηθει|

21. *νηστια·*|

24. † *καφαρναουμ'*|
   * *το διδραγμα* pro *τα διδραχμα* bis
   * *ουτε* pro *ου τελει*

25. + *ο* $\overline{ις}$ post *εισηλθεν* man 1, tamen delent man 1 et 2
   οικειαν

27. — *την*
   * *αναβαινοντα* pro *αναβαντα*

Caput XVIII

1. ¶ *μιζων*

3. *στρα|φηται*
   * *γενεσθαι* pro *γενησθε*
   εισελθηται

4. * *γαρ* pro *ουν*
   † *ταπινω|σει* pro *ταπεινωση*
   μιζων
   * *εν τη βασιλ* in ras man 1 (*του ουρα* prim scr)

5. * *τοιουτο* pro *τοιουτον*

6. * *εις* pro *επι*

7. < *εκεινω ουαι τω* $\overline{ανω}$|

8. — *εισελθειν*

10. ¶ |*οραται*
   καταφρονησηται

12. *ουχει*|
   † *ενενηκονταεννεα*

13. † *ενενηκονταεννεα*

15. ¶ * *αμαρτη* pro *αμαρτηση*
   * *ελεγξε* pro *ελεγξον*

17. — *ο* ante *εθνικος*

18. ¶ *δησηται*
   λυσηται

19. ¶ + *δε* post |*παλιν*
   < *υμιν λεγω,*
   * *ο* pro *ου*

20. *τρις*
   ειμει

21. ¶ *ποσακεις*
   † *αμαρτηση* pro *αμαρτησει*
   ε|πτακεις·|

22. ¶ 23. ¶ *συναρε*

24. *συνε|ρειν*
   οφιλετης|

27. * *το να|νιον* pro *το δανειον*

28. * |*ει τι* pro *μοι οτι*
   οφιλεις,

30. *οφιλομενον,*|

31. ¶ * *εαυτων* pro *αυτων*

32. ¶ *οφιλην*
   επι pro *ἐπει*

34. *οργεισθεις*
   † *μασα|νισταις* pro *βασανισταις*
   οφιλο|μενον

35. *ουτως*
   |*αφηται*

Caput XIX

1. ¶ * *ιου|δαιας* (*ιου* in ras man 1, *γαλιλαιας* prim scr)

3. — *οι*

4. *α|νεγνωται*

5. *καταλιψει*|
   + *αυτου* post $\overline{μρα}$
   * *κολ|ληθησεται* pro *προσκολληθησεται*
   γυναικει

7. † *μωυσης*
   ενετι|λατο

8. † *μω|υσης*
   < *επετρεψεν υμιν προς την σκληροκαρ|διαν υμων* (*υμιν* sup man 2)
   ουτως,|

9. * αυτου in ras man 1 (υμων prim scr)
— ει
πορνια
— και[1]
μοιχατε, bis
* |γαμων pro γαμησας
11. ¶ 12. ουτως,|
χωριν
13. ¶ 14. + αυτοις post ειπεν
αφεται
κωλυεται
16. < ζωην εχω
18. ¶ ante ο δε ι̅σ̅
— το
φονευσις,
μοιχευ|σις,
ψευδομαρτυρησις·|
19. αγα|πησις
21. τελιος
24. * εισελθει̅| δια τρυπηματος ραφιδος, pro δια τρυπηματος ραφιδος διελθειν
26. — εστι[2]
28. παλινγενεσια,
καθειση
† |καθησεσθαι pro καθισεσθε
† ιστραηλ,
29. * οστις pro ος
|οικειας
† λημψεται
30. + εσονται post εσχατοι[2]

Caput XX

1. πρωει
2. απεστιλεν
3. — την
4. † και εκεινοις| pro κἀκεινοις
υπαγεται
5. † εvατην|
7. υπαγεται
† λημψεσθαι,|
8. |οψειας
10. * πλιο̅| pro πλειονα
† λημψονται
12. * αυτους man 1 (αυτον prim scr et sine ras corr)
13. ετερε
15. * ως θελω pro ο θελω
ειμει,
17. ¶ 19. |ενπεξαι
20. ¶ 21. ¶ + σου post ευωνυμω̅|
22. ¶ αιτισθαι,
δυνασθαι
† πιν pro πιειν
* η pro και
23. πιεσθ(αι)|
|βαπτισθησεσθαι,
καθεισαι
+ τουτο post εμον
25. + αυτοις, post ει|πεν
26. — δε
* εσται pro εστω
27. † αν| pro εαν
< πρωτος ειναι
* εσται pro εστω
30. † δαυειδ',|
31. ¶ μιζον
† δαυειδ',|
32. θελεται
33. † ανεωχθωσιν pro ανοιχθωσιν
34. σπλανχνισθεις

Caput XXI

1. ¶ * ηλθε̅| pro ηλθον
† βηθ'σφαγη
ελεων|

απεστιλεν
2. πορευθηται
ευ|ρησεται
αγαγεται
3. ερειται,
* απο|στελλει pro αποστελει
5. * α pro ο ante βα|σιλευς
6. ¶ 7. * ε|καθεισεν pro επεκαθισεν
8. * αυτω̄| pro εαυτων
– απο των δενδρων
9. – οι^3
† δαυειδ'
10. πολεις
12. – ο
13. σπηλεον
14. < χωλοι και τυφλοι|
15. |ειδοντες
† |δαυειδ' ·
16. ¶ ante ο δε ι̅ς̅
18. * υπαγων pro επαναγων
|επινασεν,
19. * αυτης pro αυτην
* |επ αυτη, pro εν αυτη (εν prim scr man I, corr επ man eadem, vel vice versa)
21. ¶ εχηται
δια|κριθηται,
ποιη|σεται,
* και pro καν
ορι
ειπηται,|
22. † εαν pro αν
αιτη|σηται
† |λημψεσθαι ·|
23. ¶ * προσηλθε̄| pro προσηλθον
24. ειπη|ται
25. ερι

επιστευσαται
26. * ανθρωπου, pro ανθρωπων
27. < υμιν| λεγω
30. * ετερω| pro δευτερω
* απεκριθεις (ει in ras man I η prim scr)
31. ¶ ante λεγει
32. – ουκ man I, add sup man 2
* επιστευσατε (ε^3 corr man I ex ο)
μετεμεληθηται|
* τω pro του
33. – τις
34. ηγγεισεν
|απεστιλεν
35. εδιρᾱ|
απεκτιναν,
36. απεστιλεν
πλιονας
37. απεστιλεν
38. |αποκτινωμεν
39. απεκτιναν,|
41. ¶ * απολει| pro απολεσει
† εκδωσεται| pro εκδοσεται
* αποδωσωσιν| pro αποδωσουσιν
42. ανεγνωται|
43. εθνι

Caput XXII

1. – παλιν
2. † ομοιωθη
3. απε|στιλεν
4. απεστιλεν|
+ μου post σιτι|στα
5. * ος pro ο bis
6. – αυτου
απεκτιναν,
7. * και ακουσας pro ακουσας δε

\+ εκεινος post βασιλευς|
* ωργισθη (ωργισ in ras man 1; υβρισθη prim scr)
9. πορευεσθαι
ευρηται
10. ¶ 12. ετερε
13. εκβαλεται
† κλαθμος|
14. ολειγοι
15. ¶ 17. < κηνσον δουναι
18. * τας πονηριας pro την πονηριαν
πειραζεται
19. επιδιξατε|
20. ϊκων pro εικων
21. ¶ ante τοτε
κεσα|ρος[2] κεσαρι
22. † απηλθαν,| man 1, sup α[2] scr ο man 2
24. † μωυσης
† επι|γαμβρευση
27. — και
28. αναστασι
29. πλανα|σθαι
30. * γαμισκονται, pro εκγαμιζονται
32. ειμει
— ο θεος[4]
37. — τη[1] — τη[2]
38. + η ante πρωτη
\+ |η ante μεγαλη
39. αγαπησις
42–45. † δαυειδ' ter
46. * ωρας pro ημερας

Caput XXIII

1. — ο ante ι̅ς̅
2. † μω|υσεως
εκαθεισαν
γραμμα|τις
3. † εαν| pro αν
τηρειται
ποιειται, bis
4. * δε pro γαρ
κεινησαι
6. διπνοις|
7. ραββει bis
8. κληθηται
ραβ|βει,
< ο καθηγητης υμων,|
— ο χριστος
εσται,
9. καλεσηται
— τοις
10. κλη|θηται
— υμων
11. μιζων
12. ταπινωθησεται,
ταπινω|σει
13. + δε post |ουαι (13 post 14 in Stephen, 1550)
καταισθειεται
οι|κειας
† προφαει pro προφασει
† λημψε|σθαι
14. — δε
γραμματις
κλιεται
εισερχεσθαι
αφιεται
15. ¶ |υποκρειται,
περιαγεται
ποι|ειται
16. ¶ |οφιλει,
17. * τι pro τις
|μιζων
18. οφιλει,
19. μιζον,

21. * κατοικη|σαντι pro κατοικουντι

23. ¶ γραμματις

αποδεκατουνται

\+ δε post ταυτα

25. γραμματις|

καθα|ριζεται

\+ αδικειας,| post ακρασιας

27. γραμματις

παρομοιαζεται|

† κεκονιασμενοις,

ωρεοι,

28. ουτως

φαινεσθαι

εσται

29. γραμμα|τις

οικο|δομειται

κοσμειται

μνημια

30. λεγεται

31. μαρτυριται

εσται|

33. φυγηται

34. ¶ – και[3]

αποκτενιται

|σταυρωσεται,

μαστιγωσεται|

διωξεται

35. † εκχυννο|μενον

36. + οτι post υμιν

< παντα ταυτα|

37. αποκτινου|σα

* λιθοβολησασα pro λιθοβολουσα (ασ in ras man 1; λιθοβολησουσα prim scr)

|ποσακεις

* αυτης pro εαυτης

39. ιδηται

ειπηται|

Caput XXIV

1. ¶ 2. βλεπεται

– ωδε man 1, add sup man 2

– μη[2]

3. + αυτου post μαθηται

σημιον

4. βλεπεται|

5. ει|μει

6. |μελλησεται

θροεισθαι,

7. † επ pro επι[1]

< λοι|μοι και λιμοι

σισμοι

8. <|ταυτα δε παντα

9. ¶ * παραδωσωσιν pro παραδωσουσιν

εσεσθαι

11. * αναστησονται pro εγερθησονται

* υμας, pro πολλους

13. – ουτος

14. – πασι

15. ¶ ιδηται

† εστος pro εστως

† αναγιγνωσκω̄|

17. * τα pro τι

οικειας

18. † κα pro και

20. |προσευχεσθαι

< υμω̄| η φυγη

– εν

21. θλιψέις

* |ουδε pro ουδ' ου

23. πιστευσηται|

24. ση|μια

– μεγαλα man 1; ·/. sup et in marg ·/. μεγαλα man 2

26. |ταμιοις

πιστευσηται,|
29. ¶ 30. ση|μιον
31. + τοτε| post και[1]
— φωνης
32. ¶ μαθεται
* ὁ (sup ο aut littera aut spiritus asper eras)
† εκφυει,
† γιγνωσκεται|
* ευθυς pro εγγυς (υθ in ras man 3, scr man 1 εγ-γυς?)
33. ουτως
ειδηται
< ταυτα παντα,
γινωσκε|ται
36. — της[2]
38. * εκγαμισκω̅|τες, pro εκγαμιζοντες
39. + αν post εως|
41. † μυλω, pro μυλωνι
42. γρηγοριται|
* ημερα, pro ωρα
43. γινωσκεται,
† ηα|σεν pro ειασε
* τον οικον pro την οικιαν
44. γινεσθαι
δοκειται
45. * οικετιας pro θεραπειας
— αυτοις
48. ¶ 49. * τε pro δε
* μεθυστω̅| pro μεθυοντων
51. εστ(αι)|
† κλαθμος

Caput XXV

1. ¶ * ωμοιωθη pro ομοιωθησεται
2. — αι
3. * αυτω̅| pro εαυτων[1]
4. αγ|γιοις
6. εξερχεσθαι
9. * φρονιμοι (sup ο[2] scr α man 2)
* ου μη pro ουκ
|πορευεσθαι
αγορασαται
10. αγορασε
εκλισθη
11. * ηλθον pro ερχονται
13. γρηγορειται
— εν η ο υιος του ανθρωπου ερχεται
14. — γαρ
16. † |ηργασατο pro ειργασατο
19. * τινα pro πολυν
|συνερει
20. — ταλαντα[2]
ει|δε
22. ¶ — λαβων
ειδε|
23. ολειγα
24. * οπου pro οθεν
* ουκ εσκορπισας, pro ου διεσκορπισας
25. ειδε
26. ¶ ηδις
+ εγω α̅ν̅ο̅ς̅ αυστηρος ειμει, post οτι|
27. βαλιν
* τα αργυ|ρια pro το αργυριον
+ τω| ante τοκω
29. — παντι
† πε|ρισευθησεται,
30. |αχριον
* εκβαλετε pro εκβαλλετε
† κλαθμος|
32. < παντα| τα εθνη εμπροσθεν αυτου,

† αφορισει| pro αφοριει

35. |επινασα

+ |και ante εδιψησα

συνηγαγεται

36. |περιεβαλεται

επε|σκεψασθαι

† |ηλθατε

37. ιδομεν

πινωντα

38–39. ιδομεν bis

40. ¶ 41. ¶ * ευωνυμοις, pro ευωνυμων

πορευ|εσθαι

42. επινασα

εποτισαται

43. συνηγαγεται

περιε|βαλεται

επεσκεψασθαι

44. — αυτω

πινωντα

46. * ει pro εις[2]

Caput XXVI

1. ¶ * τους pro τουτους

2. < μεθ ημερας δυο| pro μετα δυο ημερας

γεινεται,

|παραδιδοτε

3. * φα|ρισαιοι, pro γραμματεις

4. < δολω κρατησωσιν|

αποκτινωσιν,|

6. οι|κεια

8. απωλια

9. † |εδυνατο

— το μυρον

10. |παρεχεται

γυναικει,

† ηργασατο pro ειργασατο

11. εχεται bis

14. * |δεκα δυο pro δωδεκα

15. |θελεται

† και εγω pro κἀγω

* παρα|δω pro παραδωσω

16. εζητι|

17. ¶ < λεγοντες τω ι̅υ̅,

— αυτω

+ απελθοντες post θελις|

18. υπαγεται

δινα

* τα pro το ante πασχα

19. * εποιησαν ουν pro και εποιησαν

20. |οψειας

+ μαθητων, post δωδεκα

22. ειμει

23. ¶ * εκει|νος pro ουτος

24. παραδιδοτε,|

25. ¶ ειμει

ραββει,|

¶ ante λεγει

26. — και[1]

* ευχαρι|στησας pro ευλογησας

27. — το

|πιεται

29. † γε|νηματος

30. ελεων,|

31. ¶ σκα̅|δαλισθησεσθαι

35. ¶ απαρνησομε:|

¶ ante ομοιως

+ δε ante και

36. ¶ < ο ι̅ς̅ μετ αυτων

† γεδ᾽σημανι,|

+ αυτου post μαθηταις

καθει|σατε

* αν pro ου

37. ζεβαιδεου

λυπι|σθαι

39. * προσελθων pro προελθων

40. ερχετε
41. |γρηγοριτε
προσευχεσθαι
* εισελ|θητε (λ in ras man ι; ρ prim scr)
42. —το ποτηριον
43. * |ευρεν pro ευρισκει
44. < προσηυξα|το παλιν
45. ¶ καθευδεται
—το
|αναπαυεσθαι,
παραδιδοτε
46. εγειρεσθαι
|ηγγεικεν
47. μαχερων
48. ση|μιον
† εαν pro αν
49. * προσηλ|θεν pro προσελθων
+ και post $\overline{\iota\upsilon}$
ραββει
50. |ετερε
* ο pro ω
¶ ante τοτε
51. αφι|λεν
52. ¶ * αυτοις pro αυτω
* αποθα|νουνται, pro απολουνται
53. παραστησι
|πλιους
54. ουτως|
55. † εξηλ|θατε
56. ¶ ante τοτε
μαθητε
59. < |θανατωσουσιν αυτον, pro αυτον θανατωσωσι
60. + τινες post |δυο
63. ¶ ante και αποκριθεις
+ του ζωντος, post $\overline{\theta\upsilon}^2$|
64. οψεσθαι
65. † |διερηξεν
χριαν
ειδε
67. † εριπισαν pro ερραπισαν
68. πεσας
70. + αυ|των post εμπροσθεν
71. |ιδεν
72. † μεταρορκου pro μεθ' ορκου
73. ¶ 74. * καταθεματιζει̅| pro καταναθεματιζειν
75. φωνη|σε

Caput XXVII

1. |πρωειας
2. η|γεμονει·|
3. ¶ 4. † δε (ε man ι corr ex ι aut η partim scr)
† οψη,
6. * εστιν pro εξεστι
βαλιν
|επι pro επει
9. ¶ † ιηρεμιου
10. * εδωκα pro εδωκαν
11. ¶ — ο ηγεμων
12. κατηγορισθαι
13. ¶ 17. θε|λεται
19. ¶ απε|στιλεν
20. επισα̅|
ετησωνται
21. ¶ θελεται
22. — αυτω
24. ειμει|
οψεσθαι,
27. ¶ στρατιωτε
πρετωριον
σπιραν,
29. * |εθηκαν pro επεθηκαν
ενεπεζον|
31. ενεπεξαν
32. ηνγαρευσα̅|

33. * ο pro ος

* λεγομενον pro λεγομενος

35. ¶ – ινα πληρωθη ···· εβαλον κληρον

39. κει|νουντες

< αυτων τας κεφαλας

40. καταβηθει

41. – δε και

εμπεζοντες

* φαρισαιω pro πρεσβυτερων

42. δυνατε

σωσε|

* πιστευσωμεν pro πιστευσομεν

* επ αυτω| pro αυτω

43. + του ante $\overline{\theta\upsilon}$

44. σπ̄|σταυρωθεντες

† ωνιδιζαν

* αυτō·| pro αυτω^{2}

45. ¶ < εγενετο σκοτος

† ενατης,|

46. † ενατην

* εβοησεν pro ανεβοησεν

* μα pro λαμα

σαβα|χθανει,

† θεε^{1} (ε^{2} sup man 2)

ενκατελειπες,|

47. ¶ * στηκοτων pro εστωτων

49. ειδωμεν

* σωζων pro σωσων

50. <|κραξας παλιν

51. ¶ † απ pro απο

* εσχισθη, pro εσεισθη

52. μνημια

* ανεωχθη, pro ανεωχθησαν

53. μνημιων

54. σισμον

55. – απο^{1}

* διακονησαι man 1, corr man 2 διακονουσαι

56. † ιωσηφ' pro ιωση

ζεβαιδεου,|

57. οψειας

αριμαθεας

58. * |προσελθω pro προσελθων

¶ ante τοτε

60. μνημιω|

* ω pro ο

* μεγα εν pro μεγαν

μνη|μιου

61. * |επι pro απεναντι

63. τρις

64. – νυκτος

65. ¶ πειλατος

εχεται

υπαγεται

ασφαλισασθαι

Caput XXVIII

1. * θεωρουσαι pro θεωρησαι

2. σισμος

* κατεβη pro καταβας

+ και post ουρανου|

4. * |ως pro ωσει

5. – δε

φοβεισθ(αι)

ζητιται|

6. ειδεται

7. οψεσθαι,

8. μνημιου

9. – ως δε επορευοντο απαγγειλαι τοις μαθηταις αυτου

¶ ante και ιδου

|χαιρεται,

10. φοβεισθαι,

υπαγεται
† **κ(αι) εκει** pro **κἀκει**
11. † **|απηγγειλον**
14. **πισομεν**
* **ποιησωμεν·|** pro **ποιησομεν**
15. ¶ — **τα**
† **μεχρις**
16. ¶ 20. **ειμει|**
— **αμην**

Subscr **ευαγγελιον κατα| μαθθεον** man 1

2. SECUNDUM IOANNEM

Quaternio *θ*, id est usque ad κραβαττον σου 5, 11, ab alia manu (*a*) scripta est

Inscr ευαγγελιον κατα ιωαννην man 2 aut *d*

Caput I

1. ¶ + ο ante $\overline{\theta\varsigma}$
3–4. * εγενετο ουδε εν· ο γεγονεν εν| αυτω ζωη·
4. — ην[1]
5. φενει|
6. ¶ * απο pro παρα
   + ην ante ὄ|νομα
8. εκινος
9. ¶ φωτιζι
11. ειδιοι
12. |γενεσθε
13. εματων
   * σαρκος· (σα in ras man *c*)
   † αλλα
14. † πληρις pro πληρης
   αληθιας·|
15. ¶ μαρτυρι
   + υμιν post ειπον|
   + ος post ερχομενος·
16. |ημις·
   + ζωην post παντες
17. † μω|υσεως
   + δε ante χαρις
   αληθια|
18. ¶ ουδις
   + ει μη post πωποτε·
   |εκινος
   + ημιν· post εξηγησατο
19. α|πεστιλαν
   ιουδεοι·
   |ιερις
   λευειτας·
   * ερωτησουσιν| pro ερωτησωσιν
20. — και[3]
   < |εγω ουκ ιμι
21. + παλιν· post αυτον|
   + συ ει· post ουν
   — ει συ
   λεγι·
   + τι ουν· post ει|μει·
22. † ειπαν
   λεγις
23. + |ευθιας ποιειτε τας τριβους αυτου·| post $\overline{\kappa\upsilon}$·
   ¶ ante καθως
24. ¶ φαρι|σεων·
25. † |ειπαν
   βαπτιζις·
   ι pro ει
   † ουδε pro ουτε bis
26. ¶ υμις
27. — αυτος εστιν
   — ος εμπροσθεν μου γεγονεν
   < ουκ ιμι| εγω
28. ¶ * βηθανια pro βηθαβαρα
   + ο ante ιωαννης
29. βλεπι
   — ο ιωαννης
   — προς αυτον
   λεγι·

*ερων τας αμαρτιας pro αιρων την αμαρτιαν

30. ¶ *υπερ pro περι

+υμιν·| οτι post ειπον

εν|προσθεν

31. ηδιν

–τω ante υδατι

* βαπτιζιν·| pro βαπτιζων

32. τεθεαμε

καταβενον

* ως| pro ωσει

* μενον pro εμεινεν

33. ηδιν

βαπτιζιν·

εκινος

ειδης

κα|ταβενον·

* αυτω· pro αυτον[2]

† ουτος| (υ sup man *b*)

34. † εορακα·

35. † |παλι pro παλιν

ιστηκι

36. λεγι·

ειδε

+ο ερων τας αμαρτιας του κοσμου| post θ̅υ̅·

37. † |κηκουσαν pro και ηκουσαν

<οι δυο αυτου

38. |στραφις

λεγι

39. ζη|τιται,

† ειπαν

ραββει·

λε|γετε

* μεθερμηνευομενον· pro ερμηνευομενον

μενις·

40. λεγι

ερχεσθαι|

* οψεσθαι· pro ιδετε

+ουν post ηλθαν

† ειδαν|

μενι·

εμιναν

εκινην·

–δε

41. +δε post |ην

σειμωνος|

42. ευρισκι

λεγι

–ο[2]

43. +και post ι̅ν̅,

–δε

* ιωαννου· pro ιωνα

ερμηνευετε

44. –ο ιησους

εξελθιν

† γαλιδεαν| pro γαλιλαιαν

ευρισκι

λεγι

+ο ι̅ς̅ post αυτω|

ακολουθι

45. –ο

46. ευρισκι

λεγι

† μωυσης

–υιον

* τω| pro του

ναζαρεθ'·

47. † ναζαρεθ,

δυνα|τε

λεγι

48. +δε post ειδεν

λεγι

ειδε

49. |λεγι

† γι|γνωσκις·

–ο ante ι̅ς̅

φωνησε|

50. + αυτω post απε|κριθη
– και λεγει αυτω
< $\overline{\text{βλευς}}$ ει pro ει ο βασιλευς
51. + οτι post σοι|
– σε
< τουτων μιζω
† οψη·
52. λεγι
– απ' αρτι
|οψεσθαι
αναβενοντας|
καταβενοντας·

Caput II

1. $\overline{\text{γ}}$ pro τριτη
* |εγινετο
γαλιλεας·|
εκι·
2. + εκι post $\overline{\text{ις}}$
3. |λεγι
4. + και ante λεγι
* συ pro σοι
ηκι
5. |λεγι
† |εαν pro αν
6. εκι|
|υδριε λιθινε
< κατα τον καθαρισ|μον των ιουδεων κιμεναι·
$\overline{\text{β}}$ pro δυο
τρις·
7. + και ante λε|γι
8. λεγι
* οι δε| pro και^3
9. ηδι
ηδισαν
|φωνι
10. λεγι
– τοτε
11. ση|μιων
γαλιλεας,|
μαθητε|
12. – εις καπερναουμ
– αυτου^1
< |και οι μαθητε αυτου ante και η $\overline{\text{μηρ}}$
– εκει
εμιναν
13. ιουδεων·
14. |κε pro και^3
* κολλυβιστας| pro κερματιστας
15. + ως post ποιησας
† εχ pro εκ^1
* |τα κερματα· pro το κερμα
* ανε|τρεψεν· pro ανεστρεψε
16. < πωλουσιν τας πε|ριστερας
+ και post εντευ|θεν·
* μη (inter μ et η est deleta littera ο?)
ενποριον·
17. * και εμνησ|θησαν pro εμνησθησαν δε
+ οτι post εστιν·
* καταφαγετε pro κατεφαγε
μαι· pro με
18. ιουδεοι
† ειπαν
ση|μιον
δικνυεις
19. ¶ – ο ante $\overline{\text{ις}}$
λυσαται|
ημερες|
20. † ειπαν
ιουδεοι|
$\overline{\text{μ}}$ $\overline{\text{και}}$ $\overline{\text{ϛ}}$ pro τεσσαρακοντα και εξ
< ο ναος ουτος οικοδο|μηθη·
ημερες
* γιρις| pro εγερεις

21. * αυτος pro εκεινος
22. * η|νεστη pro ηγερθη
— οι μαθηται
* |αυτω pro αυτου
— αυτοις
23. + τοις ante ιεροσολυ|μοις
σημια
24. * ante εαυτō| deleta est littera ο
γινωσκιν
25. χριαν,
† |εγιγνωσκεν

Caput III

1. ¶ φαρισεων
ιου|δεων·
2. * αυτον pro τον ιησουν
ραββει
† ελοιλεθας pro εληλυθας
ουδις|
< δυνατε τα σημια ταυτα
3. ¶ — ο ante $\overline{\iota\varsigma}$
δυνατε
ειδιν
4. λεγι|
— ο ante νικοδημος·
δυνατε bis
γεννηθηνε bis
εισελθιν
5. ¶ — ο ante $\overline{\iota\varsigma}$
δυνατε
εισελθιν
βασιλιαν|
7. δι pro δει
γεννη|θηνε
8. θελι πνι|
9. δυνατε|
10. — ο ante $\overline{\iota\varsigma}$
† γιγνωσκις·
11. † εορακαμεν
12. επιγια
πισ|τευεται·
* πιστευσηται· pro πιστευσετε
13. + εστιν| ος post ουδις
* ανεβη pro αναβεβηκεν
— ο ων εν τω ουρανω
14. † |μωυσης
ουτω
< δι υψωθηνε
|ανου· pro ανθρωπου
15. * εν αυτω| pro εις αυτον
— μη αποληται, αλλ'
* ζωην (ζων man *a* η corr ex ν, add ν sup man *b*)
16. ουτως
— αυτου
† |αλλα
17. α|πεστιλεν
— αυτου[1]
18. — δε
19. < αυτων πονη|ρα
20. |μισι
ερχετε
< αυτου τα εργα|
21. ¶ αληθιαν
ερχετε
* εισιν pro εστιν
ιργασμενα·|
22. ¶ † εις (ι sup man *b*)
ιουδεαν
† κακι| pro και εκει
23. + ο ante ιωαννης
ενων' pro αινων
ενγυς
σαλιμ'·
25. ¶ * ιουδεου pro ιουδαιων
26. † ηλθαν
† ειπαν
ραββει

ειδε
βαπτιζι
ερχοντε
27. δυνατε
ανος| pro ανθρωπος
λαμβανιν
28. |υμις
μαρτυριται ·
ιμι pro ειμι^{1}
— εγω
εκινου ·
29. νυμ · φιος
χαιρι ·
30. |εκινον
δι
31. † ανοθεν
— εκ της γης εστι, και
32. — και^{1}
μαρτυρι|
ουδις
λαμ|βανι ·
34. απεστιλεν
— ο θεος^{2}
35. χιρι
36. εχι
απιθων
† ουχ οψετε
μενι

Caput IV

1. ¶ φα|ρισεοι ·
πλιονας
βαπτιζι
— η
3. |ιουδεαν
|γαλιλεαν ·
4. εδι
σαμαριας ·
5. ερχετε
σαμαριας ·
* |ου pro ο
6. εκι
† οδη|πορias pro οδοιποριας
\+ δε post ωρα
* ως pro ωσει
7. + και ante ερ|χαιται
σαμαριας
αντλη|σε
λεγι
8. μαθητε
απεληλυθισαν|
9. |λεγι
σαμαριτις|
ειουδεος pro ιουδαιος
† πιν| pro πιειν
ετις pro αιτεις
<γυναικος σαμαριτιδος ουσης ·|
συνχρωνται ·
ιουδεοι
σαμαρι|ταις ·
10. ηδις
† πιν · pro πιειν
* αυτον (scr αυταον man *a* sed α^{2} del man *a* aut *b*)
11. λεγι
<το φρεαρ εστιν · βαθυ και ουτε| αντλημα εχις ·
* και ποθεν pro ποθεν ουν
* εστιν| pro εχεις^{2}
12. † μιζον pro μειζων
\+ το ζων · post φρεαρ
13. — ο ante $\overline{\iota\varsigma}$
διψησι
14. + δε post δ' αν
\+ εγω ante δωσω
15. λεγι
ερχωμε
αντλιν ·
16. λεγι

17. ¶ |λεγι
— ο ante $\overline{\iota\varsigma}$
18. $\bar{\epsilon}$ pro πεντε
εχις|
19. ¶ |λεγι
20. < τω ορι τουτω
υμις
< προσκυνιν δει·|
21. ¶ λεγι
< γυναι, post μοι
* πιστευε pro πιστευσον
ερχετε
ορι
προσκυνησεται
22. υμις|
προσκυνιται
† pro ουκ scr οοκ man *a*, corr ουκ man *b* (o^{2} del et υ suprascr)
οιδαται·
ημις
|ιουδεων
23. † αλλα
ερχετε
αληθια·
ζη|τι
† προσκυνουτας
+ εν $\overline{\pi\nu\iota}$| post αυτον
24. * ος pro ο θεος
αληθια
δι
προσκυνιν
25. λεγι|
ερ[χ]εται|
† (χριστος) χ|, id est χρ prim scr corr $\overline{\chi\varsigma}$ man *a*
εκινος
* αναγ|γελλι pro αναγγελει
* απαντα· pro παντα
26. λεγι

27. * εθαυμαζο̄| pro εθαυμασαν
* λαλει· pro ελαλει
ουδις
+ γε post μεντοι|
ζητις·
λαλις
28. λεγι
29. ειδετε
— μοι
31. * και εν pro εν δε
+ αυ|του post μαθηται
ραββει
32. φαγιν
υ|μις
οιδαται·
33. φαγιν·
34. λεγι
* ποιησω pro ποιω
τελιωσω
35. ¶ υμις
λεγεται
¶ ante επαρατε
θεασασθαι|
36. — και^{1}
λαμβανι
|συναγι
* ζων pro ζωην
— και^{3}
σπιρων
χερη
37. — ο^{2}
σπιρων
38. απεστιλα
θεριζιν·
— ο
υμις bis
|κε[κ]οπιακαται·
εισεληλυ|θαται·
39. εκινης
σαμαριτων|

40. σαμαριται·
† ηρωτουν
μινε pro μειναι
εμινεν
εκι
β̄ pro δυο
41. πλιους
42. – οτι[1]
– αληθως
– ο χριστος
43. β̄ pro δυο
εκιθεν
– και απηλθεν
γαλιλεᾱ|
44. – ο ante ι̅ς̅
εχι·
45. γαλιλεαν·
γαλιλεοι·
† εορακοτες·
* οσα pro α
+ τοις ante ιεροσολυμοις·
– αυτοι
46. – ο ιησους
γαλιλεας
ησθενι
† καφαρναουμ|
47. * ηκεν pro ηκει
ιọụ|δεας
·γαλιλεαν·
– αυτον[2]
ιασητε
|αποθνησκιν·
48. – ο ante ι̅ς̅
σημια
ειδη|τε·
πιστευσηται·
49. λεγι
|αποθανιν
50. λεγι
– και[1]
51. καταβε|νοντος·
< υπηντησαν αυτω οι δουλοι αυ|του·
απηγγιλαν
* |αυτου pro σου
52. < την ωραν πα|ρ αυτων·
* ειπον| ουν pro και ειπον
– αυτω
† εχθες pro χθες
ζ̄ pro εβδομην
53. εκινη|
54. ¶ + δε post τουτο
β̄ pro δευτερον
< εποιησεν σημιον
ιουδεας
γαλιλεαν·

Caput V

1. ιουδεων·
2. * τη ε|πιλεγομενη
† βηθσαιδα· pro βηθεσδα
ε̄ pro πεντε
3. ¶ κατεκιτο
– πολυ
4. * εκδεχομενοι pro εκδεχομενων
– αγγελος γαρ · · · κατειχετο νοσηματι
5. εκι
* μ̄ κ(αι) η̄ pro τριακοντα-οκτω
+ αυτου· post ασθενια
6. ειδω̄|
κατακιμενον·
εχι· λεγι
θελις
7. ¶ ante κ̅ε̅
* βαλη pro βαλλη
* οσω pro ω
ερχομε

καταβενι·|

8. ¶ λεγι

εγιρε

† |κραβαττον

περιπατι·|

9. ¶ – ευθεως

† κραβαττον

|περιεπατι,|

¶ ante ην δε

εκινη

10. ¶ ιουδεοι

+ και| post εστιν·

* αριν pro αραι

+ σου| post κραβαττον

11. ¶ *ο δε απεκρινατο pro απεκριθη

† ποισας| pro ποιησας

† υγιην·

εκινος

11–12. – κραββατον σου και περιπατει. ηρωτησαν ουν ····αρον τον

12. † |κραβαττον

13. ει|αθεις

14. ειδε

15. + δε post απηλθεν

+ και ειπεν| αυτοις post ιουδαιοις

υ|γειη,

16. < οι ιουδαι|οι τον $\overline{ιν}$

– και εζητουν αυτον αποκτειναι

+ τω ante σαβ|βατω,

17. – ιησους

* απεκριθη pro απεκρινατο

18. < αποκτειναι οι ιουδαιοι,

19. ¶ *|απεκριθη pro απεκρινατο

† |αμην[1] (ν sup man 3)

< αφ εαυτου ποιειν

– τι

* ο pro α

20. δικνυσιν

† δειξη

θαυμαζηται,|

21. < τους νεκρους εγειρει ο $\overline{πηρ}$|

ουτως

23. τιμωσει[2]

τειμα

24. < ουκ ερχεται εις κρισιν,

25. * ακουσωσιν pro ακουσονται

* |ζησουσιν, pro ζησονται

26. * ως pro ωσπερ

< και τω υιω ζωην| εδωκεν

27. – και[2]

28. θαυμαζεται

μνημι|οις

* ακουσωσιν pro ακουσονται

29. * εξελευσονται pro εκπορευσονται

* |και οι pro οι δε

30. – πατρος

32. μαρτυρι

34. σωθηται,

35. < προς ωραν αγαλ|λιαθηναι

36. * μειζων pro μειζω

* δεδωκεν pro εδωκε

τελιωσω

– εγω[2]

* μαρτυρουσιν pro μαρτυρει

37. * εκεινος pro αυτος

< πω|ποτε ακηκοατε,

– αυτου[2]

38. εχεται|

< |εν υμιν μενοντα,

απεστι|λεν

πιστευ|εται,

39. ερευναται

δοκειται

* αυται pro εκειναι

40. θε|λεται

ε|χηται,
42. † αλλα
εχεται
43. ¶ λαμβανεται
† |λημψεσθαι,
44. δυνασθαι
– θεου
ζητειται,
45. δοκειται|
† μωυ|σης
ηλπεικατε·
46. επι|στευεται[1]
† μωυσει,
επιστευεται[2]
47. πι|στευεται,
* |πιστευσηται :| pro πιστευσετε

Caput VI

1. ¶ 2. * ηκολουθει δε pro και ηκολουθει
* |θεωρουντες pro οτι εωρων
– αυτου
σημια
3. * ουν pro δε
– ο ante ις̅
4. ¶ 5. <τους οφθαλ|μους ο ις̅,
– τον
* αγορασωμεν pro αγορασομεν
7. + ο ante φιλιππος
– αυτων
9. – εν
* ος pro ο
10. ¶ ποιησαται
α|ναπεσιν,
† ανεπεσαν
– οι
* ως pro ωσει

πεντακισχειλιοι,|
11. * ουν pro δε[1]
– τοις μαθηταις, οι δε μαθηται
12. συναγαγεται
† |περισευσαντα
13. * επερισσευσαν pro επερισσευσε
14. ειδοντες
ση|μιον,
– ο ιησους
– οτι
15. ¶ – αυτον[2]
– παλιν
16. οψεια
– οι μαθηται αυτου
17. ενβα̅|τες
† καφαρναουμ'
* ουπω pro ουκ
18. † διηγειρετο| (ε[2] corr man 1 sine ras ex ι)
19. κε̅ η λ̅| pro εικοσιπεντε η τριακοντα
|γεινομενον
20. ειμει
φοβει|σθαι,
21. * αυτον βαλιν pro λαβειν αυτον
<εγενετο το πλοι|ον
22. † ιδον pro ιδων
– εκεινο εις ο ενεβησαν οι μαθηται αυτου
* πλοιον pro πλοιαριον[2]
23. * |πλοια pro πλοιαρια
+ της ante τιβεριαδος
– εγγυς του τοπου
24. – και[1]
* πλοιαρια pro πλοια
† καφαρναουμ
25. † ειπαν

ραββει
26. ειδεται
σημια
εφα|γεται
εχορτασθηται|
27. εργαζεσθαι
εσφρα|γεισεν
28. * αυτω, pro προς αυτον
* ποιη|σωμεν pro ποιουμεν
29. ¶ − ο ante ι̅ς̅
πιστευσηται
30. − συ
σημιον
31. * δεδωκεν pro εδωκεν
32. † μωυσης
* ε|δωκεν pro δεδωκεν
αληθεινον·|
35. − δε
ειμει|
πινασῃ,
† διψησει
36. † ἀλλα
εωρακαται
+ μοι, post |πιστευεται
38. * απο pro εκ
* ποιη|σω pro ποιω
39. − πατρος
* αυτον τη εσχατη pro αυτο εν τη εσχατη
40. * γαρ pro δε
* π̅ρ̅ς̅ μου, pro πεμψαντος με
41. ¶ ειμει
42. − και την μητερα
* νυν pro ουν
− ουτος
43. ¶ |απεκρειθη
γογγυζεται
44. ουδις|
+ προς| με· post αυτον[1]
† καγω pro και εγω
+ εν post αυτον[2]
45. − του ante θ̅υ̅
− ουν
46. < εορακε τις
* αυτος pro ουτος
εορακεν
47. ¶ − εις εμε
48. ειμει
49. <|εν τη ερημω το μαννα
51. ειμει
* ζη|σει pro ζησεται
− δε
− ην εγω δωσω
53. − μη man 1, add sup man 4
φαγη|ται
|πιηται
εχεται
54. † καγω pro και εγω
55. * αληθης pro αληθως bis
ποσεις,
56. πεινων
+ post το αιμα iterum scr |εχει ζωην αιωνιον, καγω ανα-στη|σω αυτον τη εσχατη ημερα, η γαρ σαξ| μου αληθης εστιν βρωσις, και το αιμα μ(ου)| αληθης εστιν ποσις, ο τρωγων μου| την σαρκα και πινων μου το αιμα|
57. |απεστιλεν
58. − υμων το μαννα
< τον αρτον τουτον
* ζηση| pro ζησεται
59. † καφαρνα|ουμ',
60. − εστιν
< ο λογος ουτος,
61. ιδως
62. * ειδη|ται pro θεωρητε
63. * λελαληκα pro λαλω

64. † αλλα
65. – οτι
– μου
66. < των μα|θητων αυτου απηλθον
67. ¶ θελειαι
68. – ουν
69. * |αγιος pro χριστος ο υιος
– του ζωντος
70. ¶ 71. * ισκαριωτου| pro ισκαριωτην
† εμελλεν
< παραδιδοναι αυ|τον

Caput VII

1. ¶ < μετα ταυτα περιεπατει ο ι̅ς̅
* ειχεν εξουσιαν pro ηθελεν αποκτιναι,|
2. ¶ 3. * και ειπον pro ειπον ουν
μεταβηθει|
* θεω|ρησουσιν pro θεωρησωσι
4. * αυτο pro αυτος
5. * |επιστευσαν pro επιστευον
6. ¶ – ουν
* ουδεπω| pro ουπω
7. μισιν
μεισει
8. ανα|βηται
– ταυτην[1]
< ο εμος καιρος pro ο καιρος ο εμος
9. ¶ * αυτος pro αυτοις
10. < εις την εορτην, ante τοτε|
12. < πολυς post ην
14. * μεσης| ουσης, pro μεσουσης
15. – και
+ ουν post εθαυμαζον
16. + ουν post |απεκριθη
17. – θελη
* ποιη pro ποιειν
18. αδικεια
19. † μωυσηs
ζητειται
α|ποκτιναι,
20. – και ειπε
ζητι
αποκτιναι·|
21. ¶ θαυμαζεται|
22. † μωυσης
† μωυ|σεως
περιτεμνεται
23. † |μωυσεως,
24. κρινεται
* κρινεται,| pro κρινατε
25. αποκτιναι,
26. ειδε
– αληθως[2]
27. † γιγνωσκει
28. ¶ – ο ante ι̅ς̅
– και[1]
ειμει,
αληθει|νος
29. – δε
ει|μει
απεστιλεν,|
30. * τας χειρας, pro την χειρα
31. * εκ του ου̅| οχλου πολλοι pro πολλοι δε εκ του οχλου
– οτι
* μη pro μητι
– τουτων
32. απεστιλαν
< οι αρχιερεις και οι φα|ρισαιοι
33. ¶ – αυτοις

< χρονον μικρον
ειμει
34. ζητησεται
ευ|ρησεται,
εισμει
|δυνασθαι
35. ¶ διδασκιν
36. < ο λογος ουτος
ζητησεται
ευρησεται|
εισμει
δυνασθαι|
37. ¶ – τη μεγαλη
ιστη|κει
* ει pro εαν
πεινετω,
39. * ελαμ|βανον pro εμελλον λαμβανειν
* πιστευσαντες pro πιστευοντες
– ο ante $\overline{ις}$
40. – πολλοι
< |εκ του οχλου ουν
* των| λογων αυτου pro τον λογον
41. + οτι| post ελεγον[1]
* οι pro αλλοι[2]
42. |ουχει
< ερχεται ο $\overline{χς}$,|
43. < εγενετο εν τω οχλω
45. † αυ|αυτοις pro αυτοις
ηγαγεται|
46. + αυτοις post απεκριθησαν
< ελαλησεν ουτως
– ως ουτος ο ανθρωπος
47. πεπλανησθαι,
48. – εκ[1]
49. † αλλα
* επαρατοι pro επικαταρατοι
50. ¶ – νυκτος
+ το προτερον post |αυτον
51. * πρωτον παρ αυτου pro παρ αυτου προτερον
52. απεκρειθησαν
† ειπαν|
+ τας γραφας post |ερευνησον
ειδε
* εγειρεται·| pro εγηγερται
53–VIII, 11. – και επορευθη· · · μηκετι αμαρτανε

Caput VIII

12. ¶ < αυτοις ελαλησεν ο $\overline{ις}$
* και ειπεν| pro λεγων man 1, sed > sup και et in marg λε͂γων scr man 2
εισμει
† περιπατηση
14. ¶ < η μαρτυρια μου| αληθης εστιν,
15. κρεινεται,
κρεινω
16. – και[1]
κρισεις
* αληθεινη pro αληθης
εισμει,
18. εισμει
μαρτυρι
19. ηδειται[1]|
< αν ηδειται·[2]
20. – ο ιησους
21. – ο ιησους
ζητησεται
αποθανεισθαι,|
δυνασθαι
22. δυνασθαι
23. * ελεγεν pro ειπεν
εσται, pro εστε bis
εισμει bis

< τουτου του κοσμου bis
24. – οτι[1]
αποθανεισθαι bis
πιστευσηται
ειμει|
25. ¶ * |ειπον pro ελεγον
– και[1]
26. * ειπειν pro λαλειν
† αλλα
* λαλω| pro λεγω
28. – αυτοις
|υψωσηται
γνω|σεσθαι
ειμει
εδειδαξεν|
– ο πατηρ μου
29. – ο πατηρ
30. ¶ 31. * μενηται pro μεινητε
|εσται,
32. γνωσεσθαι
33. ¶ * προς αυτον pro αυτω
– οτι
γενησεσθαι,|
34. ¶ 35. οικεια
– ο υιος μενει εις τον αιωνα
36. – ο υιος
εσεσθαι,|
37. εσται
ζητειται
αποκτιναι,
38. * |α εγω pro εγω ο
* απο του πρς ταυτα pro παρα τω πατρι μου
– ουν
* α ηκουσατε pro ο εωρακατε
* του πρς| pro τω πατρι
– υμων
|ποιειται·
39. ειπον pro ειπεν (error edit Oxon)

– αν
40. ζητει|ται
αποκτιναι
41. ποιειται
† |ειπαν
– ουν
πορνιας
† γεγε|νημεθα,
42. ¶ – ουν
+ ουκ post εμαυ|του
† αλλα
α|πεστιλεν,
43. γινωσκεται
δυνασθαι|
44. + του ante πρς[1]
εσται,
|επιθυμειας
θελεται|
† ουκ pro ουχ
45. ¶ πι|στευεται
46. – δε
* δι|ατι (δια in marg, τι in ras man 3)
– υμεις
πιστευεται
47. ακουεται
εσται,
48. – ουν
† ειπαν
σαμαριτης
49. ατιμαζεται
51. < τον εμον λογον pro τον λογον τον εμον
52. – ουν
* γευσηται pro γευσεται
53. – πατρος ημων
– συ[2]
54. ¶ * δοξασω pro δοξαζω
– μου[2]
λεγεται

* ημων pro υμων
55. † καν| pro και εαν
* υμιν pro υμων
† αλλα
56. ειδη
57. ¶ † ε|ωρακες,
58. |ειμει,
59. – δε
– διελθων δια μεσου αυτων· και παρηγεν ουτως

Caput IX

2. ραβ|βει
3. – ο ante ι̅ς̅,|
4. * ημας pro εμε
δι
* ημας pro με
* ως pro εως
5. ειμει
6. χαμε|
† του^{2} (ο man 4)
7. νειψε pro νιψαι
8. * προσετης pro τυφλος
προσετων,|
9. – οτι^{1}
* ελε|γον ουχι αλλα pro δε, οτι
ειμει>|
10. † ηνεωχθησαν
11. – και ειπεν^{1}
– την κολυμβηθραν
* τον pro του ante σιλωαμ’
* ουν pro δε
12. * και ειπαν pro ειπον ουν
14. * εν η ημερα pro οτε
† ηνεωξεν
15. <μου| επι τους οφθαλμους
16. <ουκ εστιν ουτος παρα θ̅υ̅ ο| α̅ν̅ο̅ς̅
\+ δε post |αλλοι
<σημια τοιαυτα
17. \+ ουν post λεγουσιν|
† ηνεωξεν pro ηνοιξε
18. <ην τυφλος
19. – λεγοντες
λεγεται
<βλεπει αρτι,
20. – αυτοις
† ειπαν,
21. * η τις in ras man 1 (τις prim scr)
† ηνεωξεν pro ηνοιξεν
<ηλικειαν εχει αυτος
– αυτον ερωτησατε· αυτος
* εαυτου| pro αυτου^{2}
22. * συνεθεντο pro συνετεθειντο
† αν pro εαν
23. † ειπον (corr ειπαν man 4)
ηλικειαν
* ε|περωτησατε, pro ερωτησατε
24. <τον| ανθρωπον εκ δευτερου
† ειπαν
<ουτος ο α̅ν̅ο̅ς̅
25. – και ειπεν
26. * ουν pro δε
– παλιν
† |ηνεωξεν pro ηνοιξε
27. θελεται bis
28. * και ελοιδορησαν pro ελοιδορησαν ουν
† ειπαν,
<μαθητης ει
† μωυσεως
29. † μωυσει
30. <τουτω γαρ
† ηνεωξεν pro ανεωξε
31. † αλλα
32. † ηνε|ωξεν pro ηνοιξε
34. † ειπαν

† εξεβαλαν

35. + δε post ηκουσεν

— εξω

— αυτω

* $\overline{\text{ανου}}$| pro θεου

36. — απεκριθη εκεινος

— ειπε

+ εφη post εστιν

37. — δε

† ε|ορακας

38–39. — ο δε εφη · · · · ειπεν ο ιησους

40. — και^{1}

< μετ αυτου οντες

† ειπαν

41. |ειχεται

λεγεται|

* αι αμαρτιαι pro η ουν αμαρτια

* |μενουσιν, pro μενει

Caput X

2. * εκεινος εστιν ο ποιμην pro ποιμην εστι

3. * φωνει pro καλει

4. — και^{1}

* παντα| pro προβατα^{1}

7. — παλιν

ειμει

8. < ηλθον προ| εμου

9. ειμει

† αν pro εαν

— και εισελευσεται

10. † περι|σον

11. ειμει

12. — δε

* εστιν| pro εισι

— τα προβατα^{3}

13. — ο δε μισθωτος φευγει, οτι μισθωτος εστι

14. ¶ ειμει

* γινωσκουσιν με τα| εμα, pro γινωσκομαι υπο των εμων

15. γεινωσκει

* διδωμι pro τιθημι

16. * εκ sup tamen man I

< |δει με

* |ακουσωσιν, pro ακουσουσι

* γενησονται pro γενησεται

17. τι|θημει

* αυτην| (η in ras man I, α prim scr)

18. ερει

τιθημει

+ και post εμαυτου,

* παρα (παρ in ras, α^{2} sup tamen man I, απο prim scr)

19. — ουν

20. ¶ |ακουεται·

21. * ελεγον δε αλλοι pro αλλοι ελεγον

* ανοιξαι,| pro ανοιγειν

22. ¶ * τοτε pro δε

ενκενια

— και

23. † σαλομωντος,|

24. ερεις,

25. πιστευεται,

— τω

+ αυτα| post μου,

+ τα εργα post ταυτα

* μαρτυρησει pro μαρτυρει

26. † |αλλα

πιστευεται,

* οτι ουκ pro ου γαρ

εσται|

— καθως ειπον υμιν

27. * α|κουουσιν, pro ακουει

28. < διδωμει αυτοις| ζωην αιωνιον,
29. * ο pro ος
< παντων μει|ζων
30. + μὸὺ (scr et del man 1) post ο $\overline{\pi\eta\rho}$
31. — ουν
— οι ιουδαιοι
32. ¶ — καλα
+ ουν post ποιον
— αυτων
λιθαζεται
33. — λεγοντες
34. — ο ante $\overline{\iota\varsigma}$
+ οτι post υμ$\overline{\omega}$|
εσται,
36. απεστιλεν
λεγεται
— του ante $\overline{\theta\upsilon}$
ειμει,|
37. πιστευ|εται
38. * πισ|τευεται pro πιστευητε
* πιστευεται,| pro πιστευσατε
* αναγνωτε pro ινα γνωτε
* γινωσκεται pro πιστευσητε
* τω $\overline{\pi\rho\iota}$, pro αυτω
39. < αυ|τον παλιν
40. * εμειν pro εμεινεν
41. < |εποιησεν σημιον
* ουδε εν, pro ουδεν
— ιωαννης
42. * πολ|λοι ουν επιστευσαν pro και επιστευσαν πολλοι
< εις αυτον εκει ·|

Caput XI

1. ¶ 2. αλι|ψασα
3. |απεστιλαν
ειδε
4. ασθενια|
† αλλα
7. * γωμεν pro αγωμεν man 1, corr αγωμεν man 3 (aut 2)
8. ραββει
9. — ο ante $\overline{\iota\varsigma}$
< ω|ραι εισιν
— τουτου man 1, add ·/. sup et in marg /τουτου man 2
10. |προσκοπτι
— το
12. * αυτω οι μα|θηται, pro οι μαθηται αυτου
14. — ουν
* λεγει pro ειπεν
† παρησια
15. πιστευ|σηται
† αλλα
16. συνμαθηταις|
17. < εν τω| μνημιω εχοντα,
18. — ως man 1, add sup man 2
19. * πολλοι δε pro και πολλοι
* την μαρ|θαν και την μαριαν, pro τας περι μαρθαν και μαριαν
— αυτων
20. — ο ante $\overline{\iota\varsigma}$
* εκαθητο, pro εκαθεζετο
21. < ουκ αν α|πεθανεν ο αδελφος μου, pro ο αδελφος μου ουκ αν ετεθνηκει
22. † εαν pro αν
* αιτησης pro αιτηση
23. ¶ 24. † αναστησεται (ε man 1 corr sine ras ex ι)
25. ¶ ειμει

26. — εις εμε
28. * τουτο pro ταυτα
+ οτι post ειπουσα
29. + δε| post εκεινη
* ηγερθη pro εγειρεται
* ηρχετο| pro ερχεται
30. + ετι post ην
— η ante μαρθα,|
31. οικεια
* |δοξαντες pro λεγοντες
μνημιον|
32. — ην
+ δε post ιδουσα
* |αυτου προς τους ποδας pro εις τους ποδας αυτου
< μου απεθανεν
33. ιδεν
— αυτη man I, add sup man 2
34. ειδε,
36. ειδε
37. † εδυνατο
38. * ενβριμων pro εμβριμωμενος
μνημιον,
σπηλεον|
39. * τετελευτηκοτος pro τεθνηκοτος
τεταρτεος
40. † οψη
41. — ου ην ο τεθνηκως κειμενος
42. ηδιν
απε|στιλας,
43. * εκραξεν, pro εκραυγασε
44. κιριαις,|
οψεις
< ο $\overline{\iota\varsigma}$ αυτοις
λυσαται
αφεται
45. — ο ιησους
47. < ποι|ει σημεια
48. ουτως|
* |την πολιν pro τον τοπον
49. — ων
50. * λογιζεσθαι pro διαλογιζεσθε
51. * αρχων pro αρχιερευς
† ημελλεν
* αποθνησκειν $\overline{\iota\varsigma}$ pro ο ιησους αποθνησκειν
53. ¶ * εβουλευσα̅|το pro συνεβουλευσαντο
αποκτινωσιν
54. * |ο ουν $\overline{\iota\varsigma}$ pro ιησους ουν
† ε|φρεμ
† και εκει pro κἀκει
* εμει|νεν pro διετριβε
— αυτου
57. — και[1]
* εντολας pro εντολην

Caput XII

1. — ο τεθνηκως
+ ο $\overline{\iota\varsigma}$, post νεκρων
2. |διπνον
+ αυτω, post διηκονει|
3. ηλιψε̅|
οικεια
— εκ
4. * δε ιουδας ο ισκαριω|της εις των μαθητων αυτου pro ουν εις εκ των μαθητων αυτου ιουδας σιμωνος ισκαριωτης
6. † γλωσσοκομιον
* εχον pro ειχε και
7. + ινα post αυτην
* τηρη|ση pro τετηρηκεν
8. εχεται bis

9. * ο οχλος ο πο|λυς pro οχλος πολυς εκ
— εκ νεκρων
10. αποκτινωσιν,
12. — ο ante ι̅ς̅
13. * εκραυγαζον pro εκραζον
+ και post κ̅υ̅,
14. εκαθεισεν
15. * θυγατηρ pro θυγατερ
16. — δε
— τοτε
17. |εμαρτυρι
|μνημιου
18. — ο ante οχλος
* ηκουσαν pro ηκουσε
σημιον,|
19. |θεωρειται
ωφελειται
|ειδε
20. < ελληνες τινες
* ανα|βαντων pro αναβαινοντων
21. + τω ante φιλιππω
† βηδσαιδα
22. + ο ante φιλιππος[2]
23. * αποκρινεται pro απεκρινατο
25. * |απολλυει pro απολεσει
< φυ|λαξει αυτην εις ζωην αιωνιον,|
26. < τις διακονη
< εγω ειμει
— και[3]
28. ¶ ante ηλθεν
29. * δε pro ουν
* εστηκως pro εστως
+ δε post |αλλοι
30. ¶ — ο ante ι̅ς̅
< η φω|νη αυτη
31. κρισεις
— τουτου[1]
34. + ουν post |απεκριθη
< λεγεις συ
35. * εν υμιν pro μεθ υμων
περιπατει|ται
* ως pro εως
εχεται
* λαβη, pro καταλαβη
36. * ως pro εως
ε|χεται
πιστευεται
γενησθαι,|
37. ση|μια
40. * επηρωσεν pro πεπωρωκεν
ειδωσιν
* επιστρε|ψωσιν pro επιστραφωσι
* ιασομαι pro ιασωμαι
41. * επει pro οτε
42. — και εκ
< πολλοι των αρχοντων
43. * υπερ pro ηπερ
44. < εκραξεν δε ο ι̅ς̅ pro ιησους δε εκραξε
† |αλλα
46. ¶ 47. + μη post μου
* μηδε φυλαξη,| pro και μη πιστευη
† αλλα
48. — τη ante ε|σχατη
49. < εντολην μοι
* δεδωκεν pro εδωκε
50. < εγω λαλω
|ουτως

Caput XIII

1. * ηλθεν pro εληλυθεν
2. δι|πνου
* γεινομενου
* ινα πα|ραδω αυτον ιδα σει-

μωνος ισκαριωτη| pro
ιουδα σιμωνος ισκαριω-
του ινα αυτον παραδω
3. — ο ιησους
* εδωκεν pro δεδωκεν
4. |διπνου
5. εκμασσιν
6. νιπτις|
7. * σοι pro συ
* τι,| pro αρτι
8. < μου| τους ποδας
— ο ante ι̅ς̅,
9. < πετρος σειμων,
10. * ουκ εχει χριαν ει μη pro
ου χρειαν εχει η
εσται pro εστε
11. † παραδιδουντα|
\+ οτι post ειπεν
ουχει
εσται,|
12. ¶ * εαυτου pro αυτου
* και| ανεπεσεν pro αναπε-
σων
|γινωσκεται
13. φωνειται
λεγεται
ειμει
14. ενειψα
ο|φειλεται
15. υποδιγμα
ποιηται,
16. † μει|ζον pro μειζων[2]
17. εσται
ποι|ηται
18. † |αλλα
* επηρκεν| pro επηρεν
19. πιστευσηται
ειμει,|
20. † |αν pro εαν
21. ¶ παραδωσι

23. \+ εκ post εις
— αυτου
25. * ουν pro δε
26. — ο ante ι̅ς̅,
* |δωσω ενβαι|ιας το ψωμιον,
pro βαψας το ψωμιον
επιδωσω
εν|βαψας pro εμβαψας
27. ¶ ante λεγει ουν
28. — δε
29. επι pro επει
† γλωσσοκο|μιον
— ο ante ιουδας,
30. < εξηλ|θεν ευθυς, pro ευθεως
εξηλθεν
31. \+ ουν post οτε
32. — ει ο θεος εδοξασθη εν αυτω
— και ευθυς δοξασει αυτον
33. μεικρον
ειμει,|
ζητησεται
* ειρηκα pro ειπον
— οτι
— εγω
δυνα|σθαι
34. κενην
αγαπαται[2]
35. εσται
εχηται
36. < ακολουθησεις δε υστερο̄|
— μοι[2]
37. \+ νυν post σοι
* αρτι υπερ| σου την ψυχην
μου pro αρτι; την ψυ-
χην μου υπερ σου
38. * |αποκρινεται pro απεκριθη
— αυτω
† φωνηση
* συ με| απαρνηση pro
απαρνηση με

Caput XIV

1. πιστευεται bis
2. οικεια
— αν
+ οτι| post υμιν^{1}
3. — και^{2}
† παραλημ|ψομαι
< |εγω ειμει
4. — εγω
— και^{2}
— οιδατε^{2}
5. — και
6. ειμει
7. * εγνωκε|ται pro εγνωκειτε^{1}
* γνωσεσθαι, pro εγνωκειτε^{2}
— αν
† γιγνωσκεται
8. διξον
9. * τοσουτω χρονω pro τοσουτον χρονον
ειμει
— και^{2}
10. < ποιει τα εργα αυτος|
11. πιστευεται bis
+ γε post ει δε μη
— μοι^{2}
12. — μου
13. αι|τησηται
14. ¶ + με post αιτησηται
15. αγαπαται
17. † γιγνωσκει,|
— αυτο^{2}
— δε
γινωσκεται
* αυτον pro αυτο^{3}
* εστιν, pro εσται
19. θεωρειται
ζησεσθαι,
20. — εν^{1}
|γνωσεσθαι
22. + και post | κ̅ε̅
< μελλεις ημιν|
23. — ο ante ι̅ς̅
* ποιησομέθα,| pro ποιησομεν
24. ακουεται
25. ¶ post υμιν μενω̄| amissa sunt duo folia ad verba |εαν δε πορευθω, XVI, 7

Caput XVI

10. — μου
θεωριται
11. κεκριτε·|
12. δυ|νασθαι
13. — δε
* εν τη αληθεια παση, pro εις πασαν την αληθειαν
* ακουσει pro αν ακουση
14. † |λημψεται
15. * λαμβανει pro λημψεται
16. * ουκετι| pro ου
θεωριται
ο|ψεσθαι
— οτι εγω υπαγω προς τον πατερα
17. † ειπαν
* ουκε|τι pro ου
θεωριται
|οψεσθαι
— οτι
18. < τι εστιν τουτο|
— ο λεγει
19. † |εγνοι pro εγνω
— ουν
— ο ante ι̅ς̅
* ημελλον pro ηθελον
ζητι|ται
θεωρειται

οψεσθαι
20. κλαυσεται
θρηνησεται
λυπη|θησεσθαι,
22. < νυν μεν λυπην
* εξεται man 1 pro εχετε (sup ξ scr χ man 2)
* αφερει pro αιρει
23. — εν[1]
ερωτησεται|
— οσα
αιτησηται
24. * |αιτησασθαι pro αιτειτε
† λημψεσθαι,
* πεπληρωμενη ην,| pro η πεπληρωμενη
25. — αλλ'[1]
* απαγγελω pro αναγγελω
26. < αιτησασθαι εν| τω ονοματι μου, pro εν τω ονοματι μου αιτησεσθε
28. — εξηλθον παρα του πατρος
αφιημει
29. — αυτου
ειδε
+ |εν ante παρρησια
31. — ο ante $\overline{ις}$
πιστευεται|
32. — νυν
|σκορπισθηται
αφηται,
ειμει|
33. εχηται,
* |εχεται, pro εξετε
θαρσειται

Caput XVII

1. * λελαληκεν pro ελαλησεν
* επαρας pro επηρε
— και[2] — και[3]
— σου[2]
2. * |δως αυτω pro δωση αυτοις
3. * γι|νωσκουσιν pro γινωσκωσι
— σε
αληθεινον|
* απεστιλεν pro απεστειλας
4. + σου post εργον|
* τελιωσας pro ετελειωσα
* εδωκας pro δεδωκας
6. * εδωκας pro δεδωκας bis
* σου pro σοι
* τετηρηκαν,| pro τετηρηκασι
7. * εγνωκα pro εγνωκαν
* εισιν, pro εστιν
8. * εδωκας pro δεδωκας
* εδωκα pro δεδωκα
* αυτο pro αυτοι
— και εγνωσαν
|απεστιλας,
9. * εδωκας pro δεδωκας
11. ειμει
* ω pro ους
* εδωκας pro δεδωκας
12. — εν τω κοσμω
* ω pro ους
* εδωκας pro δεδωκας
+ και post μοι,
13. * εαυτοις,| pro αυτοις
14. * εδωκα pro δεδωκα
εμεισησεν
ιμει
16. < |ουκ ειμει εκ του κοσμου,
17. — σου
+ η ante αληθεια
18. απεστιλας
|απεστιλα
19. — εγω
< |ωσιν και αυτοι

20 <μονων ε|ρωτω, pro ερωτω μονον
* υπερ pro περι^{2}
21. * $\overline{\text{πηρ}}$| pro πατερ
— ἑν^{2}
* πιστευη| pro πιστευση
απεστιλας,
22. † καγω pro και εγω
+ μου post δο|ξαν
* εδωκας pro δεδωκας (δεδωκας prim scr man 1, sed δ^{1} del man 1 et 2)
— εσμεν
23. τετελιωμενοι
— ινα^{2}
απεστιλας,|
* καμε pro εμε
24. * ο pro ους
|ειμει
† και εκεινοι pro κἀκεινοι
* θεωρουσιν man 1, corr θεωρωσιν man 2
* |δεδωκας pro εδωκας
25. <εγνων σε
απεστιλας,
26. † και ε|γω pro κἀγω

Caput XVIII

1. ¶ * |του κεδρου pro των κεδρων
* εισ|εληλυθεν pro εισηλθεν
2. πολλακεις
3. ¶ 4. ¶ * δε pro ουν
ιδως
5. |ειμει,
6. — οτι
ειμει
† απηλ|θαν
† επεσαν
χαμε,|
7. ζητειται,
8. ¶ — ο ante $\overline{\text{ις}}$
ειμει,|
ζητειται
αφεται
10. επε|σεν
* ωταριον pro ωτιον
11. — σου
12. χειλιαρχος
13. * ηγαγο̅| pro απηγαγον
— αυτον
14. συνβουλευσας
συμφερι
* απο|θανειν pro απολεσθαι
15. — ο^{1}
<γνωστος ην
16. ιστηκει
υς pro ου (error edit Oxon)
* τω pro τη
* εισηνεγκε̅| pro εισηγαγε
17. + αυτω post ουν
ειμει,
18. ιστηκεισαν
εθερμε|νοντο,
+ και post δε
<πετρος μετ αυτων| pro μετ αυτων ο πετρος
θερμενομενος,|
20. — τη ante συναγωγη
* |παντες pro παντοτε
21. * ε|ρωτας, pro επερωτας
* ερωτησον pro επερωτησον
ειδε
22. <παρε|στηκως των υπερετων,
23. * ο δε $\overline{\text{ις}}$ ειπεν| αυτω pro απεκριθη αυτω ο ιησους
* ειπον pro ελαλησα
24. + ουν post απεστιλεν
25. θερμενομενος,|

εἰμει,|
27. — ο
† ευθυς
28. πρετωριον bis
* πρωει, pro πρωια
* αλλα pro αλλ' ινα
29. < προς αυτους ο πειλατος|
+ εξω ante και
* φησιν, pro ειπε
φε|ρεται
30. * κακον ποιων pro κακοποιος
* πα|ραδεδωκειμεν pro παρεδωκαμεν
31. πειλατος,
λαβεται|
κρεινατε,
— αυτον[2]
απο|κτιναι
32. < πληρωθη ο λο|γος του ιυ
33. ¶ < παλιν εις το πρετωριο|
πειλατος
34. * και απεκρινατο pro απεκριθη αυτω
< ειπον σοι|
35. πειλατος
* μη pro μητι
|ειμει,
36. ¶ — ο ante ις
< ην εκ του| κοσμου τουτου
< οι εμοι ηγωνιζοντο αν|
37. πει|λατος
— ο ante ις
|ειμει
— εγω[2]
† γεγενημαι
38. πειλατος
39. * απολυω υμιν pro υμιν απολυσω[1]
|βουλεσθαι
+ ινα post ουν
< απολυσω υμιν| pro υμιν απολυσω[2]
40. — παντες
† βαραββαν in ras man 1; (prim scr βαρρυβαν)

Caput XIX

1. * λαβων pro ελαβεν
πειλατος
— και
3. + |και ηρχοντο προς αυτον ante και ελεγον
* εδιδο|σαν pro εδιδουν
4. — παλιν
< ο πειλατος εξω
ειδε
|γνωται
* αιτιαν εν αυτω ουχ pro εν αυτω ουδεμιαν αιτιαν
5. ¶ * ιδου pro ιδε
6. ¶ ιδον
πειλατος
λαβεται
< υμεις| αυτον
σταυρωσαται,
ουχι|
7. ¶ — αυτω
— ημων
οφιλει|
< υιον του θυ εαυτο|
8. πειλατος
9. πρετωριον
κάὶ| και pro και[2] (scr et del man 1)
10. ¶ πειλατος
11. + αυτω post |απεκριθη
< |κατ εμου ουδεμιαν
< δεδομενο| σοι
μιζονα

12. < ο πειλατος εζητι αυτον απο|λυσαι,
* εκραυγαζον| pro εκραζον
< ποιων εαυτον pro αυτον ποιων
13. πειλατος
* τω̅| λογων τουτων pro τουτον τον λογον
< τον ι̅ν̅ εξω|
εκαθεισεν
14. * ην ως pro δε ωσει
* ελε|γεν pro λεγει
ειδε
15. * ελεγον pro εκραυγασαν
¶ ante λεγει αυτοις
πειλατος
βασειλεα,[2]
10. * |οι δε παραλαβοντες pro παρελαβον δε
— και
17. + εαυτω post βασταζων
— αυτου
* ο pro ος
19. πειλατος
20. * |τοτε pro τουτον
< ανεγνωσαν πολ|λοι
— ελληνιστι
+ εβραειστι,| post ρω|μαειστι,
21. πειλατω
ειμει
22. ¶ πειλατος
23. χειτωνα|
χειτων
† αραφος
24. † |ειπαν
— εαυτοις
25. — του ιησου
26. — παρεστωτα
— αὐτου
27. * ειδε pro ιδου
28. ιδως
— ηδη
τελιωθη|
29. — ουν
— οι δε πλησαντες
+ ουν μεστον του post σπογ|γον
— και
30. — ο ante ι̅ς̅
κλεινας
* παραδεδωκεν pro παρεδωκε
31. < επι παρασκευη ην ante ι|να μη
— η ante |ημερα
32. † συνσταυρωθεντος
33. |επει pro επι
ιδον
< η|δη αυτον
34. † |αλλα
< εξηλθεν| ευθυς
35. αληθεινη
† και εκεινος pro κἀκεινος
+ και post ινα
πιστευ|σηται,
38. ¶ — ο ante ιωσηφ
† αριμα|θιας
πειλατος,
* ηλθον| pro ηλθεν
* ηραν pro ηρε
* αυτον, pro το σωμα του ιησου[2]
39. * εχων ελιγμα pro φερων μιγμα
† ζμυρ|νης
40. * ην pro εστι
41. μνημιον|
* ην τε|θειμενος, pro ετεθη
42. μνημιον

CAPUT XX

1. † μαριαμ’
— πρωι
* επι pro εις
|μνημιον,
† κα pro και
+ απο της θυρας post ηρμε|-νον
μνημιον,|
2. μνημιου
3. μνημιον|
4. * επι pro εις
μνημιον|
5. † μεντοις pro μεντοι
6. + και ο post ουν
μνη|μιον
8. μνη|μιον,
9. ηδισαν
11. ιστηκει
* |τω μνημιω pro το μνημειον[1]
< εξω κλαιουσα,|
|μνημιον[2]
13. * τεθεικασιν| pro εθηκαν
14. — και[1]
* ειδεν pro θεωρει
— ο ante ι̅ς̅
15. ¶ — ο ante ι̅ς̅
— ει
* εβαστα|ξας pro εβαστασας
< εθηκας αυτο̅|
< αρω αυτον·|
16. ¶ † μαριαμ’,
+ εβραιστι post αυτω
17. ¶ — μου[2] — μου[3]
|αναβενω
18. * αναγγελ|λουσα pro απαγγελλουσα
* εωρακα| pro εωρακε
19. οψειας
* |μιας pro τη μια των
κε|κλισμενων
— συνηγμενοι
20. * ταυτα pro τουτο
< αυτοις, post πλευραν|
— αυτου
21. < αυτοις post παλιν
— ο ιησους
22. < αυτοις και λεγει
λαβε|ται
24. ¶ 25. † εορακαμεν
< μου τον δακτυλον
< μου| την χειραν, pro την χειρα μου
26. † μετα pro μεθ’
— αυτου
— ο ante ι̅ς̅
κεκλισμενω̅|
27. ειδε|
28. ¶ — και[1]
— ο[1]
29. * |ειπεν δε pro λεγει
† εορακας
— θωμα
* ειδοτες| pro ιδοντες
30. σημια
* πεποι|ηκεν pro εποιησεν
31. πιστευση|ται
— ο ante ι̅ς̅
< ο χ̅ς̅ εστιν
εχηται|

CAPUT XXI

1. ¶ < |ο ι̅ς̅ παλιν
2. ζεβεδεου,
3. ¶ * ενεβησαν pro ανεβησαν
— ευθυς
* ουδε ε̅ ·| pro ουδεν

4. — ο ιησους εις · · · · ιησους
εστι
5. * |και λεγει pro λεγει ουν
— ο ιησους
— τι
εχεται,
6. * |λεγει pro ο δε ειπεν
βαλεται
|ευρησεται,
* οι δε εβαλον pro εβαλον ουν
< ισχυσαν ελκυσαι
8. * πλοιω pro πλοιαριω
† αλλα
† |πηχεων pro πηχων
9. * ανεβησαν pro απεβησαν
10. ¶ ενεγκαται
επιασαται
11. * |ενεβη pro ανεβη
+ ουν ante σιμων
* εις την γην pro επι της γης
< |μεγαλων ιχθυων
12. ¶ * αρισταται| pro αριστησατε
13. — ουν ο
14. — ο ιησους
— αυτου
15. ¶ * ιωαννου pro ιωνα
+ παντων post |πλειον
16. < |παλιν λεγει αυτω
* |ιωαννου pro ιωνα
17. * ιω|αννου pro ιωνα
* αγαπας pro φιλεις
* λεγει pro ειπεν^2
< παν|τα συ
† γιγνωσκεις
— ο ιησους
† προβατα man 1, προβατια man 2 (ι sup)
18. * αλλοι pro αλλος
* ζωσουσιν, pro ζωσει
* α|ποισουσιν σε pro οισει
+ συ post οπου^2
19. * ελεγεν pro ειπε
20. — δε
— ακολουθουντα
διπνω
+ αυτω post ειπεν
21. * ειπεν pro λεγει
22. < |μοι ακολουθει,|
23. < ουτος ο λογος
* |ουκ ειπεν δε pro και ουκ ειπεν
24. + και post ο^2
< αυτου| η μαρτυρια εστιν,|
— αμην
Subscr κατα ιωαννην man 1.

2. SECUNDUM LUCAM

Inscr *ευαγγελιον κατα λουκαν* man 2

Caput I

1. ¶ — *εν*
2. † *αυθοπται*
3. *ανωθε*
4. *ασφαλιᾱ* :>|
5. ¶ — *του*
   † *αβιλ'*, pro *αβια*
   * *γυνη αυτω* pro *η γυνη αυτου*
   * *αυτη*| pro *αυτης*
6. * *πασαις* (*αις* in ras man 1; duo litt prim scr)
7. * *ην ε|λισαβετ* pro *η ελισαβετ ην*
8. ¶ 9. *ιερατιας*,
10. < *ην του λαου*
11. ¶ 13. ¶ 14. * *γενεσει* pro *γεννησει*
15. *σικαιρα*
    * *εν κοιλια* pro *εκ κοιλιας*
17. † *ηλια*,| pro *ηλιου*
    απιθεις
18. ¶ *ειμει*|
19. ¶ *ειμει*
20. * *αχρις* pro *αχρι ης*
    * *πλησθησον* pro *πληρωθησονται*
21. ¶ < *εν τω| ναω αυτον*,|
23. ¶ |*λιτουργιας*
25. *ουτως*
    — ο ante *κ̅ς̅*
    † *εφειδεν* pro *επειδεν*
    — *το*
26. ¶ * *απο* pro *υπο*
27. * *εμνηστευμενην* pro *μεμνηστευμενην*
    ανδρει,
    † *δαυειδ'*,
28. ¶ — *ο αγγελος*
    — *ευλογημενη συ εν γυναιξιν*
29. ¶ — *ιδουσα*
    < *επι τω λογω διεταραχθη*
    — *αυτου*
31. † |*συνλημψη*
32. * |*αυτος* pro *ουτος*
    † *δωση* pro *δωσει*
    † *δαυειδ'*
34. ¶ * *ε|στι* pro *εσται*
    επι pro *επει*
    † *γιγνωσκω*,|
35. ¶ *δυ|ναμεις*
    * *διοτι*| pro *διο*
36. ¶ † *συνγενεις* pro *συγγενης*
    * *συνειληφεν* pro *συνειληφυια*
    * *γηρει* pro *γηρα*
37. * *του θ̅ν̅* pro *τω θεω*
38. ¶ 39. ¶ *ορινην*
41. ¶ *εσκειρτησεν*
42. * *κραυγη* pro *φωνη*
    ¶ ante *ευλογημενη*
43. — *μου*
45. * *η καρδια* pro *μακαρια*
    τελιωσεις
46. ¶ 48. *ταπινωσιν*
49. * *μεγαλα* pro *μεγαλεια*
50. * *και γενε|ας* pro *γενεων*

52. ταπινους|
53. πινωντας
εξαπεστιλεν
56. * ως pro ωσει
τρις,
57. ¶ 59. ¶ < ημερα τη ογδοη,| pro ογδοη ημερα
60. ¶ αποκριθισα
61. † ειπαν
* εκ της συγγενιας pro εν τη συγγενεια
63. ¶ 64. ¶ 65. ¶ — και[2]
|ορινη
+ και post ιουδαιας,
66. ¶ * |ταις καρδιαις pro τη καρδια
+ γαρ| post και[2]
67. ¶ † επροφητευσεν
68. — κυριος
* του λαου| pro τω λαω
69. — τω
† δαυειδ'
— του
70. — των[2]
< αυτου προφητων,
74. — των
— ημων
75. * πασαις ταις ημε|ραις pro πασας τας ημερας
— της ζωης
76. + δε post συ
* ενωπιο̅| pro προ προσωπου
77. — του ante δουναι
* αυτου, pro αυτων
78. * επισκεψε|ται pro επεσκεψατο
79. σκοτι
80. ¶ εκρατεου|το

Caput II

1. ¶ + |του ante απογραφεσθαι
2. ¶ * κυρινου,| pro κυρηνιου
3. * εαυτου pro ιδιαν
4. ¶ † δαυειδ' bis
5. * απογραφεσθαι pro απογραψασθαι
* εμνηστευμενη pro μεμνηστευμενη
— γυναικι
νεκυω ·|
6. ¶ 7. — τον πρωτοτοκον
— τη ante φατνη ·
8. ¶ 9. — ιδου
+ σφοδρα ·| post μεγαν
10. ¶ φοβεισθαι ·|
11. < κ̅ς̅ χ̅ς̅
† δαυειδ'
12. σημιον ·
ευρησεται
+ και post εσπαρ|γανωμενον
— τη ante φατνη ·|
13. εξεφνης
14. * ευδοκειας ·| pro ευδοκια
15. ¶ — και οι ανθρωποι
* ελαλου̅| pro ειπον
16. ¶ * ευρον pro ανευρον
17. * ε|γνωρισαν pro διεγνωρισαν
19. ¶ συνβαλλουσα
20. * υπεστρεψαν pro επεστρεψαν
ιδον
21. ¶ |περιτεμιν
* αυτον, pro το παιδιον
† συνλημφθηναι
22. † μω|υσεως
24. + τω ante νομω
† νοσσους pro νεοσσους

25. ¶ <ανθρωπος ην
<ην αγιον
26. ιδιν
* ειδη| pro η ιδη
— τον ante |$\overline{\chi\nu}$
27. * εισαγειν pro εισαγαγειν
εἰθεισμενον
28. ανκαλας
— αυτου
† ηυλογησεν
33. * ο πατηρ αυ|του pro ιωσηφ
— αυτου[1]
34. † ηυλογησεν
35. — δε
36. ¶ <μετα $\overline{\alpha}$|δρος ετη
$\overline{\zeta}$ pro επτα
37. + ην post |και[1]
$\overline{\pi\delta}$ pro ογδοηκοντατεσσαρων
— απο
+ τε post νηστιαις
38. — αυτη[1]
* $\overline{\theta\omega}$ pro κυριω
— εν
39. ¶ * παντα pro απαντα
* επεστρεψαν pro υπεστρεψαν
— την ante πολιν
* εαυτων pro αυτων
40. ¶ — πνευματι
* σοφια, pro σοφιας
41. ¶ † καθ pro κατ'
42. * δεκα δυο, pro δωδεκα
* ανα|βαινοντων pro αναβαντων
— εις ιεροσολυμα
43. τελιωσαντων
* εγνω|σαν οι γονεις αυτου· pro εγνω ιωσηφ και η μητηρ αυτου
44. <ειναι εν τη συνοδια·
* συγγενευσιν pro συγγενεσι
— εν[3]
45. — αυτον[1]
* ανάζητουντες pro ζητουντες
46. ¶ † μετα pro μεθ'
τρις
47. — οι ακουοντες αυτου
48. ειδο̄|τες
¶ ante και[2]
<ειπεν ante προς αυτον
† οδυνουμε|νοι
49. ¶ * ζητειτε| pro εζητειτε
* οιδατε pro ηδειτε
— μου
<με ειναι,
51. ¶. ¶ ante και[4]
* ετηρει pro διετηρει
— ταυτα
52. ¶ + ο ante $\overline{\iota\varsigma}$
+ τη ante σοφια

Caput III

1. ¶ ετι
τιβαιριου
πειλατου
* ιουδαιας·| pro ιτουραιας
— και[3]
2. * επι| αρχιερεως pro επ' αρχιερεων
¶ ante |εγενετο
— του
3. — την
4. — λεγοντος
ποιειται
5. ταπινωθησεται,|
σκολεια
7. ¶ — φυγειν
— οργης

8. * καρπον αξιον pro καρπους αξιους
αρξησθαι
|εγειρε
10. ¶ *επηρωτησαν pro επηρωτων
* ποιησωμεν, pro ποιησομεν
11. * |ειπεν pro λεγει
χειτωνας|
12. † ειπαν
* |ποιησωμεν, pro ποιησομεν
13. πρασσεται,|
14. < τι ποιησωμεν κ(αι) ημεις·| pro και ημεις τι ποιησομεν;
δια|σεισηται
συκοφαντησηται|
αρκεισθαι
15. ¶ 16. ¶ < λεγων πασιν ο ιωαννης| pro ο ιωαννης απασι λεγων
ειμει|
εικανος
17. σειτον|
18. ¶ |ευηγγελειζετο
19. ¶ < των πονηρων ων εποι|ησεν pro ων εποιησε πονηρων
21. ¶ *παν|τα pro απαντα
22. ειδι
* ως pro ωσει
¶ ante και φωνην
— λεγουσαν
23. — ο ante ι̅ς̅
< αρ|χομενος ωσει ετων λ̅ pro ωσει ετων τριακοντα αρχομενος
< υιος ως| ενομειζετο
23–38. — του ηλι, του ματθατ ····του αδαμ, του θεου

Caput IV

1. ¶ < πληρης π̅ν̅ς̅ αγιου
* εν τη ερημω· pro εις την ερημον
2. μ̅ pro τεσσαρακοντα
— υστερον
|επινασεν·|
3. * ειπεν δε pro και ειπεν
4. ¶ < προς αυτον ο ι̅ς̅ pro ιησους προς αυτον
— λεγων
— μονω
— αλλ' επι παντι ρηματι θεου
5. — ο διαβολος
— υψηλον
* γης pro οικουμενης
6. * πασα̅| ταυτην pro ταυτην απασαν
* πα|ραδιδωμι pro διδωμι
7. † εμου pro μου
8. ¶ < ο ι̅ς̅ ειπεν αυτω
— υπαγε οπισω μου σατανα
— γαρ
< κ̅ν̅ τον θ̅ν̅ σου προσκυνησεις
9. ¶ * |ηγαγεν δε pro και ηγαγεν
— ο ante υιος
10. + περι σου post περι σου
12. ¶ — οτι
γεγραπται| pro ειρηται
13. πιρασμον
16. — την ante ναζαρεθ'
* ανατεθραμ|μενος, pro τεθραμμενος
ιωθος
17. < του προφητου ησαιου·|
* ανοιξας pro αναπτυξας
— τον ante τοπον,
18. εινε|κεν

* ευαγγελισασθαι pro ευαγγελιζεσθαι
– ιασασθαι τους συντετριμμενους την καρδιαν

19. απο|στιλαι
† τεθραυμενους (αυ in ras man 3, τεθρωμενους man 1)

20. + και post βιβλιον
εκαθεισεν,
< οι οφθαλ|μοι εν τη συναγωγη

21. ¶ – οτι

22. < ουχι υ|ιος εστιν ιωσηφ' ουτος,|

23. ¶ ερειται
* εις την pro εν τη
† καφαρναουμ',

24. ¶ * ε|αυτου, pro αυτου

25. + οτι post υμιν|
εκλισθη
* μεγαλη pro μεγας

26. † σαραπτα
* σει|δωνιας pro σιδωνος

27. † ελεισεου pro ελισσαιου
< εν τω ισραηλ| ante επι
† ναιμαν| pro νεεμαν

29. – της ante οφρυος
πολεις
< ωκοδομητο αυτων
* ωστε| pro εις το

31. ¶ † καφαρναουμ'

33. ¶ – λεγων

35. * απ pro εξ
– μηδεν βλαψαν αυτον

36. † δυ|ναμει (ι sup man 1)

38. ¶ * απο pro εκ
οικειαν

39. διηκονι

40. ¶ ποικει|λαις
* ηγον pro ηγαγον
* επιτι|θεις pro επιθεις
* εθεραπευεν pro εθεραπευσεν

41. – απο
* |κραυγαζοντα pro κραζοντα
– ο χριστος
† ηα pro εια
< λαλειν| αυτα
ηδισαν

42. ¶ * |επεζητουν pro εζητουν

43. ¶ < δει με|
* επι pro εις
* απεσταλην,| pro απεσταλμαι

44. ¶ * εις τας συναγωγας pro εν ταις συναγωγαις
* τω̅| ιουδαιων, pro της γαλιλαιας

Caput V

1. + και post αυτω
– του ante ακουειν|

2. < πλοια δυο
< απ αυτων απο|βαντες
* επλυνον pro απεπλυναν

3. – του ante σιμω|νος,
ολειγον,
* καθεισας δε| pro και καθισας

4. ¶ * επαναγαγεται pro επαναγαγε
χαλασαται

5. ¶ – της
επει pro επι
* σω| ρηματι pro ρηματι σου
* τα δικτυα·| pro το δικτυον

6. < |πληθος ιχθυων
* διερρησσοντο| pro διερρηγνυτο

* τα δικτυα pro το δικτυον
7. — τοις[2]
συνλαβεσθαι
† ηλθαν
* επλησθησαν pro επλησαν
8. + ο ante σιμων
— πετρος
— του ante ι̅υ̅
ειμει
10. ζεβεδεου
¶ ante και[3]
11. ¶ + και post πλοια
12. ¶ 13. ¶ * λε|γων pro ειπων
καθαρισθητει ·
14. — αυτος
† μωυσης
15. — υπ' αυτου
αυ θενι|ων
17. ¶ * χωρας| pro κωμης
δυναμεις
* ειασθαι αυτον,| pro ιασθαι αυτους
18. ¶ 19. — δια[1]
κλεινιδιω
20. * σου αι αμαρτιαι ·| pro σοι αι αμαρτιαι σου
21. γραμ|ματις
βλασφημειας|
αφειεναι
22. δια|λογιζεσθαι
23. * |σου αι αμαρτιαι, pro σοι αι αμαρτιαι σου
εγειρε
|περιπατι ·
24. ειδηται
< ο υιος του| ανθρωπου εξουσιαν εχει
* παρα|λυτικω pro παραλελυμενω
εγειρε
25. * αυ|των (αυ in ras man 1; πα̅|των prim scr)
* εφ ο pro εφ' ω
26. — και εκστασις .... τον θεον
27. ¶ λευειν
28. * παν|τα pro απαντα
* ηκολουθει pro ηκολουθησεν
29. ¶ — ο ante λευεις|
οικεια
< |πολυς τελωνων
* αμαρτωλων, pro αλλων
30. < οι φαρισαιοι και οι γραμ|ματεις αυτων
+ των ante τελω|νων
† εσθειεται κα πει|νεται : >|
31. — ο ιησους
χρι|αν
υγειαινοντες
† |αλλα
33. ¶ † ειπαν
— διατι
34. ¶ + ι̅ς̅ post |ο δε
δυνασθαι|
36. ¶ + απο ante ιματιου
+ σχισας post και|νου
* σχεισει ·| pro σχιζει
* συμφωνησει pro συμφωνει
+ το ante ε|πιβλημα
37. * μη pro μηγε
< ο οινος ο νεος|
38. * βαλληται ·| pro βλητεον
— και αμφοτεροι συντηρουνται
39. — ευθεως
ναιον|
* χρηστος pro χρηστοτερος

Caput VI

1. ¶ — δευτεροπρωτω
— των

ησθει$\overline{ο}$|
2. — αυτοις
— εν
3. < ο $\overline{ις}$ προς αυτους ειπεν|
ανεγνωται
† δαυειδ'|
* οτε pro οποτε
επινασεν
— οντες
4. — ελαβε και
— και^{4}
5. ¶ — οτι
<του σαββα|του ο υιος του ανθρωπου,|
— και^{2}
6. ¶ — και^{1}
< ανθρωπος εκει,
7. γραμματις|
* θε|ραπευει pro θεραπευσει
+ |κατ' ante αυτου,
8. * |ειπεν δε pro και ειπε
† εγειρε (ε^{1} in ras man 1 ; ν prim scr, id est χειραν pro χειρα)
στηθει
* και pro ο δε
9. ¶ * δε pro ουν
< προς αυτους ο $\overline{ις}$,
* επερωτω pro επερωτησω
* ει pro τι
* τω σαββατω pro τοις σαββασιν
10. — αυτους
εκτινον
* |και εξετινεν, pro ο δε εποιησεν ουτω
† απεκατεσταθη|
— ως η αλλη
11. * ποιησειεν pro ποιησειαν
12. ¶ * εξελ|θειν αυτον pro εξηλθεν

14. † |σιμων pro σιμωνα
+ και| post αυτου,
+ και post ιωαννην,
* ματ'θολομεον, pro βαρθολομαιον
15. + και ante μαθθεον, (pro ματθαιον)
— τον του
16. + και ante ι|ουδαν^{1}
— και^{2}
17. ¶ + πολυς post οχλος
+ και της περεας post ιερουσαλημ'|
18. * απο| pro υπο
— και^{2}
19. * εζητουν pro εζητει
20. ¶ ante μακαριοι
* αυτων pro υμετερα
21. πι|νωντες
χορτασθησεσθαι,|
¶ ante μακαριοι^{2}
κλεοντες
* γελασουσ$\bar{ι}$·| pro γελασετε
22. ¶ εσται
— οταν^{2}
|ονιδισωσιν
† ενεκεν
23. * χαρητε pro χαιρετε
* τα αυτα pro ταυτα
24. ¶ απε|χεται
25. + νυν post ενπεπλησμενοι
|πινασεται,
— υμιν^{2}
πενθησεται
κλαυσεται,|
26. ¶ * υμιν man 1, tamen del man 1
* τα αυτα pro ταυτα
27. ¶ † |αλλα
+ μου| post ακουουσιν

+ *και* post *υμων*,
|*ποιειται*
28. *ευλογει|ται*
* *υμας*, pro *υμιν*
|*προσευχεσθαι*
* *περι* pro *υπερ*
29. * *εις*| pro *επι*
εροντος
† *χειτωνα*
30. — *δε τω*
|*εροντος*
απετει·|
31. *θελεται*
ποιειται
33. ¶ — *γαρ*
34. * *δανισηται* pro *δανειζητε*
ελπιζεται|
* *λαβειν*· pro *απολαβειν*
< *χαρις εστιν υμιν*,
— *γαρ οι*
δανιζουσι|
* *απολαμβανωσιν* pro *απολαβωσι*
35. *δανιζετε*
* *μη|δενα* pro *μηδεν*
* *εσται* pro *εσεσθε*
— *του*
36. ¶ †|*γιγνεσθαι*
— *ουν*
— *και*
37. * *ινα* pro *και ου*^{1}
+ *και* post *κριθηται*|
καταδικαζεται
* *ινα* man 1 pro *και ου*^{2} (·*και ου*· sup man 2)
απολυ|θησεσθαι,
38. — *και*^{2}
< *σεσαλευμενον πεπιεσ|μενον* (— *και*^{2})
— *και*^{3}
† *υπερεκχυννομενον*
* *ω γαρ μετρω με|τριτε* pro *τω γαρ αυτω μετρω ω μετρειτε*
39. ¶ + *και* post *δε*
* *μη* pro *μητι*
δυνα|τε
* *ενπεσουνται*,| pro *πεσουνται*
40. ¶ — *αυτου*^{1}
41. ¶ * *καλφος* pro *καρφος το*
42. ¶ ante *υποκριτα*
< *εκβαλειν*· post *α|δελφου σου*
43. ¶ * *κακον*, pro *σαπρον*
+ *παλιν* post *ουδε*
44. † |*γιγνωσκεται*·|
¶ ante *ου γαρ*
< *σταφυλην τρυγωσιν*·|
45. — *το*^{1}
— *θησαυρου της καρδιας αυτου*
— *το*^{2}
— *του*^{3}
† *περισευματος*
— *της*^{3}
47. ¶ |*υποδιξω*
48. |*οικειαν*,
† |*πλημυρης*
† *προσερη|ξεν*
οικεια
* *δια το* | *καλως οικοδομησθαι αυτην*,| pro *τεθεμελιωτο γαρ επι την πετραν*. (*δια το* in ras tamen man 1; *τε*··· prim scr)
49. * *οικοδομουντι* pro *οικοδομησαντι*
οικει|αν
* |*και* pro *η*

+ αυτη post προσερρηξεν οικειας

Caput VII

1. ¶ *δη pro δε

† καφαρναυμ',|

3. απεστιλεν

* αυτον^2 (ο in ras ν sup man 3, αυτω man 1)

4. σπουδεως

† παρεξη

5. * εποιησεν pro ωκοδομησεν

6. ¶ *εχοντος pro απεχοντος οικειας|

* αυτους pro αυτον

< φιλους ο εκατο̄|ταρχης

< εικανος ειμει

< μου υπο την| στεγην

8. ειμει

9. ¶ — ακολουθουντι αυτω

10. < |εις τον οικον οι πεμφθεντες

— ασθενουντα

11. ¶ — εν

* επορευθη pro επορευετο

— ικανοι

12. ¶ *ηγγειζεν pro ηγγισε

< μο|νογενης υιος

13. ¶ *ι̅ς̅ pro κυριος

κλεε·|

15. ανε|καθεισεν

16. ¶ 17. — εν^2

18. ¶ † απηγγειλον

19. ¶ *ετερον pro αλλον

20. * α|πεστιλεν pro απεσταλκεν

* ετερον pro αλλον

21. * εκεινη pro αυτη

— δε

22. ¶ — ο ιησους

* ειπατε pro απαγγειλατε

† ειδετε (ε^2 in ras man 3; ειδατε man 1)

— οτι

+ και post αναβλεπουσιν,

+ και post καθαριζονται|

23. † αν pro εαν

24. ¶ *εξηλθατε pro εξεληλυθατε

25. ¶ *εξηλθατε pro εξεληλυθατε

26. νε pro ναι

27. — εγω

28. * δε| pro γαρ

+ οτι post |υμιν

† μιζον pro μειζων

— προφητης

— του βαπτιστου

* |και ο pro ο δε

|μιζων

29. ¶ 30. * εαυτους| (ε sup man 1)

+ το βα|πτισμα ιωαννου·| post αυτου

31. ¶ — ειπε δε ο κυριος

32. * |αγοραις pro αγορα

* λεγοντα·|pro και λεγουσιν ωρχησασθ(αι)·|

— υμιν^2

33. ¶ + ο ante ιωαννης

* |μη pro μητε^1

< εσθιων αρτον

† μηδε pro μητε^2

< πινων οινο̄| λεγεται

34. λεγεται,

< φιλος| τελωνων

35. < παντων των| τεκνων αυτης,|

36. ¶ *τον οικον pro την οικιαν

37. ¶ < τις ην εν τη πολει pro εν τη πολει, ητις ην

+ και post αμαρ|τωλος,

* κατακει|ται pro ανακειται

οικεια
38. < οπισω ante παρα
< τοις δακρυσιν ante ηρξατο
* αυτης (ης in ras man 1, ου prim scr)
* εξεμαξεν, pro εξεμασσε
ηλι|φεν
39. ¶ – λεγων
† εγιγνωσκεν
40. ¶ < ειπεν ο $\overline{\iota\varsigma}$
< διδασκαλε φησιν
41. † |χρεοφιλεται
δανιστη
ωφιλεν
42. – ειπε
† πλε|ον pro πλειον
< αγαπησει αυτον,|
43. – αποκριθεις
< |ο δε σιμων
πλιον
\+ $\overline{\iota\varsigma}$ post ο δε
44. ¶ *τον οικον| pro την οικιαν
* υπο pro επι τους
* μοι pro μου^1
* επεδωκας| pro εδωκας
– της κεφαλης
45. διελειπεν
46. |ελεω
ηλιψας|
ηλιψεν,
– μου τους ποδας
47. † αφιενται pro αφεωνται
< αυτης αι αμαρτιαι|
|ολειγον
48. ¶ †αφιενται pro αφεωνται
49. * προς εαυτους, pro εν εαυτοις (αυτους prim scr, add ε sup man 1)

Caput VIII

1. * δεκα| δυο pro δωδεκα
2. ασθενιων·|
< $\overline{\zeta}$ δαιμονια pro δαιμονια επτα
* εξεληλυθει (ξεληλυθ in ras man 1?)
3. * αυτοις pro αυτω
* εκ pro απο
4. * εισπορευομενων pro επιπορευομενων
5. – του^1
σπιρειν
* |α pro ο^2
πετινα
– του ουρανου
6. * δια το, in ras man 1; litt septem prim scr
7. συν|φυεισαι
† απεπνιξαν (α^2 in ras man 1 aut 2; ο aut ε prim scr)
8. ε|φωνι
9. ¶ – αυτου λεγοντες
< αυ|τη ante ειη
10. δεδοτε
– της βασιλειας
* ιδωσιν· pro βλεπωσι
* συνιωσιν,| (ι^1 sup man 1)
12. ερει
13. πιρασμου
14. ¶ συνπνιγονται
16. ¶ κλεινης|
17. – γαρ
18. |βλεπεται
ακουεται·
– αν^1
† εαν| pro αν^2
19. ¶ 20. * απηγγελθη| pro απηγγελη

– λεγοντων
21. * προς αυτους, (προς αυ in ras man 1; αυτοις prim scr)
– αυτον
22. * |εγενετο δε pro και εγενετο
+ το ante πλοιον
23. λελαψ
24. * επαυσατο pro επαυσαντο
25. – εστιν[1]
26. * κατεπλευσεν pro κατεπλευσαν
† αντιπε|ρα
γαλειλαιας,|
27. – αυτω[2]
οικεια
28. – και[1]
+ αυτω, post ειπεν|
29. * παρηγγελλεν pro παρηγγειλε
εδεσμιτο
|πεδες
31. – και παρεκαλει αυτον
32. – εκει
+ του|τω, post ορι
34. ¶ * γεγονως| pro γεγενημενον
† εφυγαν
– απελθοντες
35. < τον ανθρωπον καθημε|νον,
36. ¶ ειδον|τες
37. * παν pro απαν
ενβας
38. – εδεετο δε αυτου .... ειναι συν αυτω
* εδιδασκεν pro απελυσε
39. < σοι εποιησεν
40. ¶ 42. * συν|επνιγον αυτον, (επνιγονα in ras man 1)
43. * ιατροις pro εις ιατρους
45. ¶ * συν αυτω, pro μετ' αυτου
47. ¶ – αυτω[2]
* εναντιον pro ενωπιον
* πως pro ως
ειαθη
48. ¶ θαρσι
* θυγατηρ pro θυγατερ
49. * |παρα in ras man 2 (απο man 1)
51. * ελθων pro εισελθων
< και ιωαννην και ιακωβο̄|
52. εκλεον
¶ ante ο δε ειπεν
κλαιεται
* ου γαρ pro ουκ
54. < παντας εξω,
55. < δοθηναι αυ|τη
56. |μηδενει

Caput IX

1. ¶ |συνκαλεσαμενος
– μαθητας αυτου
2. απεστιλεν
|κηρυσσιν
* ει|ασασθαι pro ιασθαι
3. ¶ ερεται|
* ραβδον pro ραβδους
† χειθωνας pro χιτωνας
4. οικειαν
εισελθηται
με|νεται,
εξερχεσθαι,|
5. * δεχωνται pro δεξωνται
– και[2]
7. ¶ γεινομενα
8. + λεγοντων post τινων δε
9. – ο
* τις (σ sup man 2)
10. † βηθ'σαιδαν ·|
11. * δεξομενος pro δεξαμενος
|ειατο ·|

12. κλειν‌ειν,
— δε
13. ¶ * αρτων pro αρτοι
< ι|χθυες δυο,
14. |πεντακεισχειλιοι,|
¶ ante ειπεν
|κατακλεινατε
15. ουτως
|ανεκλειναν
16. ¶ † ηυλογησεν
17. * |περισσευμα pro περισσευσαν
* αυτων των pro αυτοις
* |κοφινους pro κοφινοι
18. + αυτου, post μαθηται
19. αρχεων
20. ¶ |λεγεται
— ο ante πε|τρος
21. * λεγειν pro ειπειν
23. * ερχεσθαι pro ελθειν
24. — αυτου[1]
† απολεσει pro απολεση
26. επεσχυνθη
επεσχυνθησεται
27. * εστωτων, pro εστηκοτων
* γευσω̅|ται pro γευσονται
28. — τον ante |πετρον
30. † μωυσης
31. + τη ante δοξη
† ημελλεν
32. ¶ 33. — ο ante πετρος
|τρις,
< μιαν μωυσει,
ηλεια,
34. † |λεφελη pro νεφελη
35. ακουεται,|
36. εσειγησα̅|
† απηγγειλον
† εορακασιν·|
37. ¶ — εν
38. δαιομαι (ε scr man 2 sup αι)
39. εξεφνης
† μολις pro μογις
40. * |εκβαλωσιν pro εκβαλλωσιν
41. ¶ < τον υιον σου ωδε·|
42. † ερη|ξεν
43. μεγαλιοτητι
¶ ante παντων
44. θεσθαι
46. — εν
47. ¶ 48. † αποστιλοντα pro αποστειλαντα
μεικροτε|ρος
49. ¶ — ο
ιδομεν
— τα
50. ¶ κωλυεται|
* υμων pro ημων bis
51. ¶ συνπληρουσθαι
† αναλημψεως
< εστηριξεν αυτου|
52. απεστιλεν
+ τους ante αγγελους
* αυτου (sup α scr ε man 2, id est, εαυτου)
σαμαριτων
53. * εξεδεξα̅|το pro εδεξαντο
55–56. — και ειπεν····αλλα σωσαι
57. ¶ 58. πετινα
† κεφαλη pro κεφαλην
59. — πρωτον
60. < νεκρους εαυτων,
62. ¶ < ο ι̅ς̅ προς αυτον,
* επι|βαλλων pro επιβαλων

Caput X

1. απε|στιλεν
† ημελλεν

2. ¶ ολειγοι,|
|δεηθηται
* εκβαλη pro εκβαλλη
3. υπαγεται
4. βασταζεται
* ασπασασθαι,| pro ασπασησθε
5. οικειαν
εισερχησθαι
λεγεται
6. — μεν
— ο ante υιος
* επανα|πανσηται pro επαναπαυσεται
7. οικεια
μενεται
— και πινοντες
μετα|βαινεται
οικειας
8. * αν pro δ' αν
εισερχησθαι·
* |δεχονται pro δεχωνται
εσθιεται
9. θεραπευεται
λεγεται
10. ¶ εισερχησθαι
* |πλατιους pro πλατειας
11. * ημιν (η in ras man 1; υ prim scr)
— υμων man 1, add sup man 2
\+ εις τους ποδας ημων| ante απομασσομεθα
|γινωσκεται
ηγγεικεν
12. — δε
13. † |ουα pro ουαι[1]
† χορεζειν·
† βηθσαιδα̅|
— ει
† σιδονει
14. † |σιδονι
16. † αποστιλοντα
17. * εν ω pro εν τω
18. ¶ 19. *δεδωκα pro διδωμι
— του ante |πατιν
† αδικησει,|
20. χαιρεται bis
— μαλλον
21. ευ|δοκεια
22. ¶ < μοι παρεδοθη
† γιγνωσκει
* βουλεται pro βουληται
23. † καθ'|
βλεπεται,
24. βλεπε|ται
† ουχ pro ουκ[1]
α|κουεται
25. ¶ 26. † ανα|γιγνωσκεις,
28. ¶ 31. συνκυ|ριαν
* καταβαινων pro κατεβαινεν
32. — δε
λευ|ειτης
33. |σαμαριτης
34. πανδοχιον
36. <πλησι|ον δοκει σοι
37. ¶ ante ειπεν ουν
— αυτω
38. ¶ 39. *ταυτη pro τηδε
† |μαριαμ',
παρακαθεισασα
40. * ενκα|τελιψεν pro κατελιπε
41. ¶ *θορυβαζη| pro τυρβαζη
42. αφερεθησεται|

Caput XI

1. ¶ 2. *προσευχεσθαι pro προσευχησθε
λεγεται·

† ελθατω
— της ante γης,
4. † αφειομεν| (α, ε^{1}, ι, ο, in ras tamen man 1; οφιλ prim scr)
5. ¶ * ερει pro ειπη
τρις
6. * οδου in ras man 1 (α · · · prim scr)
7. * εστιν, pro εισιν
8. * φιλος| pro φιλον
αναιδιαν
† δωση pro δωσει
9. αιτιται
ζητειται
ευρησεται|
κρουεται
* ανυχθησεται pro ανοιγησεται
10. * ανηχθη|σεται:| pro ανοιγησεται
11. ¶ + εξ ante υμων
< ο υιος αιτησει|
† |η pro ει
12. † αν pro εαν
† |επιδωση pro επιδωσει
13. < δοματα αγαθα
15. * βεελζεβουλ τω αρχοντι
* |εκβαλλειν pro εκβαλλει
16. σημιον
17. * μερισθεισα pro διαμερισθεισα
18. * εμε|ρισθη, pro διεμερισθη
λεγεται
* εκ|βαλλει pro εκβαλλειν
με
19. — ει δε εγω εν βεελζεβουλ εκβαλλω τα δαιμονια
* εκβαλουσιν, pro εκβαλλουσι

< αυ|τοι κριται υμων
22. † νεικησει pro νικηση
|πανοπλειαν
ερει
24. ¶ + δε post |οταν
+ αναπαυσιν post |ευρισκον
26. γεινεται|
27. ¶ 28. ¶ * μεν ουν, pro μενουνγε
— αυτον
29. σημιον ter
30. σημιον
νινευειταις,
31. πλιον
† σολομωνος^{2}
32. ¶ * νινευειται pro νινευι
33. * κρυπτη̅| pro κρυπτον
34. + σου, post οφθαλ|μος^{1}
— ουν
φωτι|νον
σκοτινον,|
36. φωτινον bis
< μερος τι
σκοτινον,
37. † ερωτα
† αριστησει pro αριστηση
38. ειδων
39. ¶ καθαριζεται|
42. ¶ † |αλλα
|παρερχεσθαι
43. ¶ αγαπα|ται
44. εσται
— τα ante μνημια
— οι^{2}
46. ¶ φορ|τιζεται
προσψαυεται
47. ¶ οικοδομειται
μνημια|
|απεκτιναν
48. συνευδοκειται

απε|κτιναν
οικοδομει|ται
μνημια,|
49. – και[3]
* αποκτενουσῑ| man 1 αποκτεινουσῑ man 2 (ι suprascr)
– και[4]
50. † εκ|χυννομενον
52. ¶ † εισηλ|θατε
53. γραμματις|
54. – και
* κατηγορησουσιν man 1, κατηγορησωσιν man 2 (ω sup, ου non del)

Caput XII

1. επισυναχθισων
προσεχεται
|υποκρισεις·|
2. συνκεκαλυμμενον
3. ταμιοις,
4. ¶ φο|βηθηται
αποκτενοντων|
5. αποκτιναι|
< |εχοντα εξουσιαν
* βαλιν pro εμβαλειν
6. στρουθεια
< δυο| ασσαριων,
7. φοβισθαι|
8. ¶ 11. ¶ *|απολογησεσθαι, pro απολογησησθε
ειπηται,|
13. ¶ 14. ¶ 15. φυλασσεσθαι
* πασης| pro της
* αυτων pro αυτου bis
16. ¶ † ηυφορη|σεν
17. * σῡ|αξαι man 1 pro συναξω (sup αι scr ω man 2)
18. – μου[1]
† γενηματα
19. * |συ pro ψυχη[2]
21. + εν ante εαυτω
22. ¶ μεριμναται|
– υμων
φαγηται,
ενδυσησθαι,
23. πλιον
24. ταμιον,
πετινων,|
25. ¶ ηλικειαν
26. δυ|νασθαι·
27. ¶ 28. < σημερον εν αγρω| pro εν τω αγρω σημερον
κλειβανον
29. φαγηται
|πιηται,
* μετεωριζεται, pro μετεωριζεσθε
30. – του κοσμου man 1 (add sup ·/. et in marg ·/. του κοσμου man 2)
31. – ταυτα παντα
32. ¶ † ηυ|δοκησεν
33. † βαλλαντια pro βαλαντια
ανεκ|λιπτον
ενγιζει,
35. ¶ 36. * αυτων pro εαυτων
† αναλυση pro αναλυσει
37. ¶ ante αμην
38. – ελθη εν τη δευτερα φυλακη|
και
ουτως,
39. ¶ γινωσκεται
– αν[2]
40. ¶ γεινεσθαι
δοκειται
41. ¶ 42. ¶ * ο φρονιμος, pro και φρονιμος

θεραπιας
* δουναι pro του διδοναι
44. – οτι
* αυτω pro αυτου
45. αισθιειν
46. † γιγνωσκει,
– των
47. * εαυτου, (ε sup man 2)
– μηδε ποιησας
48. * ολειγα,| pro ολιγας
\+ το ante πολυ[1, 3]
49. βαλιν
* επι pro εις
50. – ου man 1 (+ οπου sup man 2)
51. |δοκειται
52. τρις
53. † επι pro εφ'
– και θυγατηρ επι μητρι
54. ειδη|ται
λεγεται
γεινεται
ουτως,|
55. λεγεται
* ερχεται, pro εσται
γεινεται,|
56. |υποκρειται·
δοκι|μαζεται,|
57. κρεινεται
58. * βαλη pro βαλλη

Caput XIII

1. ¶ εμειξε̅|
2. ¶ – ειπεν αυτοις
δοκειται
3. ουχει
απολεισθαι·
4. απεκτινεν
|δοκειται
* αυτοι pro ουτοι
5. ουχει
† μετανοειτε pro μετανοητε
απολεισθαι·|
6. ¶ < πεφυτευμενην ε̅| τω αμπελωνι αυτου,
< ζη|των καρπον
7. ¶ 8. ¶ * κοπρια· pro κοπριαν
10. ¶ 11. < ην γυ|νη
ασθενιας
– και[2]
συνκυπτουσα
12. ¶ ασθενιας
14. ¶ * αυταις pro ταυταις
θεραπευεσθαι,
15. ¶ |απεκριθη pro ακεκριθη (error edit Oxon)
* εν σαββα|τω pro τω σαββατω
† πατνης pro φατνης
17. γεινομενοις
18. ¶ 19. πετινα|
20. – και
* αυτην|ρου pro αλευρου
* ζυμωθη ολη·| pro ου εζυμωθη ολον
22. ¶ * ποριας pro πορειαν
23. ολειγοι
¶ ante ο δε
24. αγωνιζεσθ(αι)|
– λεγω υμιν
25. αρξησθαι
έσται,
26. * αρξη|σθαι pro αρξεσθε
πλατιαις|
27. εσται·|
– οι ante εργατε·
αδικειας,
28. ¶ ante οταν οψησθαι
29. ¶ – απο[2]

ανακλειθη|σονται

31. ¶ *ταυτη pro αυτη

< σε| θελει

32. ¶ αλωπεκει

|τελιουμαι·|

33. ¶ *δε pro δει

34. ¶ αποκτι|νουσα

|ποσακεις

† ορνιξ

35. αφειεται|

— ερημος· αμην

< |λεγω δε

< ιδηται με|

† ηξει pro ηξη man 1, tamen ηξοι prim scr et corr

Caput XIV

1. ¶ 3. ¶ *αυτους| pro τους

5. ¶ + ο ι̅ς̅ post αποκριθεις

< ειπεν προς αυτους|

* υιος pro ονος

* πε|σειται, pro εμπεσειται

ανασπασι

7. ¶ πρω|τοκλεισιας

8. κατακλειθης

9. ερι

† μετα pro μετ'

10. * αναπε|σε pro αναπεσον

|προσαναβηθει

11. ταπινωθησε|ται, ταπινων

12. ¶ διπνον,

13. ¶ † |αλλα

† αναπειρους

14. αναστασι

15. ¶ |φαγετε

* αριστον pro αρτον

16. ¶ διπνον

17. απεστιλεν

διπνου

ερχεσθαι|

18. παραιτισθαι|

19. δοκειμασαι|

21. — εκεινος

* εαυτου pro αυτου[1]

οργεισθεις

πλατιας

† αναπειρους

< |τυφλους και χωλους

22. ¶ 23. ¶ 24. *γευση|ται pro γευσεται

διπνου·|

25. ¶ 26. *αυτου pro εαυτου

27. * εαυτου pro αυτου

< ειναι μου

28. ¶ + ο ante θελων

† οικοδομη|σαι, καθεισας

* εις pro τα προς

29. < αυτω ενπε|ζειν

31. συνβα|λιν

|ουχει

καθεισας

χειλιασιν|

χειλιαδω̅|

32. |αποστιλας

33. — ουν

* αυτου pro εαυτου

34. ¶ † αλα pro αλας bis

Caput XV

1. ¶ < αυτω εγγιζοντες

— παντες

2. γραμ|ματις

3. ¶ — την

4. < εξ αυτων ἑν

|καταλιπει

ϟθ pro εννενηκονταεννεα

6. |συνκαλει

συνχαρηται

7. ¶ ουτως
ϙ̅θ̅
8. ¶ ουχει
απτι
οικειαν
ζητι
9. |συνκαλειται
συνχαρηται
10. |ουτως
γεινεται
11. ¶ * εσχεν pro ειχε
14. υστερισθαι,
15. πολειτων
16. + και| χορτασθηναι post κοιλιαν
— αυτου
17. * μι|σθιου pro μισθιοι
19. και
ειμει
— ποιησον με ως ενα των μισθιων σου
20. * επεσεν pro επεπεσεν
22. — την^{1}
+ αυτω post δοτε
24. — και απολωλως ην, και ευρεθη
25. οι|κεια
26. — αυτου
27. — οτι^{1}
28. — αυτου
29. < σου| εντολην
30. * σιτευτον, (sup τε scr τισ man 2, id est σιτιστον)
32. — ην^{2} και

Caput XVI

1. * αυτου^{1}| man 1, εαυτου man 2 (ε sup)
2. |γ̣α̣ρ̣
* δυνη pro δυνηση
οικονομιν,|
3. * δε αυτω (vel δ εαυτω) pro δε εν εαυτω
αφερειται
5. * |χρεωστων pro χρεωφειλετων
οφιλεις
6. † βαδους pro βατους
— αυτω
δεξε|
καθεισας
7. οφιλεις,
σειτου,
δεξε
8. αδι|κειας
9. * εαυτοις (ε corr man 1 ex α partim scr)
α|δικειας
εκλειπηται
δεξωντε|
11. εγενεσθαι
αληθεινō|
12. εγενεσθαι
13. μεισηισει,
δυνασθαι
14. — και^{2}
15. εσται|
† βδελυσμα pro βδελυγμα
— εστιν
17. ¶ |κερεαν
* παρελθειν,| pro πεσειν
20. † ειλκωμενος pro ηλκωμενος
21. † απελιχαν
22. ¶ ante απεθανεν
24. φλογει
25. * ωδε| pro οδε
26. < υμων και ημων|
εστηρικτε
— εντευθεν
27. — ουν

29. + δε post |λεγει
+ ο ante αβρααμ,
30. ουχει
31. † μωυσεως
* απελθη pro αναστη
* πιστευουσιν,| pro πεισθησονται

Caput XVII

1. + του ante μη
* pro ουαι scr ου man 1 add ϵ sup man 4
2. * λιθος pro μυλος
πε|ρικειτε
† εριπτε| pro ερριπται
3. προσεχεται
— εις σε
4. |επτακεις bis
* αμαρτηση pro αμαρτη
— επι σε
αφησις
6. * εχεται pro ειχετε
† σινηπεως
ελεγεται
7. |ερι
αναπεσε,
8. † διπνωσω pro δειπνησω
φαγεσε
πιεσε
9. — αυτω
10. ουτως|
ποιησηται
λεγεται
— οτι^{1}
αχριοι
† οφιλομεν
11. ¶ * διερχεται pro διηρχετο
|σαμαριας
12. * πορρω| pro πορρωθεν
14. επιδειξαται
15. ειαθη
16. σαμαριτης ·|
17. ¶ † ουχ pro ουχι
+ ουτοι post δεκα
20. ¶ * π̇ȯτ̇ė|ποτε pro ποτε (scr iterum et del man 1)
21. * και pro η^{1}
22. επιθυμησεται
ιδιν
† ουχ οψεσθαι|
23. — η
διωξηται,
24. — η^{2}
* υπο τον pro υπ'^{1}
— και
25. δι
26. — του^{1}
27. |ησθειου
29. † λωθ'
< θειον και πυρ
31. * εστιν pro εσται
οικεια
32. μνημονευ|εται
† λωθ',|
33. † απο|λεση pro απολεσει
34. * |αυτη pro ταυτη
< δυο εσονται
κλεινης|
— ο^{1}
† παραλημφθησεται
+ και αποκριθεντες λεγου post |αφεθησεται (scr et del man 1)
35. † |παραλημφθησεται
36. συναχθησοντε

Caput XVIII

1. + αυτους| post προσευχεσθαι
2. * $\overline{\text{ανους}}$ pro ανθρωπον
4. * ηθελε̄| pro ηθελησεν

5. — μοι
* υ|ποπταζη pro υπωπιαζη
6. αδικειας
9. — και[1]
10. ¶ 11. * ευχεται, pro ηυχετο
ειμει
12. δεις
13. ¶ *ηδυνα|το pro ηθελεν
ε|παρε,
ειλασθητι
14. ταπινωθη|σεται,
ταπινων
16. αφεται
* εμε in ras man 1 pro με (ημας? prim scr)
κωλυεται
17. ¶ †αν pro εαν
20. — σου[2]
22. |λιπει;
26. * ακουοντες pro ακουσαντες
δυνατε
27. <παρα $\overline{\theta\omega}$ εστιν, pro εστι παρα τω θεω
28. — ο
29. <υμιν λεγω,
οικειαν,
32. ενπε|χθησεται,
ενπτυσθησετ(αι)|
33. * αποκτινουσιν pro αποκτενουσιν
35. ¶ προσετ$\overline{\omega}$|
38. † δαυειδ'
39. * |σειγηση, pro σιωπηση
† δαυειδ'
40. ενγισαντος
42. — αυτω
43. * ηκολουθησεν prim scr sed corr ηκολουθει man 1 (ει sup ησ; ε̇υ̇ del)

Caput XIX

1. * εξελθων man 2 pro εισελθων (ξ in ras, εισελθων man 1)
2. † ζαχ|χαιος
— και[3]
3. ηλικεια
μεικρος
4. * προσδραμων| pro προδραμων
|ειδη
— δι'
5. † ζαχχαιε
καταβηθει,|
7. * παν|τες pro απαντες
8. † ζαχχαιος
* το ημισυ pro τα ημιση
11. ¶ <η βασιλεια του $\overline{\theta\upsilon}$ μελ|λει
12. + ην post τις
+ και post ευγενης
13. * πρα|γματευεσθαι pro πραγματευσασθε
* εν ω pro εως
14. πολει|ται
απεστιλα̅|
πρεσβιαν
15. — αυτω
— τι
* πεπραγμα|τευσατο, pro διεπραγματευσατο
17. ισθει
19. * γενου pro γινου
21. <ει αυστηρος|
ερεις
† ε|σπειρες,
22. ειμει,
ερων
23. * μ̇ο̇υ̇ το αργυριον μ(ου)

man 1 (μου[1] del et μου[2] scr in marg)
– την
+ τω ante το|κω
25. – και ειπον αυτω, κυριε, εχει δεκα μνας
29. † ε|λεωνα, pro ελαιων
απεσ̈τιλεν
30. υπαγεται
ευρησεται
εκα|θεισεν
αγαγεται,
31. λυεται
32. † ευραν|
33. λυεται
34. + οτι post ειπον
35. † επιριψαντες
36. * εαυτων pro αυτων
37. ελεων,
* ηρξατο pro ηρξαντο
* απαν|ταν pro απαν
38. – βασιλευς
39. * φα|ρισαιοι pro των φαρισαιων
40. ¶ – οτι
* σιωπησουσιν pro σιωπησωσιν
41. ηγγεισεν
* αυτην pro αυτη
42. † απ pro απο
43. – και συνεξουσι σε
46. + οτι post γεγραπται|
48. † ηυρισκον,
* ποιησουσῑ| pro ποιησωσιν

CAPUT XX

1. ¶ + αὐτῶ| (scr et del man 1) post επεστησαν
* ιερεις pro αρχιερεις
γραμματις
3. – ενα
5. * συνελογιζοντο pro συνελογισαντο
– ουν
6. * ανθρωπου pro ανθρωπων
πεπισμενος
8. ¶ 10. απεστιλε̄|
διραντες
+ αυτον post εξαπε|στιλαν
11. εξαπεστι|λαν
14. * |διελογιζοντες pro διελογιζοντο
– δευτε
αποκτινωμεν|
γενητε
16. * τουτους και δωσει (τους και δω in ras man 1; αμπ̣ε̣λ̣ω̣ν̣ος̣ prim scr)
17. απεδοκειμασαν
18. * πεσειτε pro πεση
19. < οι γραμμα|τις και οι αρχιερεις
* οχλον, pro λαον
20. * υποχωρησαντες pro παρατηρησαντες
απεστιλαν
ενκαθε|τους
21. + οιδαμε̄| ante διδασκαλε, οιδαμεν
23. πειραζεται,
24. * δει̇ξα|τε pro επιδειξατε
– δε
26. * pro εσιγησαν scr man 1 εσιωπησαν,| (sup ωπη scr -γη- man 2)
27. σαδδουκεω̄|
28. † |μωυσης
† εξαναστησει|
32. * υστερα pro υστερον
33. αναστασι|

γεινεται
34. ¶ *εκγαμιζονται| pro εκγαμισκονται
35. * της εκ νεκρων man 2 (εκ sup, ης ν in ras; των νεκρων man 1)
* εκγαμιζονται, pro εκγαμισκονται
36. * μελλουσιν, pro ετι δυνανται
37. † μωυσης
* εδη|λωσεν pro εμηνυσεν
— και τον θεον ιακωβ
38. + ο ante θεος
* αυτου| ουτοι, pro αυτω ζωσιν
41. † δαυειδ'
42. † δαυειδ'
+ των| ante ψαλμων,
44. † |δαυειδ'
45. ¶ 46. προσεχεται
διπνοις,
47. οικειας
προφασι|
† λημψον|ται

Caput XXI

2. — δε
< τινα και
3. * πλιω pro πλειον
5. † αναθεμασιν|
* |κεκοσμητο (sup ο[2] scr ε man 2) pro κεκοσμηται
6. θεωρειται|
* λιθον pro λιθω
7. |σημιον
† μελλει pro μελλη
γεινεσθαι ·|
8. βλεπεται
πλανηθηται
ειμει
πορευθηται
9. ¶ ακουσηται
πτοηθηται,
11. σισμοι
† |φοβηθρα
σημια
12. * παντων| pro απαντων
14. * |θετε pro θεσθε
15. αντι|πειν
16. παραδοθησεσθαι
† συγγε|νεων
17. εσεσθαι
19. κτησασθαι
20. ειδηται
— την
* γινωσκεται| pro γνωτε
21. εκχωριτωσαν|
— οι[3]
22. * πλησθηναι pro πληρωθηναι
23. — ταις[2]
24. * μαχαιραις, pro μαχαιρας
εχμαλωτισθησον|ται
25. σημια
συνοχη, εθνων εν α|πορεια,
+ η ως ante ηχουσης
† σαλους| pro σαλου
26. προσ|δοκειας
† οικουμε|νης, pro οικουμενη
28. γεινεσθαι,
* ανα|καλυψατε pro ανακυψατε
επαραται
απολυτρωσεις
30. * απ αυ|των pro αφ' εαυτων
γινωσκεται
31. ουτως
ει|δηται
γεινομενα

γινωσκεται
33. * παρελευσεται, man 1, corr παρελευσονται man 2 (ο corr ex ε, et ν suprascr)
† παρελευσονται, pro παρελθωσι
34. προσεχε|ται
* βαρηθωσιν pro βαρυνθωσιν
< αι καρ|διαι υμων
εφνιδιος
— η ante ημερα man 1; add sup man 2
35. παγεις
< της γης πασης,|
36. |αγρυπνιται
* κατισχυσατε pro καταξιωθητε
< παντα ταυτα|
— τα
37. — εξερχομενος
ελεων,

Caput XXII

2. γραμματις
3. ¶ — ο
* κα|λουμενον pro επικαλουμενον
6. εζητι|
7. ¶ 8. απεστιλεν
10. οικειαν
11. ερειται
οικειας
12. † αναγεον pro ανωγεον (ε corr ex ι man 1)
ετοιμασαται,|
15. — με
16. † ουκεντι
17. + το ante ποτηριον|
λαβεται
διαμερισαται
18. + νυ̅| ante γενηματος
* οτου (ο sup man 2)
19. |ποιειται
20. δι|πνησαι
* ετι pro αιματι
† εχχυννομενον,|
23. — αυτοι
* ηρξατο pro ηρξαντο
* αυτους pro εαυτους
πρασσιν,
24. φι|λονικεια
25. * εξουσιαζουσιν pro οι εξουσιαζοντες
26. μιζων|
27. μιζων,|
ουχει
— δε
ειμει
28. εσται
30. εσθειηται
|πεινηται
* καθησεσθαι pro καθισησθε
31. ¶ 33. — ετοιμος
ειμει
34. † φωνηση|
35. απεστιλα
† |βαλλαντιου
† ουθενος| pro ουδενος
36. † βαλλαντι|ον
— ο^{2}
— το
37. — ετι
* πληρωθηναι man 1, corr τελεσθηναι man 2 (·τελεσ· sup)
* ελογισθην, pro ελογισθη
* |το pro τα

38. * *και|* pro *κυριε*
μαχαιρε
εικανον
39. * *εις* in ras man I (*τω* prim scr)
|ελεων,
— *αυτου*
40. *προσευχεσθαι*
42. * *γινε|σθω,* pro *γενεσθω*
43–44. — *ωφθη δε αυτω · · · · επι την γην*
45. — *αυτου*
46. *καθευδεται,*
προσευχεσθαι
εισελθηται
47. — *δε*
* *αυτου,* pro *αυτων*
ηγγισεν| pro *εγγισε* (error edit Oxon)
49. * *επιταξομεν* pro *ει παταξομεν*
51. ¶ * *εασατε* pro *εατε*
— *αυτου*
52. ¶ 53. *εξετινατε*
* *αλλ' η* pro *αλλ'*
< *εστιν υμων*
54. *συνλαβοντες*
* *συνηγαγον* pro *εισηγαγον*
55. ¶ *|συνκαθεισαντων*
58. *ειμει,*
59. * *διαστησασης|* pro *διαστασης*
60. — *ο* ante *αλεκτωρ,*
63. *ενεπε|ζον*
64. *πεσας*
67. *πιστευσηται,*
68. *αποκριθηται*
απολυσηται·|
70. ¶ * *ουν* pro *δε*[1]
λεγεται
ειμει,

Caput XXIII

1. * *ηγαγον* pro *ηγαγεν*
πειλατον,|
3. *πειλατος*
* *αυτος* pro *ο δε αποκριθεις αυτω*
4. *πειλατος*
5. *ανασιει*
6. *πειλατος*
7. * *ιεροσολυ|μοις* (*λυμοις* in ras man I)
8. + *χρονου* post *ικανου*
σημιον
γεινομενον·|
9. *εικανοις·*
* *αυτω,* (*ω* in ras man I, *ον* prim scr)
10. *|ιστηκεισαν*
γραμμα|τις
11. † *|εξουθενισας*
— *ο*
ενπεξας,
— *τω*
πειλατω,
12. *πειλατος*
* *ο ηρωδης* (*ο* sup tamen man I)
13. *πειλατος*
συνκαλε|σαμενος
14. *κατηγορειται|*
18. * *ουν* pro *δε*
πανπληθει|
ερε
— *τον*
19. + *την* ante *φυλακην,|*
20. *πειλατος*
21. — *σταυρωσον*[2]
* *αυτον,* in ras man I (*σταυ··* prim scr)

23. επεκιντο
24. ¶ πειλατος
25. — αυτοις
* εν τη φυλακη| pro εις την φυλακην
26. — του^{1}
28. κλεεται bis
29. αιρουσιν,
στιραι
30. † πεσατε pro πεσετε
|καλυψαται
33. * τον pro ον^{2}
34. — ο δε ιησους · · · τι ποιουσι
* αυτου (ου in ras man 1)
35. * εν οις και εστηκει pro και ειστηκει
< του $\overline{θυ}$| ο pro ο του θεου
36. ενεπεζον
* προσευχομενοι pro προσερχομενοι
39. * και αυτον pro σεαυτον
40. επετειμα
* |εσμεν, pro ει
43. * ση|μερον (σ corr man 1 ex ι sine ras)
παραδισω,|
44. † ενατης|
46. * παρατιθεμαι pro παραθησομαι
* του|το δε pro και ταυτα
48. συνπαρα|γενομενοι
* αυ|των pro εαυτων
49. |ιστηκεισαν
51. συνκατατεθειμενος
αριμαθιας|
52. πειλατω
53. — αυτο^{2}
< ουδεις ουδε|πω
54. — και^{2}
* επιφαυσκεν,| pro επεφωσκε
55. — και^{1}
συνεληλυθειαι
μνημιον

Caput XXIV

2. |μνημιου,
4. διαπορισθαι
< ανδρες δυο
αισθησεσιν
5. |ενφοβων
κλει|νουσων
ζητειται
6. † αλλα|
* ανεστη, pro ηγερθη
μνησθηται
9. μνημιου
† απηγ|γειλαν
10. — ησαν δε
+ η ante ιακωβου,|
— αι^{2}
12. ¶ μνη|μιον,
— κειμενα
14. + π̇ε̇ρ̇ι̇ π̇α̇ν̇τ̇ω̇ν̇ (et del man 1) post ωμιλουν
15. † συνζητειν,|
17. αντιβαλλεται
εσται
18. — εν^{1}
20. < αυ|τον παρεδωκαν
21. † συμ πασιν
22. * ορθρειναι (ρ^{2} sup man 2) pro ορθριαι
μνημιον,|
24. μνημιον
ουτως
† ουχ pro ουκ
25. ¶ 27. † μωυ|σεως
* |διερμηνευειν pro διηρμηνευεν
* αυτου, pro εαυτου

28. ηγγεισαν
29. * εσπερας pro εσπεραν
κε|κλεικεν
30. * κα|τακεισθαι pro κατακλιθηναι
— λαβων τον αρτον
33. † υψεστρεψαν pro υπεστρεψαν
34. — οντως man 1; add sup man 2
35. * το pro τα
κλασι
36. ¶ * αυτοις| pro αυτος
+ εγω ειμει μη φοβεισθαι post λεγει αυτοις|
37. * |φοβηθεντες pro πτοηθεντες
ενφοβοι
38. εσται,
39. |ειδετε
— μου^2
ειμει,
— με
† με| pro εμε
θεωρειται
41. † τη χαρας|
42. — και απο μελισσιου κηριου
44. † μωυσεως,
45. συν|ειεναι
46. |ουτως
48. εσται
49. < εγω ιδου
επαγγελειᾱ|
καθεισατε|
ενδυσησθαι|
50. — εις man 1, add sup man 2
* βηθανιαν, (ν^2 in ras man 2; scr σ man 1)
— αυτου
† |ηυλογησεν
53. — αμην
Subscr ευαγγελιον κατα λουκαν man 1.

SECUNDUM MARCUM

Inscr *ευαγγελιον κατα μαρκον* man 2

Caput I

1. — *του*^{2}
2. — *εμπροσθεν σου*
3. *ποιειται*
+ (post *τρι|βους αυτου,*) (3 *a*) *πασα φαραγξ πληρωθησε|ται, και παν ορος και βουνος ταπινωθη|σεται, και εσται παντα τα σκολια εις ευ|θειαν, και η τραχεια εις πεδιον,* (3 *b*) *και* (*ι* sup man 1 ?) *οφθη|σεται η δοξα* κ̅υ̅*, και οψεται πασα σαρξ το| σωτηριον του* θ̅υ̅*,* (3 *c*) *οτι κς ελαλησεν φωνη| λεγοντος, βοησον και ειπα τι βοησω,* (3 *d*) *οτι| πασα σαρξ χορτος, και πασα η δοξα αυτης| ως ανθος χορτου, εξηρανθη ο χορτος και| το ανθος εξεπεσεν, το δε ρημα* κ̅υ̅ *μενει| εις τον αιωνα· και*
5. *ιεροσολυμειται|*
— *ποταμω*
6. + *ην* post |*και*^{2}
αισθιων
7. *ειμει*
* *του υπο|δηματος* pro *των υποδηματων*
8. † *βαπτιση*
9. * *εγενετο δε* pro *και εγενετο*
+ *και* post *ημεραις*
† *ναζαρεθ*
10. * |*εκ* pro *απο*
* *καταβαινον απο| του ουρανου ωσει περιστεραν και μενον|* pro *ωσει περιστεραν καταβαινον*
11. * *του ου|ρανου,* pro *των ουρανων*
† *ηυ|δοκησα,*
13. < μ̅ *ημερας* pro *ημερας τεσσαρακοντα*
14. — *ο* ante ι̅ς̅
15. *ηγ|γεικεν*
* *των ουρανων,* pro *του θεου*
μετα|νοειται
πιστευεται
16. *ιδεν*
* *αμφι|βαλλοντας* pro *βαλλοντας*
17. — *ο* ante ι̅ς̅
18. — *αυτων*
19. — *εκειθεν*
20. < *ευθεως* post *και*^{2}
< *εν τω πλοιω* post *μισθωτων*
* *ηκολου|θησαν αυτω* pro *απηλθον οπισω αυτου*
21. † *κα|φαρναουμ,*
24. — *εα*
* *συ* pro *σοι*
< *ημας απολεσαι*
+ *ωδε* ante *οιδα*
25. * |*και ειπεν* pro *ο ιησους λεγων*
* *εκ| του ανθρωπου,* pro *εξ αυτου*
25–26. + π̅ν̅α̅ *ακαθαρτον, και|*

εξηλθεν το $\overline{\pi\nu\alpha}$ ante σπαραξαν
26. — και[1]
— το πνευμα το ακαθαρτον
* ανεκραγεν pro κραξαν
* και α|πηλθεν απ pro εξηλθεν εξ
27. * εθαυμαζον| pro εθαμβηθησαν
* και συνεζητουν pro ωστε συζητειν
* εαυ|τους pro αυτους
* λεγοντες, pro λεγοντας
— τι εστι τουτο
κενη|
* η εξουσιαστικη αυτου, και οτι| pro οτι κατ' εξουσιαν και
28. * |και εξηλθεν pro εξηλθε δε
* πανταχου| pro ευθυς
29. * |εξελθων δε εκ της συναγωγης ηλθεν| pro και ευθεως εκ της συναγωγης εξελθοντες ηλθον
οικειαν
\+ ιακωβου και post ιακωβου και
30. < κατεκειτο δε η πενθερα σιμωνος|
— ευθεως
31. \+ εκτινας την χειρα| και επιλαβομενος post προσελθων
— κρατησας της χειρος αυτης
— ευθεως
διη|κονι
* αυτω, pro αυτοις
32. — και τους δαιμονιζομενους
33. πολεις
* |συνηγμενη pro επισυνηγμενη
* τας θυρας, pro την θυραν
34. ποι|κειλαις
\+ απ αυτων, post ε|ξεβαλεν λα|λιν
\+ $\overline{\chi\nu}$ ειναι· post ηδισαν αυτον|
35. — πρωι
* εννυχα pro εννυχον
— λιαν
— εξηλθ εκαι
† και εκει pro κἀκει
36. — ο
37. — και ευροντες αυτον
* λεγοντες pro λεγουσιν
* ζητου|σιν σε παντες, pro οτι παντες ζητουσι σε
38. — ινα κἀκει
* κη|ρυσσιν pro κηρυξω
* εληλυθα,| pro εξεληλυθα
39. * εις τας συναγωγας| pro εν ταις συναγωγαις
— και τα δαιμονια εκβαλλων
40. — και γονυπετων αυτον
\+ $\overline{\kappa\epsilon}$ post λεγων
— αυτω, οτι
41. εκτινας
* λεγων pro και λεγει αυτω
καθαρισθητει,
42. — ειποντος αυτου
— και εκαθαρισθη
43. — και εμβριμησαμενος αυτω, ευθεως εξεβαλεν αυτον
44. μηδενει
— μηδεν
† αλ|λα
< δειξον εαυτον pro σεαυτον δειξον

* καθαρσιου, pro καθαρισμου
* |ο pro α
† μωυσης
45. κηρυσ|σιν
— πολλα
— αυτον[1]
* επ pro εν
* παντοθεν,| pro πανταχοθεν

Caput II

1. * ερχεται pro εισηλθεν
† καρφαναουμ
— δι' ημερων
* εν οικω pro εις οικον
2. — ευθεως
χωριν,|
— μηδε τα προς την θυραν
* προς αυτους pro αυτοις
3. + ιδου ανδρες post |και
+ βασταζοντες εν κρεβαττω post αυτον|
— φεροντες, αιρομενον υπο τεσσαρων
4. * προσελθειν| pro προσεγγισαι
* απο του οχλου, pro δια τον οχλον
— εξορυξαντες
† κρα|βαττον
* εις ον pro εφ' ω
5. ¶ * σου αι| αμαρτιαι, pro σοι αι αμαρτιαι σου
6. + λεγοντες, post αυτων
7. ουτως
* αφειναι pro αφιεναι
8. — ευθεως
— αυτου
— ουτως
— εν εαυτοις
* λεγει pro ειπεν
— ταυτα
διαλογειζεσθαι
9. + γαρ post τι
— τω παραλυτικω
* σου pro σοι
εγειρε
— και αρον σου τον κραββατον
10. ειδηται
αφειεναι
— επι της γης
11. — σοι λεγω
εγειρε
† |κραβαττον
12. * ο δε εγερθεις pro και ηγερθη
— ευθεως
+ αυτου post αρας
† |κραβαττον
— εξηλθεν
* εμπροσθεν pro εναντιον
+ απηλ|θεν, post παντων
* θαυμαζειν αυτους pro εξιστασθαι παντας
— λεγοντας
< ουτως ουδεποτε|
* ειδον: pro ειδομεν
14. λευειν
αλ|φεου
* του τελωνιου| pro το τελωνιον
* ηκολουθει pro ηκολουθησεν
15. * γει|νεται pro εγενετο
* ανακειμενων αυτων pro εν τω κατακεισθαι αυτον
οι|κεια
— αυτου[1], και
|συνανεκιντο

16. * |των φαρισαιων pro και οι φαρισαιοι

— ιδοντες αυτον εσθιοντα μετα των τελωνων και αμαρτωλων

* δια τι pro τι οτι

— και πινει

17. — αυτοις

† αλλα

* εληλυθα pro ηλθον

— εις μετανοιαν

+ μαθηται post οι[2]|

— οι[4]

19. — ο ιησους

* νυμφιοι pro υιοι (νυμ in ras man 1)

— οσον χρονον μεθ' εαυτων εχουσι τον νυμφιον, ου δυνανται νηστευειν

20. * εκεινη τη ημερα, pro εκειναις ταις ημεραις

21. — και[1]

* επισυναπτι| pro επιρραπτει

— επι

ερει

+ απ αυτου| ante το[1]

— αυτου

* πλειω pro χειρον

γεινεται,

22. + |αλλ εις καινους post παλαιους

* διαρρησσον|ται οι ασκοι pro ρησσει ο οινος ο νεος τους ασκους

* απολλυνται, pro απολουνται

* βαλλουσιν,| pro βλητεον

23. * αυτον εν τοις σαββασιν| πορευεσθαι pro παραπορευεσθαι αυτον εν τοις σαββασι

* εσπαρμενων,| pro σποριμων

< οι μαθηται αυτου ηρξαντο

— οδον ποιειν

* τιλλειν| pro τιλλοντες

24. * οι δε pro και οι

ειδε

— εν

25. — αυτος

* λεγει pro ελεγεν

* |ουδε τουτο pro ουδεποτε

* τι sup man 2 (ο man 1, del man 2)

† δαυ|ειδ',

επινασεν

* μετ αυτου, (εταυτ in ras man 1)

26. * εισελθων pro εισηλθεν

— επι αβιαθαρ του αρχιερεως, και

< εφαγεν ante τους αρτους|

* και εδωκεν και τοις| μετ αυτου ους ουκ εξεστιν φαγειν ει μη| τοις ιερευσιν, pro ους ουκ εξεστι····τοις συν αυτω ουσι

27. * λεγω δε υμιν οτι pro και ελεγεν αυτοις

* εκτισθη pro εγενετο

— ουχ ο ανθρωπος δια το σαββατον

Caput III

1. * εισελθοντος αυτου pro εισηλθε παλιν

* ερχεται pro και ην εκει

+ προς αυ|τον post ανθρωπος

* εχων ξηραν pro εξηραμμενην εχων

2. * παρετη|ρουντο pro παρετηρουν

* θεραπευ|ει pro θεραπευσει

— αυτον^2

3. — εξηραμμενην

\+ ξηραν post χειρα|

εγειρε

* εκ του μεσου, pro εις το μεσον

4. * αγαθον| ποιησαι pro αγαθοποιησαι

* ου, pro κακοποιησαι

* απολεσαι·| pro αποκτειναι

5. * περιβλεψαμενος δε| pro και περιβλεψαμενος

— συλλυπουμενος

εξετινεν|

† απεκατεσταθη

— υγιης ως η αλλη

6. * |εξελθοντες δε pro και εξελθοντες

— ευθεως

συνβουλιον

* εποιουντο| pro εποιουν

7. * |ο δε pro και ο

— ηκολουθησαν αυτω

— απο^2

8. — και απο της ιδουμαιας

— οι

\+ ηκολουθουν αυτω post σιδο|να

— πληθος πολυ

* ακουοντες pro ακουσαντες

— ηλθον προς αυτον

10. * εθεραπευεν pro εθεραπευσεν

* επεπιπτο̄| pro επιπιπτειν

* αυτου man 1, αυτω man 2 (ω sup)

11. * τα πνευματα δε pro και τα πνευματα

* ιδον pro εθεωρει

* προσεπιπτον pro προσεπιπτεν

* εκραζον pro εκραζε

* λεγοντες pro λεγοντα

— οτι

12. — πολλα

* ποιωσιν, pro ποιησωσι

13. * αναβας pro αναβαινει

— και^2

* |προσεκαλεσατο pro προσκαλειται

— αυτος

14. \+ μαθητας| post $\overline{\text{ιβ}}$ (pro δεδωκα)

\+ ους post αυτου

\+ αποστολους| ωνομασεν, post και^2

* αποστιλη pro αποστελλη

\+ το ευαγγελιον, post κη|ρυσσιν

15. * εδωκεν αυ|τοις pro εχειν εκβαλλιν

\+ και περια|γοντας κηρυσσιν το ευαγγελιον,| post δαιμονια,

16. — τω

< ονομα σιμωνι

17. — και ιακωβον τον του ζεβεδαιου, και ιωαννην τον αδελφον του ιακωβου

* |κοινως δε αυτους εκαλεσεν βοαναηρ|γε, pro και επεθηκεν αυτοις ονοματα βοανεργες

18. ¶ *ησαν δε ουτοι| σιμων, και

ανδρεας, ιακωβος, και ιωᾱ|νης, φιλιππος και μαρθολομεος, και | μαθθεος, και θωμας, και ιακωβος ο του| αλφαιου, και σιμων ο κανανεος, pro και ανδρεαν····· κανανιτην

19. * ι|ουδας ισκαριωτης ο pro ιουδαν ισκαριωτην ος
* παραδους pro παρεδωκεν

20. * ερχεται pro ερχονται
† μη|δε pro μητε

21. * |περι pro οι παρ'
+ οι γραμματεις και οι λοιποι| post αυτου
† ελεγαν
* εξηρτηνται αυτου pro εξεστη

22. — οι γραμματεις
+ γραμματις,| post καταβαντες
— και οτι
τον αρχον|τα pro εν τω αρχοντι
+ και δι αυτου post δαιμονιων,

23. < εν παραβο|λαις, post αυτοις
* ειπεν pro ελεγεν
|εκβαλλιν,

25. † καν pro και εαν
οικεια[1]
— η οικια εκεινη

26. * εαν pro ει
— ανεστη
* εμερισθη, pro και μεμερισται
+ η βασιλεια αυτου post |σταθηναι

27. * ουδεις δυναται pro ου δυναται ουδεις
< διαρπασαι ante εισελθων
οι|κειαν[1]
— αυτου[1]
* τα σκευη pro την οικιαν[2]
† διαρπαση,|

28. < τα αμαρτη|ματα αφεθησεται
+ αι ante βλασφημιαι,
— οσας αν βλασφημησωσιν

29. — εις[1]
— εις τον αιωνα
† αλλα|
* αμαρτιας, pro κρισεως

30. * εχειν αυτον,| pro εχει

31. * και ερχεται pro ερχονται ουν
< αυτου η μητηρ και οι αδελ|φοι αυτου,
απεστιλᾱ|
* καλουντες pro φωνουντες

32. < περι αυτον οχλος,
* και λεγουσιν pro ειπον δε
* στηκουσιν ζητουντες pro ζητουσι

33. * ος δε pro και[1]
* και ειπεν αυτοις, pro αυτοις λεγων
— μου[1]
* και pro ἢ

34. * αυτου pro τους περι αυτον
+ τους| μαθητας post καθημενους
ειδε

35. * και ος pro ος γαρ
* ποιη pro ποιηση
< μου αδελφος
— μου[2]

Caput IV

1. <ηρξατο παλιν
* προς| pro παρα
* πλειστος, pro πολυς
< εις το πλοιον| ενβαντα
* παρα τον αιγιαλον,| pro εν τη θαλασση
* εν τω αιγιαλω pro προς την θαλασσαν
— επι της γης

2. — πολλα
* λεγων,| pro και ελεγεν
— αυτοις εν τη διδαχη αυτου

3. |ακουεται
— του

4. — εγενετο εν τω σπειρειν
* το μεν pro ο μεν
* ορνεα pro πετεινα του ουρανου

5. * |αλλα pro αλλο
* τα πετρωδη, pro το πετρωδες
* και ο|τι pro οπου
— και
* ανετει|λε, pro εξανετειλε
— δια το μη εχειν βαθος γης

6. ανατιλαντος

7. * αλλα pro αλλο
* επι pro εις
* αυ|τα pro αυτο
* εδωκαν, pro εδωκε

8. * αλλα ε|πεσαν pro αλλο επεσεν
† εδι|δει pro εδιδου
* αυξανο|μενον pro αυξανοντα
* φερει, pro εφερεν
+ το ante εν ter
$\overline{\lambda}$ pro τριακοντα
$\overline{\xi}$| pro εξηκοντα
$\overline{\rho}$ pro εκατον

9. — αυτοις

10. * |και οτε pro οτε δε
* επηρωτη|σαν pro ηρωτησαν
* μαθηται αυτου pro περι αυτον συν τοις δωδεκα
* τις η παρα|βολη αυτη, pro την παραβολην

11. * λεγει pro ελεγεν
— γνωναι
— τα ante παντα
γεινεται

12. — βλεπωσι, και
— ακουωσι, και
* συνωσιν| pro συνιωσι
— τα αμαρτηματα

13. γνωσεσθαι

15. † ευθυς
ερει
* εις αυτους,| pro εν ταις καρδιαις αυτων

16. * |ουτοι δε pro και ουτοι
— ομοιως
* οιτινες pro οι[2]

17. * και pro η
+ και post λογō|
† ευθυς
* σκανδαλιζεται, man 1, corr σκανδαλιζονται man 2

18. — και ουτοι εισιν
+ δε post οι[1]

19. * βιου pro αιωνος
— τουτου
* απαται pro η απατη
— και αι περι τα λοιπα επιθυμιαι
συνπνιγουσι

* ακαρποι γιγνονται, pro ακαρπος γινεται
20. * ουτοι| δε pro και ουτοι
* πιπτο̄|τες, pro σπαρεντες
* καρπον φερουσιν| pro καρποφορουσιν
\+ το ante εν ter
λ̄, ξ̄, ρ̄
21. * λεγει| pro ελεγεν
* καιεται pro ερχεται
κλεινην|
* αλλ’ pro ουχ
* τεθη, pro επιτεθη
22. * ουδεν| pro ου
− τι
* αλλ’ ινα pro ο εαν μη
24. ¶ βλεπε|ται
ακουεται,
μετρειται|
− και προστεθησεται υμιν τοις ακουουσιν
25. * εχει pro αν εχη
26. * ανο̄ς οταν pro εαν ανθρωπος
− τον
* την γην pro της γης
27. * εγει|ρεται pro εγειρηται
* |βλαστα pro βλαστανη
* μηκυνεται pro μηκυνηται
28. * πλη|ρης ο σειτος pro πληρη σιτον
σταχυει,
29. − δε
− ευθεως
30. * πως pro τινι
* τινι την παραβο|λην δωμεν, pro ποια παραβολη παραβαλωμεν
− αυτην
31. * κοκκον pro κοκκω
* οπο|ταν pro ος οταν
* την γην pro της γης
* μικροτερον man 1, μικροτερος man 2
\+ ω̄| ante παντων
− εστι
32. − και οταν σπαρη
* αυξει pro αναβαινει
γεινεται
< μειζον (pro μειζων) ante πᾱ|των
λαχανων κ in ras man 1 (κ̣α̣ι̣ · · · · prim scr)
< αυτου υπο τη̄| σκιαν πετινα
33. − πολλαις
† εδυναν|το
34. † καθ ειδιαν
* αυτας·| pro παντα
35. |οψειας
36. * αφιουσιν pro αφεντες
\+ και post οχλον
* αμα πολλοι ησαν pro αλλα δε πλοιαρια ην
37. γεινεται
λελαψ
* μεγαλου ανεμου·| pro ανεμου μεγαλη
* και τα pro τα δε
* εισεβαλλεν pro επεβαλλεν
38. * εν pro επι[1]
* προσ|κεφαλαιου pro το προσκεφαλαιον
* διεγειρᾱ|τες pro διεγειρουσιν
− και[3]
− αυτω
39. * εγερθεις pro διεγερθεις
* τη θαλασση και ειπεν pro ειπε τη θαλασση

— σιωπα
* φιμωθητι ·| pro πεφιμωσο
— μεγαλη
40. * λεγει pro ειπεν
διλοι
ε|σται
ουτως
— πως ουκ
εχεται
41. * η θαλασσα και οι ανεμοι pro και ο ανεμος και η θαλασσα

Caput V

1. † ηλθαν
† την (ν sup man 3)
* |γεργυστηνων, pro γαδαρηνων
2. * εξελθοντων αυ|των pro εξελθοντι αυτω
— ευθεως
< |α̅ν̅ο̅ς̅ εκ των μνημιων (αν in ras man 1, τ̣· prim scr)
3. < ειχεν την κατοικησιν μνημιοις ·
† ουδε pro ουτε
* αλυσι αυτον| ουκετι εδυναντο pro αλυσεσιν ουδεις ηδυνατο αυτον
4. * πολ|λακεις αυτον δεδεσθαι και πεδες και |αλυσεσι · pro αυτον πολλακις πεδαις και αλυσεσι δεδεσθαι
* διεσπαρκεναι δε pro και διεσπασθαι
— υπ' αυτου
αλυσις|
* συντετριφεναι,| pro συντετριφθαι

* μηδενα δε ισχυειν αυτον ετι pro και ουδεις αυτον ισχυε
5. * |νυκτος δε και ημερας διαπαντος pro και διαπαντος νυκτος και ημερας
* μνημιοις pro μνημασιν
6. ¶ — απο
* προσεδρα|μεν pro εδραμε
7. * λεγει, pro ειπε
* συ| pro σοι
— του[1]
9. < ονομα σοι|
* λεγει αυτω pro απεκριθη λεγων
10. * αποστιλη αυτον| pro αυτους αποστειλη
11. < προς τω ορι (pro προς τα ορη) post μεγαλη
12. * παρακαλεσαντες αυτον ειπα̅| pro παρεκαλεσαν αυτον παντες οι δαιμονες λεγοντες
13. — ευθεως ο ιησους
† εισηλθαν
— ησαν δε
14. * |και οι pro οι δε
* αυτους pro τους χοιρους
† |ανηγγειλον
15. * ευρισκουσιν pro θεωρουσι
— καθημενον και ιματισμενον και
16. * ειδοτες pro ιδοντες
18. * ενβε|νοντος pro εμβαντος
< μετ αυ|του η
19. * και pro ο δε ιησους
* διαγγειλον pro αναγγειλον
* πεποιηκεν pro εποιησε
* ηλεηκεν pro ηλεησε
20. κηρυσσιν

21. * διαπερα|σαντες pro διαπερασαντος
< εν τω πλοιω του ι̅υ̅
22. * τις pro εις
* ω ο|νομα pro ονοματι
ειδων
* προσπι|πτι pro πιπτει
23. < τας χειρας αυτη
* ινα pro οπως
25. — τις
< ι̅β̅ ετη pro ετη δωδεκα
26. — παρ'
27. + και ante ακουσασα
— ελθουσα
— του ιματιου
28. < αψωμαι αυτου
29. * ειαθη pro ιαται
30. * ειπεν, pro ελεγε
31. — αυτου
* συντριβοντα pro συνθλιβοντα
32. — ιδειν
* πεποιηκυιαν, pro ποιησασαν
33. ιδυια
+ εμπροσθεν πα̅|των post αυτω[2]
* αιτιαν αυτης,| pro αληθειαν
34. * θυγατηρ pro θυγατερ
ι|σθει
υγειης
35. σκυλλις
36. — ευθεως
* παρακουσας pro ακουσας
37. < αυτω ουδενα
* παρακο|λουθησε, pro συνακολουθησαι
+ μονον post ει μη
38. + και post θορυβον|
39. θορυβι|σθαι
40. + ειδοτες οτι απεθανεν,| post |αυτου[1]
* παντας pro απαντας
παραλαμβανι|
* εαυτου, pro μετ' αυτου
* κατακειμενον| pro ανακειμενον
41. — αυτη
† ταβιθα pro ταλιθα
— κουμι
εγ̅ειρε|
42. ι̅β̅ pro δωδεκα
43. διεστιλατο
† γνοι pro γνω

Caput VI

1. — εκειθεν, και ηλθεν
2. ‖ ηρξαντο pro ηρξατο
— οτι
δυναμις
γεινονται·|
3. + της| ante μαριας
αδελφε pro αδελφαι
4. — αυτοις
συνγενεσιν
οικεια|
5. † εδυνατο
* ουκετι pro εκει ουδεμιαν
< ποι|ησαι δυναμιν,
ολειγοις
6. < κυκλω κωμας
7. ι̅β̅ pro δωδεκα
* εδωκεν pro εδιδου
8. * παρηγ|γελλεν pro παρηγγειλεν
* αρωσιν pro αιρωσιν
* πηραν pro ζωνην
9. ενδυσησθαι
χειτωνας

10. — αυτοις
† αν pro εαν
οικειᾱ|
11. * ος pro οσοι
+ τοπος post αν
* δεξηται| pro δεξωνται
* ακουση pro ακουσωσιν
* αυτων,| pro αυτοις
— αμην λεγω υμιν · · · πολει εκεινη
12. * μετα|νοωσιν pro μετανοησωσι
13. * εξεπεμ|πον pro εξεβαλλον
ηλιφον
+ αυτους,| post εθεραπευον
14. * |ελεγον pro ελεγεν
* βαπτιστης pro βαπτιζων
* αυτου, (man 1) pro εν αυτω (ω sup ου man 2)
15. + δε post αλλοι[1]
— εστιν η
16. * ον εγω| ον pro ον εγω (ον[1] sup man 2)
— εστιν· αυτος
— εκ νεκρων
17. — ο ante ηρωδης
αποστιλας
18. < γυναικα εχειν pro εχειν την γυναικα
20. ιδως
συνετηρι
* ηπορειτο pro εποιει
21. διπνον
* εποιησεν pro εποιει
χειλιαρχοις|
22. — της[2]
* |ετησαι pro αιτησον
* δαν pro εαν
23. — και ωμοσεν αυτη, οτι ο εαν με αιτησης, δωσω σοι
* |ημισυ pro ημισους
— μου
24. * αιτησωμαι,| pro αιτησομαι
+ αιτησε post ειπεν[2]
25. † |ευθυς
— προς τον βασιλεα, ητησατο λεγουσα
* δω|σης pro δως
— εξ αυτης
πινακει
26. * ακναειμενους pro συνανακειμενους
27. απο|στιλας
— ο βασιλευς
† σφεκουλατορα pro σπεκουλατωρα
+ επι πινα|κει, post αυτου
28. * και pro ο δε
† φυλακη (η corr man 1 ex ει sine ras)
πινακει
— αυτην[1]
29. * |κηδευσαι pro και ηραν
* αυτον pro αυτο
— τω ante μνημιω·
30. † απηγ|γειλον
* εποιησεν| pro εποιησαν
— οσα[2]
* εδιδασκεν pro εδιδαξαν
31. — αυτοι
αναπαυεσθαι
* λοιπον, pro ολιγον
— οι[2]
ηυκερουν,
32. † και (ι sup man 2)
33. ιδον
* αυτον pro αυτους[1]
* υπαγοντες pro υπαγοντας
— αυτον[1]

— και προηλθον αυτους, και
  συνηλθον προς αυτον

34. — ο ιησους
  εσπλανχνισθη
  * ηρξαντο pro ηρξατο

35. — αυτου
  * παρηλθεν, pro πολλη

36. — αρτους
  — γαρ
  — ουκ εχουσιν

37. * δηναριων ρ̅ pro διακοσιων
  δηναριων
  + ινα εκα|στος αυτων βραχυ
  τι λαβη,| post φαγειν

38. υπαγεται
  — και[1]
  ειδεται,

39. συνποσια[1]
  συμποσια[2]

40. † ανεπεσαν
  * |ανδρες ρ̅ pro ανα εκατον
  ν̅, pro πεντηκοντα

41. † ηυλογη|σεν·
  + πεντε post τους[3]
  * παρατιθωσιν pro παραθω-
  σιν

43. ι̅β̅ pro δωδεκα
  * πληρωματα| pro πληρεις

44. — τους αρτους, ωσει
  πεντακεισχειλιοι

45. † ευθυς
  ενβηναι
  — εις το περαν
  † βηθαιδαν
  + αν post εως

47. οψειας

48. * ιδων pro ειδεν
  + σφοδρα, post αυτοις
  ερχε|τε
  — προς αυτους

49. < φαντασμα εδοξᾱ|

50. < θαρσιτε μη φοβεισθαι εγω
  ειμι|

51. — λιαν
  * αυτοις pro εαυτοις

52. † συνηκον pro συνηκαν
  < αυτων η καρδια

53. † ηλθαν
  + εις post γην|
  — και προσωρμισθησαν

54. † ευθυς
  + οι ανδρες του τοπου post
  |αυτον

55. * περιεδρα|μον pro περιδρα-
  μοντες
  + εις ante ολην
  + και post εκεινην·|
  * κρεβαττοις pro τοις κραβ-
  βατοις
  * οτι pro οπου
  < εστιν εκει,

56. * οποταν pro οπου αν
  * εισεπορευ|οντο pro εισεπο-
  ρευετο
  * ηψαντο pro ηπτοντο

Caput VII

2. * |τινες pro τινας
  + τινας post αυτου
  + τους ante αρτους

3. * πυκνα pro πυγμη
  αισθιουσιν,

4. † απ pro απο
  + δε οταν ελθωσιν post α|γο-
  ρας
  αισθιουσιν,
  κρατιν,
  κλεινων,

5. επιτα
  * ερωτω|σιν pro επερωτωσιν

+ λεγοντες · post γραμματις|
* κοιναις ταις pro ανιπτοις αισθιουσιν

6. † επροεφητευσεν
* αγαπα, pro τιμα
* εχει pro απεχει

8. – γαρ
κρατιτε
– βαπτισμους ξεστων και ποτηριων, και αλλα παρομοια τοιαυτα πολλα ποιειτε

9. * στησηται, pro τηρησητε

10. † μωυσης|
* αθετων pro κακολογων

11. λεγεται
† αν pro εαν^{2}

12. αφιεται
– αυτου bis

13. + την εντολην post λογον|
παραδοσι
* παρεδοτε, pro παρεδωκατε
– και παρομοια τοιαυτα πολλα ποιειτε

14. |ακουεται
συνιεται|

15. * αυτον^{1} (ν sup man 2)
* εκ του $\overline{\text{ανου}}$ εκπο|ρευομενα pro εκπορευομενα απ' αυτου

17. * εισηλθον pro εισηλθεν

18. |ουτως
εσται,
|κοινωσε,

19. * διανοιαν, pro καρδιαν
† αλλα
* χωρει, pro εκπορευεται
* καθα|ριζων pro καθαριζον

21. – οι^{2}

21–22. <μοιχιαι,| πορνιαι, κλοπαι, φονος (corr ex φονοι man 1) πλεονεξια| πονηρια, pro μοιχειαι··· πονηριαι

23. – ταυτα
εκπορευετε

24. – εκειθεν
* |ορια pro μεθορια
– και σιδωνος
οι|κειαν

25. – αυτης
* εν $\overline{\text{πνι}}$ ακαθαρτω pro πνευμα ακαθαρτον

26. <η δε γυνη| ην
† συραφοινισσα
* εκ|βαλη pro εκβαλλη

28. – και λεγει
* |λεγουσα $\overline{\text{κε}}$, και pro ναι, κυριε· και γαρ
* εσθιουσιν pro εσθιει
† ψιχων| pro ψιχιων

30. – αυτης

31. ¶ * εις pro προς
* εις| την δεκαπολιν, pro δεκαπολεως

32. + και post |κωφον
† μογγιλαλον

33. * προσλαβομενος pro απολαβομενος
– τους ante δακτυλους
– αυτου^{1}
<πτυσας| ante εις τα ωτα
† γλωσ|σας pro γλωσσης

34. † |εφεθθα, pro εφφαθα
† διανυχθητι,

35. * διηνυγησαν pro διηνοιχθησαν

36. διεστιλατο
* λεγωσιν,| pro ειπωσιν
* οσω pro οσον

— αυτος
37. † υπερπε|ρισσω
* πεποιηκεν pro ποιει
— τους αλαλους

Caput VIII

1. ¶ + δε post εκειναις
* παλιν πολ|λου pro παμπολλου
+ αυτω̅| post εχοντων
— ο ιησους
— αυτοις
2. σπλαγχνιζομε|
* τω οχλω pro τον οχλον
* ημερε pro ημερας
τρις
3. + εως| post νηστις
εκλυθησοντε
* |και τινες pro τινες γαρ
+ απο ante μακροθεν
4. + λε|γοντες, post μαθηται
— αυτου
* ωδε δυνασαι αυτους| pro τουτους δυνησεται τις ωδε
ερημειας,|
5. * |ο δε ηρωτησεν pro και επηρωτα
+ ωδε post ποσους
< αρ|τους εχετε,
† ειπαν
6. † κα pro και[1]
αναπεσιν
ζ̅ pro επτα
* αυτοις pro τοις μαθηταις αυτου
7. † ειχαν
ολειγα,
+ αυτα post και[2]
8. — αυτα
— δε
† περισευματα
— κλασματων
ζ̅ pro επτα
+ πληρεις, post σπυ|ριδας
9. τετρακεισχειλιοι
10. ¶ < ενβας ευθυς pro ευθεως εμβας
— το
+ και post αυτου
* προς το ορος| δαλμουναι, pro εις τα μερη δαλμανουθα
11. † συνζητειν
* απ pro παρ᾿
σημιον
* εκ pro απο
12. — αυτου
σημιον bis
— λεγω υμιν
* ου pro ει
δοθησετε
< ταυτη τη γενεα
13. < παλιν ενβας
14. * απελθοντες| pro επελαθοντο
+ οι μαθηται αυτου ante λαβειν
— και ει μη
* μονο̅| εχοντες αρτον pro αρτον ουκ ειχον
15. βλε|πεται
† φαριοεων,
+ απο post και[2]|
* των ηρωδιανων, pro ηρωδου
16. * οι δε pro και
— λεγοντες
* εχουσιν, pro εχομεν
17. + εν εαυτοις ολιγοπιστοι| post διαλογειζεσθαι

εχεται bis
συνιεται
— ετι
18. * εχετε και pro εχοντες bis
* βλεπουσιν, pro βλεπετε
α|κουεται·
— και^{2}
μνημονευεται
19. πεντακισχειλι|ους (ε^{2} sup man 2)
20. + αρτους post $\overline{\zeta}$ (pro επτα)
τετρακισχειλιους|
— κλασματων
† ειπαν
$\overline{\zeta}$, pro επτα
21. * λεγει pro ελεγεν
* ου|πω pro ου
συνιεται,
22. * ερχονται pro ερχεται
† βηθαιδ$\overline{\alpha}$·|
23. * αυτου pro του τυφλου
* ενπτυσας pro πτυσας
+ και post αυτου
+ |επ ante αυτω
* ηρωτα pro επηρωτα
— τι
24. * ο δε pro και
* λεγει, pro ελεγε
— οτι
— ορω
25. + αυτου post χειρας
— εποιησεν αυτον
* διεβλεψεν pro αναβλεψαι
† απεκατεσταθη|
* ανεβλεπεν man 1 pro ενεβλεψεν (ενεβλεπεν man 2)
* παντα τηλαυγως, pro τηλαυγως απαντας
26. α|πεστιλεν
* |μη pro μηδε^{1}
— μηδε ειπης τινι εν τη κωμη
27. καισαριας
< επη|ρωτα post αυτου^{2}
28. + λεγον|τες, οι μεν post αποκριθησαν
* |αλλοι δε pro και αλλοι
29. — και αυτος
|λεγεται,
— ειναι
+ ο υιος του $\overline{\theta\upsilon}$ του ζωντος·| post $\overline{\chi\varsigma}$
30. * λεγου|σιν pro λεγωσι
31. + απο τοτε post και^{1}
* απο prim scr, corr υπο man 1
+ τ$\overline{\omega}$| ante αρχιερεων
* τη τριτη ημερα pro μετα τρεις ημερας
32. † παρησια
33. * ιδως pro ιδων
34. — αυτοις
* |ει τις pro οστις
* ακολουθειν pro ελθειν
* αρας pro αρατω
— αυτου^{2}, και
35. < εαυτου ψυχην, pro ψυχην αυτου^{2}
— ουτος
36. * ωφελει τον $\overline{\alpha\nu o\nu}$ pro ωφελησει ανθρωπον
< εαυ|του ψυχην, pro ψυχην αυτου
37. * τι γαρ pro η τι
38. επεσχ$\overline{\upsilon}$|θη
— λογους
— ταυτη
μοι|χαλιδει
επεσχυνθησεται
* και pro μετα

Caput IX

1. ¶ − αν
εληλυθειαν
2. † καθ pro κατ'
+ εν τω| προσευχεσθαι αυτους post και^{5}
+ ο $\overline{\iota\varsigma}$ post μετεμορφωθη|
3. − χιων, οια
4. + ιδου post και^{1}
* αυτος pro αυτοις
† |μωυση pro μωσει
συνλαλουντες
5. * ειπεν πετρος pro ο πετρος λεγει
|ραββει
< ωδε ημας
* θελεις ποιησω ωδε pro ποιησωμεν
τρις,
† μωυση
6. * λαλει pro λαληση
7. + ιδου post |και^{1}
* |αυτους, pro αυτοις
− ηλθε
< ακουετε αυτου,
8. * περι|βλεπομενοι pro περιβλεψαμενοι
9. |διεστιλατο
* α ειδον| εξηγησονται, pro διηγησωνται α ειδον
10. * οι δε pro και
† συνζητουντες
* ε|στιν οταν pro εστι το
* αναστη, pro αναστηναι
11. * επη|ρωτησαν pro επηρωτων
* τι ουν pro οτι^{1}
γραμματις
12. − μεν
* πρωτος pro πρωτον
* αποκαθιστανι pro αποκαθιστα
† εξουθενηθη| pro εξουδενωθη
13. * ηδη pro και^{1}
* ηλθεν| pro εληλυθε
* αυτω· pro αυτον
14. * ελθοντες pro ελθων
* ιδον pro ειδεν
− πολυν
γραμματις
† συνζητουντας
* προς αυτους| pro αυτοις
15. † ευθυς
* ιδοντες pro ιδων
* εξεθαμ|βηθησαν pro εξεθαμβηθη
16. * αυτους, pro τους γραμματεις
† συν|ζητειτε
* εαυτους, pro αυτους
17. < εις post οχλου
+ αυτω, post ειπεν
18. − αυτον^{2}
− αυτου
ξηρενετε,
† ειπα pro ειπον
* ηδυνηθησā| εκβαλειν αυτο, pro ισχυσαν
19. * και pro ο δε
* αυτοις| pro αυτω
+ ο $\overline{\iota\varsigma}$ ante λεγει,
* απιστε pro απιστος
+ και διεστραμ|μενη ante ἑως
* ανεξωμαι pro ανεξομαι
φερεται
20. − και^{2}
− αυτον^{4}
21. < αυτου τον $\overline{\pi\rho\alpha}$

+ λεγων| ante ποσος
* εξ ου pro ως
* εκπαιδοθεν, pro παιδιοθεν
22. πολ|λακεις
— και^{2}
† αλλα
* δυνη| pro δυνασαι
23. * τουτο pro το
* δυνη pro δυνασαι
— πιστευσαι
24. * το $\overline{\text{πνα}}$ pro ο πατηρ
* παιδαριον pro παιδιου
— μετα δακρυων
* ειπεν· pro ελεγε
— κυριε
* βοηθησον pro βοηθει
25. * συντρεχει pro επισυντρεχει
+ ο ante οχλος
— τω ακαθαρτω
* το αλαλον κ(αι)| κωφον $\overline{\text{πνα}}$ pro το πνευμα το αλαλον και κωφον
< επιτασσω σοι
26. * κραξας pro κραξαν
* σπαραξας pro σπαραξαν
— αυτον
27. — αυτον^{1}
— και ανεστη
28. * εισελθοντος αυτου pro εισελθοντα αυτον
+ προσηλ|θον αυτω post οικον
+ κατ ιδιαν και post μαθηται
— αυτου
* επη|ρωτησαν pro επηρωτων
+ λεγοντες, post αυτον^{2}
— κατ' ιδιαν
29. δυνα|τε
νηστια·|
30. ¶ 31. * λεγει pro ελεγεν
παραδιδοτε
* εγειρεται· pro αναστησεται
32. * ερω|τησαι pro επερωτησαι
33. * ηλθον pro ηλθεν
† καφαρναουμ',|
οικεια
* διελεχθητε προς εαυ|τους· pro προς εαυτους διελογιζεσθε
34. * αυτων μιζō| ειη, pro μειζων
35. — και^{1}
καθεισας
$\overline{\text{ιβ}}$ pro δωδεκα
εστε|
36. — αυτο εν
εναγκαλισαμενος
37. † αν pro εαν bis
* εκ pro εν
* παιδιον pro παιδιων
* |εν pro επι
απο|στιλαντα
38. * και αποκριθεις pro απεκριθη δε
* ειπεν, pro λεγων
+ |εν ante τω ονοματι
* ηκολουθει pro ακολουθει^{1}
— οτι ουκ ακολουθει ημιν
39. — ιησους
* εν| pro επι
* δυνησονται pro δυνησεται
— ταχυ
< με κα|κολογησαι,
40. * ημων pro υμων bis
41. < αν γαρ pro γαρ αν
— τω
* $\overline{\text{χρς}}$ pro χριστου

|εσται;

<+ οτι post υμιν

42. + μου post μικρων

— αυτω

* περιεκει|το μυλον ονικον pro περικειται λιθος μυλικος

* εβληθη pro βεβληται

43. * |σκανδαλιση pro σκανδαλιζη

< |κυλλον, post εισελθεῖ,

— την γεενναν, εις

44. — οπου ο σκωληξ · · · ου σβεννυται

45. * σκανδαλιση pro σκανδαλιζη

* κοψον pro αποκοψον

< σοι εστιν

* απελθει| pro βληθηναι

46. — εις το πυρ · · · · ου σβεννυται

47. * ει pro εαν

* |σκανδαλιση pro σκανδαλιζη

— σοι

— βληθηναι

— του πυρος

48. * σβεννυεται ·| pro σβεννυται

49. * αλις γηθησεται · pro αλισθησεται

— και πασα θυσια αλι αλισθησεται

50. † αλα pro αλας ter

* μωρανθη pro αναλον γενηται

* αρτυ|σηται · pro αρτυσετε

+ υμεις ουν post αρτυσηται

< εν εαυτοις εχεται

ειρηνευεται

Caput X

1. † και εκειθε͞| pro κἀκειθεν

— δια του

* συνπορευεται pro συμπορευονται

— παλιν[1]

* ο|χλος pro οχλοι

ιωθει

2. * οι δε φαρισαιοι προσελ|θοντες pro και προσελθοντες οι φαρισαιοι

* αυτου pro αυτον[1] man 1, corr αυτον man 2 (υ[2] eras et ν scr)

3. ενετιλατο

† μωυσης,

4. † ειπαν|

† μωυσης

5. εγραψε

— υμιν

6. ¶ — αυτους

7. + και ειπεν, ante ενεκεν

|καταλιψει

* εκαστος pro ανθρωπος

8. * ουκ pro ουκετι

< σαρξ| μια,

9. * εζευξεν pro συνεζευξεν

10. οικεια

< επηρω|τησαν ante οι μαθηται

— περι του αυτου

— αυτον

11. — ος εαν απολυση · · · μοιχαται επ᾽ αυτην

12. — και[1]

< απολυση γυνη

* γαμηση αλλον pro γαμηθη αλλω

+ και| εαν ανηρ απολυση την γυναικα μοιχατ(αι)| post μοιχαται,
14. + επιτει|μησας post και^{1}
< αυτοις ειπεν,
αφεται
† εμε pro με
− και^{2}
κωλυεται
* των ουρανων·| pro του θεου
15. † αν pro εαν
16. ενανκαλεισαμενος
* επιτιθει pro τιθεις
+ και post αυτα^{2}
† ευλογει|
17. + ιδου τις πλουσιος post οδ$\overline{\text{ο}}$|
− εἶς
− αυτον^{1}
+ λεγων, post αυτον^{2}
19. − μη αποστερησης
+ σου, post |$\overline{\mu\rho\alpha}$
20. + τι υστερω ετι,| post μου
21. − ο δε
ενβλεψας
+ ει θελεις τελιος ειναι post αυτω,^{2}
* σε pro σοι
− τοις ante |πτωχοις
* ουρανοις| pro ουρανω
< αρας τον σταυρον σου ante δευρο
ακολουθι
22. * απο του λογου pro επι τω λογω
+ α|π αυτου post απηλθεν
24. ¶ ante ο δε $\overline{\iota\varsigma}$
− παλιν
− τους πεποιθοτας επι τοις χρημασιν
+ πλουσιον, post εισελθειν
25. − της bis
† τρωμαλιας pro τρυμαλιας
< πλουσιον post $\overline{\theta\upsilon}$
26. * δυνησεται pro δυναται
27. + μεν| post παρα^{1}
+ τουτο post $\overline{\alpha\nu o\iota\varsigma}$
† αλλα
− εστι παρα
28. − και^{1}
< αυτω λεγειν ο πετρος
− ιδου ημεις
< παντα α|φηκαμεν
* ηκολουθηκαμεν pro ηκολουθησαμεν
29. − δε
οικειαν
< η $\overline{\mu\rho\alpha}$ η $\overline{\pi\rho\alpha}$
− η γυναικα
+ ενεκεν post και
30. οικει|ας
− αδελφους και
* $\overline{\mu\rho\alpha}$ pro μητερας
31. − οι
32. − και^{3}
+ αυτω, post ακολου|θουντες
− εφοβουντο
$\overline{\iota\beta}$ pro δωδεκα
33. − τοις^{2}
− αυτον^{2}
34. ενπεξουσιν
* ενπτυσωσιν pro εμπτυσουσιν
35. * προσηλθον pro προσπορευονται (προσελθοντες prim scr man 1; litt τες del man (1) et 2 et 3; ε^{1} eras et η scr man 3)
* θελωμεν pro θελομεν
† $\overline{\alpha}$| pro εαν

+ σε post α̅
* αιτησωμεθα pro αιτησωμεν
36. θελεται
<με ποιησαι (με sup man 2)
37. — σου^{2}
* βασιλεια της δοξης,| pro δοξη σου
38. + αποκριθεις post ι̅ς̅
* αυτω pro αυτοις
* |το pro τι
αιτισθαι,
δυνασθαι
* η pro και
39. † ειπαν|
— αυτω
— ο δε ιησους ειπεν αυτοις
πιεσθαι·
βα|πτιζομε
βαπτισθησεσθαι,
40. κα|θεισαι
* η pro και
— μου^{2}
42. — ιησους
— αυτους
* ου μεγα|λοι pro οι μεγαλοι
— αυτων^{3}
43. ουτως|
— δε
* εστιν pro εσται
* οστις αν pro ος εαν
<εν υ|μιν μεγας γενεσθαι
<υμων διακο|νος,
44. * ειναι pro γενεσθαι
+ υμων post |εσται
45. † λουτρον
46. + ο ante υιος
— βαρτιμαιος ο
47. * ναζαρηνος pro ναζωραιος
48. — και επετιμων ··· ελεησον με
49. — αυτω
* θαρ|ρων pro θαρσει
εγειρε
φωνι
51. θελις
† ραββουνι|
52. — ιησους
* αυτω pro τω ιησου

Caput XI

1. ενγιζουσιν
† ιεροσολυμα
ελεω̅|
2. — και^{1}
* λε|γων pro λεγει
υπαγεται
<κατεναν|τι κωμην, pro κωμην την κατεναντι
— υμων
ευρησεται
* ω pro εφ' ον
+ ου|πω ante ουδεις
* επικεκαθεικεν pro κεκαθικε
3. — ποιειτε τουτο
4. — τον
— την
5. * |τινες δε pro και τινες
* εστωτων pro εστηκοτων
6. * ειπεν αυτοις pro ενετειλατο
7. * αγουσιν pro ηγαγον
* επιβαλλουσιν pro επεβαλον
— αυτων
* καθιζει pro εκαθισεν
8. — αυτων
* |εστρωννυον pro εστρωσαν
— αλλοι δε στοιβαδας ···· εις την οδον

9. — ωσαννα
10. |βασειλια
— εν ονοματι κυριου
* ειρηνη pro ωσαννα
11. — ο ιησους, και
ο|ψειας
— ηδη
ι̅β̅· pro δωδεκα
12. * αυριο̅| pro επαυριον
* εις βηθανιαν pro απο βηθανιας
επι|νασεν,
13. * απομακροθεν συκην| pro συκην μακροθεν
+ εις αυτην, post ηλθεν
< |τι ευρησει
* εις αυτην, pro εν αυτη
+ μονον| post φυλλα
+ υ ante καιρος
14. < ειπεν αυτη ο ι̅ς̅,
< εις τον αιωνα| εκ σου καρπον μηδεις
* φαγη· κ(αι) ηκουσαν| pro φαγοι. και ηκουον
15. — ο ιησους
— και αγοραζοντας
† εν τω ιερω (ν τω ιερω in ras man 1; prim scr ε τω ιερω)
+ εξεχεε̅·| post κολλυβιστων
17. εθνεσι·
|σπηλεον
18. < οι αρχι|ερεις και οι γραμματις,
* απολεσωσιν pro απολεσουσιν
* |πας γαρ pro οτι πας
19. * οταν pro οτε
* εγεινετο
* εξω| της πολεως εξεπορευοντο, pro εξεπορευετο εξω της πολεως
20. < παραπο|ρευομενοι πρωει
εξη|ρανμενην
21. ραββει,
ειδε
22. — και
εχεται
+ του ante θ̅υ̅·|
23. — οτι[1]
ορι|
* αρθηναι pro αρθητι
* βληθηναι pro βληθητι
— ο εαν ειπη
24. — αν
αιτισθαι,
* ελαβετε pro λαμβανετε
25. στηκηται
* ανη pro αφη
26. — ει δε υμεις··· παραπτωματα υμων
28. * |ελεγον pro λεγουσιν
< ταυτην την εξουσιαν
— ινα ταυτη ποιης
29. ¶ * επερωτω| pro επερωτησω
— και[1]
* τινι pro ποια
30. * απ pro εξ[1]
αποκριθηται
31. * διελογιζο̅|το pro ελογιζοντο
* αυτους pro εαυτους
+ οτι post λεγοντες,
+ ημιν post ερει
— ουν
32. * φοβουμεθα pro εφοβουντο
* παντες pro απαντες
* |ηδισαν pro ειχον
33. < τω ι̅υ̅ λεγουσι̅|

† οιδομεν, man 1, corr οιδαμεν man 3

CAPUT XII

1. * λαλειν, pro λεγειν
* $\overline{ανος}$ τις εφυ|τευσεν αμπελωνα, pro αμπελωνα εφυτευσεν ανθρωπος
+ αυ|τω post περιεθηκεν
— και[3]
* εξωρυξεν pro ωρυξεν
2. απεστιλεν
— προς τους γεωργους
3. + και απεκτιναν post |εδιραν
απεστιλαν
4. — παλιν
απεστιλεν
— λιθοβολησαντες
* κεφαλεωσαντες pro εκεφαλαιωσαν και
απεστιλαν|
* ητιμασμενον, pro ητιμωμενον
5. απεστι|λεν,
— κἀκεινον απεκτειναν
* δε pro μεν
αποκτινοντες,
6. * υστερον δε| pro ετι ουν
+ τον ante αγαπητον
απε|στιλεν
— και αυτον
— οτι
7. < ειπαν, post εαυτους
αποκτι|νωμεν
8. απεκτ.ν$\overline{α}$|
10. * ανεγνωκατε, pro ανεγνωτε
α|πεδοκειμασαν
12. — και αφεντες αυτον, απηλθον
14. * ηρξαντο ερωταν αυτ$\overline{ο}$| εν δολω· pro λεγουσιν αυτω
— ου[1]
+ |ειπον ουν ημιν ante εξεστιν
< δουναι κηνσον καισαρι| (κηνσον sup man 2)
15. + υποκριται, post πειραζετε
ειδω,
16. † ειπαν
— αυτω
17. — ο ιησους
< τα καισα|ρος αποδοτε
18. |σαδδουκεοι
19. † μωυσης|
* εχη pro καταλιπη
* τεκνον| pro τεκνα
— αυτου[1, 2]
20. * απεθανεν και pro αποθνησκων
21. — και[1]
— και απεθανε
— και[4]
22. — και ελαβον αυτην
$\overline{ζ}$ pro επτα
* εσχατον pro εσχατη
< η γυνη α|πεθανεν, pro απεθανε και η γυνη
23. — ουν
αναστασι
* ουν αυτ$\overline{ω}$| τινος pro οταν αναστωσι, τινος αυτων
$\overline{ζ}$ pro επτα
24. * αποκριθεις δε pro και αποκριθεις
πλανασθαι|
25. γαμι|σκοντε,
+ οι ante αγγελοι
26. * ει pro οτι
εγειρ$\overline{ο}$|τε

* *ανεγνωκατε* pro *ανεγνωτε*
† *μωυ|σεως*
< *ο* $\overline{\theta\varsigma}$ *λεγ*$\overline{\omega}$| *αυτω˙*
— *ο* ante $\overline{\theta\varsigma}$[2,3,4]
27. — *ο* ante $\overline{\theta\varsigma}$[1]
— *θεος*[2]
— *υμεις ουν*
πλανασθαι,|
28. * *προελθων* pro *προσελθων*
* |*ακουων* pro *ακουσας*
† *συνζητουντων*
* *ιδ*$\overline{\omega}$| pro *ειδως*
< *απεκριθη αυτοις,*
— *πασων*
29. * *ειπεν* pro *ιησους απεκριθη*
— *οτι*
* *παντων πρωτη,* pro *πρωτη πασων των εντολων*
† *ιστραηλ',*
— *εις*
30. *αγαπησις*
— *εντολη*
31. * |*ομοιως* pro *ομοια*
αγαπησις
μιζων
32. < $\overline{\theta\varsigma}$ *εστιν*
33. * *κα το* pro *και*[2]
— *και εξ ολης της ψυχης*
+ *σου* post *πλησιον*
* *σε|αυτον,* pro *εαυτον*
πλιον
— *των* bis
34. — *αυτον*[1]
+ *οτι* post *αυτω,*|
βασειλιας
< *ετολμα αυτον ουκετι*
* *επερωταν*| pro *επερωτησαι*
35. — *ο ιησους*
* *λεγει* pro *ελεγεν*
γραμματις
— *ο* ante $\overline{\chi\varsigma}$
36. — *γαρ*
— *τω* ante $\overline{\pi\nu\iota}$
— *τω* ante *αγιω,*
† |*εκχθρους*
* *υποκατω* pro *υποποδιον*
37. — *ουν*
* *πως* pro *ποθεν*
— *ο*
38. — *αυτοις*
+ *ταις* ante *στολαις*
39. *διπνοις,*
40. — *τας* ante *οικειας*
— *των* ante *χηρ*$\overline{\omega}$|
+ |*και ορφανων,* post *χηρ*$\overline{\omega}$
προφασι
* *οιτινες* pro *ουτοι*
† *λημψονται*
* *περισσοι* pro *περισσοτερον*
41. * *εστως* pro *καθισας*
+ *παντας,* post *εθεωρι*
+ *τον* ante *χαλκον*
43. — *αυτου*
— *οτι*
|*πλιον*
— *των βαλοντων*
44. * *περισσευμα|τος αυτων* pro *περισσευοντος αυτοις*
— *παντα οσα ειχεν*

Caput XIII

1. — *ιδε*
ποταπε
2. — *ο ιησους*
+ *ωδε* post |*αφεθη*
* *λιθον* pro *λιθω*
* *αφε|θη ουδε διαλυθησεται˙* pro *καταλυθη*

+ και δια τριων η|μερων αλλος αναστησεται ανευ χειρω̅·| ante καθημενου of verse 3.

3. * καθημενου δε pro και καθημενου

ε|λεων

* επηρωτα| pro επηρωτων

4. * ειπον pro ειπε

σημιον

— παντα

5. < και αποκριθεις αυτοις ο ι̅ς̅

|βλεπεται

6. — γαρ

+ ο χ̅ς̅, post ειμει

7. ακουσηται

θροεισθαι,

— γαρ

8. γαρ

|βασειλιαν

— και^{2}

σισμοι

— και εσονται

— και^{4}

8–9. — αρχαι ωδινων ταυτα. βλεπετε δε υμεις εαυτους

9. * και δωσουσιν pro παραδωσουσι γαρ

δαρησεσθ(αι)·|

σταθησε|σθαι

10. * πρωτον δε δει| pro δει πρωτον

11. * αγω|σιν pro αγαγωσιν

λαλησηται,

— μηδε μελετατε

† αν pro εαν

* εκεινο pro τουτο

λαλειται,

εσται|

12. * αναστησο̅|ται pro επαναστησονται

13. εσεσθαι

— ουτος

14. ειδηται|

— το ρηθεν υπο δανιηλ του προφητου

* στηκον pro εστος

15. οικειαν,

αρε

< τι, post αυτου

οικειας

16. αρε

* τα| ιματια pro το ιματιον

17. — ταις^{2}

18. προσευχεσθαι

— η φυγη υμων

19. θλιψεις

— κτισεως

20. — κυριος

21. ειδου bis

* κ̅ς̅ pro χριστος η

* πι|στευεται pro πιστευσητε

22. + πολλοι post γαρ

σημια

* πλαναν| pro αποπλαναν

23. — ιδου

24. † αλλα

δωσι

25. + εκ ante του ουρανου

* πε|σουντε, pro εσονται εκπιπτοντες

— αι^{2}

* τοις ουρανοις| corr man 2 ex τω ουρανω man 1

26. * νεφελη| pro νεφελαις

27. — αυτου bis

* ε|πισυνστρεψουσιν pro επισυναξει

+ της ante γης|

* ακρων ουρανων, pro ακρου ουρανου

28\. — ηδη

γινωσκεται

29\. |ουτως

ειδητε

γει|νομενα,

30\. + δε post αμην

* εως pro μεχρις ου

31\. * παρελευσετε| pro παρελευσονται

33\. + δε| post βλεπεται

αγρυπνιτε

προσευχεσθαι,

+ ει μη ο π̅η̅ρ̅ και ο υιος post γαρ,

κερος ·|

— εστιν

34\. * ωσπερ γαρ pro ως

οι|κειαν

ενετιλατο

35\. |γρηγοριται

οικειας

* μεσανυκτιō| pro μεσονυκτιου

πρωει,

36\. |εξεφνης

37\. — λεγω

γρηγοριται,|

Caput XIV

1\. * |φαρισαιοι pro γραμματεις

— εν

* κρατησοντες|

|αποκτινωσιν,

3\. οικεια|

* γυνη προσηλθεν pro ηλθε γυνη

* πολυ|τιμου, pro πολυτελους

— κατα

4\. + των μαθητων post τινες

— του μυρου

5\. εδυ|νατο

— τουτο

+ το μυρον post πραθηναι

< δη|ναριων τ̄ pro τριακοσιων δηναριων ·

* ενεβριμουντο pro ενεβριμωντο

6\. + αυτοις, post ειπεν

* κοπον pro κοπους

παρεχεται ·

+ γαρ post καλον

† ηργασατο

* εν εμοι, pro εις εμε

7\. εχεται bis

* υμων, pro εαυτων

θεληται

δυνασθαι

* αυτοις pro αυτους

8\. — αυτη

9\. + οτι post υμιν|

— τουτο

10\. + ιδου post |και

ιβ| pro δωδεκα

* παρα|δοι pro παραδω

— αυτοις

11\. εζητι

< αυτον ευκαι|ρως

* παραδοι · pro παραδω

13\. * αποστιλας pro αποστελλει

< δυο post αυτου

— και[2]

|υπαγεται

+ εισελθō|των υμων post και[3]

14\. — και

† αν pro εαν

+ μου, post καταλυμα

* φαγο|μαι · pro φαγω

15\. † αναγιον| pro ανωγεον

ετοι|μασαται
16. + ετοιμασαι| post εξηλθον
17. $\overline{ιβ}$, pro δωδεκα
18. ¶ ante αμην
† υμω pro υμων
< με παρα|δωσει
19. |λυπισθαι
— και αλλος, μη τι εγω
20. — εκ
$\overline{ιβ}$ pro δωδεκα
ενβαπτομενος
21. + πα|ραδιδοτε ante υπαγει
παραδιδοτε,
— ην
22. — αυτων
— ο ιησους
* εδιδου pro εδωκεν
+ αυτοις,| post ειπεν
λαβεται
— φαγετε
— εστι
23. * τοις| μαθηταις pro αυτοις
24. — καινης
* υπερ pro περι
+ εις αφεσιν αμαρτιων,| post εκχ$\overline{υ}$|νομενον
25. — ουκετι
† γε|νηματος
26. ελεων,|
27. ¶ * σκανδα|λισθησεσθαι (εσθαι in ras man 1, οντε prim scr)
* τα προβατα σκορπισθησεται, pro διασκορπισθησεται τα προβατα
28. + εκ νεκρων post με
29. ¶ * αποκριθεις λεγει pro εφη
< ει κ(αι)|
† αλλ' (λ' sup man 2)
30. — σοι
+ συ post οτι
— εν
— η δις
* με αρνηση, pro απαρνηση με
31. * ο δε πετρος μαλ|λον περισσως ελεγεν, οτι pro ο δε εκ περισσου ελεγε μαλλον
32. * εξερχονται pro ερχονται
† |γεσσημανιν,
καθεισατε
33. + τον ante ιωαννην|
* μετ αυτου, pro μεθ' εαυτου
εκθαμβισθαι|
34. |μιναται
γρηγορειται,|
35. * την| γην pro της γης
< |ινα post εστ$\overline{ι}$
36. + μου post $\overline{πηρ}$
+ εστ$\overline{ι}$| post σοι
< τουτο απ εμου·|
† αλλα
38. γρηγορειται
προσευ|χεσθαι
εισελθηται
πιρασμ$\overline{ο}$·|
40. * καταβαρου|μενοι, pro βεβαρημενοι
ηδισαν
41. καθευδεται
— το ante λοιπον
αναπαυ|εσθαι
+ το τελος, ιδου post απεχει
* |και pro ιδου
παραδιδοτε
42. εγειρεσθαι|
43. ¶ — ευθεως
— ων
$\overline{ιβ}$, pro δωδεκα

— των[3, 4]
44. † συσημον
< λεγων αυτοις,
* αγαγεται pro απαγαγετε
45. + χαιρε| post λεγει,
* ραββει pro ραββι ραββι
46. — επ αυτον
* εκρα|τουν pro εκρατησαν
47. * και εις pro εις δε
* παρεστω|των pro παρεστηκοτων
— την
επεσεν|
αφιλε̄|
48. † εξηλ|θατε
συνλα|βειν
49. + των προφητων·| post γρα|φαι
50. * τοτε pro και
+ οι μαθηται αυτου ante αφεντες
51. η|κολουθι
— επι γυμνου
* |οι δε νεανισκοι εκρατησαν αυτον, pro και κρατουσιν αυτον οι νεανισκοι
53. + καιαφαν, post αρχιερεα
* συνπο|ρευονται pro συνερχονται αυτω
* οι[2] (ι sup tamen man 1)
54. * ηκολουθει pro ηκολουθησεν
|συνκαθημενος
— και[3]
|θερμενομενος
55. † ηυρισκον·|
56–57. — και ισαι αι μαρτυριαι ··· κατ᾽ αυτου
59. < ην ειση
60. — το
— ουκ αποκρινη ουδεν
* |οτι pro τι
61. + και ante πα|λιν
— ο αρχιερευς
+ εκ δευτερου post αυτον
* ευλογημε|νου, pro ευλογητου
62. + αποκριθεις post ι̅ς̅
+ αυτω,| post ειπεν
ειμει·
οψεσθαι
< |εκ δεξιων καθημενον
* της δυναμεως·| pro των νεφελων
63. + ευθυς post αρχιερευς
† διαρηξας|
χειτωνας
64. + παντες post ηκουσατε
* την| βλασφημιαν του στοματος αυτου pro της βλασφημιας
< φαι|νεται υμιν,
* και pro οι δε
65. ενπτυειν
περικαλυ|πτιν
— αυτω[2]
+ νυν χ̅ε̅| τις εστιν ο πεσας σε, post προφητευσον
υπηρετε
* ελαμβανον, pro εβαλλον
66. — του[1]
67. θερμενομενον
* ης·| pro ησθα
68. * ουτε pro ουκ
† ουτε pro ουδε
< συ τι
* εις την| εξω αυλην, pro εξω εις το προαυλιον
— και αλεκτωρ εφωνησε
69. — παλιν

70. * ηρνη|σατο, pro ηρνειτο
μεικρον
* περιε|στηκοτες pro παρεστωτες
— και γαρ γαλιλαιος ει, και η λαλια σου ομοιαζει
71. λεγεται,
72. + ευθεως post και[1]
* ανα|μνησθεις pro ανεμνησθη
— δις
< |τρις με απαρνηση
— και[3]

Caput XV

1. πρωει
+ των ante γραμματεων
* απηγαγον,| pro απηνεγκαν
+ αυτον post παρεδωκαν
2. + λεγω̄| post πειλατος
— αυτω
3. + αυτος δε ου|δεν απεκρινατο, post πολλα,
4. πειλατος
* επηρωτα pro επηρωτησεν
ειδε
< σου ποσα
* κατηγορου|σιν, pro καταμαρτυρουσιν
5. πειλατον·|
6. + ιωθει ο ηγεμων post εορτην
* απολυ|ειν pro απελυεν
* ον pro ονπερ
7. * τοτε ο λεγομενος βαρναβας pro ο γενομενος (error edit Oxon) βαραββας
* στασιαστων pro συστασιαστων
στασι
8. αιτισθαι|
— αει
9. πειλατος|
θελεται
10. * |ηδει pro εγινωσκε
* παρεδωκαν pro παραδεδωκεισαν
11. ανε|σισαν
† βαρ|ναβαν pro βαραββαν
12. ¶ πειλατος
— παλιν
— θελετε
* τον pro ον λεγετε
post των ιουδαιω̄| amissum est unum folium ad verba απ ανωθεν εως κατω, XV, 38
39. * παρεστως pro ο παρεστηκως
— εξ εναντιας
* αυτω pro αυτου
— ουτω
40. — και[2]
* μαριαμ[2] pro μαρια[1]
— του[1]
† ιωση| (ι sup man 2)
41. — αι bis
* διηκονουσαν| pro διηκονουν
42. επι pro επει
43. * ελθων pro ηλθεν
† ιωσης pro ιωσηφ
* ο man 1, del man eadem
† αριμαθειας|
+ τον ante πειλατο̄|
44. πειλατος
* ηδη τεθνηκεν| pro παλαι απεθανε
45. * παρα pro απο
† ιωση, pro ιωσηφ

46. + ευθεως ηνεγκεν, post σιν|-δονα
* εις την σινδονα pro τη σινδονι
* ε|θηκεν pro κατεθηκεν
μνημιω
+ της ante πετρας,
προσεκυλεισε|
μνημιον,|
47. * η ιωση| $\overline{μηρ}$ pro ιωση

CAPUT XVI

1. − του²
† κα pro και³
* εισελθουσαι pro ελθουσαι
αλι|ψωσιν
2. − και λιαν
πρωει
* μια των σαββατων| pro της μιας σαββατων
* μνημα ετι pro μνημειον
ανατιλαντος|
3. † |αποκυλιση pro αποκυλισει
* απο pro εκ
μνημιου,
4. < σφοδρα μεγας,
5. μνημιον
* θεωρουσιν pro ειδον
6. * |φοβεισθαι, οιδα γαρ οτι pro εκθαμβεισθε
< τον ναζαρη|νον ζητιται
* ειδετε εκει pro ιδε
+ αυτου εστιν post τοπος|
7. † |αλλα
+ και post υπαγετε
* ιδου προ|αγω pro προαγει
|οψεσθαι
8. * ακουσασαι εξηλθον και pro εξελθουσαι ταχυ
μνημιου,
* εσχεν γαρ pro ειχε δε
* φοβος| pro τρομος
9. πρωει
− πρωτον
* παρ pro αφ'
10. − και κλαιουσι
12. εφανερωθ[η ε]ν|
13. * απηγγελον pro απηγγειλαν
14. − αυτοις
* $\overline{ιβ}$ pro ενδεκα
ω|νιδισεν
+ (post επιστευσαν,|) (14 a)| κακεινοι απελογουντε λεγοντες, οτι ο| αιων ουτος της ανομιας και της απιστιας| υπο τον σαταναν εστιν, ο μη εων τα υπο| των $\overline{πνατων}$ ακαθαρτα. την αληθειαν| του $\overline{θυ}$ καταλαβεσθαι δυναμιν, (14 b) δια| τουτο αποκαλυψον σου την δικαιοσυ|νην ηδη, εκεινοι ελεγον τω $\overline{χω}$, (14 c) και ο| $\overline{χς}$ εκεινοις προσελεγεν, οτι πεπληρω|ται ο ορος των ετων της εξουσιας του| σατανα, αλλα εγγιζει, αλλα δινα και υ|περ ων εγω αμαρτησαντων παρεδοθη̅| εις θανατον, ινα υποστρεψωσιν εις τη̅| αληθειαν και μηκετι αμαρτησωσιν·| ινα την εν τω ουρανω $\overline{πνι}$κην, και α|φθαρτον της δικαιοσυνης δοξαν| κληρονομησωσιν,
15. * αλλα pro και ειπεν αυτοις
16. * κατακριθεις, ου σωθησεται·| pro κατακριθησεται
17. |σημια
|δ[αι]μονια

καινες,

18. † βλαψη ·|

19. ¶ — ουν

\+ ι̅ς̅ χ̅ς̅ post κ̅ς̅

† ανε|λημφθη

εκαθεισε̄|

20. σημιων : >—

<· αμην ·> non in textu sed add man 1.

Subscr *ευαγγελιον κατα μαρκον* man 1.

Subscr man 5 (et 6 et 7) ⳨ *χριστε αγιε συ μετα του δουλου σου τιμοθεου* ⳨| (*υ σου τιμοθεου* ⳨ in ras man 7; scr man 5 *υ τ*···········; man 6 *υ του* ······*ου*); add man 6 *και παντων των αυτου* ⳨

In sup marg legitur ··λλου *ναως* man 8.

University of Michigan Studies

HUMANISTIC SERIES

Size, 22.7 × 15.2 cm. 8°. Bound in cloth

VOL. I. ROMAN HISTORICAL SOURCES AND INSTITUTIONS. Edited by Professor Henry A Sanders, University of Michigan. Pp. viii + 402. $2.50 net.

CONTENTS

1. THE MYTH ABOUT TARPEIA: Professor Henry A. Sanders.
2. THE MOVEMENTS OF THE CHORUS CHANTING THE CARMEN SAECULARE: Professor Walter Dennison, Swarthmore College.
3. STUDIES IN THE LIVES OF ROMAN EMPRESSES, JULIA MAMAEA: Professor Mary Gilmore Williams, Mt. Holyoke College.
4. THE ATTITUDE OF DIO CASSIUS TOWARD EPIGRAPHIC SOURCES: Professor Duane Reed Stuart, Princeton University.
5. THE LOST EPITOME OF LIVY: Professor Henry A. Sanders.
6. THE PRINCIPALES OF THE EARLY EMPIRE: Professor Joseph H. Drake, University of Michigan.
7. CENTURIONS AS SUBSTITUTE COMMANDERS OF AUXILIARY CORPS: Professor George H. Allen, University of Cincinnati.

VOL. II. WORD FORMATION IN PROVENÇAL. By Dr. Edward L. Adams, University of Michigan. (*In Press.*)

VOL. III. LATIN PHILOLOGY. Edited by Professor Clarence Linton Meader, University of Michigan. Pp. viii + 290. $2.00 net.

Parts Sold Separately in Paper Covers:

Part I. THE USE OF IDEM, IPSE AND WORDS OF RELATED MEANING. By Clarence L. Meader. Pp. 1–112. $0.75.

Part II. A STUDY IN LATIN ABSTRACT SUBSTANTIVES. By Professor Manson A. Stewart, Yankton College. Pp. 113–78. $0.40.

Part III. THE USE OF THE ADJECTIVE AS A SUBSTANTIVE IN THE DE RERUM NATURA OF LUCRETIUS. By Dr. Frederick T. Swan. Pp. 179–214. $0.40.

Part IV. AUTOBIOGRAPHIC ELEMENTS IN LATIN INSCRIPTIONS. By Dr. Henry H. Armstrong, Princeton University. Pp. 215–86. $0.40.

Vol. IV. Roman History and Mythology. Edited by Professor Henry A. Sanders. Pp. viii + 427. $2.50 net.

Parts Sold Separately in Paper Covers:

Part I. Studies in the Life of Heliogabalus. By Professor Orma Fitch Butler, Belmont College. Pp. 1–169. $1.25 net.

Part II. The Myth of Hercules at Rome. By Professor John G. Winter, University of Michigan. Pp. 171–273. $0.50 net.

Part III. Roman Law Studies in Livy. By Professor Alvin E. Evans, Washington State College. Pp. 275–354. $0.40 net.

Part IV. Reminiscences of Ennius in Silius Italicus. By Dr. Loura B. Woodruff. Pp. 355–424. $0.40 net.

Size, 28 × 18.5 cm. 4°.

Vol. VI. Athenian Lekythoi with Outline Drawing in Glaze Varnish on a White Ground. By Arthur Fairbanks, Director of the Museum of Fine Arts, Boston. With 15 plates, and 57 illustrations in the text. Pp. x + 371. Bound in cloth. $4.00 net.

Vol. VII. Athenian Lekythoi with Outline Drawing in Dull Color on a White Ground, and an Appendix: Additional Lekythoi with Outline Drawing in Glaze Varnish on a White Ground. By Arthur Fairbanks. Illustrated. (*In Press.*)

Vol. VIII. The Old Testament Manuscripts in the Freer Collection. By Professor Henry A. Sanders, University of Michigan.

Part I. The Washington Manuscript of Deuteronomy and Joshua. With 3 folding plates of pages of the Manuscript in facsimile. Pp. vi + 104. Paper covers. $1.00.

Part II. The Washington Manuscript of the Psalms. (*In Preparation.*)

Vol. IX. The New Testament Manuscripts in the Freer Collection. By Professor Henry A. Sanders, University of Michigan.

Part I. The Washington Manuscript of the Four Gospels. With 5 plates. Pp. viii + 247. Paper covers. $2.00.

Part II. The Washington Fragments of the Epistles of Paul. (*In Preparation.*)

Vol. X. The Coptic Manuscripts in the Freer Collection. By Professor William H. Worrell, Hartford Theological Seminary. (*In Preparation.*)